W9-BCL-732

EL

ICCIONARIO

DEL

ESPAÑOL CHICANO

THE

DICTIONARY

OF

CHICANO SPANISH

Compiled by
Roberto A. Galván, Southwest Texas State University
Richard V. Teschner, University of Texas at El Paso

National Textbook Company
NTC a division of *NTC Publishing Group* • Lincolnwood, Illinois USA

1992 Printing

Published by National Textbook Company, a division of NTC Publishing Group.
© 1989, 1985, 1977 by NTC Publishing Group, 4255 West Touhy Avenue,
Lincolnwood (Chicago), Illinois 60646-1975 U.S.A.
2 3 4 5 6 7 8 9 ML 9 8 7 6 5 4 3

Índice de materias/Table of Contents

Abreviaturas usadas en este diccionario / List of Abbreviations

abbrev.	abbreviation / abreviatura
adj.	adjective / adjetivo
adv.	adverb / adverbio
Ang.	Anglicism (word or phrase historically Spanish but altered in meaning through English influence) / anglicismo (palabra o frase de origen castellano pero que se alteró luego por influencia del inglés)
ant.	antiquated / anticuado -da
aut.	automotive, automobile / automovilístico -ca, carro
cf.	compare / compárese
coll.	colloquial / coloquial
conj.	conjunction / conjunción
dim.	diminutive / diminutivo
e.g.	for example / por ejemplo
Eng.	word from English borrowed into Spanish / palabra prestada del inglés al español (cf. Ang.)
esp.	especially / especialmente
et al.	and others / y otros -tras
euph.	euphemism, euphemistic / eufemismo, eufemístico -ca
fam.	familiar / familiar
f.	feminine / femenino -na
fig.	figurative / figurado -da
fpl.	f. plural / plural f.
fsg.	f. singular / singular f.
ger.	gerund / gerundio
hum.	humorous(ly) / festivo -va
id.	identical (to) / lo mismo (que)
i.e.	that is to say / es decir
imperf.	imperfect tense / tiempo imperfecto
ind.	indicative (mode) / (modo) indicativo
infra	below / abajo
interj.	interjection / exclamación
iron.	irony, ironic / inronía, irónico -ca
m.	masculine / masculino -na
mf.	either m. or f. according to sex of human referent / m. o f. según el sexo
m. & f.	word taking either gender / palabra de ambos géneros

mfsg.	singular (either m. or f.) / singular (o m. o f.)
mpl.	m. plural / plural m.
msg.	m. singular / singular m.
n. place	no place of publication indicated / no se indica el lugar de imprenta
orthog.	orthographic / ortográfico -ca
pej.	pejorative / peyorativo -va
pers.	person (e.g., 1st person sg. = *yo*) / persona (e.g., 1ª persona de sg. = *yo*)
pl.	plural
poss.	possible / posible
pr.	pronounced / se pronuncia
pres.	present tense / tiempo presente
ppart.	past participle / participio pasado
pret.	preterite tense / tiempo pretérito
prob.	probably / probablemente
pron.	pronoun / pronombre
q.v.	which see / véase
ref.	reference, refer(s) / referencia, se refiere(n)
resp.	respectively / respectivamente
rus.	rustic, rural or small town / rústico -ca, de pueblo chico
s.	see / véase
sg.	singular
Std.	standard Spanish, normative usage / español normativo
subj.	subjunctive mode / subjuntivo
supra	above / arriba
underw.	underworld / del hampa
va.	active (transitive) verb / verbo activo (transitivo)
var.	variant / variante
vn.	neutral (intransitive) verb / verbo intransitivo
vr.	reflexive verb / verbo reflexivo
vulg.	vulgar, obscene / obsceno -na, ordinario -ria

Preface

The Chicano language, as it is spoken and written in the United States today, is constantly in flux. New words are coined to express various cultural and technological changes, while old words acquire slightly different meanings, and pronunciation slowly evolves. *The Dictionary of Chicano Spanish* will serve as an invaluable reference for anyone involved with the dynamic Chicano culture. The wordlist of this unique dictionary comprises 8,000 items frequently used in the Chicano language.

Designed for students, business people, educators, and service professionals, *The Dictionary of Chicano Spanish* features words and expressions not usually found in standard references and purposely excludes words easily located in commonly available dictionaries. In this way, it is an excellent supplement to any monolingual Spanish or bilingual Spanish and English dictionary.

Many terms in *The Dictionary of Chicano Spanish* have been labeled according to their current usage in Chicano speech: *slang, colloquial, vulgar, euphemistic, antiquated*, etc. Thus, users of this dictionary will be able to know quickly the appropriate social connotations of the words they look up.

Also included, as separate or coordinate entries, are words whose pronunciation results in a variant spelling–thus avoiding the need to search for words pronounced differently from standard Spanish. For example, the word *degual* is listed as a variation of the word *desigual; malición* is listed as a rustic variation of *maldición*. Likewise, *espeletiar* appears alongside *espeletear; maniar* alongside *manear*. Words containing variations such as *güe-* or *bue-* for *hue-* (*huerta* > *güerta, huevo* > *buevo*) and *j* for *h* (*hijo* > *jijo*) are also listed separately. Because of the relative simplicity of the change, the dropped *d* close to or at the end of words (e.g., *bondad* > *bondá* or *hablado* > *hablao*) has not been shown in separate entries.

At the back of the book you will find an appendix of 550 up-to-date proverbs and sayings commonly used in everyday speech as well as a bibliography of secondary sources. The practical bibliography provides both a scholarly list of resources consulted in compiling this dictionary and a rich source of reading and research material for all those wishing to expand their knowledge of the Chicano language.

A Note to Users

Unless otherwise indicated, nouns or adjectives ending in -*o* or -*a* are masculine and feminine respectively.

Likewise, unless otherwise indicated, nouns and adjectives ending in -*on* and -*ona* are masculine and feminine respectively.

Since Spanish is almost always pronounced as it is written, this dictionary does not provide phonetic transcriptions for its entries.

Prólogo

Una característica de todo idioma vivo es su constante cambio. Con el fin de expresar cambios culturales y avances tecnológicos se idean nuevas palabras, algunas voces adquieren nuevos significados y la pronunciación cambia gradualmente.

El diccionario del español chicano será un libro de consulta de incalculable valor para todo aquél que se relacione con la dinámica comunidad chicana de los Estados Unidos. Su léxico de 8.000 artículos refleja el habla chicana, verbal y escrita, de los Estados Unidos de hoy.

Los estudiantes, empresarios, educadores y profesionales del campo de servicios encontrarán en *El diccionario del español chicano* palabras y expresiones que no se suelen hallar en los libros de consulta tradicionales. Como suplemento a los muchos diccionarios monolingües o bilingües actualmente en venta, es una obra incomparable. Sus autores han excluido espicíficamente las palabras que figuran en uno o más de los diccionarios de mayor circulación.

Tras largos años de investigación de campo y de revisión de fuentes primarias y secundarias, los autores han clasificado muchas voces según su uso actual en el habla chicana: voces jergales o caló *(slang)*, coloquiales *(colloquial)*, vulgares *(vulgar)*, eufemísticas *(euphemistic)*, anticuadas *(antiquated)* y así sucesivamente. De este modo, el usario de este diccionario podrá sentirse seguro de conocer las connotaciones sociales de la palabra consultada.

El diccionario del español chicano es fácil de usar. Para hallar un artículo en él no se necesita ser un especialista en lingüística. Con miras a facilitar su uso, los autores han incluido palabras que se pronuncian y deletrean de varios modos, evitándole así al lector tener que buscar aquí y allá palabras cuya pronunciación varía del español corriente. Estas palabras pueden figurar como artículos separados o en el mismo artículo en que aparece la forma principal. Por ejemplo, la palabra *degual* aparece como una variación de *desigual; malición* aparece como una variación rústica de *maldición*. Del mismo modo, *espeletiar* está catalogada al lado de *espeletear* y *maniar* al lado de *manear*. Las palabras que contienen variantes como *güe-* o *bue-* por *hue- (huerta > güerta; huevo > buevo)* y *j* por *h (hijo > jijo)* también se presentan por separado. Debido al cambio relativamente simple de la supresión de la *d* al final de algunas palabras (e.g., *bondad > bondá* o *hablado > hablao*), no aparecen por separado. De este modo, *El diccionario del español chicano* consta de artículos que reflejan el uso, la pronunciación y la escritura actual, no sólo en la conversación y escritura informal, sino en la dinámica y vigorosa literatura chicana.

El apéndice titulado *Proverbs and Sayings/Proverbios y refranes* presenta una lista actualizada de 550 proverbios y refranes que le añaden vivacidad al habla chicana de todos los días.

Un tercer apéndice contiene una bibliografía de fuentes secundarias que se consultaron en la elaboración de este diccionario. Además de documentar las obras de consulta revisadas, dicha bibliografía ofrece a los lectores interesados en ampliar su conocimiento del léxico chicano un importante caudal de materiales de lectura e investigación.

Nota al lector

De no indicarse lo contrario, los sustantivos y adjetivos que terminan en -*o* y -*a* son respectivamente masculinos y femeninos.

De igual manera, a menos que se indique lo contrario, los sustantivos y adjetivos de parejas que terminan en -*ón* y -*ona* son respectivamente masculinos y femeninos.

Como el español casi siempre se pronuncia como se escribe, este diccionario no ofrece transcripciones fonéticas.

El diccionario del español chicano

El diccionario del español chicano

A

A: A CA (var. of a casa de): "Voy a ca mamá" 'I'm going over to mom's house'; A CARRILLA hurriedly, rapidly; A CAS DE (var. of) a casa de: "Voy a cas de Chucho" 'I'm going to Chucho's house'; A CAS E (var. of a casa de); A COMO DE LUGAR one way or another, any way it can be done: "¿Cómo piensan hacerlo?-- A como dé lugar;" A FUERZA QUE SÍ most likely, in all likelihood, more likely than not: "¿Tendrán frío los gatos?-- A fuerza que sí" 'Are the cats cold?--More likely than not.'; A HUEVO by force, forcibly; A LA BRAVA seriously; genuinely; A LA BUENA voluntarily, willingly; A LA BUENA O A LA MALA willingly or else: "Lo haces a la buena o a la mala" 'You'll do it willingly or else'; A LA HORA DE LA HORA/A L'HORA DEL HORA when it comes right down to it, at the moment of truth, when all is said and done; A LA MALA by force (cf. A LA BUENA); A LA MEJOR probably, likely as not (cf. Std. a lo mejor); AL NO SER QUE (var. of a no ser que); A MANOS tied (in a sports competition); even, all paid up; A PATIN on foot; A PESPUNTE (slang) on foot; A PINCEL (slang) on foot; A PLATA LIMPIA innocent, blameless; A POCO perhaps (often used as interj.: 'You don't say!' --used when the speaker dares a braggard to make good a threat; also used to register surprise or incredulity); A POCO RATO shortly, soon thereafter; A RAIZ (said of a person dressed too sparingly for the weather); A RATO afterwards, in a while; A TIRO DE QUE although, despite; A TODA FUERZA in full swing: "El baile estaba a toda fuerza" 'The dance was in full swing'; A TODA MADRE super, great, tremendous (etc.); rapidly, quickly; A TODA MÁQUINA very fast, rapidly; A TODO DAR very good, tremendous, great, super (etc.); A TODO ESTO while we're speaking about that, while we're on the subject: "Bueno, y a todo esto, ¿qué hiciste con el reloj?" 'Well, while we're on the subject, what did you do with the watch?'; A TODOS TIROS always; A TODO TREN very good, excellent, super (etc.); ¡A VOLAR! (interj.) Get out of here!, Beat it! (coll.); ¡A VOLAR CON ALAS! Beat it! Scram!; AL RATÓN (var. of) al rato 'in a short while'

ABANICAR EL AIRE (slang) vn. to strike out (baseball)

ABANICO (slang) easy out (ref., in baseball, to person who strikes out easily)

ABARROTES mpl. groceries; groceries and other items sold at grocery stores

ABOCANADO -DA running wild (ref. to horses); (ref. to persons, hum.) footloose, wild, fancy-free

ABOCANAR vr. to rear up and run wild (said of horses and, hum., of persons)

ABOLIADO -DA (see ABOLILLADO -DA)

ABOLIAR (see ABOLILLAR)

ABOLILLADO -DA (coll.) gringo-like, gringoized (see also BOLILLO-LLA)

ABOLILLAR va. to cause to become like a gringo, gringoize; vr. to act like a gringo

ABRELIO (var. of) Aurelio (proper name)

ABREMOS (var. of) abrimos (1st pers. pl. pres. ind. of abrir)

ABRICIAS (var. of) albricias

ABRIDERO -DA act of opening a door, a container, a drawer, etc., repeatedly: "Siempre anda con esa abridera de puerta" 'He just keeps on opening and closing the door'

ABRIDO -DA (var. of) abierto -ta
(ppart. of abrir)
ABRIDURA act of repeatedly opening
a door, a container, etc. (cf.
ABRIDERO -RA)
ABRILES (usually mpl.) (coll.) years,
years old: "¿Cuántos abriles
tienes?" 'How old are you?'
ABRORA (var. of) aurora 'dawn'
ABRORA (var. of) Aurora (proper
name)
ABRUJA (var. of) aguja
ABUELITO -TA (slang) friend
ABUJA (slang, underw.) joint of a
narcotic cigarette; injection
(of a narcotic substance), fix
(slang); (also: var. of aguja)
ABUJAZO (slang, underw.) injection
of a narcotic substance, fix
(slang) (cf. ABUJA)
ABUJERADO -DA (var. of) agujerado-da
ABUJERAR (var. of) agujerar
ABUJERO (var. of) agujero
ABURI (var. of) bure et al. (see
also DE ABURI et al.)
ABUSADO -DA bully; clever person;
wealthy person; miser
ABUSAR vr. to be alert; to become
alert
ABUSON -SONA abusive, bully-like
ACÁ: ¿DE CUÁNDO ACÁ? Since when?,
What do you mean by that?
(statements indicating incre-
dulity and often intended as a
form of challenge to the speak-
er); ACÁ GARCÍA (see GARCÍA,
IR ACÁ GARCÍA); ACA LA MADRE DE
LOS BURROS/ACÁ LA MADRE DE LOS
CABALLOS (fig.) a long way away,
half way to hell and gone
(slang)
ACABADO -DA old, worn out
ACABAR va. to age, wear down, fa-
tigue: "Me estás acabando con
tus pleitos"; vr. to wear oneself down, become run down; to
die
ACAPRICHAR (var. of) encaprichar
ACARREAR vn. to spread tales, bear
rumors
ACARTONADO -DA lean, thin (ref. to
persons)
ACARRIAR (var. of) acarrear
ACE (Eng.) mf. ace (person who ex-
cels in an activity)
ACOMEDIDO -DA accommodating, oblig-
ing (see also COMEDIDO -DA)
ACOMEDIR vr. to serve or help without being asked; to be helpful,
accomodating
ACCENTO (Eng.) accent
ACEITAR (var. of) aceptar
ACEITE m. kerosene; ACEITE DE CARRO
motor oil; ACEITE DE COMER

cooking oil, olive oil
ACELGA (fsg., also fpl.: ACELGAS)
spinach
ACERO frying pan
ACETAR (var. of) aceptar
ÁCIDO msg. amphetamines, (slang)
acid (="hard" drug used for
narcotic purposes)
ACOMODADO -DA opportunistic
ACTOBÚS (var. of) autobús
ACTOMOBIL (var. of) automóbil
ACTOR -TORA mf. (vars. of) autor
-tora
ACTUAL (Ang.) actual, real, factual
ACU (interj. said to babies) (non-
sense syllables, probably onoma-
topoetic) coo, kitchy-kitchy coo
ACUADUCTO (var. of) acueducto
ACUAL (var. of) cual
ACULTRADO -DA (pej.) gringo-like,
gringoized
ACUPAR (Ang?, or var. of?) ocupar
ACHANTAR (var. of) chantar
ACHAR (var. of) echar
ACHICHORRANAR (var. of) achicharrar
ACHINADO -DA curly (ref. to hair)
ACHINAR (var. of) chinar
ADELFINA (var. of) Delfina
ADIO' (interj. of incredulity)
Really?, You don't say?!
ADITORIO (var. of) auditorio
ADOLORADO -DA hypochondriac
ADOLORIDO -DA hypochondriac
ADOPTADO -DA adoptive; artificial,
unreal
AFECTADO -DA tubercular, suffering
from tuberculosis
AFECTAR vr. to become tubercular
AFILAR vr. to form a line; to stand
in line; to march in a line; to
take a walk
AFILERIAR (slang) va. to knife
AFILORIAR (slang) va. to knife
AFLOJAR va. to let out (clothing);
(coll.) to cough up (money),
pay; vr. to fart (vulg.), break
wind
AFRAÑAR va. to understand
AGABACHADO -DA (pej.) gringo-like,
gringoized
AGACHADO -DA humble, lowly
AGARRADERA (var. of) agarradero;
fpl. love handles (slang), small
rolls of fat on the human waist;
breasts; TENER BUENAS AGARRADE-
RAS to have a good shape (ref.
to female body) (and therefore)
to be sexually attractive
AGARRADO -DA: TENER AGARRADO -DA
to have under arrest
AGARRAR va. to catch on, get
(coll.), comprehend; to take in,
reduce the dimensions of (e.g.,
clothes which are too large);

AGARRAR ABAJO to keep someone
in his/her place, keep down
(coll.); AGARRAR AIRE to get
caught in cold air (folk medicine's belief is that such ex-
posure will precipitate muscular
pains or spasms); AGARRARLE A
ALGUIEN DE SU CUENTA to have
someone on a string (fig.),
maintain in a position of dependency: "Ya déjalo, ya lo
agarraste bastante de tu cuenta";
AGARRAR BIEN AGARRADITO -TA
to grasp very tightly; to trap
a criminal beyond the possibi-
lity of escape; AGARRAR CHANZA
to take a chance, to risk;
AGARRAR CLASES/CURSOS to take
courses (in school); AGARRAR DE
PURO PEDO to hound someone to
death; AGARRAR DE UNA CUENTA
to harp on the same theme; to
hound someone to death (fig.),
annoy in an extreme fashion;
AGARRAR EL CHIVO (Ang.) to
get someone's goat (fig.):
"Juan le agarró el chivo a Pepe,
por eso se peliaron" 'Juan got
Pepe's goat, and that's why
they got into a fight'; AGARRAR
EL SUEÑO to fall asleep: "Me
tomé una píldora pero no pude
agarrar el sueño"; AGARRAR EN
to fall into the habit of, to
take a notion to: "En estos
días ha agarrado en comer huevos
y tortillas" 'Recently he's
taken a notion to eating eggs
and tortillas'; AGARRAR PA'
TRAS (Ang.) to retract, take
back (i.e., someone one has
said); vn. AGARRAR CORRENTIA
to gain momentum; AGARRAR GUSTO
to develop a taste for: "Ya
le agarró gusto a la cerveza"
'He's already developed a taste
for beer'; AGARRAR LA BOTELLA
to hit the bottle (coll.),
drink to excess habitually;
AGARRARLA SUAVE (coll.) to
take it easy, be unconcerned;
AGARRAR LA TETERA to hit the
bottle (coll.), drink to excess
habitually; AGARRAR PARA to
go off to, head for: "¿Pa dónde
agarró Pepe?" 'Where was Pepe
going off to?'; AGARRAR PATADA
DE (Ang.) to get a kick out of
(coll.), receive gratification
from; vr. to fight; AGARRAR
TESÓN CON to harp on (a subject); to use or wear (repeatedly): "Agarró tesón con la
corbata nueva" 'He kept on wear-

ing the new tie'; AGARRAR VUELO
to get a running start; AGARRAR-
SE A CANCOS to come to blows
(in a fight); AGARRARSE AL
TIRÓN to fight, AGARRARSE A
PORRAZOS to fight, get into
a fight; AGARRARSE A REATAZOS/
RIATAZOS to fight; AGARRARSE
A LAS MECHAS or AGARRARSE DE
LAS MECHAS to pull hair while
fighting (usually said of wom-
en); AGARRARSE CON ALGUIEN to
take up (relations) with (ref.
to amorous relationships):
"Dicen que Cuca se agarró con
un cubano" 'They say that Cuca
has taken up with a Cuban'
(Note: it is usually the woman
who "se agarra" with the man,
not the reverse)
AGARRÓN (see DAR UN AGARRÓN)
AGOSOMAR vr. to become frightened
or intimidated
AGRESIVO mf. agressor
AGRICOLTURA (var. of) agricultura
AGRINGADO -DA (pej.) gringo-like
AGRINGOLADO -DA (pej.) gringo-like
AGRINGOLAR va. to gringoize, cause
to act like a gringo (Anglo-
Saxon); vr. to become or act
like a gringo
AGRITO prickly desert shrub
AGRURAS fpl. acidity, acid stomach
condition; gaseous stomach
condition, stomach gas
AGUA f. rain; (interj.) Watch out!;
adj. DE AGUA soft, delicate
(ref. to persons); effeminate;
HACER (ALGO) COMO AGUA to
perform a task with ease: "Para
hacer eso se requiere bastante
inteligencia.--Pues yo lo hago
como agua"; HACER AGUA to
urinate
AGUACERAL m. heavy rain shower,
cloudburst
AGUADO -DA dilute, watered (said
of liquids that lose the
desired thickness when excessive amounts of water or, in
the case of paint, thinners are
added); soft, delicate; VENIR
AGUADO to be no match for:
"Sé que ese tipo me viene muy
aguado" 'I know that guy is no
match for me'
AGUADOR m. water-boy; (fig.) person
always alert to shifts in the
political wind
AGUANTADOR -DORA patient, forebearing
AGUANTAR: AGUANTAR BURI BARILLA
to tolerate heavy kidding;

AGUANTAR LA VARA COMO VENGA (coll.) to withstand whatever comes, take whatever fortune brings; AGUANTAR MULETA to tolerate heavy kidding; vr. to resign oneself, be resigned to

AGUANTE m. strength to endure heavy emotional and physical stress

AGUANTON -TONA patient, forebearing, able to tolerate a great deal

AGUAZAL m. downpour, heavy rain shower

AGÜELO -LA (var. of) abuelo - la

AGUERRIDO -DA stubborn; relentless

ÁGUILA, EL (coll., Hispanization of) Eagle Pass, Texas

ÁGUILA (interj.) Watch out!, Be careful!; AGUILA AHI (interj.) Watch out!, Be careful!; ÁGUILA CON LOS V LISES (interj., coll.) Watch out!; ÁGUILAS (interj.) Watch out!, adj. alert, quick, careful, shrewd; ANDAR AGUILA to be on the alert, be watchful; PONERSE AGUILA to become alert, get smart (coll.)

AGUILIA (var. of) aguililla

AGUILILLA buzzard (Buteo)

¡AGUILUCHAS TRUCHAS! (interj., slang) Watch out! Be careful!

AGÜITA drizzle, persistent light rain; annoyance, bother (frequently used as interj.: "¡Qué agüita!" 'What a bother!')

AGUITADO - DA downcast, sad; afflicted; frustrated; nervous; frightened; tired

AGÜITAR va. to make sad; to bore; to tire out; to frighten; to aflict; to make nervous; vr. to become frustrated, afflicted, frightened, bored, sad, tired, nervous, etc.

AGÜITE m. sadness; fear, fatigue; boredom; nervousness

AGUJERADO -DA (ref. to a baseball player who fails to snare grounders or other hits rolling on the ground); (vulg.)(f.) (ref. to any woman who is no longer a virgin);

AGUJERO -R A (vulg.) m. anus; vagina; f. hairpin

AGUZADILLO LA (coll.) smart-aleck kid, mischievous child

AGUZADÍO -IA (var. of) aguzadillo- lla

AGUZADO -DA (var. of) abusado -da

AHI (var. of) ahí

AHIJADO -DA mf. ward (person, usually a child, under the protection of an adult guardian)

AHINCADO -DA (var. of) hincado - da 'kneeling'

AHINCAR (var.) of hincar

AHOGADITO ring (child's game played with marbles)

AHOGADO -DA (slang) dead drunk

AHOGAR vr. (slang) to get soused (coll.), get very drunk

AHORA adv. today; AHORA PRONTO recently: "¿Cuándo pasó todo eso?-- Ahora pronto"

AHORCAR vr. (slang) to get married

AHOY (var. of) hoy

AHUA (var. of) agua

AHUEVADO -DA adamant, insistent, stubborn

AHUICHOTE m. pimp, whoremaster

AHUICHOTEAR or AHUICHOTIAR to encourage, stimulate

AHUITADO -DA (var. of) agüitado -da

AI (var. of ahí)

AIGRE (var. of) aire m.

AIGRIO -GRIA (var. of) agrio -gria

AIGRONAZO violent wind

AIRE m. (anal) gas; (interj., coll.) Scram!, Beat it!, AIRE AL QUEQUE (slang) Scram!, Beat it!, Bug off! (slang); DARLE AIRE A ALGUIEN to get rid of someone; to fire someone from a job; to give someone the brush off (slang), dismiss; EN TANTO QUE EL AIRE in a jiffy, in a split second, in no time at all

AIREPURETO (var. of) aeropuerto

AIROPLANO (var. of) aeroplano

AISCRIM (Eng.) (var. of) aiscrín

AISCRÍN (Eng.) m. ice cream

AISCRINERO -RA ice-cream vendor

AJEAR vr. to become wrinkled

AJERA (var. of) afuera

AJILAR (var. of) afilar

AJOLOTE m. salamander

AJUERA (var. of) afuera

AJUEVADO -DA (var. of) ahuevado -da

AJUEVAR (var. of) ahuevar

AJUITADO -DA (var. of) agüitado -da

AJUITAR (var. of) agüitar

ALA: ¡A VOLAR CON ALAS! Beat it! Scram! DAR ALAS to give free rein to; to side with someone

ALACRANADO -DA mad, angry; blond; (slang) feminine

ALACRANESCO -CA evil-tongued, malicious, viciously gossipy

ALAGARTO (var. of) lagarto

ALAMBRAZO telephone call; telephone message

ALAMBRE ELECTRICO (hum.) thin, skinny (ref. to persons)

ALAMBRISTA mf. illegal Mexican immigrant into the United States (so named for his/her skill in jumping or otherwise crossing

the wire fence that forms the
border between California and
Baja California)
ALAMBRITO inter-uterine device, coil,
loop (form of contraception)
ALARMA: ALARMA DE LUMBRE fire
alarm
ALARME m. (var. of) alarma
ALAVANTAR (var. of) levantar
ALBA: ¡AL ALBA! (interj., coll.)
Cut it out!, Stop it!; Watch
out!, Be careful; PONERSE AL
ALBA to become alert, be care-
ful; SER AL ALBA to be clever,
astute, alert
ALBAJÓN m. (var. of) arvejón
ALBAYALDE m. face powder
ALBOCHARNAR (var. of) abochornar
ALBOROTADO -DA: ANDAR ALBOROTADO -DA
CON to have a crush on, be smit-
ten by
ALCAGÜETE mf. (var. of) alcahuete
ALCASO (var. of) acaso
ALCATRAZ m. paper bag
ALCOHOLISTA mf. alcoholic
ALCOL m. (var. of) alcohol
ALDABA f. small latch, catch (i.e.,
of a screen door, window screen,
small box, etc.)
ALDILLA groin
ALDREDE (var. of) adrede
ALE (Eng.) m. alley
ALEBRASTAR or ALEBRESTAR vr. to
brighten up, cheer up, regain
one's good spirits (often said
with ref. to sick persons on the
road to recovery); (coll.) to
smarten up, get smart
ALEGAR vn. to dispute, argue
ALEGRÓN -GRONA mf. flirt; good-
time Charlie/Charlotte (coll.)
f. woman of ill repute, pros-
titute
ALELADO -DA stupid, simple-minded
ALELUYA mf. (pej.) Protestant
ALERTO -TA intelligent
ALEVADOR (var. of) elevador
ALEVANTAR m. (var. of) levantar
ALFIDER m. (var. of) alfiler
ALFILEAR or ALFILIAR va. to cut
(someone) with a knife, stab
ALFILERIAR (slang) va. to knife
ALFIREL (var. of) alfiler m.
(cf. ALFIDER)
ALFOMBRÍA or ALFOMBRILLA (type of
verbenaceous plant used as a
ground cover in dry climates);
German measles, rubella
ALFRENTE (var. of) enfrente
ALGODÓN m. cottonwood tree (Pop-
ulus deltoides)
ALGODONERO -RA freeloader, sponge(r)
(slang)
ALGOTRO -TRA (var. of) algún otro/

alguna otra (Std. otro -tra)
ALGUATE m. cactus sticker, cactus
spine
ALGUEN (var. of) alguien pron.
ALIENTO -TA illegal Mexican immigrant to the United States
ALIMAL mf. (var. of) animal
ALIMAR mf. (var. of animal)
ALINEADO -DA or ALINIADO -DA dressed
up, elegant; straight (slang)
(i.e., not in trouble with the
law)
ALINEAR or ALINIAR vr. to get dressed; to go straight (slang)
cease to be in trouble with the
law
ALIÑAR (var. of) alinear/aliniar
ALISTAR va. to dress up; vr. to get
dressed up
ALIVIADO -DA adj. well, cured (of an
illness)
ALIVIANADO -DA (slang) "high" on narcotics, "turned on" by a narcotic drug
ALIVIANAR va. to straighten (someone)
out (e.g., to straighten out a
criminal, assist a criminal in
reforming); to lend a helping
hand; vr. to go "straight" (case
to engage in a criminal behav-
ior)
ALIVIAR va. to cure; vr. to get well,
cease to be sick; to end preg-
nancy by giving birth
ALÍZ (Hispanization of) Alice, Texas
ALMA: COMO CUANDO DIOS SE LLEVA UN
ALMA in the twinkling of an eye
(coll.), quite rapidly; TENER
EL ALMA EN EL CUERPO to wear
one's heart on one's sleeve
ALMETIR (var. of) admitir
ALMIRAR (var. of) admirar
ALMITIR (var. of) admitir
ALMUADA (var. of) almohada
ALMUERZAR (var.) of almorzar
ALÓ (Eng.) hello
ALOJA (interj., coll.) Hello!, Hi
there!; Goodbye!
ALQUERIR (var. of) adquirir
ALREVESADO -DA (var. of) al revés
ALTA (see DAR DE ALTA)
ALTERO m. high pile of objects
ALTO: PARAR EL ALTO to put a stop
to abusive behavior or to per-
sonal excesses: "Se está ata-
cando mucho; hay que pararle el
alto" 'He's becoming very abu-
sive; we'll have to make him
cut it out' (coll.); to put
someone in his/her place, cut
someone down to size (coll.);
PONERSE ALTO (coll.) to get high,
get drunk; DAR DE ALTA to discharge, fire (from a job);

PARAR LA ALTA (var. of) parar
el alto
ALUMBRADO -DA (slang) drunk
ALUMINO (var. of) aluminio
ALUZAR va. to light up, cause light
to shine or enter into (a room,
etc.)
ALVERTIR (var. of) advertir
ALZADITO -TA (coll.) imprisoned
ALZADO -DA mf. loner, lone-wolf
(coll.) (said of person who
dislikes the company of others)
ALZAR va. to put away, return to an
assigned place of storage (e.g.,
clothes, toys, etc., to their
respective drawers); ALZAR LA
CASA to clean house; vr.: AL-
ZARSE UNA BOLA to rise up, form
(said of wounds on the human
body): "A Juanito se le alzó
una bola en el brazo" 'Juanito
got a lump on his arm'
ALLÁ: ALLÁ A LAS QUINIENTAS or ALLÁ
A LAS CUANTAS after a long period of time (often ref. to a
delayed reaction; also ref. to
solutions or assistance coming
too late to be of any good);
ALLÁ EL that's up to him, that's
his business (coll.)
AMÁ (var. of) mamá
AMACANAR vr. to grab something tightly; to refuse to budge from a
place, refuse to move
AMACIZAR va. to tighten; to get a
firm grip on; vr. to brace oneself; to make love, posses sexually: "Se amacizó con ella"
'He had his way with her' (coll.)
AMACHADO -DA stubborn, insistent
AMACHAR vr. to be stubborn: to 'resist
AMACHIMBRAR vr. to surrender, give up
AMACHINAR vr. to take what one wants:
"Se amachinó con el libro" 'He
made off with the book'; to
strike a blow; to take sexual
possession; to neck (coll.), pet
(ant. slang), engage in non-
copulative amatory activities
AMACHÓN -CHONA stubborn
AMAR: SABER LO QUE E S AMAR A DIOS
EN TIERRA AJENA to know firsthand what trouble really is
AMARIHUANAR(SE) (var. of) en-
marihuanar-(se)
AMARRADO -DA married, tied down
(slang)
AMARRADOR -DORA employee who ties
or bundles (e.g., vegetables
into bunches, wool into packs,
etc.)
AMARRAR va. to marry; vr. to get

married, tie the knot (slang);
AMARRARSE LA TRIPA to tighten
one's belt (fig.), economize;
to endure hunger; AMARRARSE
LOS PANTALONES (fig.) to act re-
solutely
AMBALANCIA (var. of) ambulancia
AMBASADOR -DORA (Eng.) m. f. am-
bassador
AMBUSTERO -RA (var. of) embustero -ra
AMEJORAR (var. of) mejorar
AMENORAR (var. of) aminorar
AMERICANO -CA (non-pej.) Anglo-
Saxon, gringo
AMIGUERO -RA person who makes friends
easily
AMILCADO -DA (Eng.) milk, contain-
ing milk
AMOLADO -DA ruined, down and out
(coll.)
AMOLAR va. to ruin, harm; vr. to ruin
oneself, harm oneself; PARA
ACABARLA DE AMOLAR on top of all
that, to make things worse
(fixed expressions): "Y para
acabarla de amolar, robaron tam-
bién la ropa y el carro"
AMOLINAR (var. of) arremolinar
AMONOS (var. of) vámonos
AMOS (var. of) vamos
AMOSOMADO -DA dull; ill-humored,
sour (fig.)
AMOSOMAR (var. of) agosomar
ANCA prep. at the house of: "Estoy
anca Juan" 'I'm at Juan's
house' (Std. Estoy en casa
de Juan)
ANCLAR vn. to arrive
ANCLEAR or ANCLIAR vn. to settle
down permanently, establish
permanent residence
ANCHETA (coll.) thingamagig, thin-
gummy (said with ref. to an
item whose name one has forgotten)
ANDA, VETE or ANDAVETE (command)
Get out of here!
ANDADA distance covered by foot;
very long walk
ANDADITO -TA m., f. manner of walking, gait, carriage
ANDANCIA light epidemic
ANDAR: ANDAR ALUMBRADO -DA (slang)
to be drunk; ANDARLE A ALGUIEN
to be in a very tight spot
(fig.), be in serious trouble:
"Ya me andaba" 'I was really up
against the wall' (fig.,slang);
ANDAR A LA LINEA to be well
dressed; ANDAR AL ALBA to be on
the alert, careful; ANDAR AL
TROTE CON ALGO/ANDAR AL TROTE
CON ALGUIEN to be wrapped up in

something/someone (fig.), be very involved with something/someone: "El niño anda al trote con el juguete que le compramos", ANDAR ÁGUILA to be on the alert, be careful; ANDAR AGÜITADO -DA to be downcast, sad, frustrated, tired, nervous (etc.); ANDAR ANDANDO to be up and about after an illness (said with ref. to persons who are sufficiently recuperated to be able to leave their sickbeds); ANDA QUE NO SE SIENTA/ANDA QUE NO SE AGUANTA (also pl.: ANDAN QUE NO SE SIENTAN, etc.) he's got ants in his pants (slang), he's extremely restless; ANDAR BAILANDO to be missing; ANDAR BOMBO to be drunk; to be dazed; ANDAR BRUJO/BRUJA to be penniless, stone broke (coll.) (note: only a man may ANDAR BRUJO while either sex may ANDAR BRUJA); ANDAR CABALLÓN -LLONA to be drunk; to be high on narcotic drugs; ANDAR CANICA(S) to be passionately in love; ANDAR CARGA to be carrying narcotic drugs; ANDAR CARGADO -DA to be carrying (to have possession of) narcotic drugs; ANDAR CATARRÍN to be drunk; ANDAR CLAVADO -DA to possess stolen money; to be in the money; (coll.), to possess a certain quantity of money in excess of the amount one is accustomed to have; ANDAR COMO BURRO SIN MECATE to run wild and free (said with ref. to persons); ANDAR CON ALGUIEN (coll.) to go steady, date one person exclusively; ANDAR CON EL RABO CAÍDO to feel depressed, low (coll.); ANDAR CON PELOTA (vulg.) to be passionately in love with (someone); to be carrying the torch for someone (coll.), suffer from unrequited love for; ANDAR CORTADO -DA DE DINERO to be low on funds; ANDAR CORTO -TA to be low on funds; ANDAR CRUDO -DA to have a hangover; ANDAR CHARCA to be well dressed; ANDAR CHIFLADO -DA to be love-lorn, obsessively in love; ANDAR CHUECO -CA to be involved in shady deals (coll.), be involved in dubious business practices; ANDAR DE A TIRO or ANDAR DIATIRO to be very drunk; ANDAR DE JACALERO -RA to go from house to house visiting or gossiping; ANDAR DE JILO to run

rapidly, go like a bat out of hell (coll.); ANDAR DE MOJADO -DA to be an illegal immigrant from Mexico (see also MOJADO); ANDAR DE PASEO to be out on the town, to celebrate publicly (in various places of entertainment); ANDAR DE PUCHE to act as if one were the boss; ANDAR DE PUNTOS to walk on tiptoes; ANDAR (DE) SUELTO -TA to run around wild and free; ANDAR DE HOQUIS et al. (see DI HOQUIS et al.); ANDAR EL CUERPO to defecate (cf. HACER EL CUERPO); ANDAR ELÉCTRICO -CA to be drunk; ANDAR EMPALMADO -DA to be heavily bundled up (for protection against cold weather); ANDAR EMPELOTADO -DA to be passionately in love with (someone), to be carrying the torch for (someone), suffer from unrequited love for; ANDAR EN (+ ___ years of age) to be ___ years old: "Andrés anda en los 34"; ANDAR EN EL BABAY to be out on the town, to celebrate publicly (in various places of entertainment); ANDAR EN EL RESBALÓN to be having a love affair, having sexual relations; ANDAR EN LA LÍNEA to be drunk; ANDAR EN LA MOVIDA (slang) to sleep around (slang), have sexual relations frequently and promiscuously; to sow one's wild oats (fig.), behave wildly (esp. while one is young); to carouse; ANDAR EN LAS NUBES to be drunk; ANDAR EN PEDO CON (slang) to be in trouble with; ANDAR EN PELOTAS (vulg.) to go around mother-naked (vulg.), walk around completely nude; ANDAR ENTONADO -DA to be drunk; ANDAR ENTRADO -DA to be tipsy, slightly drunk; ANDAR FICHA to be broke, without money; ANDAR FICHA LISA (coll.) to be flat broke, completely without a cent; ANDAR HASTA EL COPETE (slang) to be very drunk; ANDAR HASTA LA RAYA COLORADA to be very drunk; ANDAR HASTA LAS CACHAS / ANDAR HASTA LAS CACHITAS to be very drunk; ANDAR HASTA LAS MANITAS to be very drunk; ANDAR JUNTOS to go steady (coll.), date one person exclusively; ANDAR LANA MORADA to be in love (note the process of disguise: enamorado > lana-morado); ANDAR LOCO -CA to be drunk; to be high on narcotic drugs, ANDAR LOCOTE drunk; high on narcotic

drugs; ANDAR MAL to be involved in an illicit love
affair; to be involved in
a shady (questionable) business
deal; ANDAR MEDIO SUATO -TA
to be tipsy; ANDAR MOTEADO
-DA / ANDAR MOTIADO -DA to be
high on marihuana; ANDAR MOTO-
ROL to be tipsy, slightly
drunk; ANDAR MANITOS / ANDAR
MUY MANITOS to be real buddy-
buddy (slang), be on very
friendly terms; ANDAR PANDO
-DA to be staggering drunk,
falling-down drunk; ANDAR PARA
ARRIBA Y PARA ABAJO / ANDAR
PARRIBA Y PABAJO to run a-
round like a chicken with its
head cut off (fig.), to rush
about rapidly; ANDAR PEDO -DA
to be drunk; ANDAR PIOCHA to
be dressed neatly; ANDAR PISTO
-TA to be drunk; ANDAR PLOCHA
to be dressed neatly; ANDAR
PUERCO -CA to be dirty,
filthy; ANDAR QUE APENAS to
be extremely drunk (so drunk
one can scarcely walk); ANDAR
QUEBRADO -DA (Ang?) to be
broke, without money; ANDAR
QUEDANDO BIEN to be trying to
make a very favorable impression on someone (usually the
object of one's amorous inten-
tions--most often said of a
male trying to ingratiate himself with a female): 'Héctor
anda quedando bien con Yolanda'; ANDAR RAYADO -DA to have
money on hand; to be in the
money (coll.), be unaccustom-
edly wealthy; ANDAR RECORTADO
-DA DE DINERO to be very low
on funds; ANDAR ROSADO -DA
(see ROSADO); ANDAR SOBRES (
andar sobre alguien) to pur-
sue a member of the opposite
sex, run after someone (coll.);
ANDAR SOCADO -DA to be cleaned
out (said of someone who has
lost his/her money in a game
of chance); ANDAR SOCAS to be
cleaned out (cf. ANDAR SOCADO);
ANDAR SOLARES to be alone (cf.
andar a solas); ANDAR SONAMBULO
-LA to be high on narcotic
drugs or alcohol; ANDAR
SOQUEADO -DA / ANDAR SOQUIADO
-DA to be cleaned out (cf.
ANDAR SOCADO); ANDAR SUBIDO
-DA to be high on narcotic
drugs or alcohol; ANDAR
TINIADO -DA (Eng., thinner)
to be high from sniffing paint

thinner; ANDAR VOLADO -DA to
go beserk; to be distracted
ANDAR VOLANDO BAJO to be feeling low (coll.), sad, depressed
ANDARIEGO -GA m. adulteror, f. a-
dultress
ANDARINO (var. of) andarín
ANDARON (var. of) anduvieron (3rd
pers. pl. pret. of andar)
ANDASTE (var. of) anduviste (2nd
pers. fam. sg. pret. of andar)
ANDATE PASEANDO / ANDATE PASIANDO
(coll.) That's it! Now you've
got it! (i.e., the correct
answer to a question, the solu-
tion to a problem, etc.)
ANDURIEGO -GA (var. of) andariego
-ga
ANGINAS fpl. tonsils
ANIMAS: ANIMAS (SANTAS) QUE interj.
If only . . . ! (similar in
intent and function to Std.
Ojalá que . . .)
ANONERO -RA exaggerator
ANQUE (var. of) aunque; (var. of)
anca (q.v. supra)
ANSÍ (var. of) así
ANSIA: COMER ANSIA to be impatient
ANTECRISTO (var. of) anticristo
ANTES: MAS ANTES before, before-
hand (Std. antes)
ANTICO -CA identical, similar
ANTICONCEPTIVO -VA contraceptive
ANTIFRÍS (Eng.) m. antifreeze
ANTIGÜIDAD (var. of) antigüedad f.
ANTINOCHE (var. of) anteanoche
ANTIOJOS (var. of) anteojos 'eye-
glasses'
ANTONCES (var. of) entonces
ANUNCIO: DECIR UN ANUNCIO to
announce; to advertise
AÑALES mpl. many years
AÑIDIR (var. of) añadir
AÑO DEL CALDO (coll.) very old; m.
yesteryear, olden days, times
gone by
AOLER (var. of) oler
APÁ (var. of) papá
APACHADO -DA (var. of) apapachado
-da
APACHAR (var. of) apapachar
APACHURRADO -DA smashed, crushed;
wrinkled (ref. to clothes)
APACHURRAR va. to smash, crush,
squash; APACHURRAR (LA) OREJA
(slang) to sleep; vr. to
become smashed, crushed,
squashed
APACHURRÓN m. act of smashing,
crushing
APAGADORA fire engine
APAGAR: APAGAR LOS OJOS to give
(someone) a black eye (in a
fight): "Le apagaron los ojos

en el bochinche" 'They gave him a black eye in the brawl'

APALANCAR vr. to lift with a lever; to open with a level

APALIAR (var. of) <u>apalear</u>

APANTALLAR vn. to act important, show off

APAÑAR: APAÑAR AIRE to escape from (someone): "Tuvieron que apañar aire porque vieron venir a la polecía" 'They had to escape because they saw the police coming'; to steal

APAPACHADO -DA spoiled, pampered (ref. to children)

APAPACHAR va. to spoil, pamper (ref. to children); to encourage

APARADOR m. showcase, store counter; m. grass catcher (type of basket attached to rear or side of a lawn-mower)

APARAR va. to buy

APARATITO inter-uterine device, coil, loop (contraceptive)

APARATO msg. buttocks

APARENCIA (var. of) <u>apariencia</u>

APARTADO part (division in human hair)

APARTE reserved, somewhat standoffish (ref. to people); SER MUY APARTE to be a loner, be shy of human company

APELATIVO -VA surname (cf. Std. <u>apellido</u>)

APENADO -DA ashamed

APENAR va. to shame, make someone feel ashamed; vr. to be ashamed

APENAS: ANDAR QUE APENAS to be extremely drunk, be falling-down drunk

APENDIS m. (var. of) <u>apéndice</u>

APENTERAR va. to frighten; to surpass; to degrade, humiliate

APERLADO -DA pearl-colored (ref. to skin coloration mid-way between "white" and "brown")

APESTAR vn. to become out-of-date, passé: "Esa canción ya apesta" 'That song is already out-of-date'

APLADIR (var. of) <u>aplaudir</u>

APLANADORA steam roller

APLANAR va. to press, bear down upon

APLASTAR va. to leave speechless, cut down, put in one's place; vr. to overstay one's welcome; to sit down with the intention of staying a long while; to butt in, enter unwelcomed into (e.g., a conversation)

APLASTÓN m. unexpected scolding or punishment, reprimand; DARLE A ALGUIEN UN APLASTÓN to put

someone in his/her place; ECHARLE A ALGUIEN UN APLASTÓN to put someone in his/her place

APLICACIÓN (Ang.) f. application (for funds, a job, admission to a school, etc.) (Std. <u>solicitud</u> etc.)

APLOGAR vr. to regain one's composure, become calm

APLOMAR vr. to be slow to react (because of inability, laziness, lack of preparation, etc.)

APORREADO -DA / APORRIADO -DA beaten up, thrashed (in a fight, etc.)

APORREAR or APORRIAR vr. to fight

APOYO last squirt of milk from a cow's udder

APREBAR (var. of) <u>aprobar</u>

APRECIO: HACER APRECIO to pay attention

APRENDER (Ang.) to find out, become aware of: "Aprendí que iba a venir el jueves" 'I learned (=found out) that he was coming Thursday'

APRENTERAR va. to outshine; to belittle; to scare

APRETADO -DA tight-fitting (ref. to clothes): "El vestido le queda muy apretado" 'The dress is too tight on her'

APRETADOR m. brassiere

APRETAR: APRETAR EL MONO to bewitch, hex: "A Pedro le están apretando el mono, por eso se está portando así"

APRETONES (see DAR APRETONES)

APRONTAR vr. to arrive unexpectedly

APROVECHADO -DA bully-like (said of persons), viciously aggresive

APROVECHAR vr. to bully someone

¡APUCHA! interj. (expression of surprise or astonishment)

APUCHAR (Eng.) (var. of) <u>puchar</u>

APUERCADO -DA poorly dressed

APURACIÓN f. haste, hurry

APURADO -DA in a hurry; in a tight spot (fig.), in trouble

APURAR vr. to hurry

APURÓN -RONA impatient (ref. to people)

APURREADO -DA / APURRIADO -DA (vars. of) <u>aporriado -da</u>

AQUELLA (see DE AQUELLA)

AQUELLO: POR AQUELLO DE LAS DUDAS just in case: "Lo voy a llamar por teléfono por aquello de las dudas"

AQUEO -A (var. of) <u>aquello -lla</u>

AQUÍ: AQUÍ ASÍ right here (Note: this fixed expression is accompanied by the speaker's pointing with his/her finger

ARACLÁN m. (var. of) alacrán

ARAÑADO -DA stolen
ARAÑAR va. to steal; (coll.) to
    try to get something for noth-
    ing
ARAÑON m. scratch
ARAS (var. of) arras fpl.
ARBOLERA (var. of) arboleda
ARCAS fpl. (seldom fsg.) armpits
ARCO: ARCO IRES (var. of arco iris m.
AREDOR (var. of) alrededor
ARENGUE m. trouble, difficulty
ARENTRO (rus.) (var. of) adentro
ARFILER (var. of) alfiler m.
ARGENTE adj. m. & f. accommodating
ARGOLLA wedding ring
ARGÜENDA m. piece of gossip
ARGÜENDERO -RA gossiper, gossip-
    monger
ARGULLO (var. of) orgullo
ARGUMENTO (Ang.) argument, dispute,
    verbal fight
ARISCAR va. to fight; ARISCAR MAN-
    GAS (coll.) to roll up one's
    sleeves (in preparation for a
    fight)
ARISCO -CA suspicious, distrustful;
    skittish; jealous
ARISMÉTICA (var. of) aritmética
ARMADO -DA flushed (slang), loaded
    (=possessed of considerable
    money or other assets)
ARMAR vr. to have it made (coll.),
    be assured of success or for-
    tune; to have a stroke of good
    luck, come into good times
ARME (Eng.) m. army
AROPLANO (var. of) aeroplano
AROPUERTO (var. of aeropuerto
ARVEJÓN m. chick-pea (Cicer
    arietinum)
ARRACADA any type of earring
ARRACLE m. & f. show-off
ARRANADO -DA (hum.) married, hitched
    (hum.); peaceful; docile
ARRANAR va. to marry, marry off,
    hitch (hum.); vr. to get mar-
    ried, get hitched (hum.); to
    sit comfortably
ARRANCADO -DA penniless, broke
    (slang)
ARRANCAR vr. to move off rapidly
    from a standing position
ARRANE m. matrimony, married state
ARRANQUE: SER DE ARRANQUE(S) to be
    unpredictable; to be tempera-
    mental; ARRANQUES mpl. periods
    of strange and unusual be-
    havior; TENER SUS ARRANQUES to
    anger quickly; to become angry
    unexpectedly
ARRASTRADERO: IRSE POR EL ARR-
    ASTRADERO to be guided by the
    tracks of an animal

ARRASTRADO-DA mean, despicable; mis-
    chievous, tricky; (slang) lousy,
    crumby, damned (coll.): ¡So-
    siégate, huerco arrastrado!"
    'Stop it, you damned little
    brat!"
ARRASTRAR va. to be good at do-
    ing things, excel: "A Juan le
    arrastra para jugar al tenis"
    'Juan is very good at playing
    tennis'; ARRASTRAR EL APARATO
    to be good at doing things,
    excel
ARREADOR -DORA or ARRIADOR -DORA
    chauffeur, driver of a car
ARREAR or ARRIAR va. to drive
    (horses, mules, etc.); to
    drive any vehicle (including
    motorized vehicles)
ARREGLADA fsg. repairs; act of
    straightening out (the life of
    a person previously engaged in
    crime or otherwise "crooked"
    business); act of hexing or
    bewitching
ARREGLAR va. to hex, bewitch;
    ARREGLAR CUENTAS to settle a
    matter; vr. to reform, straight-
    en oneself out (fig.)
ARREJUNTAR vr. (coll.) to cohab-
    itate, live together out of
    wedlock, shack up (vulg. &
    slang)
ARREMPUJÓN m. (var. of) rempujón
ARRENDAR va. to return, give back:
    "¿Qué hiciste con la camisa?
    ¿Se la arrendaste?" 'What did
    you do with the shirt? Did you
    give it back to him?'; vr. to
    turn back after having started
    out, return: "Se arrendó antes
    de llegar a la casa"
ARREPENTIR vr. to change one's
    mind
ARREQUINTADO -DA tight-fitting;
    tightly pressed together (ref.
    to persons, e.g., in a crowd);
    mf. high-pressure artist (per-
    son who puts others under pres-
    sure, keeps them in a state of
    tension)
ARREQUINTAR var. to tighten (a
    wire); to get someone into
    trouble; to force someone into
    a corner; vr. to press tightly
    against someone (esp. while
    dancing)
ARRESTRAR (var. of) arrestar
ARRIADOR -DORA (var. of) ARREADOR -
    DORA
ARRIAR (var. of) ARREAR
ARRIESGAR vr.: ARRIEGARSE EL CUERO
    to risk one's neck

ARRIMADO: ESTAR DE ARRIMADOS to live with someone and be dependent upon them (often said with ref. to relatives who "move in with" a family)

ARRIMAR vr. to move in with a family (often relatives) and depend on them financially; ARRIMARLE A ALGUIEN LA CHANCLA to spank

ARRINCONAR va. to put in a corner

ARROLEAR or ARROLIAR (coll.) to go for a ride (in a car); to go for a walk

ARROÑA (var. of) roña

ARRUINAR: PARA ACABARLA DE ARRUINAR to make matters worse (set expressions)

ARRUMBADO -DA (var. of) rumbado -da

ASARRUCHAR (var. of) aserruchar

ASCO (see PONER DEL ASCO)

ASCRINERO -RA (var. of) aiscrinero -ra (Eng.)

ASEGÚN (var. of) según

ASEGURANZA (var. of) seguranza

ASEGURAR: NO ASEGURAR to not expect someone to live: "No la aseguran" 'They don't expect her to live'

ASEGURO (var. of) seguro

ASENTAR va. to tamp down, smooth, level, smooth out (press clothing lightly with a clothes-press or an iron)

ASÍ: ASÍ ES QUE so, therefore (conj.): "Nos quieren allí a las seis de la tarde en punto, así es que no vengas tarde"; ASÍ SÍ (SE VALE) That's more like it (general expression of approval); ASÍ NO (SE VALE) That's not it at all, That's just not right; That's not fair (Note: así no enjoys greater frequency than así sí); ASÍ Y ASADO so-and-so (used to ref. to person whose name one wishes to avoid mentioning): "¿Por qué te pones a hablar con ese así y asado?" 'Why do you talk with that old so-and-so?'

ASIENTO: mpl. ASIENTOS coffee grounds

ASIGUN (var. of) (a)según

ASILENCIAR (var. of) silenciar

ASINA (var. of) así

ASISTENTE -TA (Ang.) mf. assistant (Std. ayudante)

ASISTIR vr. to serve oneself (food); to eat

ASOLEADO -DA or ASOLIADO -DA scatterbrained, lame-brained, stupid; crazy, loony (slang); (said of a person dazed or stunned from overexposure to the sun's rays); TONTO ASOLEADO crazy old fool

ASOLEAR vr. to overexpose oneself to the rays or heat of the sun; to show the effects of being out in the hot sun (by perspiring, being short of breath, etc.)

ASPERINA (var. of) aspirina

ASPIRINO -NA (coll.) person who becomes intoxicated by aspirins, person who "turns on" with aspirins

ASQUELA mosquito (Culicidae)

ASQUEROSO -SA squeamish

ASTRACTO -TA (var. of) abstracto -ta

ASTRONOTA mf. (var. of) astronauta

ASUAVIZAR (var. of) suavizar

ASUMIR (Ang.) to assume (i.e., that something has happened), suppose, conjecture (Std. suponer etc.)

ASUSTÓN -TONA (coll.) fraidy-cat (coll.), person easily frightened

ATACADO -DA (coll.) stuffed, full, filled (e.g., with food); opportunistic; abusive, vulgar, gross; tight fitting: "El vestido le queda muy atacado" 'The dress is too tight-fitting on her'

ATACAR vr. to overdo in a vulgar or greedy fashion; to behave abusively; to take more than one should (e.g., food); (coll.) to make a pig of oneself through overeating

ATACÓN -CONA bully(-like), abusive; stingy, cheap, parsimonious

ATAJO (pej.) bunch, group (of persons); ATAJO DE PENDEJOS bunch of idiots (fig.), group of fools

ATARANTADO -DA in trouble; absent-minded

ATARIADO -DA (var. of) atareado -da

ATASCADA (see DAR UNA ATASCADA)

ATASCADERO mess, jam (coll.), difficult situation

ATASCADO -DA ignorant; good-for-nothing; mean, base, vile; filthy, dirty

ATASCAR va. to jam (an object) into an opening; ATASCARLA (vulg.) to insert the male organ into the vagina; to force one's way in, crash (e.g., a party) (slang)

ATASCOSO -SA muddy

ATAÚR (var. of) ataúd m.

ATENDER (Ang.) va. to attend, be present at, go to (Std. asistir)

ATENDIENTE mf. clerk, attendant

ATENER vr. to depend upon someone to do one's work or dis-

charge one's responsibilities:
"Si vienes a atenerte, es mejor
que te vayas"

ATENIDO -DA dependent upon others to
do one's work

ATEXANADO -DA Texanized, Texan-like

ATIBIARSE A HACER ALGO to get a
move on (fig.), get busy doing
something

ATIRANTADO -DA dead

ATIRANTAR vr. to go to bed, stretch
out (fig.)

ATIRICIADO -DA sad, depressed

ATIRICIAR vr. to become sad

ATIZAR va. to stir, poke (a fire);
to strike (someone); ¡ATIZALE!
interj. Move it!, Get a move
on!, Shake a leg! (coll.)

ATOCAR (var. of) tocar

ATOL m. (var. of) atole

ATOLE m. drink made of water, corn
meal, sugar and sometimes chocolate and other ingredients; m.
cream of wheat (cereal); ATOLE/
ATOLE DE AVENA oatmeal (cereal);
DAR ATOLE CON EL DEDO to deceive
one's husband with another woman;
DESPUÉS DE ATOLE too late to do
any good; HACER ATOLE to flatten,
break every bone in one's body
(ref. to person run over by a
heavy vehicle); HACERSE ATOLE
to become over-dilute, watery
(usually said of food losing con-
sistency while being prepared):
"El arroz se hizo atole porque
le echaste(s) mucha agua y lo
dejaste(s) una hora sobre la
lumbre"

ATOLERO -RA person who makes or sells
atole; (also, pej. designation
for any vulgar or ill-mannered
person)

ATOLLADERO tight spot, jam (coll.),
difficulty

ATOLLAR va. to anger; vn. to wan-
der, roam; vr. to get confused,
mixed up

ATOMOBIL (var. of) automóbil m.

ATOMÓBIL (var. of) automóbil m.

ATONTADO -DA dazed, stunned (as
from a blow on the head)

ATOR -RA m., f. (var. of) autor -ra

ATORNILLADO -DA prudent, having common sense

ATOTACHADO adv. rapidly

ATRABANCADO -DA reckless

ATRABANCAR va. to act recklessly

ATRANCAR va. to latch (usually a
screen door), lock (a door),
bar

ATRASADO -DA (coll.) backward, slow
to learn, dense; half-baked

(coll.); relapsed, set back
(said of medical patients);
willfully ill-informed; ESTAR
ATRASADO -DA to be incorre-
gible; (as a reprimand for abusive behavior:) "¡Estás atrasado!" 'You're really something
else again!' (iron.)

ATRASAR va. to cause a medical
patient to suffer a relapse:
"El doctor en vez de aliviarlo,
lo atrasó"; vr. to have a relapse, suffer a setback: "Anoche
estaba muy bien, pero esta mañana se atrasó"

ATREVIDO -DA insolent, abusive

ATROCIDADO -DA opportunistic, abusive

ATROJADO -DA behind, running slow
(ref. to clocks and watches);
behind schedule

ATROJAR vr. to fall behind, run
slow (ref. to clocks and watches): "Voy a darle cuerda a mi
reloj para que no se atroje otra
vez"; to fall behind in one's
work, on one's payments, etc.:
"Me van a quitar la casa porque
me atrojé en mis pagos"

ATUFAR vr. to become proud

ATULLAR (var. of) atollar

AUCUPADO -DA (vars. of) ocupado -da

AUDITOR (Ang?) m. bookkeeper

AÚJA (var. of) aguja

AURA (var. of) ahora

AUROPLANO (var. of) aeroplano

AUTOBUSERO -RA busdriver

AUTORIDAD fsg. the police, police
force

AVENTAR va. to push; to throw (an
object); vr. to fight; to excel,
do well; AVENTAR A LOCO to ignore; AVENTAR A LEÓN to ignore

AVENTÓN m. lift, ride (in a car);
push, shove

AVERIGUACIÓN f. dispute, argument

AVERIGUADERO dispute, argument

AVERIGUADOR -DORA argumentative person

AVERIGUAR va. to argue; vn. to argue; vr. AVERIGUÁRSELAS to
resolve one's problems: "Carlos
nunca se las va a averiguar"

AVERIGUATA noise and confusion
created by an argument

AVIENTE mf. decoy; police informer

AVIROTE adj., mf. naked, nude

AVISPA bee

AVISPERO: PONERSE (EN EL) AVISPERO
to become alert

AY: ¡AY TÚ!, ¡AY TÚ PEPE!, ¡AY TÚ
PEPE, CUIDADO QUE TE VOY A

PEGAR!, ¡AY TÚ TÚ!, ¡AY TÚ PEPE,
TÚ LA TRAIS!, ¡AY TÚ CHOCHÓN!
interjs. (hum. or pej.) (used
to mark or make fun of an effeminate person or else to mark or
make fun of an effeminate-sound-
ing statement); (var. of) ahí,
(also of) allí; interj. Will you
look at that!; ¡AY MIRA NOMÁS!
Will you look at that!; AY NOS
VEMOS / AY TE GUACHO / AY TE
MIRO (coll.) See ya 'round, So
long, Be seein' ya (coll.);
AY TE MIRO, CASIMIRO / AY TE
GUACHO, CUCARACHO (slang) (roughly equivalent to Eng. 'See ya
later, alligator', etc.); POR AY/
POR AY NOMAS (just) over there;
more or less, approximately; AY
VOY I'm coming (also AY VAMOS,
AY VAN, etc.)
AZADONEAR or AZADONIAR (var. of)
azadonar
AZODONEAR or AZADONIAR (var. of)
azadonar
AZONZADO -DA stunned, dazed (from
a blow, over-exposure to the sun,
etc.)
AZONZAR va. to stun, stupify; vr.
to become stunned, bewildered
AZORRILLAR va. to intimidate, fright-
en; vr. to become frightened;
to become confused
AZOTAR va. to give (a present); to
pay, fork over (coll.); vn. to
yield, submit; to die; vn. to
fall down hard, fall down with
a bang; AZOTAR LA RES (var. of)
caer la res; AZOTAR MUY FEO
(slang) to die tragically
AZTLÁN m. ancient homeland of the
Aztec people, roughly coincident
with what is now the southwestern
part of the United States (Texas,
New Mexico, Arizona, California,
etc.)
AZUCADERA (var. of) azucarera sugar
bowl
AZUFRE (slang) m. heroin
AZUL (slang) m. policeman, "man
in blue"
AZURCA f. (child language, var. of)
azúcar

B

BABAY (Eng.) bye-bye (<good-bye);
IR DE BABAY to take a walk;
IR AL BABAY to "go out" (coll.)
leave in search of amusement
BABICHE msg. beet(s); bitch; son-
of-a-bitch (vulg.) (origin of
BABICHE uncertain--possible
blend of baba and biche
bitch?)
BABITO (dim.) (Eng.) Bobby
BABOSADA foolish act; stupid idea,
remark or act
BABOSO -SA ignorant, stupid
BABUCH (slang) foolish;stupid
BACALADO (var. of) bacalao
BACIERO chief shepherd
BACÍN m. bassinet; bed pan; slop
jar
BACHA cigarette butt; (Eng.) (slang)
badge, identification plate;
barge, flat boat
BACHICHA (slang) cigarette butt
(esp. marihuana cigarette
butt)
BADÍA (var. of) bahía
BAI (Eng.) interj. good-bye;
BAI BAI good-bye
BAICA (Eng.) bicycle
BAILADOR -DORA mf. fond of danc-
ing; good dancer
BAILAR vr. BAILARSE A ALGUIEN to
whip or spank someone; to de-
feat someone in a fight
BAILE: BAILE-CENA (Ang.) m. din-
ner-dance; BAILE ZAPATEADO/
ZAPOTIADO Mazurka (type of
dance)
BAISA (coll. & underw. slang) hand
(prob.< baes 'manos' in
Spanish Romani [Gypsy] lan-
guage)
BAISICLE (Eng.) m. bicycle
BAISICLETA (Eng.) bicycle
BAISÍQUEL (Eng.) m. bicycle
BAISO -SA (slang) young person
BAJAR: BAJAR PARA ABAJO (pleo-
nasm) to go down, descend;
to get off, climb down from;
BAJAR DE ARRIBA to leave
prison legally; BAJARLE LA
REGLA A ALGUIEN to flow (said
of menstrual fluid), have one's
period

BAJO mpl. lower floors (of a building)

BALA m. or f. clever person, astute person; flirt, (f.) loose woman

BALACEADA or BALACIADA act or effect of firing a volley of shots (bullets); riddling (of a person with bullet shots)

BALACEAR or BALACIAR va. to riddle or spray with bullets, fire a volley of bullets

BALDE (dim. of) Baltasar

BALERINA (var. of) bailarina

BALONE or BALONI (Eng.) m. baloney sausage; (hum.) penis

BALÚN (Eng.) m. balloon

BAMBA Cuban dance; trick; accident

BANCO (Ang.) river bank; BANCO DE MADERA lumber yard; BANCO DE SANGRE blood bank

BANDA (Ang?) bandage, band-aid

BANDEJA washbasin; BANDEJAS fpl. pots and pans: "¿Por qué no has lavado las bandejas?"

BANDOLERO -RA lazybones (coll.), indolent (person)

BANQUEAR or BANQUIAR va. to bank, deposit money in a bank

BANQUETEAR or BANQUETIAR vn. to have a good time

BAÑO: BAÑO DE PIES foot bath; BAÑO DE REGADERA shower bath; BAÑO DE TOALLA sponge bath; DARSE BAÑOS DE PUREZA to glorify oneself, take a holier than thou attitude (coll.)

BAQUEAR or BAQUIAR (Eng.) va. & vr. to back up (a car), cause to move backwards; to support, back up; to back down, go back on one's word, chicken out (slang)

BARAJEAR or BARAJIAR (var. of barajar) va. to mix, jumble together; vn. to mix with a crowd (said of persons)

BARAJERO -RA card freak (slang), inordinately fond of playing cards

BARAÑA unkempt head of hair; (coll. & underw.) tomorrow; (coll. & underw.) morning; thickets, branches (fsg.)

BARATA bargain sale; BARATA DE QUEMAZÓN fire sale (sale at reduced prices of merchandise slightly damaged in a fire)

BARATEAR or BARATIAR vr. to mix with a crowd (said of persons)

BARATO deadbeat (coll.), person unwilling to pay and eager to borrow

BARATÓN -TONA ill-bred, coarse, vulgar

BARBA: HACER LA BARBA to apple-polish (coll.), flatter; BARBA DE ELOTE corn tassel (Zea mays) (herb prepared as a tea and used to treat kidney ailments); fpl. BARBAS TENGAS or BARBAS TENGAS Y CON ELLAS TE MANTENGAS (expression used mainly by children to taunt other children, roughly equivalent to Eng. "Phooey on you!")

BARBACOBA (var. of) barbacoa

BARBARO -RA excessive; tremendous, wonderful, marvellous; daring

BARBEAR or BARBIAR va. to apple-polish (coll.), flatter

BARER (var. of) barrer

BARRA bar (of metal); bar (barroom counter; the barroom itself)

BARRACA (Ang.) barrack (military)

BARRAL (coll. & underw.) m. muscular man

BARRANCO slope, hillside

BARRANQUEÑA: HACER BARRANQUEÑA to gather and take possession of a large number of articles for one's own use

BARREADA or BARRIADA fsg. citizenry of a barrio (collective reference to all persons in a given neighborhood)

BARRER va. to make the sign of the cross with wide, sweeping motions on a person's body to break the spell of a hex or an incantation (the act is performed by the healer as he/she recites several Our Fathers, Hail Marys and Credos)

BARRILITO -TA (coll.) chubby, tubby

BARRIO neighborhood (esp. with ref. to a Mexican-American neighborhood)

BARRO acne

BARRÓN -RRONA m.,f. materialist(ic)

BARROTE m. rafter

BAS (Eng.) m. bus

BASCA vomit

BÁSCULA (coll. & underw.) search; DAR BÁSCULA to frisk; PASAR BÁSCULA to frisk

BASE: BASE POR BOLAS (baseball slang) base on balls

BASQUEAR or BASQUIAR vr. to vomit

BASUDERO -RA (var. of) basurero -ra

BASURA scum of society (pej. ref. to persons); BASURA BLANCA (Ang.) (pej.) white trash (lower-class Anglo-Saxons); (see also PONER DE LA BASURA)

BASURITA foreign object that has gotten into one's eye

BATEAR or BATIAR (Eng.) va. to bat

a ball (in baseball)
BATEO (Eng.) act or effect of batting a ball (in baseball)
BATERÍA (electrical) battery; flashlight; a hard time: "No quiero que me den tanta batería" 'I don't want them to give me such a hard time'
BATERO -RA (Eng.) batter (of a ball, in baseball)
BATIADOR -RA mf. (var. of) bateador -dora (Eng.)
BATIAR (Eng.) (var. of) batear
BATIDERO disorderly and messy place
BATIDO -DA dirty, soiled (often ref. to persons)
BATIR vr. to get dirty: "Acabo de cambiarte; no te vayas a batir con ese chocolate"
BATO -TA (coll. & underw.) f. gal; m. guy, dude (slang); BATO CALOTE big guy; BATO DE COLEGIO educated person; guy who thinks he's smart; BATO RELAJE punk; ridiculous punk; BATO TIRILÍ Pachuco (q.v.); BATO TIRILONGO member of an adolescent or criminal gang; dude (slang); hood (slang)
BAUL (var. of) baúl
BAXEO (var. of boxeo
BAYONESA (var. of) mayonesa
BEBE va. to drink intoxicating beverages
BEBIDA act or effects of drinking intoxicating beverages
BECERRO -RRA ignorant person
BEDERO (var. of) babero
BEIBI (Eng.) mf. (var. of) bebé (cf. BEBE)
BEIBISIRA (Eng.) mf. baby-sitter
BEIBISIRIN (Eng.) m. baby-sitting
BEIQUINPAUDA or BEIQUINPAURA (Eng.) m. baking powder
BEIS (Eng.) m. base (in baseball)
BELDUQUE m. knife
BENDECIDO (var. of) bendicho (ppart. of bendecir)
BENDÉI (Eng.) m. band-aid
BENITO (dim. of) Benjamín
BENQUEAR or BENQUIAR (vars. of) banquear/banquiar
BEO -A (var. of) bello -lla
BEQUEAR or BEQUIAR (vars. of) baquear / baquiar (Eng.)
BEQUENPAURA or BEQUINPAUDA or BEQUINPAURA (Eng.) m. baking powder (cf. BEIQUINPAUDA et al.)
BERRONGO -GA bothersome (person)
BESBOL (Eng.) m. baseball
BESOTEAR or BESOTIAR va. to kiss repeatedly
BESUQUIAR (var. of) besuquear

BET (Eng.) m. baseball bat
BETABEL msg. sugar beet(s)
BETABELERO -RA harvester of sugar beets
BETEAR or BETIAR (vars. of) batear/batiar (q.v.)
BETEO (var. of) bateo (q.v.)
BETERO -RA (var. of) batero -ra (q.v.)
BETO -TA (dims. resp. of) Alberto -ta, Gilberto, Heriberto, Humberto, Roberto -ta
BI (Eng.) (dim. of) Beatriz
BIBEL or BIBÉL (Hispanizations of) Beeville, Texas
BICA (slang) money
BICARBONATO: BICARBONATO DE SODA bicarbonate of soda
BICECLETA tricycle
BICICLETERÍA bicycle shop
BICOCA (slang) money
BICORBONATE (var. of) bicarbonato
BIEN: BIEN DADO -DA wealthy, rich; (with ref. to a blow to the body) good solid blow, thorough blow or beating: "Te voy a dar una paliza bien dada"; ¡BIEN HAIGA! 'Good for you!' (expression of approbation); BIEN PARECIDO -DA handsome; BIEN SENTADO -DA rich, sitting pretty (coll.)
BIL (Eng.) m. bill of sale; tab, restaurant check
BINGO (Eng.) m. (game of) bingo
BINOCULAR (Ang.) mpl. binoculars
BIRONGA (coll. & underw.) beer
BIRONGUEAR or BIRONGUIAR (coll. & underw.) to drink beer; to drink any alcoholic beverage
BIRONGUERO -RA (slang) beer-drinker
BIROTE m. French bread
BÍRREA or BIRRIA barbecue; (Eng.) beer
BIRRIONGA (slang) beer
BÍSQUETE (Eng.) m. biscuit
BÍTARO beet; sugar
BITOQUE m. nozzle of a syringe used for enemas; nozzle of a hose
BIURE (Hispanization of) Buda, Texas
BIURE CHAP or BIURI CHAP (Eng.) m. or f. beauty shop, beauty parlor
BLAF (Eng.) m. bluff (deception, deliberate misleading)
BLANCANIEVE (var. of) Blancanieves
BLANQUILLO -LLA mf. (pej.) Anglo-Saxon; m. (euph.) testicle, ball (vulg.)
BLANQUÍO (var. of) blanquillo
BLICH or BLICHE or BLICHI (Eng.)

m. bleach

BLICHAR or BLICHEAR or BLICHIAR (Eng.) va. to bleach (hair)

BLOAUT (Eng.) m. blowout (of a car's tire)

BLOC (Eng.) m. block

BLOFE (Eng.) m. bluff (deception, etc.--cf. BLAF)

BLOFEADOR -DORA or BLOFIADOR -DORA (Eng.) bluffer (deceiver)

BLOFEAR (Eng.) va. to bluff, deceive

BLOQUE (Ang.) m. city block; cement block

BOBITO (dim.) (Eng.) Bobby

BOBITO eye gnat (hippelates)

BOBO -BA (slang) drunk; crazy, nuts (coll.); m. balloon

BOCA: BOCA DE CHANCLA thick-lipped; BOCA DEL ESTOMAGO esophagus, gullet; BOCA GRANDE (coll.) big mouth, excessive talker; HACERSE (DE) BOCA CHICA to pretend to be a small eater; TENER BOCA CHICA to talk very little

BOCON -CONA adj. (coll.) defamatory; mf. defamer; liar; gossiper; foul-mouthed person; loud-mouth (excessive and noisy talker)

BOCHINCHE m. gathering or crowd of lower-class or delinquent persons; party, celebration; melee

BOFO -FA soft, spongy; fat; VIEJA BOFA fat old bitch (vulg.); whore

BOGANVILIA (var. of) buganvilla

BOGUE (Eng.) m. buggy (esp. baby buggy)

BOICOTE (Eng.) m. boycott

BOICOTEAR or BOICOTIAR (Eng.) va. to boycott

BOI ESCAUT (Eng.) m. boy scout

BOILA (Eng.) boiler

BOITELAS interj. (coll.) Hot damn!, Gol-lee!

BOLA dollar; group of people; mob, disorderly gathering; baseball (Std. pelota); BOLAS fpl. knots (type of tissue swelling) "Dicen que las bolas en la nuca vienen de la nerviosidad" BOLA DE CARNE meatball; BOLA DE LA PUERTA door knob; HACER BOLA to confuse, puzzle, bewilder; HACERSE BOLA to mill around (said of groups of people); to become confused; VOLVERSE BOLA to become confused; (see also DAR CON BOLA); fpl. testicles, balls (vulg.)

BOLADO -DA m. adulteror; f. adultress

BOLEADA or BOLIADA shoe-shine

BOLEADOR or BOLIADOR m. shoeshine boy

BOLEAR or BOLIAR va. to shine shoes

BOLERO -RA m. shoeshine boy; f. mumps

BOLETO ticket; (pej.) gringo, Anglo-Saxon

BOLEVEAR or BELEVIAR vn. to dance

BOLILLO -LLA (pej.) gringo- Anglo-Saxon; BOLILLO CON COLA PRIETA gringoized Mexican-American, coconut (slang--ref. to Chicano who is "brown on the outside but white on the inside")

BOLIO -LIA (var. of) bolillo -lla

BOLITA yolk of egg; clay marble (used in game of marbles)

BOLO dollar, peso; gift; bunch of pennies traditionally thrown to children at baptisms by godfathers

BOLON m. multitude

BOLSA pocket (in trousers); BOLSA CHIQUITA watch pocket; BOLSA DE AGUAS amniotic sac: "El feto crece en la bolsa de aguas"; douche bag; enema bag

BOLSITA watch pocket, small pocket for storing watches

BOLSUDO -DA (coll.) monied, loaded (coll.); (said of clothes having an excessive number of large pockets)

BOLUDO -DA lumpy, full of lumps

BOMBO -BA (slang) rich, wealthy; tired; ANDAR BOMBO -BA to be drunk; to be dazed: VIEJO BOMBO / VIEJA BOMBA interjs. (pej.) You damned old bastard / bitch!

BOMBONES mpl. okra

BOMPA (Eng.) (automobile's) bumper

BOMPEAR or BOMPIAR (Eng.) va. to bump, bump into

BOMPER (Eng.) m. (automobile's) bumper (cf. BOMPA)

BONCHE or BONCHI (Eng.) m. bunch, handful; (coll.) gang, bunch (of persons)

BONGALO bungalow

BONITO -TA handsome; QUE BONITO!, ¿NO? (iron.) Nice going! (iron.) (expression used to reprimand people for their improper behavior)

BONQUE (Eng.) (slang) m. bunk (type of bed); TIRAR BONQUE (coll.) to go to sleep

BONQUEAR or BONQUIAR (Eng.) vn. to sleep

BOÑUELO (var. of) buñuelo

BOQUINETA m. cleft palate

BORCELANA small chamber pot

BORCHINCHE (var. of) bochinche

BORDERA (Eng.) owner and operator of a boarding house

BORDO small dam or dike; (Eng.) food dispensed in a boarding house

BORLO dance; movie theater; agitated situation; any festivity

BORLOTE m. noise, agitation, tumult; scandal; trouble; HACER BORLOTE to make trouble; to liven things up, raise hell (coll.)

BORLOTEAR or BORLOTIAR vn. to raise hell (coll.), liven things up; to make trouble

BORLOTERO -RA mf. trouble-maker; agitator; adj. turbulent, noisy, rowdy

BOROL (Eng.) m. bottle

BORUCA: HACER BORUCA to confuse, disorient

BORUQUEAR or BORUQUIAR va. to confuse, disorient

BORRACHALES (usually mfsg.) habitual drunkard, lush (coll.)

BORRACHÍN -CHINA habitual drunkard

BORRACHINTO -TA alcoholic, drunkard

BORRADO -DA greenish-colored (esp. ref. to eyes)

BORRAR vr. to beat it (coll.), scram (coll.); BORRAR DEL MAPA (coll.) to kill (someone)

BORREGO -GA sheep; veal

BORREGUERO -RA country person, hick (coll. & pej.)

BOS (Eng.) m. bus; boss

BOSGO -GA glutton

BOSLAIN (Eng.) m. transportation network, busline; bus terminal

BOSTECEAR or BOSTECIAR (vars. of) bostezar

BOSTEZADA yawn

BOSTECEADA or BOSTECIADA (var. of) bostezada

BOTANA taco given free to tavern patrons

BOTE m. pail, bucket; bottle (in general); baby bottle; (slang) jail; ECHAR EN EL BOTE / ECHAR AL BOTE to hex, bewitch

BOTEA (var. of) botella

BOTELLA fsg. intoxicating beverages; AGARRAR LA BOTELLA to take to the bottle (fig.), become a habitual drunkard

BOTI (var. of) bote

BOTIJÓN -JONA large-bellied (usually ref. to women)

BOTO -TA alcoholic; PONERSE LAS BOTAS to take advantage of a situation

BOTÓN very young boy who constitutes the male half of the "miniture couple" at formal Catholic wedding ceremonies

BOX (Eng.) (var. of) boxeo m.

BÓXAR or BÓXER (Eng.) m. boxer (Std. pugilista)

BOXIAR (var. of) boxear

BOXIN (Eng.) m. boxing, fisticuffs

BRACA (Eng.) break, chance, opportunity

BRACERO day-laborer, esp. one of Mexican origin;(by extension) Mexican immigrant to the United States

BRANDI (Eng.) m. brandy

BRAVO -VA: A LA BRAVA by force

BRAZO: MÁS VALEN LAS PIERNAS QUE LOS BRAZOS (said by mothers when they see their sons paying more attention to their wives than to Mother)

BRECA (Eng.) break, rest period; brake (on a car or other vehicle)

BRENDI (Eng.) (var. of) brandi

BREÑA (var. of) greña

BREQUE (Eng.) m. brake (aut.)

BREQUEAR or BREQUIAR (Eng.) va. to brake, apply the brakes to stop a moving vehicle

BRETE m. eagerness to act

BRICH or BRICHE (Eng.) m. bridge (card game)

BRILLA (var. of) brillantina

BRILLANTINA (Eng?) hair tonic, hair oil

BRINCACHARCOS msg. high-water pants

BRINCAR: BRINCAR EL CHARCO to cross the river (understood to ref. to the Rio Grande/Río Bravo between Texas and Mexico); (by extension) to immigrate from Mexico to the United States

BRIZNA drizzle, light rain; crumb; chip, splinter, piece

BRÓCOLO (Eng.) m. broccoli

BRODA (Eng.) m. (coll.) brother

BROITA (Eng.) m. (var. of) brodita (dim. of broda, q.v.)

BRÓMFIL (Hispanization of) New Braunfels, Texas

BRÓNSVIL (Hispanization of) Brownsville, Texas

BRUJA broke (coll.), without money; ANDAR BRUJA to be penniless

BRUJO medicine man, curandero

BRUJEAR or BRUJIAR to go without sleep

BRUTAL (coll.) super, terrific, great, keen (etc.) (adj. of general approbation)

BRUTÁLICO -CA (coll.) super, terrific, great (etc.) (adj. of

general approbation)
BRUTO -TA (coll.) intelligent;
    tremendous, terrific; (said of
    problems or tasks that are very
    difficult to resolve or com-
    plete); stupid, dumb; f.
    sexually attractive
BUCA (slang) girl
BUCHACA billiard table pocket
BUCHE (vulg.) m. ass, buttocks;
    PESARLE A ALGUIEN EL BUCHE to
    be lazy; mpl.: HACER BUCHES
    (DE SAL) to fill one's mouth
    with warm salt water so as to
    kill germs and lessen the pain
    of a toothache
BUELITO -TA (var. of) abuelito -ta
BUEN adv. well (used instead of
    Std. bien)
BUENO -NA fine (e.g., BUEN TIEMPO
    fine weather); BUEN TIEMPO
    (Ang.) good time, enjoyable
    experience; BUENO PARA NADA
    (Ang.) good for nothing, lazy,
    useless; BUENO Y SANO healthy;
    ESTAR BUENO to be enough
    (said with ref. to actions the
    speaker finds excessive and
    wishes to terminate): "Ya
    está bueno con esa canción"
    'That's enough of that song';
    ESTAR DE BUENAS to be in a
    good mood
BUENOTE -TA (slang) sexually attrac-
    tive, very good-looking
BUEVO (var. of) huevo
BUEY m. cuckold; adj. ignorant,
    dumb
BUEYADA (var. of) boyada
BUGANVILIA (var. of) buganvilla
BUIGA, BÚIGAS, BÚIGA, BÚIGAMOS/
    BÚIGANOS, BÚIGAN (vars. of)
    bulla, bullas, etc. (pres.
    subjunctive of bullir)
BÚIGO (var. of) bullo (1st pers.
    pres. indic. of bullir)
BUJERO (var. of) agujero
BÚLAVA (Eng.) boulevard
BULCHITEAR or BULCHITIAR (Eng.)
    (vulg.) to bullshit (vulg.)
BULCHITERO -RA (Eng.) (vulg.)
    bullshitter (vulg.)
BULE (Eng.) mf. bully (person who
    intimidates others)
BULÍO -A (var. of) bolillo -lla
BULLIR va. to incite, provoke;
    BULLIR LA LENGUA to gossip,
    speak ill of (someone); to
    talk frequently
BULTO ghost, phantom
BUQUÉ m. bouquet (of flowers)
BUQUEAR or BUQUIAR (Eng.) va. to
    book (i.e., to enter a purchase
    as debit against future wages;

this practice is typically
    carried out by owners of com-
    pany stores
BUQUI -QUIA m., f. child, kid,
    youngster
BURE or BURI (slang) much, many,
    very
BURLISTA mf. joker; mocker
BURUCA (var. of) boruca
BURRO (fig.) dumbbell (coll.),
    stupid; ENTRE MENOS BURROS MÁS
    OLOTES the less you eat the
    more there'll be for someone
    else
BUS m. (var. of) autobús
BUSCAMOSCAS mfsg. agitator,
    trouble-maker
BUSCAPLEITOS mfsg. troublemaker;
    person who is always looking
    for a fight
BUSCAR va. to look for trouble;
    to incite, provoke; BUSCARLE
    LA CARA A ALGUIEN to seek
    someone out so as to effect a
    reconciliation; BUSCAR PEDO
    to look for trouble; BUSCARLE
    RUIDO AL CHICHARRÓN to make
    trouble for oneself needlessly;
    EL QUE LA BUSCA LA HALLA if
    you look for· trouble you'll
    find it; (see also LADO--
    BUSCARLE A ALGUIEN POR SU LADO-
BUSCATOQUES (slang & underw.) mfsg.
    addict in search of a narcotic
    fix
BUSCÓN -CONA troublemaker; sharpie
    (coll.), wheeler-dealer
    (slang); arriviste, person on
    the make (coll.)
BUSGO -GA dog; glutton; SER UN
    BUSGO to have a hollow leg
    (coll.), desire to eat inces-
    santly
BUSO -SA clever, smart
BUSQUITA little extra advantage
    obtained in a business deal
BUTACA hope chest
BUTE or BUTI (vars. of) bure or bu-
    ri (q.v.)
BUTLEGA or BUTLÉGUER (Eng.) mf.
    bootlegger

C

CABALLADA (coll.) group of disorderly or riotous persons

CABALLITOS (var. of) caballito 'merry-go-round'

CABALLO n. clumsy person; CABALLO CUATROALBO horse with four white hooves; CABALLO PINTO pinto horse; METER CABALLO (coll.) to put in a bad word about someone

CABALLÓN -LLONA high on drugs: "Pepe anda caballón" 'Pepe's high on drugs'; large; tall (both with ref. to persons)

CABANUELAS (var. of) cabañuelas

CABAR (var. of) acabar

CABARETEAR or CABARETIAR vn. to go nightclubbing

CABARETERO -RA frequenter (habitué) of nightclubs; worker in a nightclub

CABECILLA head (of a bed, table, etc.)

CABECITA (euph.) head of penis; CABECITA DE VENA red dots on the skin, angiomata

CABELLERA wig, toupee

CABEZA (underw.) U.S. black; CABEZA DE BÚFALO (pej.) U.S. black; ECHARLE POR LA CABEZA A ALGUIEN to tell on someone (coll.), betray a confidence; TENER BUENA CABEZA to have a good head (coll.) be intelligent; VOLTEARLE A ALGUIEN LA CABEZA to give someone a swell head (fig.), cause someone to assume an exaggerated sense of importance

CABEZUDO -DA hard-headed, recalcitrant

CABINETE (Eng.) m. cabinet

CABLAR (var. of) clavar

CABLE: CABLE DE BOCA word of mouth

CABO (var. of Std.) quepo (1st pers. sg. indic. of caber)

CABOI (Eng.) m. cowboy

CABRA: CABRA QUE DA LECHE (said of a person with great promise)

CABRÓN m. husband deceived by an adulterous wife; (general term of insult, usually vulg.: son of a bitch, bastard, etc

CABRONAZO hard blow (with fist or

blunt instrument)

CABRONZOTE -TA m.,f. large; tall (ref. to persons)

CÁBULA discord; mf. competitor

CABULEAR or CABULIAR va. to complete a chore

CABURRO (hum.) cowboy

CABÚS (Eng.) m. caboose; (hum.) buttocks; large buttocks, big butt (coll.) (ref. is usually to the posterior region of the female)

CACA (vulg.) excrement (Std. mierda)

CACAHUATE m. pill; barbituate pill; (slang) NO VALER UN CACAHUATE not to be worth a damn

CÁCARA (slang) girl; person with acne; acne

CACARAQUEAR or CACARAQUIAR (vars. of) cacarear or cacariar

CACARAQUEO (var. of) cacareo

CACAREAR or CACARIAR vn. to gossip

CACEROLA cooking pot

CACHAR (Eng.) va. to catch; to cash (a check, etc.)

CACHETADA slap

CACHETAR va. to slap (the face) (see also CACHETEAR et al.)

CACHETE m. cheek; EL OTRO CACHETE Mexico (= el otro cachete de la misma cara)

CACHETEAR or CACHETIAR va. to slap

CACHETÓN -TONA plump-cheeked; CACHETÓN DEL PURO m. fat man (esp. one who smokes cigars constantly)

CACHIRUL m. large comb, back comb

CACHO -CHA: CACHAS facial expressions of worry or displeasure; side of a gun's handle; ANDAR HASTA LAS CACHAS to be dead drunk; TRAER LAS CACHAS COLGANDO to be wearing a long face, have a hang-dog expression (coll.); CACHO bit, small amount, fraction: "Son las siete y cacho" 'It's a little after seven o'clock'

CACHUCHA drug supply; heroin capsule; (pej.) police, police force; hat

CACHUCHÓN m. mean or vengeful policeman

CACHUDO -DA stern-faced

CACHUMBEAR or CACHUMBIAR va. to nick, chip; (fig.) to neck (kiss and embrace)

CACHUQUEAR or CACHUQUIAR (slang) va. to blow a job (coll.), mess up (coll.); to doublecross

CADA: (DE) CADA EN CUANDO from
time to time; once in a while
CADENA: CADENA DE TELEVISIÓN tele-
vision channel; CADENA DE TIEN-
DAS chain stores
CADE (var. of) cadilaque m.
CADILAQUE (Eng.) m. Cadillac
(brand of automobile); any large,
expensive car
CADILEC (Eng.) m. Cadillac (cf.
CADILAQUE)
CAEDRÉ, CAEDRÁS, etc. (vars. of
Std.) caeré, caerás, etc. (fu-
ture forms of caer)
CAER va. to swoop down upon, catch
off guard, fall upon; vr. to
come across with (coll.), pay
up, pay one's debts; vr. to
scratch (in pool or billiards);
CAER AGUA(S) to rain; CAER
ATRAVESADO to rub someone the
wrong way; CAERLE A ALGUIEN LA
CHANCLA to receive a reprimand;
CAER COMO LA BASURA / CAER COMO
LA CHINGADA to be repellent;
CAER CON ALGO to catch or come
down with (coll.) a disease;
CAER DE ESA / CAER COMO LA
PATADA to be repellent, repulsive: "Ese bato me cayó como
la patada" 'That guy really
turned me off'; CAER DE AQUELLA
to please, turn on (slang), be
atractive to; CAER GACHO / CAER
GORDO / CAER PESADO / CAER
PESETA / CAER SURA to displease,
turn off (slang), be unattrac-
tive to, be repellent, etc.
(cf. CAER COMO LA BASURA et al.,
supra); CAER LA RES to fall into a trap; CAER TIERRA to get
into trouble, get caught; CAERLE
LA TIERRA A ALGUIEN to surprise,
sweep down upon by surprise; to
yield (said of someone who falls
prey to the calculating advances
or machinations of the opposite
sex in a romantic involvement),
fall into a trap, CAER TOSTÓN
to turn off, displease, be repellent, etc.; NO TENER EN QUÉ
CAERSE MUERTO to be destitute,
dirt-poor (coll.); ¡CÁETE! /
¡CÁETE MUERTO! (coll.) Pay up!,
Fork over!
CAFÉ: CAFÉ CON LECHE brownish or
tan colored; CAFÉ CON LLANTAS
(hum.) coffee with doughnuts;
CAFÉ CON MOSCA (hum.) coffee
with sweetroll; CAFÉ NEGRO
(Ang?) coffee without cream
CAFECERO -RA coffee-fiend, person
who drinks a great deal of

coffee
CAFESES (var. of) cafés (Std. pl.
of café)
CAFIRO (slang) coffee
CAFIRUCHO (slang) bad-tasting
coffee
CAFRO (slang) coffee
CAGADERA (vulg.) diarrhea
CAGADERO (vulg.) bathroom, toilet;
pile of excrement
CAGADO -DA (vulg.) angry, tired,
infuriated; f. (vulg.) excrement
underw.) heroin; (vulg.) brat,
obstreperous child; CAGADA f.
blunder, mess: "Hizo su cagada como siempre" 'He blew it
as usual'
CAGÓN -GONA (said of persons who
defecate with frequency); m.f.
quick-tempered (person)
CAGUILLAS mfsg. quick-tempered
person; scaredy-cat, person
who is easily frightened
CAI (Hispanization of) Kyle, Texas
CAIBA, CAIBAS, CAIBA, CÁIBAMOS /
CÁIBANOS, CAIBAN (vars. of)
caía, caías, etc. (imperf.
forms of caer)
CAIDO -DA (var. of) caído -da
(ppart. of caer)
CAINDO (var. of) cayendo (ger.
of caer)
CAIR (var. of) caer
CAIRÉ, CAIRÁS, etc. (vars. of) caeré,
caerás, etc. (future forms of
caer)
CAIS, CAI, CAIMOS/CAYEMOS/CAYIMOS,
CAIN (vars. of) caes, etc.
(pres. ind. forms of caer)
CAITE (Eng.) m. kite
CAJA: CAJA DE COLORES crayon box;
CAJA DE CORREO (Ang.) mail box
(Std. buzón)
CAJETA small round wooden box con-
taining caramel candy
CAJETUDA adj. sexy (said of women);
f. headache
CAJÓN DE CARTAS (Ang.) m. letter
box, mail box
CAJONERÍA mortuary
CAJONERO -RA box-maker; funeral
director
CALABACITA squash (vegetable);
(coll. & hum.) woman's leg;
fpl. little white lies
(coll.), minor untruths
CALABAZA dummy, stupid person; air-
filter of an automobile's car-
burator; (see also DAR CALA-
BAZAS)
CALABOZ m. (var. of) calabozo
CALABURNIA stupid; eccentric
CALACA death; sign of death

CALAMBRE m. part of the human body
fallen into a comatose state:
"Tengo un calambre en la pierna
derecha" 'My right leg has fallen asleep'

CALANGO -GA ambitious

CALAR va. to try out, test; to attack (e.g., hunger pangs): "Me
está calando el hambre"; to
hurt (fig.), offend: "Me caló
lo que me dijo" 'What he said
offended me'; vr. to have a
try (at doing something), give
it a try: "Se me hace que no
lo puedo hacer porque ya me
calé"

CALAVERA drunkard; stupid person,
dullard; combination tractor
and plow

CALCEAR or CALCIAR vn. to walk bare-
footed

CALCETA stocking, sock; DESENRROLLAR
LA CALCETA (hum.) to dance

CALCETÍN: CALCETIN DE SEDA (hum.)
upper class, silk-stocking
(fig.)

CALCO (slang) shoe

CALCOMANÍA decal; process and result of transfering a design to
a wet surface

CALDEADO -DA or CALDIADO -DA angry,
boiling mad

CALDEAR or CALDIAR va. to anger;
to make love to; vr. to become
angry

CALDO soup; AÑO DEL CALDO yesteryear, days gone by

CALENTADORA: ¡CALENTADORAS! interj.
(slang) Shut up! (form of
linguistic disguise--note the
partial resemblance between the
first syllables of this form and
cállate)

CALENTAR va. to excite sexually;
vr. to be in heat (said of
animals), become sexually excited (said of persons)

CALENTÓN: DAR UN CALENTÓN to arouse
sexually; to arouse anger;
DARSE UN CALENTÓN to become
aroused sexually; to become angry

CALIENTE adj. hot, sexually excited; ESTAR CALIENTE to be
sexually excited; (Ang.) to be
hot (ref. to the weather);
(Ang.) to be hot, feel hot
(ref. to one's body temperature)

CALIFA(S) California; m.& f. Cali-
fornian

CÁLIZ: HACER EL CÁLIZ to try, make
an effort: "No sabe si puede
ganar, pero quiere hacer el
cáliz"

CALMANTE m. snack before meals;
¡CALMANTES MONTES! (slang)
interj. Quiet down!, Knock it
off! (coll.), Take it easy!,
etc.

CALMAR vr. to wait

CALMEROZ (slang) interj. Take it
easy!, Knock it off!, etc.

CALO nickle, five cent piece; penny; attempt, effort

CALÓ slang (esp. Pachuco slang);
dialect; jargon

CALOFRÍO hot flash (of the sort experience by women reaching the
"change of life")

CALORCITO intense heat

CALOTA (slang) beautiful woman

CALOTE (slang) mf., adj. big;
politically active; effect-
ive in politics

CALVITO (slang) God, the Deity

CALZONCILLOS mpl. man's long
underwear

CALZONCÍOS (var. of) calzoncillos

CALZONES mpl. man's undershorts;
woman's panties; trousers

CALZONUDO -DA (said of person wearing baggy trousers)

CALLEJA alley

CALLO: PAJUELEAR/PAJUELIAR EL CALLO
to stink (said of feet); TENER
CALLO to be experienced; to be
callous

CAMADA: SER DE LA MISMA CAMADA
(slang) to belong to the same
generation; to be on the same
social level

CAMALEÓN or CAMALIÓN: m. horned
toad; FUMAR COMO UN CAMALEÓN
to smoke like a chimney (fig.),
smoke excessively

CAMARÁ (var. of) camarada

CAMBACHEAR or CAMBACHAR (vars. of)
cambalachear or cambalachar

CAMBEADO -DA or CAMBIADO -DA m.
homosexual; f. lesbian

CAMBEAR (var. of) cambiar

CAMBIAR: CAMBIAR CHAQUETA to
change allegiance, be a turn-
coat; CAMBIAR EL DISCO to
change the subject; to stop
harping on the same theme

CAMEADOR -DORA or CAMIADOR -DORA
hard worker

CAMEAR or CAMELLAR (vars. of) camiar

CAMELLO or CAMEO (slang) work, labor; job, employment

CAMIAR (slang) to work, labor

CAMINO: CAMINO DE FIERRO railroad

CAMITA baby's bed, crib; (slang)
buddy, friend

CAMOTAZOS (slang) blows with the

fists or with a solid object
CAMPAMOCHA walking stick
CAMPANA electrical buzzer
CAMPEAR or CAMPIAR vn. to go camp-
    ing
CAMPECHANO -NA countrified; mf.
    country person, peasant; f.
    type of Mexican sweetbread
CÁMPER (Eng.) m. camper (recreation-
    al vehicle)
CAMPIÓN -PIONA (var. of) campeón -
    peona
CAMPIONATO (var. of) campeonato
CAMPO: CAMPO TURISTA (Ang.) tourist
    camp; motel
CAMPOSANTERO -RA cemetery care-
    taker
CANA: CANAS VERDES: SACARLE A UNO
    CANAS VERDES (used by parents
    to reprimand children when they
    misbehave: "Espérate, tú también
    vas a ser padre, y tus hijos te
    van a sacar canas verdes"; the
    implication is that the next gen-
    eration will be even harder to
    manage if the present generation
    misbehaves; CANAS VERDES is
    roughly equivalent to 'premature
    gray hairs')
CANALEAR or CANALIAR va. to cut
CANALERO -RA canal worker
CANCO (slang) blow with the hand or
    fist; mpl. fist fight; AGARR-
    ARSE A CANCOS / DARSE CANCOS /
    METERSE CANCOS to have a fist
    fight; to beat up (coll.) on one
    another
CANDE (dim. of) Candelario -ria
CANDELÍA or CANDELILLA icicle
CANDELIAR or CANDELILLAR vn. to
    fall lightly (said of freezing
    rain or hail)
CANDI m. candy
CANDILAR va. to lure into a trap
CANICA: ANDAR CANICA(S) / CARGAR
    CANICA (slang) to be passionate-
    ly in love with, carry the torch
    for (coll.)
CANIJO -JA mischievous person, lit-
    tle devil (coll. & hum.)
CANILLA wrist
CANQUEAR or CANQUIAR va. to beat
    someone up in a fight; vn. to
    fight with the fists; vr. to
    have a fist fight; to beat up
    on (coll.) one another
CANQUIZA beating, thrashing (in a
    fight)
CANTAR (slang) va. to ask for; to
    degrade, humiliate; to tell off
    (coll.), reprimand severely
CANTEAR or CANTIAR vr. to incline,
    lay on edge

CANTINERA dance-hall girl
CANTO (slang) house; home
CANTÓN (slang) m. house EL CANTÓN
    DE LA PERRA GALGA (hum.) the
    Greyhound bus terminal
CANUTILLO herbal tea ("Mormon tea,"
    ephedra trifurca) used to treat
    anemia
CANUTO (see SALIR CANUTO)
CAÑONETA (var. of) camioneta
CAPA raincoat; (slang) heroin cap-
    sule; CAPA DE AGUA raincoat
CAPABLE (Ang.) capable
CAPACETA m. convertible top (of
    an automobile)
CAPEAR or CAPIAR va. to catch; to
    put heroin in capsules; vn. to
    tattle on someone
CAPIROTADA m. dessert made out of
    bread, cheese, raisins, honey
    and shortening; the same type of
    dish made with meat and without
    any form of sweetening
CAPIRUCHE or CAPIRUCHO m. captain
CAPITAL f. capitol (building) (Std.
    capitolio)
CAPÓN -PONA sterile (ref. to persons
    unable to bear or procreate
    children)
CAPOTE (see DAR CAPOTE)
CAPOTEADA (see DAR CAPOTEADA)
CAPOTEAR or CAPOTIAR va. to snatch
    an object (usually a ball) on
    way to its intended receiver;
    to leave scoreless in an athlet-
    ic competition, to blank (coll.)
CAPOTIZA: DAR UNA CAPOTIZA to leave
    scoreless, blank (in an athletic
    competition); to shellack
    (coll.), achieve a high number
    of points while leaving the
    opponent scoreless
CAPOTUDO: OJOS CAPOTUDOS bulging
    eyes, pop eyes (slang); droop-
    ing eyelids
CAPTIVO -VA (var. of) cautivo -va
CAQUIS msg. fecal matter (euph.
    often applied to babies' feces);
    CAQUIS MAQUIS: ESTAR CAQUIS
    MAQUIS--"El bebito está caquis
    maquis" 'The baby is "dirty"'
    (i.e., the baby had defecated
    in his/her pants)
CARA: ECHAR EN CARA to hold some-
    thing over someone: "Después
    del favor que me hiciste ahora
    quieres echármelo en cara";
    TENER CUERPO DE TENTACIÓN Y
    CARA DE ARREPENTIMIENTO to have
    a beautiful body and a homely
    face (said of a woman); TORCER
    LA CARA to snub; (see also
    DAR EN CARA)

CARÁCTER (Ang.) personage in a play,
    character; odd-ball (slang),
    eccentric person
CARÁCTERES (var. of Std. pl.)
    caracteres
CARAJADA booboo, stupid thing, dumb
    act
CARAJAZO blow (with fist or object)
CARAJO interj. (mild or violent
    according to intonation); CA-
    RAJOS (var. of) carajo:
    "¿Qué carajos quieres?" 'What
    in the Sam Hill/tarnation (etc.)
    do you want?'; CARAJO -JA
    mischievous, tricky; difficult,
    hard to resolve
CARAMELO peppermint stick
CARANCHADA trick, mischief; stroke
    of bad luck
CARANCHO -CHA mischievous, tricky
CARANTIZAR (var. of) garantizar
CARÁTULA (slang) face
CARBULADOR (var. of) carburador m.
CARCACHA old car, jalopy (coll.)
CARCAJEAR or CARCAJIAR vn. to laugh
    heartily, guffaw
CARCAMONÍA (var. of) calcomanía
CARCELEJA type of children's game
    played with marbles
CAREADO -DA adj. at par, begin-
    ning a sports competition on an
    equal footing; f. sports com-
    petition not involving a handi-
    cap
CARGA (slang & underw.) load of
    narcotics
CARGADO -DA bothersome; overbearing;
    boring; strong (e.g., strong
    coffee): "El café está muy car-
    gado" 'The coffee is too strong';
    thick (e.g., beard or hair);
    ANDAR CARGADO -DA (underw.) to
    be carrying drugs
CARGADOR m. pall bearer
CARGAR va. to charge (merchandise
    to an account); CARGAR CANICA
    to be passionately in love with,
    carry the forch for (coll.);
    CARGAR LA CALENTURA to increase
    or persist (ref. to fever):
    "Anoche le cargó la calentura al
    niño" 'The child's fever went
    up last night'; CARGAR LA CARR-
    ETA (for one person to do most
    of the work in a supposedly co-
    operative venture, to take the
    lion's share of the burden);
    CARGAR LA EDUCACIÓN EN LA PUNTA
    DE LOS PIES/CARGAR LA EDUCACIÓN
    EN LOS TALONES (ref. to an
    educated person who behaves in
    an ill-bred manner); CARGAR
    PELOTA (slang) to be passionate-

ly in love with, carry the
    torch for (coll.); CARGÁRSELE
    A ALGUIEN MUCHO to take some-
    one's death very hard: "A
    Julio se le cargó mucho la
    muerte de su bisabuela"
CARGO: HACERLE CARGOS A ALGUIEN
    (Ang.) to bring charges against
    someone (in a law suit)
CARGUERO freight train
CARIÑOSO -SA likeable
CARITA flirt, tease
CARLANGO -GA raggedy; m. coat
    (in general)
CARLANGUIENTO -TA raggedy; sickly-
    looking
CARMESA (var. of) quermés or quer-
    mese (also spelled kermés, ker-
    mese)
CARMÍN m. lipstick
CARNAL (slang) m. brother
CARNALA (slang) f. sister
CARNALISMO comradeship
CARNALONGO -GA (slang) m. big broth-
    er; f. big sister
CARNE: BOLAS DE CARNE meat balls;
    CARNE DEL DIABLO devilled
    ham; CARNE MOLIDA hamburger
    meat, ground meat; CARNE PICADA
    hamburger meat, ground meat
CARNOSIDAD: CARNOSIDAD DEL OJO
    fleshy eye growth (pterigium)
CARPANTA multitude
CARPETA (Ang.) rug
CARTELÓN m. placard
CARTITA small card (e.g., a filing
    card)
CARTUCHERA holster
CARTÚN (Eng.) m. cartoon
CARRANCLÁN m. type of cloth used for
    women's dresses
CARRAZO luxurious automobile
CARREREAR or CARRERIAR va. to hur-
    ry someone along; vn. to hur-
    ry, rush
CARRERÍA mass or bunch of automo-
    biles
CARRETÍA or CARRETILLA spool (e.g.,
    spool of thread)
CARRETÓN m. child's toy wagon
CARRÍA or CARRILLA: ¡CARRILLA!
    interj. Hurry up!; AGARRAR A
    CARRILLA to give chase to; DAR
    CARRILLA to bother, pester;
    ECHAR EN CARRILLA to give chase
    to; HACER ALGO A CARRILLA to
    do something hurriedly
CARRITO streetcar, tram; TENER CARR-
    ITO to harp on the same subject
CARRIZO fishing rod
CARRUCHA (coll.) jalopy, clunker
    (slang), old worthless car
CARRUCHAR va. to cart off, carry

off; vn. to ride in a car

CARRUCHO automobile (usually pej.)

CARRUMFLA (slang) jalopy, old car; (hum.) face

CASA: CASA DE ALTO two-story house; CASA DE APARTAMENTOS (Ang.) apartment house, apartment building; CASA DE BORDE or CASA DE BORDEROS *or* CASA DE BORDOS (Eng.) boarding house; CASA DE CAMBIO currency exchange; CASA DE CORTE (S) (Ang.) courthouse; CASA DE RENTA (Ang.) house for rent; rented house; CASA GRANDE (Ang?) (slang) big house (i.e., penitentiary); CASA MORTUORIA funeral home; CASA REDONDA (Ang.) round house (for the switching and repairing of trains)

CASANOVA m. adulteror

CASCAR va. to ask for and receive something

CASCAREAR or CASCARIAR vn. to use one's last ounce of strength in order to accomplish something

CASCARÓN (used mainly in mpl.: CASCARONES) egg shells filled with confetti, then painted, and subsequently broken over people's heads, festively, at Eastertime

CAS: CAS DE (see A CAS DE)

CASE prep. at the home of: "Está case Felipe" 'He's at Felipe's house'

CASERA babysitter; person who enjoys doing household chores

CASIMIRO GUERRA (slang & hum.) m. young man about to be drafted

CASITA out-house, privvy

CASPIENTO -TA full of dandruff

CASQUETA masturbation; HACERSE LA CASQUETA to masturbate

CASQUETEAR or CASQUETIAR va. & vr. to masturbate

CASQUILLA cartridge case; empty cartridge

CASTAÑO chest, trunk

CATÁGALO or CATÁGOLO (vars. of) catálogo

CATAPLÚN (var. of) cataplum (interj.)

CATARINO -NA (var. of) Catalino -na

CATARRIENTO -TA (var. of) catarroso -sa

CATARRO: CATARRO CONSTIPADO chronic cold in the head; hay fever

CATE (dim. of) Catalino -na, Catarino -na

CATEADO -DA or CATIADO -DA mf. victim of a beating

CATEAR or CATIAR (slang) va.to beat

up (in a fight); vr. to beat up on one another in a fight

CATIZA (slang) beating, thrashing (in a fight)

CATO (slang) blow with a fist; CATOS fist fight; boxing match; AGARRARSE A CATOS to have a fist fight; METERSE CATOS to beat up on one another in a fight

CATOLECISMO (var. of) catolicismo

¡CATORCE! interj. (of varying intensity according to intonation)

CATORRAZO heavy blow with the fist; heavy slap

CATRÍN m. dandy, fop, dude, (slang)

CAUBÓI (Eng.) m. cowboy

CAUCH or CAUCHO (Eng.) m. couch, sofa

CAUSULA (var. of) cápsula

CAVARRUBIAS (var. of) Covarrubias (surname)

CAYER (var. of) caer

CAYÍ, CAYISTE, CAYIMOS (vars. of) caí, caíste, caímos (various pret. forms of caer)

CAYO (dim. of) Arcadio

CAZO large kettle used for boiling clothes; bowl

CAZUELEJA children's game played with tops

CEBOLLA (hum.) watch, wristwatch

CEBOLLITA children's game similar to tug-of-war

CEDRÓN m. bucket

CELAFÁN or CELAFÉIN (Eng.) m. cellophane

CELEBRAR: ¿QUÉ CELEBRAS? (set expression) What are you up to?, What are you doing?; What is wrong with you?

CÉLEBRE adj. thankful; cute

CELEBRE (var. of) célebre

CELEBRO (var. of) cerebro

CELGA (var. of) acelga

CEMETERIO (var. of) cementerio

CEMITA (var. of) acemita 'bran bread'

CENCIA (var. of) ciencia

CENICERA (var. of) cenicero ashtray

CENTRO: CENTRO ABARROTERO shopping center

CENTURA (var. of) cintura

CENZONCLE or CENZONTE or CENZONTLE mf. mocking bird (Mimus polyglottos)

CEQUIA (var. of) acequia

CER (var. of) hacer

CERCA adj. m. & f. stingy

CERCAS (var. of) cerca

CEREBRO nape of neck

CERILLO any type of match (Std.

fósforo)
CERO kindergarten
CEROTE large-statured, tall
CERVECERO -RA very fond of beer
CERRADO: CERRADO DE BARBA thick-bearded
CERRAR: CERRAR EL PICO (coll.) to shut up, be quiet
CESTÓN m. kitchen cupboard
CICLETA (var. of) bicicleta 'bicycle'; tricycle
CIELO (vocative) darling
CIEN (var. of) ciento (when Std. requires the full form, e.g.:) "cien treinta" "ciento treinta", etc. (also in adjectival constructions:) "¿Cuántos libros tienes? -- Cien."
CIENTÍFICO -CA well-educated, knowledgeable
CIERTO -TA: CIERTOS ELOTES (VERDES) /CIERTOS ELOTES Y CAÑAS HELADAS certain so-and-sos (said to avoid naming someone specifically)
CIGARRERA ash-tray
CIMENTERO -RA (var. of) cementero -ra
CIMENTO (var. of) cemento
CINC (Eng.) m. sink (for washing dishes)
CINCO nickel, five cents; DAR CINCO: "Dame cinco" (slang) 'Shake hands', 'Slap me five' (slang)
CINCHO (Eng.) (slang) cinch, sure thing; DE CINCHO certainly, for sure
CINIA (Eng.) zinnia
CINQUE (coll.) five; fifteen
CINTA shoelace
CINTO woman's belt (never ref. to male belt)
CINTURA small of back, area surrounding the small of the back
CINZONCLE or CINZONTE or CINZONTLE (vars. of) CENZONCLE et al.
CIODI (Eng.) m. C.O.D. (abbrev. of Collect On Delivery; the abbrev. has been reconstituted in Spanish as Cobrar o devolver)
CIRGÜELA f. or CIRGÜELO m. (vars. of) ciruela
CIRQUERO -RA fond of circuses; mf. circus performer; person working for a circus
CISCA shame
CISCAR va. to frighten away
CISCO (dim. of) Francisco
CISNERO -RA liar
CIZOTE m. sore; wound
CLAB (Eng.) m. (var. of) club
CLACO (slang) nickel, five cents

CLAPIAR (Eng.) va. to applaud; to cut in on someone at a dance; vn. to clap, applaud
CLARIDOSO -SA frank, blunt
CLAS or CLASIA (vars. of) clase f.
CLAVADO -DA (underw.) stolen; ECHARSE UN CLAVADO / TIRARSE UN CLAVADO to dive into water
CLAVAR (slang) vr. to steal; to fail to return a borrowed item; CLAVAR LA UÑA to sell (often through high-pressure tactics); to borrow money; to stab
CLAVEL (slang) adj. thieving; m. thief (ref. to male thieves only)
CLAVELITO -TA (slang) adj. thieving; mf. thief
CLAVETE (slang) adj. thieving; m. thief (ref. to male thieves only)
CLAVETEAR or CLAVETIAR (slang) (vars. of) clavar
CLAVETÍN (slang) m. robbery
CLEIMIAR (Eng.) va. & vn. to claim
CLEMO (slang) penny, one-cent piece
CLEPEAR or CLEPIAR (Eng.) (vars. of) clapiar
CLEPTO -TA (var. of) cleptomaníaco -ca
CLETA (dim. of) Henriqueta
CLETA (var. of) bicicleta, tricicleta
CLÍNERS (Eng.) mpl. cleaners, dry cleaners; LLEVAR A LOS CLÍNERS (slang) to clean someone out (fig.), impoverish someone
CLIPA (Eng.) f. (usually fpl.: CLIPAS) clippers, shears
CLOB (var. of Eng.) club m.
CLOCHE (Eng.) m. clutch (automotive)
CLORAX or CLOROX (Eng.) m. bleach, chlorine
CLOROFORME (var. of) cloroformo
COBIJA(S): PEGÁRSELE A ALGUIEN LA(S) COBIJA(S) to oversleep
COBRADOR -DORA persistent in collecting money that is due
COBRE m. penny, one-cent piece
COBRÓN -BRONA persistent in collecting money that is due
CÓCCIZ m. tailbone, coccyx
COCEDOR m. oven
COCINIAR (var. of) cocinar
COCO (hum.) head, skull; (child language) hurt, injury
COCOLES mpl. beans
COCOMALETAS msg. bogyman
COCOLMECA herbal tea (sarsaparilla, Smilax mexicana) used to treat kidney ailments
CÓCONO turkey; gigolo; (slang)

male homosexual; mf. person high on drugs

COCTEL or CÓCTEL or COCTEIL (Eng.) m. cocktail party; cocktail (alcoholic drink)

COCHE (Eng.) m. coach, athletic trainer

COCHINO -NA nasty; indecent

COCHITO -TA conformist, square (coll.)

COCHOTAS: COCHOTAS DE PAPÁ (term of endearment with a slight tinge of vulgarity to it; possible Eng. equivalent: 'Daddy's sweet mama')

COCHOTE -TA m. sugar daddy; f. sweet mamma (terms of endearment, often used in the vocative; cf. COCHOTAS supra); mf. fat person

CODO stingy; EMPINAR EL CODO to drink (usually intoxicating beverages)

COGEDERA (vulg.) fornication

COGEDOR -DORA m. sex fiend, satyr; f. nymphomaniac

COGER (vulg.) va. to fornicate, COGER EN LAS MORAS (coll.) to catch red-handed; COGER FRÍO (Ang.) to catch cold, get a cold; COGER PARA to head toward, go in the direction of; COGERSE ALGO to steal

COGIDO -DA (vulg.) adj. screwed (vulg. slang); f. screwing (vulg.), fornication: "Le dieron su buena cogida" 'They really ____ her over'

COIL (Eng.) m. inter-uterine device, coil, loop (contraceptive)

COJÍN m. adultress; unmarried woman who enjoys sex frequently

COLA fsg. buttocks; (Eng.) long-distance telephone call; (fig. and slang) tail, shadow, probation officer (i.e., anyone who "follows" a criminal, a suspect or an ex-criminal); COLA AFUERA (Eng.) long-distance telephone call; COLA LARGA sly, astute, tricky; PONER COLA to put a tail on (someone) (e.g., to have someone follow a suspect); SALIR CON COLA to travel with one's family; to leave prison on parole; TENER COLA to be on probation; NO TENER COLA QUE LE PISEN to have nothing to be ashamed of, have no skeletons in the closet; TRAER COLA (for underclothing to be showing)

COLAR vr. to slip in and out, sneak in and out

COLCRIM or COLCRÍN (Eng.) m. cold-cream

COLCHA: ¡¿CUÁLES COLCHAS?! (interj.) What do you mean?, What the hell are you talking about?! (esp. with the implication: I didn't promise you anything); PEGARSE LAS COLCHAS to oversleep: "A Luis se le pegaron las colchas, por eso llegó tarde"

COLEAR or COLIAR va. to follow, tail (slang); to grab by the seat of the pants or by the skirt; to borrow; to color (var. of colorear)

COLECTADOR -DORA collector (e.g., of taxes)

COLECTAR va. to collect

COLEGIANTE mf. student; college student

COLEREAR or COLERIAR va. to borrow

COLERO -RA sponger, freeloader (coll.)

COLGAR: COLGAR LOS GUANTES (fig.) to retire from boxing; COLGAR LOS TENIS (fig. & hum.) to die (<tennis shoes)

COLICHE mf. tag-along, person (usually youngster) who follows others wherever they go

COLMAR: COLMARLE A ALGUIEN EL PLATO to cause someone to come to the end of his/her rope (coll.): "Ya me colmaste el plato con tu abuso. ¡Vete!"

COLMENA bee

COLOPEAR or COLOPIAR to go out on the town (coll.), have a good time in nightclubs, etc. (<columpiar 'to swing'?)

COLOR: COLORES mpl. type of children's game; DAR COLORES to show off

COLORADA (slang) secconal capsule; blood; SACAR LA COLORADA to give someone a bloody nose

COLOTE (var. of) culote m.

COLTURA (var. of) cultura

COLUDO -DA showing, hanging out (said of underclothing, shirt-tails, etc.)

COLUMPIO -PIA tight-wad (coll.), person who never pays; person who walks with an exaggerated swinging gait; CADA CHANGO A SU COLUMPIO Y A COLUMPIARSE LUEGO let each one attend to his/her own affairs

COMA (var. of) goma

COMBIAR (Eng.) va. to comb

COMELÓN -LONA glutton

COMENZÓN (var. of) comezón

COMER: COMER ANSIA to be impatient;

COMER CON LA VISTA to devour with glances; COMER GALLO to become agressive; to hit foul balls (note bilingual pun: foul--baseball term--equated with fowl 'gallo'); COMERSE UNA CARTA to fail to answer a letter; COMERSE A UNA PERSONA to browbeat someone; COMERSE A ALGUIEN CON LOS OJOS to stare at someone with hatred or anxiety; COMERSE A ALGUIEN VIVO to tell someone where to get off (slang) in no uncertain terms, reprimand someone severely; COMERSE ALGUIEN SUS PALABRAS (Ang.) to eat one's words (fig.), retract something one has said

COMIDO -DA full, awash with, blighted by: "Tiene la cara comida de espinillas" 'His face is full of pimples'; COMIDA DE BUFÉ (Eng.) buffet supper; f. COMIDA EMPACADA canned food

COMIDOR (var. of) comedor m.

COMILÓN -LONA (var. of) comelón -lona

COMO: COMO ALMA QUE (SE) LLEVA EL DIABLO/COMO CUANDO DIOS SE LLEVA UN ALMA in the twinkling of an eye (fig.), very rapidly; COMO ÉL SOLO as only he can be: "Es loco como él solo" 'He's crazy as only he can be' (also: COMO ELLA SOLA, COMO ELLOS SOLOS, etc.); ¿COMO LES QUEDÓ EL OJO? (slang) How does that grab you?, How do you like them apples? (slang)

COMPA (<compadre) (slang) m. Mac, Bub, Jack, mister, etc. (frequent vocative used to address person whose name one does not know): "Ese, compa, páseme un frajo" 'Hey Mac, gimme a cigarette'

COMPANIA (var. of) compañía

COMPAÑERO: EL＿＿＿ ÉSE MI COMPAÑE-RO (ironic or festive reference to a quality shared by both the speaker and the person referred to; the remark is sometimes made to take revenge on an initial criticism from the person referred to, e.g., "el chaparro ése mi compañero" 'that guy was just as short as I am')

COMPITA (var. of) compadre, compa m.

COMPLEAÑOS or COMPLIAÑOS msg. (vars. of) cumpleaños

COMPLETAR: COMPLETAR CON to take care of as well, finish up the job with (you) too: "Y si tú te entremetes, completo contigo" 'And if you stick your nose into this, I'll take care of you afterwards' (i.e., after having defeated the original antagonist, as in a fight)

COMPONEDOR -DORA handy-man, Mr. Fix-It (coll.); distorter of the truth

COMPONER va. to cast a spell, bewitch; vr. to reform, go straight (after a life of crime); to clear up (said of cloudy skies)

COMPRAR: COMPRAR A TIEMPO (Ang.) to buy on time (coll.), buy on the installment plan

COMPROMISO debt

COMPUESTITO -TA (coll.) straightened out (i.e., after having led a life of crime); bewitched, hexed (often used in the context of I-told-you-so, or He-had-it-coming-to-him, e.g., "Pues ya está compuestito" 'I told you they would put a spell on him sooner or later')

CON (Eng.): CON DE NIEVE (var. of) cono de nieve

CON prep. CON SAFOS or CON ZAFOS (insulting) The same to you!, The same goes for you!, Now I've said the last word!; CON EL GORDO hitch-hiking; (Eng.) m. cone (Std. cono); (see also CON DON--v.s. DON)

CONCENCIA (var. of) consciencia

CONCUÑO (var. of) concuñado

CONCHA (dim. of) Concepción

CONCHABAR vr. to live in free union, form a common-law marriage

CONDENADO -DA (pej.) bastard, son-of-a-bitch (terms of insult)

CONDO (rus.) (var. of) cuando

CONDUCÍ, CONDUCISTE, CONDUCIÓ, CON-DUCIMOS, CONDUCIERON (vars. of) conduje, condujiste, etc. (pret. forms of conducir)

CONDUCTOR -TORA or CONDUTOR -TORA railroad conductor, ticket collector

CONE (Eng., dim. of) Connie

CONECTACIÓN (var. of) conexión

CONEJO msg. biceps

CONFERENCIAL m. meeting; small conference meeting

CONFIDENCIA (Ang.) trust, confidence

CONFIDENTE -TA faithful; CONFIDENTE

m. sofa (in general)

CONFORMAR va. to adjust, harmonize, reconcile; vr. to reconcile

CONFORME reconciled (adj.)

CONGA type of Cuban dance

CONGAL (slang) m. brothel, whorehouse; beer joint

CONO: CONO DE NIEVE ice cream cone

CONOCENCIA acquaintanceship, group of friends

CONQUIÁN m. type of card game similar to whist

CONSCIENCIA: TENER LA CONSCIENCIA LIMPIA to have a clear conscience; TENER LA CONSCIENCIA SUCIA to have a guilty conscience

CONSECUENTAR va. to tolerate, bear with

CONSERVATIVO -VA stingy, tight-fisted

CONSIGUIR (var. of) conseguir

CONSTIPADO -DA (Ang.) constipated, unable to move one's bowels

CONTAR: CONTAR LAS MUELAS to pull the wool over someone's eyes (coll.), to deceive

CONTENTAR va. to reconcile; vr. to become reconciled

CONTENTO -TA reconciled

CONTESTABLE (var. of) condestable

CONTIMÁS (var. of) cuantimás 'at least'

CONTOY TODO (var. of) con todo y todo 'lock, stock and barrel' (coll.=absolutely everything)

CONTRA (see DAR LA CONTRA)

CONTRABANDISTA mf. illegal immigrant (esp. one from Mexico to the United States)

CONTRABANDO illegal (male) immigrant

CONTRECHO -CHA contradictory

CONTROL -LA (slang) m. gang leader; f. (hum.) wife

CONVENENCIA (var. of) conveniencia

CONVENCIERO -RA or CONVENENCIERO -RA opportunistic

CONVERTIBLE m. (Ang.) convertible (car with folding roof); pick up truck

CONVIENCIA (var. of) conveniencia

CONVITE m. group of persons announcing a forthcoming event from a truck

CÓNYUGUE (var. of) cónyuge

COPALA perch (perca flavescens)

COPEAR (var. of) copiar

COPEÓN -PEONA or COPIÓN -PIONA m., f. copycat

COPEQUIEC (Eng.) m. cupcake

COPETÓN -TONA (ref. to person whose hair is piled up high in front)

COPERAR (var. of) cooperar

COPETE m. top rim of a measuring glass; ANDAR HASTA EL COPETE to be very drunk; ESTAR HASTA EL COPETE to come to the end of the road (fig.), be completely fed up with (fig.), want nothing more with: "Ya estoy hasta el copete con Enrique" 'I've just come to the end of the road with Henry'; TENERLE A ALGUIEN HASTA EL COPETE: "Ya me tienes hasta el copete" 'I've just had it up to here with you'

COPETEAR or COPETIAR va. to fill a glass to the brim

COPQUEIC (Eng.) (var. of) copequiec

CORA (var. of) corazón m.; (see also DE CORA)

CORAJE: m. pathologically angry condition believed to cause miscarriage, spoil breast milk, etc.; DA-CORAJE (hum. or ironic) m. Cadillac (or any other expensive brand of automobile)

CORBATA: CORBATA DE GATO (hum.) bowtie

CORBATERO tie rack (perch for hanging neckties); man fond of wearing neckties

CORBEADOR -DORA or CORBIADOR -DORA freeloader, sponge (coll.)

CORBERO -RA freeloader, sponge (coll.)

CORCHOLATA bottle cap

CORDÓN m. string; street curb

CORONA V.I.P., big-shot (coll.), important or influential person CORONA DE SAN DIEGO climbing red rose (Antigonon leptopus)

CORPOS (Hispanization or var. of) Corpus Christi, Texas

CORSAJE m. corsage

CORTADO -DA m. (var. of) cortadura; ANDAR CORTADO DE DINERO to be low on funds; ANDAR RECORTADO DE DINERO to be very low on funds

CORTAR va. to put down (slang), put someone in his/her place, deprecate; vr. (slang) to leave; CORTAR EL MITO to stop talking (used esp. as a command: "¡Corta el mito"); CORTAR LAS NUBES to "cut" storm clouds (acc. to folk belief, if an innocent child makes the sign of the cross with a knife out of doors, storm clouds will disappear); CORTARSE LA CALENTURA (for a fever to break, cease to be intense): "Anoche se le cortó la calentura" 'His fever broke last night'

CORTE (Ang.) f. court, courthouse;

slight trim (haircut)
CASA DE CORTE(S) (Ang.) court-
house
CORTINA: ¡CORTINAS! (slang) Cut it
out!, Stop it!
CORTO -TA f. short film preced-
ing the main feature; m. (coll.)
brushoff; (elec.) short circuit;
ANDAR CORTO DE DINERO to be low
on funds
CORTÓN m. brushoff, snub
CORVAS fpl. TEMBLARLE A ALGUIEN
LAS CORVAS to be afraid
CORRE (casa de corrección) (underw.)
f. prison, jail
CORREA immigration or customs of-
ficer (esp. U.S. immigration
officer on the U.S.-Mexican bor-
der)
CORRECTAR (Ang.) va. to correct
CORREDERA diarrhea
CORRELÓN -LONA scaredy-cat (slang)
(said of person who consistently runs away from a situation
which he/she finds threatening)
CORRELLÓN or CORREÓN m. thick belt
(article of clothing)
CORRENTÍA impetus, momentum; AGARRAR
CORRENTÍA to get a running start
CORRENTÓN -TONA common, ordinary,
cheap
CORRER va. to chase; (Ang.) to run
off, reproduce, duplicate:
"¿Cuántas copias corriste?";
(Ang.) to operate, run (e.g., a
business); va. (Ang.) to run,
supervise; CORRER EL CUERPO to
defecate; CORRER LA CABEZA to
talk excessively; CORRER PARA
UNA OFICINA (Ang.) to run for
political office
CORRETEAR or CORRETIAR va. to run
ragged
CORRIDA: EN CORRIDA written by hand
CORRIENTE ordinary, common, cheap,
lowclass
COSA: CREERSE LA GRAN COSA / HACERSE
LA GRAN COSA to act superior;
COSA QUE conj. therefore, and
so, hence; LA OTRA COSA (any
narcotic drug substitute); ¡QUÉ
COSAS! (fixed expression of
endearment and approbation frequently used with ref. to a
child's actions) How nice!, How
adorable!, etc.
COSITA: fpl. HACER COSITAS (euph.)
to copulate
COSOTA: fpl. COSOTAS (DE MAMÁ)
(term of endearment usually used
when addressing one's female
sweetheart; poss. Eng. equiva-

lent: 'Sweet mamma'); COSOTAS
(DE PAPÁ) (term of endearment
with a slight tinge of vulgarity;
poss. Eng. equivalent: 'Daddy's
sweet mamma'); (cf. COCHOTAS et
al.)
COSTAL: SER HARINA DEL MISMO COSTAL
to share the same charcteristics,
be cut from the same cloth (fig.);
SER HARINA DE OTRO COSTAL to belong to a different tribe (fig.),
belong to someone else (often
said sarcastically be parents
to married offspring who seldom
return to the parental home to
visit)
COSTALAZO precipitous tumble, heavy
fall; DAR EL COSTALAZO to keel
over, go down like a sack of
meal (fig.)
COSTEAR or COSTIAR to be worth the
trouble, worthwile
COSTILLA f. girl friend; f. boy
friend; girl who keeps a gigolo
COSTILLITA: SER MUY COSTILLITA to
be a stinker (slang), be disagreeable to others
COSTIPADO -DA (vars. of) constipado -
da
COSTURERÍA seamstress's shop
COTACO (Eng.) m. "Kotex" (female
sanitary napkin)
COTACHÍS (Eng.) m. cottage cheese
COTIN m. cloth used to cover chairs
or sofas; slip cover
COTINCHÓN -CHONA meddler (usually
ref. to man who meddles in wom-
en's affairs)
COTORRAZO blow, heavy hit
COTORREAR or COTORRIAR vn. to converse amiable, gossip, chat
COTORRO -RRA talkative person, chatterbox, gossip
COUC (Eng.) f. coca-cola (soft
drink)
COUCH (Eng.) mf. coach, trainer
COYOTE mf. youngest member of a
family; person easily frightened; exploiter; unscrupulous politician; halfbreed; person who
works for a commission (fixed
rate of pay)
COYOTEAR or COYOTIAR va. to rob;
vn. to goof off (slang), fool
around, enjoy oneself aimlessly
COZCO devil
CRACA (Eng.) wise crack, would-be
clever remark
CRANQUE (Eng.) m. crank (tool);
crank (grumpy person)
CRAQUEADO -DA or CRAQUIADO -DA (Eng.)
cracked (slang), crazy
CRAQUEAR or CRAQUIAR (Eng.) va. to

crack, break open

CREADA (var. of) criada

CREATURA (var. of) criatura

CRECER vn. to mature, gain experience

CRECIDOTE -TA ponderous and overgrown young person

CREER: CREERSE LA DIVINA GARZA ENVUELTA EN TORTILLA / CREERSE LA DIVINA GRACIA / CREERSE LA GRAN COSA / CREERSE LA GRAN CACA (vulg.) / CREERSE MUY MALDITO -TA / CREERSE MUY CHICOTUDO -DA / CREERSE MUY CHICHO -CHA to consider oneself superior / CREERSE MUY MACHÍN to consider oneself to be a real stud (slang): "Él se cree muy machín" 'He thinks he's a real stud'; / CREERSE SABROSO -SA to feel superior, consider oneself superior; ¡NO CREAS! (interj., iron.) Don't doubt it for a moment!

CREIBA, CREIBAS, etc. (vars. of) creía, etc. (imperf. conjugation of creer)

CREÍDO -DA credulous, gullible, vain, presumptuous

CREIDO -DA (var. of) creído -da (ppart. of creer)

CRENQUEAR or CRENQUIAR (Eng.) va. to crank a car

CREP or CREPÉ: CREPÉ ROMANO type of coarse cloth

CREPA (Eng.) (vulg.) crapper (i.e., toilet)

CREQUEAR or CREQUIAR (Eng.)(vars. of) craquear or craquiar

CRER (var. of) creer

CRESTA: IR LA CRESTA to rise (said of bodies of water during floods)

CREYER (var. of) creer

CREYON (Eng.) m. crayon

CRIAR: CRIAR CON PECHO to breast feed

CRIS (dim. of) Cristóbal

CRISMAS or CRISMES (Eng.) msg. Christmas (season); Christmas present

CRISTAL m. multicolored marble; mf. (mildly pej.) Anglo-Saxon; (dim. of) Crystal City, Texas

CRO (var. of) creo (1st pers. sg. pres. ind. of creer)

CRUCIFICO (var. of) crucifijo

CRUDO -DA adj. hungover; mf. person suffering from a hangover

CRÚNER (Eng.) m. crooner, singer of popular love songs

CRUZ: HACER LA CRUZ to make one's first sale of the day (said of merchants)

CRUZACALLES mfsg. gadabout, loafer

CRUZADO -DA halfbreed

CUACO horn of an animal; mpl. animal horns; handle bars of a bicycle

CUACHA chicken dung; HACER CUACHA (vulg., slang) to make mincemeat of (fig.), beat up soundly (in a fight)

CUACHALOTE ugly; bad; clumsy

CUACHÓN -CHONA fat and flabby; slovenly dresser, infrequent bather

CUACHONÓN -NONA very fat and flabby

CUADRO field for cultivation; field under cultivation

CUAI (cuate) m. buddy, pal (slang)

CUAJAR vn. to lie, tell falsehoods

CUALQUIERA prostitute, whore

CUANDO: (DE) CADA EN CUANDO from time to time

CUANTIMÁS (coll.) at least; let alone

CUANTO -TA: ¡A LAS CUÁNTAS! It's about time!, ¿A QUIÉN Y A CUÁNTOS? What business is that of anyone's?

CUARENTAIDÓS or CUARENTAIUNO (slang) male homosexual (so named after the disputed number of men caught in flagrante delicto at a private party by the police in Mexico City in the late 1930's)

CUARENTENA forty days following parturition (birth of a child): "Antes, las mujeres tenían que evitar baños y varios alimentos durante la cuarentena"

CUARTA belt (article of clothing)

CUARTADA spanking or whipping with a belt

CUARTAZO msg. single blow with a belt; mpl. spanking, whipping (with a belt)

CUARTERÓN -RONA person of mixed Hispanic and African ancestry

CUARTILLA quarter, twenty-five cent piece

CUARTITO outhouse, outdoor toilet

CUARTIZA spanking or whipping with a belt

CUARTO: CUARTO REDONDO (Ang.) quarter round (piece of corner furniture similar to a night stand)

CUATE -TA twin; pal, buddy (coll.); peer, equal; m. double-barreled shotgun; CUATES mpl. (slang) testicles

CUATEZÓN -ZONA intimate friend

CUATROJOS (slang) mfsg. four-eyes (i.e., person who wears eyeglasses)

CUATRO: CUATRO REALES / RIALES fifty cent piece
CUAY m. guy, fellow
CUBRIDO (var. of) cubierto (ppart. of cubrir)
CUCARACHA (coll.) jalopy, old car
CUCARACHERO place infested with cockroaches
CUCARACHO (var. of) cucaracha
CUCO or CUCA (dims. of) Refugio (m. & f.)
CUCOMALETAS (var. of) cocomaletas
¡CÚCHALE! or ¡CÚCHELE! interj. Sic'- em! (said to animals as encouragement to attack someone or retrieve something)
CUCHARA: CUCHARA DE VIERNES busybody, interfering person
CUCHÍA or CUCHILLA: PANTALONES DE CUCHILLA bellbottomed trousers
CUCHILLERO -RA troublemaker
CUCHO -CHA twisted, misshapen; harelipped
CUELA or CUÉLALE or CUÉLATE or CUELE or CUÉLELE or CUÉLESE interjs. (slang) Scram!, Beat it!, Bug off!, etc.
CUELLO: CUELLO DE LA MATRIZ cervix, entrance to the uterus
CUENTA: GARRAR ALGO DE UNA CUENTA to keep harping on something; HACER DE CUENTA QUE to suppose, assume
CUENTAZO several related pieces of gossip (all of which make for a long story)
CUENTO: pretext: "Ahora con el cuento de que está enfermo se porta como niño" 'Acting now under the pretext that he is sick, he's behaving like a child' CUENTO CHINO (often mpl.) lie, falsehood; CON EL CUENTO DE QUE under the pretext that: "Con el cuento de que estaba enfermo, no quiso hacer el trabajo"; ESTAR MALO EL CUENTO (said of situations which have become precarious): "Si mandaron traer (a) la ley, es que está malo el cuento" 'If they sent for the cops then things have really gotten bad'
CUERA (slang) girl friend, sweetheart; (pej.) mistress, kept woman; woman of considerable beauty
CUERAZO (slang) sexually attractive or very beautiful woman
CUERDO -DA (slang) adj. reckless, bold; (slang) f. boss, leader; ¡CUERDA! interj. What!, Bam!, Pow!; CUERDA DE LEÑA cord of

wood
CUERERÍA leather goods shop
CUERÍN m. scab (over a wound on the skin); trap for small animals (e.g., mouse trap)
CUERITO scab (over a wound on the skin)
CUERIZA spanking
CUERNO -NA mean; wicked; PONER CUERNOS to deceive one's spouse through adultery
CUERNADO -DA buck-toothed; lean-faced
CUERO -RA (slang) handsome (m.), pretty (f.); m. fiancé, sweetheart; man living in free union with a woman, common-law husband; m. gang, circle of friends; ARRIESGAR EL CUERO to risk one's life, rise one's hide (slang); CUERO DE RANA dollar bill, greenback (slang)
CUERPAZO sexy female body
CUERPO (slang) woman with a sexy body; ANDAR EL CUERPO / CORRER EL CUERPO to defecate; CUERPO DE COCA-COLA shapely (ref. to a woman's body) CUERPO DE ESTUDIANTES (Ang.) student body, totality of students (Std. estudiantado); HACER EL CUERPO to defecate; HACÉRSELE EL CUERPO CHINITO A ALGUIEN to get goose-pimples; TENER EL ALMA EN EL CUERPO to be sensitive about things, wear one's heart on one's sleeve (coll.)
CUERVO (pej.) U.S. black person
CUESTIÓN (Ang.) f. question (i.e., one that asks for information; Std. pregunta)
CUETAZO pistol shot; shot from any weapon
CUETE drunk, high as a kite (coll.); m. drunken binge; gun, pistol; CUETES mpl. curls, ringlets
CUETEAR or CUETIAR va. to shoot
CUEVA (vulg. slang) vagina
CUEVENO -NA light-colored (usually said of eyes)
CUIDADO: PONER CUIDADO to pay attention
CUIDADORA babysitter
CUIDANDERA babysitter
CUIDANIÑOS fsg. babysitter
CUIDAR: CUIDAR A LA ESPOSA for a man to "take care of" his wife by ejaculating outside of the uterus
CUIJA personal defect attracting sympathy
CUILCA cover, blanket, quilt
CUILMAS: SAN CUILMAS (hum.) San

Antonio, Texas; (hum.) (name
applied to any town one wishes
to burlesque)
CUILTA (Eng.) quilt, blanket
CUININICHE mf. uncooperative person
CUIRA (slang) quarter, twenty-
five cent piece
CUIZA (slang) prostitute (cf. huiza)
CUITEAR or CUITIAR (Eng.) va. to
quit
CULA (slang, vulg.) (var. of) culo
CULEBRA: CULEBRA DE AGUA sudden
storm, cloudburst
CULEBRÍA or CULEBRILLA undulating
line
CULECO -CA brooding (said of hens);
adj. m. recently become a
father (said of a man whose
first child has just been born)
CULEQUILLAS: EN CULEQUILLAS (var.
of) en cuclillas
CÚLER (Eng.) m. water cooler,
drinking fountain
CULERO -RA cowardly, fearful; eccentric; m. (slang & vulg.)
homosexual; mf. (slang &
vulg.) son-of-a-bitch
CULO fear, fright; CULO AGUADO large,
flabby ass (vulg.; ref. is
usually to the feminine posterior); FRUNCÍRSELE A ALGUIEN
EL CULO to be afraid, become
frightened
CULÓN -LONA (slang & vulg.) son-of-
a-bitch
CULOTE m. female buttocks (ref.
may be pej. or flattering, de-
pending on the context)
CUMPRIAÑOS (var. of) cumpleaños
CUÑADO (term used to address a
stranger)
CUOTIZAR va. & vr. to set the
price on an article
CUQUEAR or CUQUIAR (Eng.) va. to
cook
CUQUI (Eng.) f. cookie
CURA (slang) f. fix (of a narcotic
drug); medicinal preparation
for someone with a hangover
CURANDERO -RA witch doctor cum
herbalist
CURAR va. to remove a hex or spell;
to provide an addict with a
fix (slang); CURAR DE SUSTO
to cure, by sorcery, the after-
affects of a traumatic experience; CURARLE A ALGUIEN LOS
CALLOS to stop annoying someone; CURARSE (DE) LA CRUDA to
"cure" a hangover by drinking
more alcohol; to cure a hang-

over by drinking menudo (q.v.)
CURIOSITO -TA m. & f. cartoon film
or humorous short feature shown
before the main feature in movie
theaters; comic relief, in a
play or movie
CURIOSO -SA funny, humorous; fpl.
comic strips in a newspaper;
comic relief in a play or movie
CURITA (Eng., through metonymy
Curity) band-aid, bandage
CURSI embittered, sour
CURSIENTO -TA diarrhetic, suffering
from diarrhea
CURSIO (var. of) curso
CURSO (normally msg.) loose bowels,
diarrhea
CURVAR (Ang.) va. to curve, grade
on a curve (manner of assign-
ing grades on examinations)
CURVIA insinuation, innuendo
CUSQUEAR or CUSQUIAR va. to pick
up with a utensil; to eat
CUTE (Eng.) m. coat

CH

CHABACÁN (var. of) chabacano
'apricot'
CHABELA (dim. of) Isabel(a)
CHACOTEAR or CHACOTIAR vn. to
engage in lewd behavior
CHACUACO (slang) cigarette; cigar
butt
CHACHALACA talkative
CHACHALAQUERO -RA talkative
CHACHO -CHA (vars. of) muchacho -
cha
CHAFO -FA worthless, substandard;
tired, fatigued
CHAGO (dim. of) Santiago
CHÁGÜER or CHAHUER (Eng.) m.
shower (bath and apparatus);
party (at which gifts are
given in honor of a new-born
baby or a woman engaged to be
married
CHAHUA or CHÁHUER (Eng.) m. shower,
party to bestow gifts
CHAIN (Eng.) m. shine, polish;
shoeshine; DAR CHAIN to shine
or polish (esp. shoes)
CHAINADA (Eng.) shine, polish,
(esp. of shoes)
CHAINAR or CHAINEAR or CHAINIAR
(Eng.) va. to shine or polish

(esp. shoes)
CHAINERO (Eng.) shoe-shine boy
CHAIRA (slang) watch chain; sweet-
heart; fiancée
CHALÁN m. shoe
CHALAR (used only as interj.:)
¡CHÁLESE! or ¡CHALE! Shut up!,
Cool it!, Knock it off!, etc.
CHALE (dim. of) Carlos
CHALE (vulg.) m. penis
CHALECO: DE CHALECO as a freeload-
er, without paying; free, gratis
CHALICE (Eng.) m. & f. chalice
CHALITO (dim. of) Carlos
CHALITO (vulg.) penis
CHALUPA shoe
CHALLO -LLA (dim. of) Rosario (m. &
f.)
CHAMACO -CA m. boy; f. girl
CHAMARRA sweater
CHAMBA (coll.) job
CHAMBEAR or CHAMBIAR vn. to work
at a job
CHAMBELÁN or CHAMBERLÁN or CHAMBELÁIN
m. escort
CHAMBONEAR or CHAMBONIAR vn. to do
a job awkwardly
CHAMORRO calf (of the leg)
CHAMPIÓN -PIONA (Eng.) champion
CHAMPIONATO (Eng.) championship
CHAMPÚ (see DARSE CHAMPÚ)
CHAMPUCERO -RA (vars. of) chapucero -
ra
CHAMPURRADO gruel made of sugar,
chocolate and corn meal
CHAMUCO devil
CHAMUSCADO -DA scorched, burnt
CHANATE adj. black; m. coffee;
(pej.) U.S. black person
CHANCAQUÍA or CHANCAQUILLA thistle,
burr
CHANCLA slipper (bedroom slipper);
ARRIMAR LA CHANCLA to dance;
to spank; CAERLE A ALGUIEN LA
CHANCLA to receive a reprimand
(esp. said of husbands whose
wives put a stop to their flirta-
tions or other misbehavings);
TIRAR CHANCLA to dance
CHANCLAR or CHANCLEAR or CHANCLIAR
va. to spank; vn. to dance;
to walk
CHANCLAZO spanking; dance, party
CHANCLE m. dance; TIRAR CHANCLE
to dance
CHANCLEO dance, party
CHANCLETEAR or CHANCLETIAR (vars. of)
chanclar et al.
CHANCLÓN -CLONA good dancer
¡CHANE (SU PICO)! or ¡CHÁNESE! in-
terjs. Shut up!, Cool it!
(slang), etc.
CHANGARRETE m. business establish-

ment
CHANGLE mf. & adj. useless, good-
for-nothing (usually ref. to
persons)
CHANGO -GA monkey; (slang) young
person; (pej.) U.S. black person; (slang) fiancé(e); f. tomboy; f. amusing little show-
offish girl; CADA CHANGO A SU
COLUMPIO Y A COLUMPIARSE LUEGO /
CADA CHANGO A SU MECATE Y A DAR-
SE VUELO everyone (should) mind
his/her own business; every man
for himself; PONERSE CHANGO to
become alert, get smart; to get
all dressed up
CHANGUEAR or CHANGUIAR va. to
imitate, mock, ape (coll.)
CHANO (dim. of) Feliciano, Graciano,
Luciano
CHANQUILEAR or CHANQUILIAR vn. to
walk, take a walk
CHANSA (common orthog. var. of)
chanza
CHANSIAR (slang) va. to two-time
(slang), commit adultery
CHANTAR vn. to live, dwell; vr.
to get married; (coll. & vulg.)
to shack up (Std. vivir amance-
bados)
CHANTE m. house, home
CHANZA (Eng.) f. chance, opportunity;
risk; mumps; adv. perhaps;
AGARRAR CHANZA to take a chance,
risk; (HAY) CHANZA QUE there's
a chance that, it's possible
that
CHAPA door knob; door latch; (Eng.)
porkchop; any chop of meat; fpl.
(Ang.) false teeth, choppers
(slang)
CHAPANECAS fpl. popular Mexican
dance
CHAPANECO -CA short-statured
CHAPARRAL m. road runner (Geoco-
ccyx californianius)
CHAPARRO -RRA short person; ¡QUÉ
SUERTE TAN CHAPARRA! What
lousy luck!
CHAPEADO -DA or CHAPIADO -DA flushed
(said of cheeks)
CHAPEAR or CHAPIAR vr. to blush;
to apply rouge to cheeks
CHAPETA earring; diaper
CHAPETE f. (var. of) chapeta; ¡QUÉ
CHAPETE! What a bod! (slang--
said of an attractive woman);
CHAPETE'S PLEIS (Eng.) (said of
a sexually attractive woman's
body): "¿Tú conoces a Mariana?--
Uj, ¡Chapete's Pleis!"
CHAPETEADO -DA or CHAPETIADO -DA rosy-
cheeked

CHAPETEAR or CHAPETIAR va. to rouge
   one's cheeks; to fornicate
CHAPETONA: ¡QUÉ CHAPETONA! What a
   bod! (slang--said of sexually
   attractive woman's body)
CHAPETUDA sexy woman
CHAPETURA (var. of) chapetuda
CHAPÍN -PINA misshapen (said of legs)
CHAPO -PA short-statured (person);
   (coll. & hum.) Japanese
CHAPOPOTE (var. of) chapapote
CHAPOTE m. live-oak tree (Quercus
   virginiana)
CHAPUCEAR or CHAPUCIAR va. to de-
   ceive, cheat
CHAPUCERO -RA cheat, deceiver
CHAPUL m. child
CHAPULÍN -LINA grasshopper
CHAPULINADA group of children (fig.);
   swarm of grasshoppers
CHAPUZA fraud, deception; HACER
   CHAPUZA A ALGUIEN to cheat
   someone
CHAPUZAR va. to cheat, deceive
CHAQUETEAR or CHAQUETIAR va. to be-
   tray
CHAQUETERO -RA turn-coat, betrayer
CHÁQUIRA (Eng.) (slang) jacket
CHARA (Eng.) charter
CHARAMUSCA taffy in twisted or spiral
   form
CHARCA: ANDAR CHARCA to be well
   dressed
CHARCO: AHOGARSE EN CUALQUIER CHARCO
   to be incapable of doing any-
   thing right, not able to fight
   one's way out of a paper bag
   (fig.); BRINCAR EL CHARCO to
   cross the Rio Grande/Río Bravo
   (Texas-Mexican border) (said
   with ref. to persons immigra-
   ting from Mexico to Texas)
CHARCHAR or CHARCHIAR (Eng.) va. to
   charge purchases on a charge
   account
CHARCHINA jalopy, old car; (slang)
   girl
CHARIFE (var. of) cherife (Eng.)
CHARLADOR -DORA liar
CHAROLA tray (of whatever sort); fpl.
   pots and pans
CHARPIAR (Eng.) va. to sharpen
CHARRASQUEAR or CHARRASQUIAR va. to
   scar with a knife
CHARREADA or CHARRIADA party or get-
   together of charros
CHASÍS m. SER EL PURO CHASÍS to be
   nothing but skin and bones
   (coll.), be extremely thin
CHAT (Eng.) m. shot, injection
CHATO -TA (term of endearment used
   between husband and wife); f.
   marihuana; CHATOS mpl. crab

lice (usually found in the genital region); HACERSE CHATO -TA
   to turn a deaf ear (coll.)
CHAVAL -VALA sweetheart; m. fiancé;
   f. fiancée
CHAVALÓN -LONA child
CHAVETA (slang) head (Std. cabeza);
   fiancée; sweetheart (f.)
CHAVO -VA (slang) young person;
   sweetheart
CHAYO (dim. of) Eduardo; CHAYO -YA
   (dim. of) Rosario (m. & f.)
CHAYOTE m. tom-boy; (slang) dollar
CHECADITA (Eng.) check-up, examina-
   tion
CHECAR (Eng.) va. to review; to
   verify; to check; to correct;
   to examine
CHECHE (m.), -CHA (f.) young child,
   little shaver (coll.)
CHEIQUEAR or CHEIQUIAR (Eng.) va. to
   shake, agitate
CHELA (dim. of) Graciela, Celia
CHELO (dim. of) Consuelo
CHEMA m. (dim. of) José María
CHEMBI (slang) adv. perhaps, maybe
CHENCHO -CHA (dim. of) Cresencia,
   Cresencio (m. & f.), Inocencio
   (m. & f.)
CHENDO -DA (dims. of, resp.: Rosendo,
   Rosenda)
CHENTE -TA (dims. of, resp.: Vicente,
   Vicenta)
CHEPE mf. hypocrite
CHEQUE (Eng.) m. investigation,
   examination (see also DAR SU
   CHEQUE)
CHEQUEADITA or CHEQUIADITA (Eng.)
   (vars. of) checadita
CHEQUEADOR -DORA or CHEQUIADOR -
   RA m., f. (Eng.) checker, in-
   spector
CHEQUEAR or CHEQUIAR (Eng.) (vars.
   of) checar
CHEQUEO (Eng.) check, check-up;
   examination
CHÉRBET (Eng.) m. sherbert
CHERIFE (Eng.) m. sherrif
CHERMÉS m. silk cloth
CHI f. (vulg.) urine; HACER (LA)
   CHI (var. of) hacer chis
CHIAPANECO -CA (var. of) chapaneco -
   ca
CHICABACHO -CHA chicano (Mexican-
   American) who acts and thinks
   like an Anglo-Saxon (gabacho,
   q.v.)
CHICAGO (slang, vulg. & hum.) toilet,
   restroom, bathroom (etc.) (<
   chi 'urine' + cago 'I defecate')
CHICALES mpl. corn-meal stew
CHICANADA (slang) action or behavior
   typifying a Chicano; group of

Chicanos

CHICANEADA or CHICANIADA (slang)
(vars. of) chicanada

CHICANEAR or CHICANIAR (slang)
vn. to behave in a Chicano-
like fashion; (coll., said of
Chicanos) to do one's thing
(slang), act as one feels like
acting

CHICANEO action or behavior typifying a Chicano

CHICANERIA (slang) (id. to CHICANEO)

CHICANGLO Chicano who acts like an
Anglo-Saxon; Anglo-Saxon who
identifies with the Chicano and
the Chicano cause(s)

CHICANISMO ideology and ethnic spir-
it typifying the Chicano Move-
ment(s)

CHICANO -NA Mexican-American, person
of Mexican heritage born and
raised in the United States or
person born in Mexico of Mexican
ethnic background who has become a United States citizen
or permanent resident; any person of Mexican ethnic background

CHICLE m. tar; asphalt; pest, un-
invited person, tag-along (colloquial)

CHICLOSO -SA pest, tag-along (coll.);
m. (vulg.) anus

CHICO -CA mocking-bird (Mimun polyglottos); adj. mf. (iron.) big,
large; CHICAS PATAS mfsg. Mexican: "Él es un chicas patas";
A LAS CHICAS PATAS in the Mexican fashion

CHICOLITO -TA small, tiny

CHICOTAZO whiplash, blow with a
whip

CHICOTE (slang) m. penis

CHICOTEADA or CHICOTIADA whipping,
lashing

CHICOTEAR or CHICOTIAR (slang): CHICO-
TEARLE A ALGUIEN EL APARATO /
EL MANGO / CHICOTEARLE A AL-
GUIEN PARA HACER ALGO: to excell
at doing something: "A él le
chicotea para jugar a la pelota"
'He is really good at playing
ball'

CHICOTUDO -DA very large; difficult;
m. extremely handsome male, an
Adonis (coll.); (slang) V.I.P.,
man of considerable importance

CHICURA ragweed herb (Ambrosia ambro-
coides) (whose roots are made
into a douching solution)

CHICHARO pea, green or sweet pea
(Lathyrus odoratus); (slang)
mpl. household goods (e.g., furniture, etc.)

CHICHARRO (hum.) cigar

CHICHARRONEAR or CHICHARRONIAR va.
to burn to a crisp

CHICHARRON: BUSCARLE RUIDO AL
CHICHARRON to look for trouble;
HACER CHICHARRON to burn to a
crisp

CHICHE or CHICHI f. breast (female)
sinecure, soft job (coll.) often obtained as a political
favor; DAR CHICHE to breast-
feed a child; MAMAR CHICHE to
sponge (coll.), live off other
people, live at someone's expense

CHICHECANO -NA or CHICHICANO -NA
(slang) Chicano who enjoys a
sinecure (cf. CHICHE/CHICHI)
(the word appears to have been
born in 1968 at the Kelly Air
Force Base in San Antonio, Texas)

CHICHERO (coll. & mildly vulg.)
brassiere, bra

CHICHITA welt

CHICHO (dim. of Narciso; CHICHO-
CHA adj., mf. crazy, daffy,
screwy (slang); wonderful, great

CHICHON -CHONA large-breasted
(usually f., ref. to women)

CHIFLADO -DA daffy, scatter-brained
(coll.); stuck up (coll.), presumptuous; smitten, head over
heels in love (coll.); ANDAR
CHIFLADO -DA to be smitten in
love

CHIFLAR va. to elate; to cause to
swell with a (false) sense of
pride or self-importance; to
spoil, pamper; vr. to swell
with a (false) sense of pride

CHIFLETA (var. of) chiflete; (var.
of) chufleta; f. sarcastic remark, innuendo

CHIFLON -FLONA person very suscep-
tible to the flattery of others

CHIFON m. chiffon

CHIFONIA chiffonier, chest of drawers

CHIHUA or CHIHUAHUA interj. (of
varying intensity of meaning,
according to intonation, e.g.,
everything from 'Goodness gra-
cious' through 'Hell!')

CHILE m. penis; CHILE PARADO erect
penis, hard-on (slang); CHILE
PELON (in the sexual act, penis
not encased in a condom); IR
HECHO CHILE to go like a bat
out of hell (slang), move very
quickly; chilli pepper (and the
following variant types) CHILE
ANCHO bell pepper; CHILE BOLITA

small round red pepper; CHILE
CASCABEL dry red pepper whose
seeds rattle inside the cask;
CHILE DEL MONTE round red pepper measuring one centimeter in
diameter; CHILE DULCE sweet
pepper; CHILE EN ESCABECHE
chile preserved in vinagre;
CHILE JALAPEÑO large and piquant green pepper; CHILE JAPO-
NÉS elongated piquant red pepper about four centimeters in
length; CHILE PIQUÍN very piquant caper-sized green or red
pepper; CHILE PISADO large
red dry pepper measuring about
ten centimeters in length and
six in width; CHILE PITÍN
(var. of) chile piquín; CHILE
RELLENO large green pepper
filled with meat and sauces and
then baked

CHILERO -RA fond of eating chilli
peppers; m. small yellow bird
with gray wings (Pitangus sul-
furatus)

CHILETE m. (id. to chilipiquín or
CHILE PIQUÍN) (Capsicum baccatum)

CHILPASÍA dry and ripe chile arti-
ficially dried in the sun

CHILPAYATE mf. small child

CHILPITIN (var. of) chile piquín/
chile pitín

CHILUCA (slang, underw.) head (human)

CHILUDO m. (vulg.) man with a big
penis

CHILLA: ESTAR EN LA CHILLA to be
hardpressed financially (usually for just a short time)

CHILLADOR -DORA: TROMPO CHILLADOR
wind-up top which makes a
whining noise when spinning;
(VÍBORA) CHILLADORA rattle-
snake

CHILLANTE loud (said of colors)

CHILLAR vn. to cry; vr. to become
very angry

CHILLÓN -LLONA cry-baby

CHIMENEA: TENER LA CHIMENEA MUY
CERCA to be very hot-tempered

CHIMINEA (var. of) chimenea

CHIMOLEAR or CHIMOLIAR (vars. of)
chismorrear or chismorriar

CHIMOLERO -RA (var. of) chismolero -
ra

CHIMPA hair

CHIMUELO -LA lacking teeth, with
some teeth missing

CHINANERO any stick used to remove
a hot lid from a kettle

CHINAR va. to comb; vr. CHINÁRSELE
EL CUERPO A ALGUIEN to get

goosebumps (goosepimples)

CHINCORRAZO blow on the head

CHINCUALES mpl. type of small skin
eruption; (fig.) nervousness:
"Parece que traes chincuales"
'You'd think you had ants in
your pants' (coll.) (said of
persons, usually children, who
are restless and who continually
squirm around)

CHINCUÍS m. ocular sty

CHINCHE adj. miserly; m. & f.
CHINCHE PEDORRA / CHINCHE
PERRODA stink-bug (Pentato-
mida); HACERSE CHINCHE to act
stingy, miserly; to overstay
one's welcome; TENER LA SANGRE
DE CHINCHE to be repugnant to,
repellent to (said of persons)

CHINCHERÍA squalor, filth; place
infested with chinch bugs (bed
bugs)

CHINCHERO messy room; messy house;
any room, mattress, etc., infested with bed-bugs; (hum.)
small business establishment;
jail

¡CHINELAS! interj. (slightly euph.)
'Son of a . . . .'

CHINGADA (lit., woman on whom the
act of coition has been performed) (vulg.); ESTAR COMO LA
CHINGADA to be as ugly/mean/
timid/insensitive (etc.) as one
can possibly be; ¡HIJO DE LA
CHINGADA MADRE! interj. (strong-
est and most vulg. interj. possible) 'XXXXXXX XXXX!'; ¡HIJO
DE TU CHINGADA MADRE! (very
vulg.); MANDAR A LA CHINGADA to
tell someone to go to hell;
¡¿QUÉ CHINGADOS QUIERES?!
(very strong and vulg.) What
the hell ya want?; ¡ME LLEVA
LA CHINGADA! (strong and vulg.)
I'll be God-damned! ¡VÁMONOS A
LA CHINGADA! Let's get the hell
out of here!

CHINGADAZO (var. of) chingazo

CHINGADERA nuisance, annoyance;
damn(ed) thing

CHINGAL: UN CHINGAL a great deal,
to a high degree (cf. UN
CHINGATAL)

CHINGAR (vulg.) va. to copulate
(etc.); to cheat; to avenge;
to defeat (in a contest); to
get what one is after: "Ya
chingó" 'He got what he wanted';
vr. (slang & vulg.) to get
married; interjs.: ¡CHINGA
CAGADA! (very strong and vulg.)
'XXXXXX XXXX!'; CHINGAR LA

PACIENCIA to bother; PARA ACA-
BARLA DE CHINGAR to make matters worse

CHINGATAL: UN CHINGATAL a great
deal, to a high degree (cf. UN
CHINGAL)

CHINGAZO blow with the hand or with
a heavy object; CHINGAZOS mpl.
a fist fight; AGARRARSE A CHIN-
GAZOS to get into a fist fight

CHINGÓN -GONA: large; tall (ref. to
persons); EL MERO CHINGÓN (hum.)
the big boss, the big cheese
(slang)

CHINGONÓN -NONA (var. of) chingonote

CHINGOS mpl. (used adjectivally)
several, many; (used adverbial-
ly) a great deal, to a considerable extent

CHINGUIZA (see DAR UNA CHINGUIZA)

CHINITA: ¡CHINITA POR TU AMOR! interj. (slightly euph.) Son of
a ... !; ¡CHINITAS! interj.
(slightly euph.)

CHINITO: HACÉRSELE A ALGUIEN EL
CUERPO CHINITO to get goosebumps (goose-pimples); TRAER
LOS OJOS CHINITOS to have
sleepy(-looking) eyes

CHINO -NA m. curl (of hair); comb
(in general); comb for removing
body lice or hair lice; mf.
darling (term of endearment);
CHINA POBLANA Mexican regional
costume (worn by women); PAPEL
DE CHINA tissue paper

CHIPIAR vn. to drizzle, rain very
lightly

CHIPIL or CHÍPILI mf. spoiled or
overindulged child (cf. CHIPLE)

CHIPÓN -PONA spoiled child

CHIQUEADOR -DORA or CHIQUIADOR -DORA
mf. pamperer (person who pampers);
adj. fond of pampering

CHIQUEAR or CHIQUIAR va. & vr. to
spoil, pamper; vr. to play
hard to get, be evasive (esp.
in amorous games)

CHIQUEO act or effect of pampering

CHEQUEÓN -QUEONA or CHIQUIÓN -QUIONA
spoiled child; person who enjoys being pampered

CHIQUERO dirty and messy place,
pigpen (fig.)

CHIQUETE m. chewing gum; asphalt;
tar

CHIQUININGO -GA or CHIQUIRRINGO -GA
or CHIQUITINGO -GA small child

CHIQUITO -TA son/daughter who bears
the first name of the parent of
the same sex (esp. used after
parent's first name with ref.
to the child, e.g., "Eva chi-

quita"; also used when ref. to
a child who imitates the parent, even though the two are
not identically named); m.
(slang) buttocks; (vulg.) anus

CHIRA (Eng.) mf. cheater, deceiver

CHIRIAR (Eng.) va. & vn. to cheat,
defraud

CHIRINOLA gossiper; group of gos-
sips; fuss, bother

CHIRIÓN -RIONA cheater, deceiver

CHIRIPADA (var. of) chiripá

CHIRRIONA (var. of) chirona

CHISCA or CHISCURA bicycle

CHISMARAJO gossiping, gossip

CHISMOLEAR or CHISMOLIAR (vars. of)
chismorrear

CHISMOLERO -RA gossiper

CHISPA f. (ref. to both men and
women) astute, sly, sharp;
¡CHISPAS! (mild interj.) Holy
cow!, Golly!

CHISPUDO -DA curly (said of hair);
daffy, crazy, screwy (coll.)

CHISQUEADO -DA or CHISQUIADO -DA
(slang) adv. very rapidly,
like crazy (coll.)

CHISQUEAR or CHISQUIAR va. to drive
crazy, madden; vr. to become
crazy

CHISTAR or CHISTEAR or CHISTIAR vn.
to complain (esp. with interj.
ichst! as to request silence
in a theater), to shush

CHISTE m. NO TENER CHISTE to be
worthless, of no importance; to
be dull (said of persons); to
to be easy to accomplish: "Eso
no tiene chiste" 'There's nothing to doing that'

CHITO -TA (muchachito -ta) m. (dim.)
little boy; f. (dim.) little
girl

CHITO -TA (dims. of) Jesús, Jesusa;
Felícito, Felícita

CHIVAS fpl. trinkets, objects of
little value; (slang) interj.
Give me whatever you have!
(used for example by a thief to
a victim: 'Hand it over!')

CHIVATO -TA mischievous youngster,
"kid" (coll.)

¡CHIVE! (slang) interj. Don't be
frightened!

CHIVEAR or CHIVIAR vr. to back
down, back out, retract (a
statement), be afraid or bashful

CHIVERO -RA skittish person, scaredy-
cat (coll.); (pej.) Anglo-Saxon;
m. goatherd; f. young girl

CHIVETAL m. fold for goats (young
goats)

CHIVETE m. fear

CHIVETERO -RA frightened; m. fold for kids (young goats)

CHIVINOLERA gossipy person

CHIVO -VA (slang) adj. afraid, shy; handsome, beautiful; mf. (slang) coward; f. ten dollar bill; heroin; thingamagig (used as a substitute for a forgotten designation); coin; nanny goat; AGARRAR EL CHIVO (Ang.) to get someone's goat (fig.): "Juan le agarró el chivo a Pepe, por eso se peliaron" 'Juan got Pepe's goat, and that's why they got into a fight'; HACERLE A ALGUIEN LOS TAMALES DE CHIVO (fig.) to deceive a spouse, commit adultery

CHIVOTE (slang) m. handsome man

CHO (Eng.) show, spectacle, exhibition; movie theater

CHOC (Eng.) m. shock; choke (automotive); chalk (writing instrument)

CHOCADO -DA at odds with one another (said of two or more persons); ESTAR CHOCADOS not to be on speaking terms

CHOCANTE ˌrepugnant; presumptuous

CHOCANTERIA repugnant act

CHOCANTÓN -TONA repulsive, repugnant (usually ref. to persons)

CHOCAR va. to shock, repel, be repulsive to: "Ese tipo me choca mucho"; vr. to become enemies; to cease to be on speaking terms: "¿Por qué no invitastes a María y a Juana?--Porque ayer se chocaron"; CHOCAR LAS MANOS to shake hands

CHOCLE (Eng.) m. chalk (writing instrument)

CHOCHE m. small boy; (Eng.) George; (Hispanization of) George West, Texas (city in south Texas) (cf. YOCHE)

CHOCHO -CHA chubby; slow-moving; f. small girl

CHOCHÓN -CHONA (term of endearment)

CHOFERO -RA chauffeur, driver of a car

CHOFLEAR or CHOFLIAR (Eng.) vn. to shuffle

CHOLA or CHOLE (dim. of) Soledad f.

¡CHOLE! or ¡CHÓLESE! (slang) Shut up!, Knock it off!, Cool it!, etc.

CHOLENCO -CA weak, worn, weary; (said of persons who appear to be coming down with an illness); sickly, prone to infirmities

CHOLENQUE m.,f. (var. of) cholenco -ca

CHOMPA or CHOMPE or CHOMPETA (slang) f. head (human)

CHON or CHONA (dims. of) Asunción, Encarnación (m. & f.) (dims. of) Concepción (f. only)

CHONES mpl. (calzones) long underwear

CHONGO knot of hair tied up in the back of the head; AGARRARSE DE LOS CHONGOS to fight by pulling one another's hair

CHONGUEADA or CHONGUIADA fight wherein one woman pulls another's hair

CHONTE m. mocking bird (Mimus polyglottos)

CHOPA (f.) or CHOPE (m.) (Eng.) shop, store

CHOPETEAR or CHOPETIAR (slang) vn. to have sexual intercourse

CHOQUEAR or CHOQUIAR (Eng.) va. to choke, manipulate the choke (on a car); vr. (var. of chocar 'to shake hands')

CHOPO (hum.) nose

CHOPUCERO -RA (var. of) chapucero -ra

CHORA sweetheart, fiancée; cigarette butt

CHORALO -LA small child

CHORCHA (Eng.) (little used) church; (more frequently) group of people; HACERSE LA CHORCHA for a group to form, congregate

CHORE (Eng.) m. short-statured

CHORICERO -RA sausage vendor; member of the family of a sausage vendor

CHORIZO type of Mexican sausage; (vulg.) penis, etc.

CHORREADO -DA or CHORRIADO -DA dirty, soiled

CHORREAR or CHORRIAR va. to soil with a liquid, make dirty; vr. to spill a liquid on oneself; to drip: "La pompa está chorriando"

CHORRERA or CHORRERIA diarrhea; (id. to chorrero)

CHORRERO long string of (things or person): "Traiba un chorrero de huercos" 'He had with him a long string of brats' (see also CHORRERIA)

CHORRO diarrhea; multitude (of people);(euph.) gonorrhea; LLOVER A CHORROS to rain cats and dogs (fig.), rain heavily

CHORROS (Eng. sure) (slang) (affirmative response to a question) "¿Vas al pueblo?-- Chorros"

CHOT (Eng.) (var. of chat, also Eng.)

CHOTA (slang) policeman; police

force

CHOTEADO -DA or CHOTIADO -DA (slang, vulg.) promiscuous, loose-living (usually ref. to women), with a lot of mileage on (slang)

CHOTEAR or CHOTIAR va. to use to excess; to abuse; to ridicule; to defame, ruin; to make a fool of someone; to caress heavily, pet (slang)

CHOTEO act and effect of using to excess, abusing, ridiculing, defaming, etc. (see CHOTEAR, supra)

CHOU (Eng.) (var. of cho, also Eng.)

CHUCO , EL (slang) El Paso, Texas

CHUCO -CA (slang) (var. of) pachuco-ca

CHUCHALUCAR va. to take advantage of a woman sexually

CHUCHO -CHA (dims. of) Jesús, María de Jesús

CHUCHO -CHA sly, astute, foxy (coll.) m. dog

CHUCHULUCO little toy

CHUECO -CA twisted, not straight, tilted; bowlegged; crooked, dishonest

CHUGA (pej.) U.S. black person

CHÚINGOM (Eng.) m. chewing gum

CHULADA cute remark or gesture (can be used ironically, e.g., "¡Qué chulada!" 'Well isn't that just something!')

CHULEAR or CHULIAR va. to caress; to speak affectionately to; to flatter (usually 'to flatter a woman'); to primp; vr. to pimp

CHULO -LA pretty (often said to children)

CHUPACHARCOS (slang) mpl. tennis shoes; homosexual

CHUPADA pull, inhalation (on a cigar or cigarette)

CHUPADERA act of smoking; chain smoking, continual smoking of cigarettes

CHUPADOR -DORA smoker; heavy smoker

CHUPAMIEL m. unscrupulous politician

CHUPÓN -PONA (slang., vulg.) homosexual

CHUPONCITO puff on a cigar or cigarette

CHUPARROSA humming bird (Trochilidae)

CHUSAR or CHUSEAR or CHUSIAR (Eng.) va. to choose, select

CHUSEADOR -DORA or CHUSIADOR -DORA (Eng.) person who does the choosing

CHUTAR or CHUTEAR or CHUTIAR (Eng.) va. to shoot

CHUTEADO -DA or CHUTIADO -DA embar-

rassed

CHUTEO (Eng.) act of shooting; shoot-out (with guns, between two or more people); (var. of) choteo

CHUY (dim. of) Jesús

D

DA-CORAJE (see CORAJE)

DAGAZO stab with a dagger

DAILEAR or DAILIAR or DALEAR or DALIAR (Eng.) va. to dial (a telephone)

DAIME (Eng.) m. dime, ten cent piece

DALLAS (see IR A DALLAS)

DAMA: DAMA DE HONOR bridesmaid

DAMIANA damiana (Turnera diffusa) (herb prepared as a solution and either drunk or else used as a douch for treatment of FRÍO DE LA MATRIZ, q.v. infra)

DAR va. to show, project (a film); A MÍ NO ME LA DAS You can't fool me!; DAR A BAJAR to illtreat, mistreat; DAR AIRE to fire, discharge; to dismiss one's boy-(girl) friend; give him/her the air (slang); to give cause to suspect: "No le des aire de lo que ha pasado aquí; DAR ALAS to give someone free rein; to side with someone (in a dispute, etc.) DAR A OLER to give cause to suspect: "No le den a oler que su amigo se murió ayer" 'Don't give him cause to suspect that his friend died yesterday'; A COMO DÉ LUGAR one way or another, any way it can be done: "¿Cómo piensan hacerlo?-- A como dé lugar."; DAR APRETONES (folk medicine:) sharp squeezes administered, from behind, to a sick person, typically one with a cold and aching bones and muscles; the sick person grabs himself by the hands behind the neck so that the elbows jut out from the body at a 90° angle; the treatment is said to cure the cold and relieve the muscular ache; DAR ATOLE CON EL DEDO to deceive one's spouse with another person, have adulterous sexual relations; DAR BÁSCULA to frisk for concealed weapons, stolen goods, etc.; DAR BEBITO (coll.) to impregnate, make pregnant; DAR BOLA to cause unnecessary problems; DAR CALABAZAS to give someone the air (slang), reject (as a suitor); to make a fool out of someone; DAR CAPOTE to blank (sports slang), hold an opponent to zero points in a game; DAR CAPOTEADA/DAR CAPOTIADA to blank (sports slang), achieve a very high score while holding the opponent to zero points; DAR CAPOTIZA (id. to DAR CAPOTEADA); DAR CARRILLA to bother, molest; DAR CATOS (coll.) to beat someone up, usually with one's fists; DAR COLOR to show something off (usually a new possession); DAR CHAMPÚ to shampoo someone's hair; DAR DE ALTA to discharge (i.e., from a hospital); to discharge from the armed forces (usually ref. to an honorable dischange); DAR DE PECHO to breast feed; DAR DE SÍ to yield, be reasonable, be willing to compromise (the expression is used more frequently in the negative: NO DAR DE SÍ to be adamant, uncompromising, hard to convince, etc.); to stretch (said of clothing); DAR EL GOLPE AL CIGARRO to inhale deeply on a cigarette; DAR EN CARA to be fed up with (coll.), satiated with: "Ya me dio en cara esa sopa"; DAR EN EL (MERO) MATE to hit where it hurts; to hit right on the button; DAR EN EL MOCO to punch on the nose; to administer a beating (usually in a fist fight); DAR EN LA MADRE (id. to DAR EN EL MOCO); DAR EN LA MERA MADRE to administer a severe beating; DAR EN LA TORRE to administer a beating (usually in a fist fight); DAR EN TODA LA MADRE to give someone a severe beating (usually in a fist fight) DAR FAMA to praise, eulogize; DAR GUERRA to annoy, irritate, bother; DAR LA CONTRA to contradict, oppose, disagree with; DAR (LA) LATA to bother, pester: "Llévate ese niño pa' fuera, está dando mucha lata"; DAR LA PATADA to dismiss, fire (from a job); to sever ties, break with, terminate (e.g. an amorous relation-

ship); to stink, emit a foul odor; DARLAS to have sexual intercourse promiscuously, be up for (grabs) (slang) (usually said of women), put out (slang) (cf. IR A DALLAS); DAR LAS DOCE to be in a tight spot: "Ya me daban las doce" 'I was sure in a tight spot'; to be worried stiff: "Ya me daban las doce con el niño porque tenía una calentura de 105°"; DAR LAS NALGAS (hum.) to lose in a game or sports contest; to have sexual intercourse promiscuously, be up for grabs (slang) (usually said of women); DAR LÁSTIMA CON to feel sorry for: "Me dio lástima con Juan" 'I felt sorry for Juan'; DAR LA SUAVE to humor; DAR LA VUELTA to look in on (someone): "Dame la vuelta mientras me baño, no vaya a ser que me desmaye" 'Look in on me while I'm taking a bath, just to make sure I haven't fainted'; DARLE AL GAS (Ang.?) to step on the gas (fig.), hurry (also vn.: ·to hurry, speed up, get a move on [slang]; DARLE DE REVERSA to back up, reverse (a vehicle); DARLE GAS to speed up (esp. a motor vehicle); DAR LIJA to put the finishing touches on a job; DAR LUZ to give the go-ahead, approve a request; to give a light (to someone lighting a cigarette, etc.); (var. of dar a luz 'to give birth to'); DAR MADERA to flatter, apple-polish (coll.), give a snow job (slang); DAR PA' DENTRO (vulg.) to copulate (vulg.): "Le dio pa' dentro"; DAR PATADAS DE AHOGADO/DIOGADO to be in a tight spot, a precarious situation; to fight a losing battle: "Ese pobre señor está dando patadas de ahogado"; DAR PA' FUERA to fire, dismiss (from a job); DAR PA' TRAS (Ang.) to return, give back; to back up, reverse: "Le dio pa' tras al coche" 'He backed up his car'; DAR PENA to embarrass: "Me da mucha pena" 'It embarrasses me'; DAR POR to take a notion to: "Le dio por irse temprano" 'He got it into his head to go early'; DAR POR SU LADO to humor: "Dale por su lado para

que te dé lo que quieres"; DAR
PUERTA to show the body's
"private parts" (genitalia,
etc.) or to show one's under-
garments unintentionally; DAR
QUEBRADA (Ang.) to give a break,
allow to have a chance; DAR
REATAZOS/RIATAZOS to administer
a beating (usually with fists);
DAR SU CHEQUE to fire (coll.),
dismiss, discharge from a job;
DAR SU LONCHE to put someone
in his/her place, tell someone
where to get off (slang): "Mamá te está esperando para darte
tu lonche" 'Ma is waiting to
give you what you've got coming
to you', DAR UN AGARRÓN to
scold; to browbeat; (vulg.) to
copulate (with); DAR UN APLAS-
TÓN to humiliate, cut down
(coll.); DAR UN REATAZO/RIATAZO
to strike a blow with one's
fist; DAR UNA CHINGUIZA to
administer a beating (usually
with fists); DAR UNA ATASCADA
(vulg.) to copulate; DAR UNA
FREGUIZA to beat up (coll.),
administer a beating (usually
with fists); DAR UNA MANITA
to lend a helping hand; DAR
UNA MANO (id. to DAR UNA
MANITA); DAR UNA METIDA (vulg.)
to copulate, (coll.) slip it
in (vulg. slang); DAR UNA
PALIZA to beat (coll.), soundly triumph over (in a sport's
competition); DAR UNA REATIZA/
RIATIZA to give a severe beating (usually with fists) (cf.
DAR REATAZOS, DAR UN REATAZO);
DAR UNA TAMBORIZA to administer a severe beating, beat to
a pulp (coll.); DAR UNA TIRADA
(vulg.) to copulate (vulg.); vn.
to go off in a specific direction (usually used as a command): "Dale pa' la casa"
'Get on home': DAR ABASTO to
suffice, be enough (usually
employed in the negative):
"Estas tortillas no dan abasto"
'These tortillas aren't going
to be enough to feed the number
of people expected'; to be coped
with: "Estos niños no dan a-
basto; se ensucian la ropa
cuatro veces por día"; DAR CON
BOLA to realize one's goals;
DAR LA VUELTA to pass by, drop
by (a place), drop over (for a
visit): "Mañana no dejes de
dar la vuelta" 'Don't forget
to come by tomorrow'; DAR UNA

VUELTA to make a complete
turn; to go for a stroll or a
ride; DAR UN RAUND (Eng.) to
last out a round (said of box-
ers in a boxing match); vr. to
give up, yield, produce: "Este
año se van a dar muchas nue-
ces"; to submit to sexual advances; DARSE A BAJAR to act
in such a manner as to bring
on ill treatment or abuse:
"Te tratan así porque das a
bajar" 'They treat you like
that because you bring it on
yourself'; DARSE BAÑOS DE PU-
REZA to boast of one's decorum
and behavior; to justify one's
words and deeds; DARSE CABRONA-
ZOS to beat up on one another
(usually in a fist fight);
DARSE CANCOS to have a fist
fight; DARSE CATOS to have a
fist fight; DARSE CHAMPÚ to
shampoo one's own hair; DARSE
CHINGAZOS to beat up one another (usually in a fist fight);
DARSE DE SANTOS to thank one's
lucky stars (coll.), be thankful for favors received; DARSE
EN to bump: "El niño se dio
en la cabeza con la mesa"
'The child bumped his head on
the table'; DARSE FREGADAZOS/
DARSE FREGAZOS to beat up on
one another (usually in a fist
fight); DARSE GUSTO to have
fun, have a good time; DÁRSELA
A ALGUIEN to fool, deceive
(used only in the negative):
"Tú no me la das" 'You can't
fool me'; DARSE LIJA to exalt
oneself, praise oneself; DARSE
MADERA (id. to DARSE LIJA);
DARSE PAQUETE to give oneself
importance, boast of one's
abilities; DARSE TOPES to
bump heads; to try to outdo
each other (said of two or more
persons); DARSE TROMPA to become aware of something; DARSE
TROMPAZOS to beat up one another; DARSE UNA AGARRADA/
DARSE UN AGARRÓN to get into
an argument; to get into a fist
fight; DARSE UNA CHINGUIZA to
beat up one another severely
(usually in a fist fight);
DARSE UNA REATIZA/RIATIZA to
give one another a severe beating; DARSE UN AGARRÓN (vulg.)
to engage in copulation; DARSE
UN CALENTÓN to become sexually
excited; to anger one another;
DARSE UN FREGADAZO/DARSE UN

FREGAZO to hit oneself on an object
DANDO Y DANDO (said as a request for simultaneous exchange of objects, roughly equivalent to Eng. 'Share and share alike')
DE: DE ABURI many; DE AGUA incomplete; weak, soft (said of persons); effeminate, faggy (slang); DE A MADRE totally, completely; a great deal, a considerable amount; super, magnificent, swell; DE AQUELLA very nice, super, neat, swell (etc.) (all coll.); DE AQUELLA MELAZA terrific, super, swell (etc.); DE A TIRO totally, completely; DE A VOLADA fast, rapidly, quickly; DE CINCHO assuredly, certainly (cf. CINCHO); DE CORA enthusiastically; ¿DE CUÁNDO ACÁ? Since when? (used to indicate disbelief and incredulity): "Ahora ya no le tengo rencor a nadie porque he cambiado.--¿De cuándo acá?"; DE CHALECO free, gratis; DE DEVERAS in truth, in earnest, seriously; DE DIARIO daily, every day; DE HILO in a straight line, directly; very fast; DE HOQUIS in vain; with no strings attached (coll.), with no hidden complications; DE JILO (var. of) de hilo; DE MALAS: at least: "De malas ya mero pagamos por la casa" 'At least we've almost paid for the house'; DE OQUIS (orthog. var. of) de hoquis; DE PASADA on the way to; DE PASO on the way to; DE PATITAS feet first (i.e., to go out feet first, be thrown out of a place feet first in a prone position); DE POR SÍ QUE as things now stand; as it is: "No hables de él; de por sí que no quiere venir a la fiesta"; DE PRIMERO at first, in the beginning; DE PUERTA nice, swell, good, excellent (etc.); DE RANCHO from the sticks, countrified, hickish, farm-fresh (fig.): "Mi primo es bien de rancho" 'My cousin is straight from the farm' (fig.); DE SEGUNDO second-hand; DE SEGURO for sure, a certainty, a sure thing; DE TODO VUELO beautiful, enticing, shapely, sexy, (etc.) (said of women); DE UN SOPETÓN in one gulp; DE VOLADA (see DE A VOLADA); DE VUELTA again; after returning; DEL (contraction): DEL OTRO LADO

(coll.) from Mexico; DEL TIRO totally, completely
DEÁN (Ang.) m. dean (of a college)
DEBELIDAD (var. of) debilidad
DEBELITAR (var. of) debilitar
DECEDIR (var. of) decidir
DECIDO (rus.) (var. of) dicho (ppart. of decir)
DECINUEVE (var. of) diecinueve
DECIOCHO (var. of) dieciocho
DECIR: A (inf) SE HA DICHO Let's (inf.) : "A comer se ha dicho" 'Let's eat'; DECIR BIEN to predict accurately: "Te dije que iba a venir.--Dijiste bien"; DECIR MAL to err in what one has said, misspeak oneself: "Ya se fue ... No no, digo mal, todavía está aquí" 'He went off already ... No, I'm wrong, he's still here'; DECIR PA' TRAS (Ang.) to talk back to, respond aggresively: "No te dejes; dile pa' tras" 'Don't just stand there and take it, talk back to him'; DECIR UN ANUNCIO to announce; NO DECIR NI MI ALMA to say nary a word, keep absolute silence (esp. after a scolding); ¿NO TE DIGO? (also ¿NO LE(S) DIGO?) interj. Well I'll be!, Son of a pup! (etc.); QUE SE DIGA so to speak, to speak of: "Él no tiene muy buena voz, que se diga"; USTED DIRÁ It's up to you; you tell me
DECISÉIS (var. of) dieciséis
DECISIETE (var. of) diecisiete
DECORA (Hispanization of) (North and South) Dakota
DEDAL (coll.) m. finger
DEDO: APUNTAR EL DEDO to tell on someone, tattle on someone; DEDO CHIQUITO little finger (fifth finger on the hand); DEDO DE LOS ANILLOS ring finger (fourth finger); METER DEDO (slang, vulg.) to simulate copulation, insert the finger into a woman's vagina to simulate coition; PONER EL DEDO (id. to APUNTAR EL DEDO)
DEFENSA: DEFENSA DEL CARRO bumper (automobile)
DEFENSIA (var. of) defensa
DEFÍCIL (var. of) difícil
DEFOULT (Eng.) m. default (in a sports competition)
DEFUNTO (var. of) difunto
DEGUAL (var. of) desigual
DEIT (Eng.) m. date, social appointment
DEJADO -DA negligent in dress and

personal hygiene, slovenly; lazy; meek
DEJAR: DEJAR A LA DESIDIA to pro-
crastinate; DEJAR LA PUERTA
ABIERTA to leave good feelings
behind; DEJAR PLANTADO -DA to
fail to keep a date or an appointment; DEJARSE (CAER) to
yield to the seductive advances
of the opposite sex; DEJAR SA-
BER to inform, advise; NO DE-
JARSE to take nothing from nobody (slang), refuse to accept
insult, abuse, etc.; to fight
back, return insult for insult;
(NOMÁS) POR NO DEJAR (just) to
while the time away (to do
something just to be doing something); DEJAR POR LA PAZ to
quit, let something rest,
leave something be, leave well
enough alone; vr. (slang, vulg.)
to put out, give freely of one's
sexual favors: "¿Te dejas?"
'Do you 'do' it?' 'Do you put
out?'
DEJÓN -NA person who lets others
bully or manipulate him/her
DELANTAR (var. of) delantal m.
DELGADO -DA thin (ref. to persons
only; flaco -ca is applied
by many to both animals and
persons, though some insist
that flaco designates animal
thinness only)
DELINCUENTE: DELINCUENTE JUVENIL
mf. (Ang.) juvenile delinquent
DEMO(N)STRACIÓN (Ang.) f. demonstration (ref. to political
demonstration) (Std. manifesta-
ción)
DEMO(N)STRAR (Ang.) vn. to demon-
strate (for a political cause,
etc.)
DEN (Eng.) m. secluded room for
studying or relaxing, den
DENDE (var. of) desde
DENGUE m. gesture (body or facial)
DENTRAR (var. of) entrar
DENUNCIANTE m. cruel and ruthless
policeman
DEO (var. of) dedo
DEODORANTE (Eng.) m. (var. of)
desodorante
DEPACHAR (var. of) despachar
DEPENDER: DEPENDER EN (Ang.) (var.
of) depender de
DEPONER va. to vomit
DEPRESIÓN (Ang.) f. economic de-
pression
DEPUÉS (var. of) después
DEPUTADO -DA (var. of) diputado -da
DERECHAZO hard blow with the right
fist (usually in a boxing match)

DERECHERO -RA straight shooter,
person whose aim is consistent-
ly accurate
DERECHITO adv. straight ahead (said
in giving route directions)
DERECHO: DECIR POR DERECHO to
speak frankly, get to the point
(coll.)
DERRAME: DERRAME DEL CEREBRO stroke,
cerebral hemorrhage
DERRITIR (var. of) derretir
DESABROCHADOR m. clasp, fastener,
clip
DESACOMEDIDO -DA non-accommodating,
disobliging
DESAFANAR vn. to get out of jail
DESAFISFECHO -CHA (Eng.) (var. of)
desatisfecho -cha (Eng.)
DESAHIJAR va. to prune (plants)
DESAHIJE m. act or affect of
pruning (plants)
DESAIGRAR (var. of) desairar
DESANIVELADO -DA (var. of) des-
nivelado -da
DESANIVELAR (var. of) desnivelar
DESAPARECIDO -DA (euph.) deceased,
dead
DESAPARTAR (var. of) apartar
DESARMADOR m. screwdriver
DESATINAR: HACER DESATINAR A AL-
GUIEN to make someone lose
his cool (slang), cause some-
one to become very angry and
quite disoriented
DESATISFECHO -CHA mean, base, dis-
picable (ref. to persons)
DESAYUNO light breakfast taken
during the early part of the
morning
DESBALAGADO -DA dispersed, spread
out; lost
DESBARATAR va. to change a larger
monetary unit unto smaller ones
DESBORRADOR m. eraser
DESBORRAR va. to erase; to expunge
DESCADECIMIENTO (var. of) des-
caecimiento 'weakness, lack of
energy'
DESCARAPELAR (var. of) escarapelar
DESCARGADOR -RA freeloader (coll.),
sponger, parasite
DESCARRILADO -DA crazy, screwy
(coll.), off one's rocker (fig.)
DESCÍPULO (var. of) discípulo
DESCOGER (var. of) escoger
DESCOLGAR vn. to leave unannounced,
take French leave (coll.)
DESCOLORIDO -DA (pej.) Anglo-Saxon
DESCOMPASAR vr. to overstep the
bounds of reasonable behavior
or decorum
DESCONCHI(N)FLADO -DA in a state of
disrepair, in poor working order

DESCONCHINFLAR va. to put out of order, render unusable; vr. to
break down, become inoperative
DESCONTAR (slang) vr. to beat it
(slang), go away, leave; vr. to
avenge oneself; to settle a financial debt
DESCONTROLADO -DA out of control,
uncontrolled
DESCONTROLAR vr. to lose control
of oneself
DESCOSER vr. (fig.) to shout it
from the rooftops (coll.), open
up and tell everything
DESCUACHARRANGADO -DA (slang) broken,
shattered; in a bad state of
disrepair
DESCUACHARRANGAR (slang) va. to put
out of order, render inoperable;
vr. to break down, become inoperative
DESCUALIFICAR (Eng.) va. to dis-
qualify
DESCHARCHAR (Eng.) va. to discharge
(from the armed forces); (hum.)
to break off an amorous relation-
ship, give the gate to one's
sweetheart (slang)
DESCHARCHE or DESCHARCHI (Eng.) m.
discharge from the armed forces
(ref. to the act of discharge
or the document certifying same);
(hum.) dismissal given to the
partner in an amorous relation-
ship, walking papers (slang),
the old heave-ho (slang)
DESDE: adv. DESDE CUANDO for a
long time now: "Eso ya lo sé
desde cuando" 'I've known
that for a long time now'
DESEMBARAÑADOR m. comb
DESEMBARAÑAR va. to comb hair
DESENRAICE m. act and effect of
uprooting (i.e., plants, shrubs,
etc.)
DESENRAIZADO -DA bad off (coll.),
hopeless, incorrigible; LOCO
DESENRAIZADO crazy old fool
DESENRAIZAR va. to uproot (plants)
DESENROLLAR: DESENROLLAR LA CALCETA
(slang) to dance
DESEPAQUETAR (var. of) desempaquetar
DESFENDER (var. of) defender
DESFLECHADO -DA disoriented
DESFROZAR (Eng.) va. to defrost
DESGANCHAR (var. of) desenganchar
DESGARRADO -DA ragged, in rags
DESGARRANCHADO -DA raggedy, torn,
worn out (ref. to clothes and
also to person wearing such
clothes)
DESGARRANCHAR vr. to tear one's
clothes to shreds

DESGARRAR (var. of) esgarrar 'to
cough up phlegm'
DESGARREATE or DESGARRIATE m. heavy
destruction of property; up-
heaval
DESGASNATAR vr. to yell, shout; to
talk too freely
DESGOTADO -DA (var. of) escotado -da
'low (of neckline, i.e., dress
which barely reaches above
wearer's breast)'
DESGRACIADO -DA (pej.) base, vile,
mean, son-of-a-bitch
DESGRACIAR va. to ruin, injure badly
DESGRANAR va. to tear apart; vr.
(hum.) DESGRANARSE LA MAZORCA
to fall down (said of persons)
DESGUSTAR (var. of) disgustar
DESHERMANABLE unbrotherly, unsis-
terly (said of person who mis-
treats his/her siblings)
DESIAR (var. of) desear
DESIDIOSO -SA procrastinating;
negligent
DESIMULAR (var. of) disimular
DESINFESTANTE (var. of) desinfec-
tante
DESINFESTAR (Ang.) va. to disinfect
DESMADRAR va. to beat up (in a
fight); to destroy or deface
maliciously; vr. to hurt oneself
DESMANCHAR va. to remove spots
DESMECHAR va. & vr. to pull at one
another's hair in a fight
DESNARIZADO -DA (var. of) desnari-
gado -da
DESOBLIGADO -DA irresponsible
DESOCUPAR va. to dismiss from a
job, fire
DESPACHADOR -RA mf. store clerk
DESPAGAR va. to cut weeds
DESPARRAMAR va. to broadcast news
or gossip far and wide
DESPENSA medicine cabinet
DESPERCUDIDO -DA light-complexioned,
light-skinned; pale
DESPERJUICIO (var. of) perjuicio
DESPIDIR (var. of) despedir
DESPILFARRERO (var. of) despilfarro
DESPLUMAR va. to defeat (in a con-
test)
DESPUÉS: DESPUÉS DE: (Ang.) in
honor of, after: "Lo nombraron
después de Benito Juárez"
'They named him after Benito
Juárez'; DESPUÉS DE ATOLE (said
of solutions or assistance ap-
pearing too late to do any
good)
DESPUESITO adv. right after, immediately after: "Se fue des-
puesito de ti" 'He left just

after you did'
DESPUESTO -TA (var. of) dispuesto
DESPULMONAR vr. to work hard (of-
　　ten to excess)
DESTAPADO -DA hatless, without a
　　head covering
DESTAPADOR m. plunger (used to
　　clean out clogged drains, etc.)
DESTAPAR vr. to obtain relief from
　　constipation; vr. to remove one's
　　headgear, uncover one's. head
DESTENDER (var. of) extender; DES-
　　TENDER LA CAMA to make the bed
DESTETE m. weaning
DESTORNUDAR (var. of) estornudar
DESTORNUDO (var. of) estornudo
DESTRAÍDO -DA or DESTRAIDO -DA (vars.
　　of) distraído -da
DESTRIBUIDOR (var. of) distribuidor
　　m.
DESTRUIGO, DESTRUIGUES, etc. (vars.
　　of) destruyo, destruyes, etc.
　　(pres. ind. forms of destruir)
DETECTA (Eng?) m. detective
DETECTIVA mf. (var. of) detective
DETENIDO -DA freeloader (coll.),
　　stingy person
DETIRAR (var. of) retirar
DETRATO (var. of) retrato
DETUR m. (Eng.) detour
DEVALGAR (var. of) divulgar
DEVERAS (see DE DEVERAS)
DEVERTIR (var. of) divertir
DEVINO (var. of) divino
DEVISAR (var. of) divisar
DEVOLVER: DEVOLVER PA' TRAS (Ang.)
　　va. to return, take back;
　　vr. (var. of volverse 'to
　　turn back, return')
DEVORCIO (var. of) divorcio
DÍA m. (EL) DÍA DE FINADOS All
　　Souls' Day (Nov. 2nd); (EL)
　　DÍA DE LA CONEJA Easter,
　　Easter Sunday; (EL)DÍA DE
　　VALENTÍN (St.) Valentine's Day
DI AY (var. of) de ahí: "Di ay se
　　jueron a casa" 'From there they
　　went on home' or 'And then
　　they went on home'
DIÁLAGO (var. of) diálogo
DIAME (Eng.) m. dime, ten-cent
　　piece (cf. DAIME, DIME et al.)
DIANTRE mf. devil; DIANTRE DE:
　　"¡Diantre de huerquito éste!"
　　'You damnable mischievous little
　　brat, you!
¡DIANTRES! interj. (var. of)¡¡dian-
　　tre!
DIAVOLADA (see DE A VOLADA)
DIBILIDAD (var. of) debilidad f.
DIBILITAR (var. of) debilitar
DICEMOS or DICIMOS (var. of) decimos
　　(1st pers pl. pres. ind. of
　　decir)

DICER or DICIR (vars. of) decir
　　(cf. DIJIR)
DICINUEVE (var. of) diecinueve
DICIOCHO (var. of) dieciocho
DICIPELA (var. of) ericipela erysi-
　　pelas (type of contagious skin
　　disease)
DICISIETE (var. of) diecisiete
DICHE (Eng.) m. irrigation canal;
　　any type of ditch
DIEGO (DE RIVERA) (slang) m. dime,
　　ten-cent piece
DIENTE: DIENTE PICADO tooth with
　　a cavity or tooth decay; PELAR
　　EL DIENTE to smile; to show
　　one's teeth (often in anger)
DIENTISTA (var. of) dentista
DIENTÓN -TONA (var. of) dentudo -da
DIFORME (var. of) deforme
DIGNATARIO -A (var. of) dignitario -a
DIJÍA, DIJÍAS, etc. (vars. of) decía,
　　decías, etc. (imperfect forms
　　of decir)
DIJIERA, DIJIERAS, etc. (vars. of)
　　dijera, dijeras, etc. (past
　　subj. of decir)
DIJIERON (var. of) dijeron (3rd
　　pers. pl. pret of decir)
DIJIR (var. of) decir
DIJUNTO -TA (vars. of) difunto -ta
DILE (Hispanization of) Dilley,
　　Texas
DILEAR or DILIAR (Eng.) vn. to deal
　　or traffic in narcotic drugs
DILICADO -DA (vars. of) delicado -
　　da
DIMA or DIMO (Eng.) (slang) dime,
　　ten-cent piece (cf. DAIME,
　　DIAME et al.)
DINERO-ORO United States currency
　　(cf. DINERO-PLATA)
DINERO-PLATA Mexican currency
DINO -NA (var. of) digno -na
DINTISTA (var. of) dentista mf.
DIONDE (var. of) donde
DIOQUIS (see OQUIS, also DE HOQUIS)
DIOS: ¡DIOS NOS (ME) FAVOREZCA!
　　DIOS NO LO QUIERA Heaven for-
　　bid!; EN EL NOMBRE SEA DE DIOS
　　Amen, So be it; ¡NI LO MANDE
　　DIOS! Heaven forbid!, Saints
　　preserve us!; SEA POR DIOS
　　Amen, So be it; (slang) That's
　　the way the cookie crumbles
　　(slang); SI DIOS ES SERVIDO
　　God willing: "Buenas noches,
　　hasta mañana.--Si Dios es ser-
　　vido"; SI DIOS ES SERVIDO
　　God willing; SABER LO QUE ES
　　AMAR A DIOS EN TIERRA AJENA
　　to know firsthand what trouble
　　really is
DIPA (Eng.) dipper, ladle
DIPARTAMENTO (var. of) departamento

DIPO (Eng.) depot, train station

DIPTONGUIZAR (var. of) diptongar

DIPUTADO deputy policeman

DIRECCIÓN f. steering wheel (automobile)

DIRRETIR or DIRRITIR (vars. of) derretir

DISCHARCHAR (var. of) descharchar (Eng.)

DISCO: CAMBIAR EL DISCO to stop harping on the same theme, change the topic of conversation; DISCO RAYADO (fig.) (said of a person who keeps harping on the same theme; the "harped-upon" conversational theme itself)

DISCONFIADO -DA (vars. of) desconfiado - da

DISCUTO (var. of) discurso m. 'discourse'

DISGUSTADO -DA hard to please

DISINTERESADO -DA (vars. of) desinteresado -da

DISISÉIS (var. of) dieciséis

DISMINUIGO (var. of) disminuyo (1st pers. pres. ind. sg. of disminuir)

DISPACIO (var. of) despacio

DISPEDIR (var. of) despedir

DISPERTAR (var. of) despertar

DISPIERTO, DISPIERTAS, etc. (vars. of) despierto, despiertas, etc. (pres. ind. --conjugation of despertar)

DISPUÉS (var. of) después

DISTRAIDO -DA (var. of) distraído - da

DISTRICTO (var. of) distrito

DISTRITAL adj. mf. of or pertaining to a district

DISTRUIGO, DISTRUIGUES, etc. (vars. of) destruyo, destruyes, etc. (pres. ind. conjugation of destruir) (cf. destruigo et al.)

DISVARIAR (var. of) desvariar

DITADO (var. of) dictado

DITECTO (Eng?) detective

DITUR (Eng.) m. detour

DIVIRSIÓN (var. of) diversión f.

DIVURCEAR or DIVURCIAR (vars. of) divorciar

DIVURCIO (var. of) divorcio

DIZQUE (var. of) dice que

DOBLEPLEY (Eng.) m. double play (in baseball)

DOCE (see DAR LAS DOCE)

DOCTOR: VISITA DE DOCTOR very brief visit (expression usually in the form of a complaint voiced by a host when visitors depart after a stay the host feels was too brief; the complaint is common among members of the same family who feel they should "see" each other more frequently)

DOCHE (Eng.) m. Dodge (brand of automobile)

DOLER: DOLER LA CINTURA to have a backache

DÓLOR (var. of) dólar m. 'dollar'

DOLOR: DOLOR DE BAZO spleen pain, "stitch in the side"; DOLOR DE CINTURA backache (esp. in the lower back); HACÉRSELE DOLOR A ALGUIEN HACER ALGO for it to hurt (fig.) someone to do something (ref. to ungenerous attitude): "Se te hizo dolor darme un pedacito de manzana" 'It hurt you to give me a little piece of the apple'

DOMÁS (var. of) nomás adv.

DOMECILIO (var. of) domicilio

DOMINGUERO suit of clothes reserved for formal occasions, "Sunday best" (coll.); DOMINGUERO -RA mf. & adj. (said of person who enjoys going out to have a good time or to visit on Sundays)

DOMPE (Eng.) m. garbage dump; dump truck; (fig.) house or room in a filthy condition

DOMPEAR or DOMPIAR (Eng.) va. to dump, dispose of; to vomit; to dump, give someone the slip (fig.), get rid of someone

DON: AY VA CON DON (hum. and also vulg.) (said of a passing woman; double entendre: 'There she goes with Don' and also 'There she goes with a condom')

DONA (Eng.) doughnut

DOÑAJUANITA (slang) marihuana

DORMELÓN -LONA (var. of) dormilón - lona

DORMIERA, DORMIERAS, etc. (past subj. forms of dormir) (vars. of) durmiera, durmieras, etc.

DORMIÓ, DORMIERON, DORMIENDO (vars. of) durmió, durmieron, durmiendo (resp. 3rd pers. sg. pret. 3rd pers. pl pret., and ger. of dormir)

DORMIR: DORMIR COMO UN TRONCO to sleep like a log (fig.), sleep very soundly; DORMIR LA BORRACHERA to sleep off an alcoholic binge; DORMIR LA CRUDA to sleep off a hangover; DORMÍRSELE A ALGUIEN EL GALLO to be caught napping, caught off guard (e.g. in a business deal or other competitive effort); to fail to take advantage of a favorable situation; to fail in the sex act (said of men who lose their

erection); PONER A DORMIR to
knock out in a fist fight or
boxing match
DORMITORIO (Ang.) dormitory (student residence)
DORREALES or DORRIALES (vars. of)
dos reales
DOS: EN UN DOS POR TRES in the
twinkling of an eye (coll.),
with extreme rapidity; DOS
REALES or DOS RIALES quarter,
twenty-five cent piece
DOSTEAR or DOSTIAR (Eng.) va. to
dust, remove dust (as in clean-
ing a room)
DOTA (Eng?) m. doctor, physician
DOTOR (var. of) doctor m.
DRAIVEAR or DRAIVIAR (Eng.) va. to
drive (an automobile)
DRENAJE m. drain, catheter
DRIBLEAR or DRIBLIAR (Eng.) va. to
dribble (a ball, in basketball)
DRINC or DRINQUE (Eng.) m. drink
(esp. an alcoholic drink)
DROGA (slang) debt
DROMA (Eng.) m. traveling sales-
man (<drummer [dated slang ex-
pression for traveling salesman])
DROPEAR or DROPIAR (Eng.) va. to
drop, let fall
DUÉRMAMOS (var. of) durmamos (1st
pers. pl. subjunc. of dormir)
DULCE: SER DE DULCE (slang, pej.)
to be a pansy (slang, pej.), be
a homosexual; DULCE CON SAL m.
hog skin crackling; DULCE DE
PALITO m. (any sweet object
embedded on a stick, e.g., an
all-day sucker)
DUQUE m. tobacco (loan metonymy,<
Duke brand tobacco?)
DURMIR (var. of) dormir
DURO -RA (slang) stiff (slang),dead

E

EA (var. of) ella
ECHADA f. boast; bluff, fib; brooding hen; SER MÁS LAS ECHADAS QUE
LAS CULECAS (lit., for there
to be more hens on the nest than
the number that are actually
laying eggs; said of persons
who claim to have accomplished
much but who actually have not)
ECHADOR -DORA mf. braggart; bluffer
ECHAR va. ECHAR A CUESTAS to
throw someone on his/her back;

ECHAR CARNES to curse; ECHAR
DE PATITAS A LA CALLE to fire,
dismiss (from a job) in short
order; to run off, tell to
leave (e.g., a home--usually
ref. to the manner in which one
common law partner tells the
other to depart); ECHAR UN A-
PLASTÓN / ECHAR UN TAPÓN to
put someone in his/her place,
put someone down (slang), tell
someone where to get off (slang),
reprimand; ECHAR A LA BOLSA /
ECHAR EN LA BOLSA to defeat;
ECHAR AL BOTE to bewitch; ECHAR
A PERDER to spoil, pamper (esp.
ref. to children); ECHAR DE LA
MADRE to curse at someone (the
taboo word madre is usually included in the cursing); ECHAR
EL GATO A RETOZAR to let out
a secret, let the cat out of
the bag (coll.); ECHAR EN
CARRILLA to give chase to,
chase away: "Juan le echaron
en carrilla porque estaba molestando mucho"; ECHAR HABLADAS
to insinuate; ECHAR LA SAL to
jinx, bring bad luck; ECHAR LA
TRANCA to latch (usually ref.
to a screen door); ECHAR (SU)
LONCHE to put someone in his/
her place, tell someone where
to get off (slang): "Pásale,
papá va a echarte tu lonche"
'Come on, daddy's going to give
you what you've got coming'
(said to a child who has mis-
behaved); ECHAR MADRES to curse,
cuss out (cf. ECHAR DE LA MA-
DRE); ECHARLE LA LEY A ALGUIEN
to get the law after someone;
to bring a lawsuit against
someone; ECHAR MENOS (var. of)
echar de menos; ECHAR MOSCA
to tease; ECHAR PAPAS to tell
lies, lie; ECHAR UN PEDO (vulg.)
to expel wind; ECHAR PIQUETE
to provoke, needle (coll.);
ECHAR POR LA CABEZA to betray,
tell the secrets of someone
else: "Primitivo se enojó con
Inocencio porque le echó por la
cabeza"; ECHAR TRANCA (A LA
PUERTA) to lock (a door with
a key), latch (a screen door);
vn. ECHAR(SELAS) DE LADO to
brag, boast; ECHAR MAROMAS to
do somersaults; ECHAR PULGAS
to cause trouble; ECHAR(SE)
UNA POLCA to dance a polka
(or another other dance); ECHAR
UN PALITO (slang) (for a male
to have sexual intercourse);

vr. to lie down (said only of
animals or, in anger or sarcastically, of humans); ECHARLO AL
JUEGO (var. of) echarlo a juego
to tell as a joke, tell in fun;
ECHARSE AL PLATO / ECHÁRSELO
to get the best of someone, beat
someone out; to seduce; to kill;
ECHARSE DE VER to be evident,
show: "Es muy mezquino. --Se
echa de ver." 'He's very stingy.
--It shows.' ECHARSE EL TROMPO
EN LA UÑA (usually said as a
command:) "¡Échate el trompo
en la uña!" 'Put that in your
pipe and smoke it!' (said as
an admonishment or by way of
revenge); ECHARSE ENCIMA to
jump on someone; ECHARSE TRACA-
LA(S) to fall into debt;
ECHARSE UN PEDO to expel wind;
ECHARSE UN PEDO DE AQUELLOS
(slang, vulg.) to let out a real
stinker (ref. to a very bad-
smelling expulsion of bodily
wind)
EDEFICIO (var. of) edificio
EDITOR (Ang.) m. newspaper editor
(Std. redactor)
EDUCACIÓN (Ang.) f. education (in
all senses of the word in Eng.,
not solely 'upbringing' as per
Std.)
EDUCACIONAL (Ang.) adj. educational,
that which serves to enhance the
learning process
¡EIT! or ¡ÉITALE! (slang, used to
call a person's attention:)
Hey you!
¡ÉJELE! interj. (used to poke fun
at someone:) "¡Éjele, perdieron
el juego!"
EJIR (rus.) (var. of) decir
EJOTE msg. string beans, green
beans
ELANTE (var. of) delante
ELÁSTICO rubber band
ELBA (slang) m. barber (< el·
ba ⌈rbero⌋)
ELECTAR (Eng.) va. to elect, elect
to office
ELECTRECIDAD (var. of) electrici-
dad f.
ELÉCTRICO -CA (slang) drunk
ELIGIR (var. of) elegir
ELOISA (var. of) Eloísa
ELOTE: CIERTOS ELOTES certain
(well-known) persons, certain
so-and-sos (would-be oblique
ref. to persons whom one coyly
does not wish to name)
EMBACHICHAR va. to con, dupe,
swindle
EMBARADO -DA bloated (ref. to stom-

ach bloated from indigestion)
EMBARAZADO -DA (Ang.) embarrassed
EMBARRADA (var. of) embarradura
EMBARAÑADO -DA (var. of) enmaraña-
do -da
EMBARRAR. va. to run over (e.g. a
person with a vehicle); to
spread (e.g. butter on a slice
of bread)
EMBIJAR va. to paint; to smear,
grease
EMBOLAR va. to confuse, mix up; vr.
to get confused or mixed up
EMBOLIO (var. of) embolia 'stroke'
EMBONO (var. of) abono
EMBORUCAR va. to confuse, mix up;
vr. to get confused or mixed up
EMBORRACHAR va. to make dizzy; vr.
to become dizzy
EMBUSTEROSO -SA liar
EMITERIO (var. of) Emeterio
EMPACADOR -DORA mf. packer (person
who works in a packing house)
EMPACAR (slang) va. to eat; vr. to
stuff oneself (coll.), eat to
satiation
EMPACHADO -DA fed up (fig.), extremely annoyed (with)
EMPACHAR va. to irritate, annoy
EMPALMADO -DA bundled up, wearing
lots of clothes
EMPALMAR va. to pile up items
one top of the other; vr. to
bundle up, wear plenty of clothing (as for protection against
the cold)
EMPALME: TRAER EMPALME to be heavily bundled up, be wearing many
clothes
EMPANADA semi-circular-shaped jelly
roll or doughnut
EMPANAL m. type of small bread roll
EMPANTURRAR va. to stuff (a person)
with food; vr. to stuff oneself
with food, eat to excess
EMPANZADO -DA stuffed, full (said
of stomachs replete with food)
EMPANZAR va. to stuff (a person)
with food; vr. to stuff oneself
with food, eat gluttonously
EMPAQUE (slang) m. chow (slang),
food, meal, dinner; tooth packing (temporary filling for cavity)
EMPAREJAR vr. to tie the score in
a game; to avenge
EMPEDAR vr. to get drunk (cf. PEDO)
EMPELOTADO -DA passionately in love
EMPELOTAR vr. to be passionately in
love
EMPINADO -DA bent over
EMPINAR va. to bend (usually ref.
to persons); vr. to bend over
EMPISTOLADO -DA armed with a gun

EMPLEADO -DA or EMPLIADO -DA police
    officer; (esp.) immigration
    officer
EMPLUMAR vn. to become of age
EN: EN CAS DE (var. of) en casa de;
    EN EL COLORADO (Ang.) in the red
    (slang), in debt; (DE) EN SEGUIDA
    DE alongside, next door: "Vive
    en la casa de en seguida de no-
    sotros"; EN TANTO QUE NADA in
    a jiffy, very quickly; EN UN
    DOS POR CUATRO/EN UN TRES POR
    CUATRO (vars. of) en un dos
    por tres in a jiffy, in a wink;
    EN VECES (var. of Std. a veces
    'at times'); EN VISITAS (var.
    of Std. de visita 'on a visit')
ENAMORAR: ENAMORARSE CON (Ang., var.
    of Std. enamorarse de)
ENCÁ or ENCA prep. (var. of) en casa
    de
ENCAJAR va. to blame; vr. to climb
    on someone's back; to get on top
    of one's partner to have sexual
    intercourse
ENCALMADO -DA dying of thirst, ex-
    tremely thirsty
ENCAMORRADO -DA ill-tempered
ENCANDILADO -DA tired
ENCANDILAR va. to tire; to lure,
    tempt; vr. to get tired, tire
    out
ENCANICADO -DA (slang) passionately
    in love
ENCANICAR vr. to fall passionately
    in love
ENCANTONEADO -DA or ENCANTONIADO -DA
    (slang) married, hitched (slang)
ENCANTONEAR or ENCANTONIAR (slang)
    vr. to get married, get hitched
    (slang)
ENCAPUCHADO -DA (slang) well-dressed
ENCARAMADO -DA on top of
ENCARAMAR vr. to mount a horse; to
    "mount" someone to have sexual
    intercourse
ENCARTADO -DA halfbreed, of mixed
    racial background
ENCEBAR vr. to get grease on one's
    hands
ENCENDIDO m. match (used for ignit-
    ing
ENCIMAR vr. to be where one is not
    wanted; to be or become a pest
ENCIMÓN -MONA (vars. of) encimoso -
    sa: ANDAR ENCIMÓN or SER ENCI-
    MÓN to be a pest (fig.), be
    bothersome
ENCIMOSO -SA pest, annoying person
ENCONTONEAR or ENCONTONIAR (vars.
    of) encantonear, encantoniar
ENCORRALAR va. to corner
ENCUERADO -DA naked
ENCUERAR va. to strip, take the

clothes off of; vr. to undress
ENCUETAR va. to inebriate; vr. to
    get drunk
ENCHALECAR (slang) va. to shoplift
ENCHAQUETAR va. to help (someone)
    put on a jacket; vr. to put on
    one's jacket
ENCHARCADO -DA adj. stuck in the
    mud; m. mistake
ENCHARCAR vr. to make a mistake;
    to get stuck in the mud
ENCHILADA m. burned mouth or tongue
    (resulting from the ingestion
    of any type of food that con-
    tains hot chile)
ENCHILADO -DA infuriated, outraged
ENCHILAR va. to burn someone's
    tongue with hot food; vr. to
    burn oneself (in the mouth)
    with hot food (esp. food con-
    taining hot chile)
ENCHINADO -DA in curls
ENCHINADOR m. hair curler
ENCHINAR va. & vr. to curl hair;
    vr. ENCHINÁRSELE EL CUERPO A
    ALGUIEN to get goosepimples
    (goosebumps)
ENCHINCHADO -DA infested with chinch
    bugs
ENCHINCHAR va. to fill with bed-
    bugs; vr. to become infested
    with bedbugs (usually said of
    mattresses)
ENCHUECAR va. to twist; vr. to
    become twisted
ENDENANTES adv. a little while ago
ENDEREZAR va. to straighten out
    (fig.), reform, rehabilitate;
    vr. to straighten oneself out,
    reform oneself
ENDEVERAS (var. of) de veras
ENDOMINGAR vr. to dress up in style,
    dress up in one's "Sunday best"
ENDROGAR va. to get someone into
    debt; vr. to get into debt
ENFAJAR va. to put a belt or sash
    on someone; vr. to put on one's
    belt or sash
ENFATIZAR va. to emphasize
ENFERMA adj. f. (euph.) menstruat-
    ing, having one's period
ENFERMAR va. to hex, make sick
    through witchcraft; vr. to
    begin labor pains; to be in
    labor
ENFERMEDAD: ENFERMEDAD DE ANDANCIA
    disease that is "going around,"
    mild epidemic (cf. ENFERMEDAD
    QUE ANDA): ENFERMEDAD DEL CA-
    RACTER character disorder, di-
    sease of social pathology
    (often considered innate);
    ENFERMEDAD ENDAÑADA disease
    resulting from an act of witch-

craft; ENFERMEDAD QUE ANDA disease that is "going around,"
mild epidemic; ENFERMEDAD SECRE-
TA venereal disease

ENFLACAR va. to cause someone to
become thin: "Lo enflacó de tan-
tas penas"; vr. to become thin,
lose weight; to diet (so as to
lose weight)

ENFRIFOLAR or ENFRIJOLAR vr. to eat
an excessive amount of beans,
stuff oneself with beans (usually pinto beans)

ENGANCHAR va. to hook or trick into
marriage; vr. (hum.) to become
engaged to be married; to get
married, get "hooked" (slang)

ENGANCHE m. engagement, promise to
marry; downpayment; contract to
obtain bracero laborers

ENGANCHISTA m. (sometimes pej.) con-
tractor of bracero labor

ENGARRUÑAR vr. to get into a fight;
to double up, shrink (esp. when
extremely angry)

ENGARTUSAR (var. of) engatusar

ENGRASADA shoe-shine; DAR UNA ENGRA-
SADA to apply shoe paste to
shoes (as to shine them)

ENGRASAR va. to apply shoe paste to
shoes (so as to shine them)

ENGRASE m. applications of shoe paste
to shoes for purposes of shining

ENGREÍR vr. to become attached to,
fond of

ENGRIDO -DA (var. of) engreído -da

ENGRIFAR va. to administer marihuana;
to someone; vr. to take marihuana;
to feel the effects of marihuana

ENGRINGOLAR va. to cause someone to
become gringo-like, to gringoize;
vr. to become like a gringo

ENGUAYNAR (Eng.) va. to get someone
drunk on wine; vr. to get drunk
on wine

ENGÜERAR vr. to become addled (ref.
to people); to become rotten
(ref. to eggs)

ENGUSANAR vr. to become wormy (ref.
to animals and persons who fall
prey to worms in their intestines)

ENHUEVAR vr. to become stubborn

ENJAULADO -DA jailed, in jail

ENJAULE (slang) m. jail

ENJETADO -DA (said of person who is
pouting; also said of person making a facial expression denoting
anger

ENLISTAR (Eng.) vr. to enlist in the
armed forces

ENMAIZADO -DA: LOCO -CA ENMAIZADO
-DA screwball (coll.), crazy
old fool

ENMANTECAR va. to dirty with grease
or lard; vr. to become dirty
with grease or lard

ENMAÑADO -DA deceptive, fraudulent,
tricky (ref. to persons)

ENMARIHUANAR va. to administer
marihuana to, cause to take
marihuana; vr. to take marihuana

ENMUGRAR (var. of) enmugrecer

ENMUGRENTAR to soil, dirty

ENMULAR vr. to become obstinate,
stubborn

ENRAIZADO -DA: LOCO -CA ENRAIZADO
-DA screwball (coll.), crazy
old fool (cf. ENMAIZADO)

ENREDADO -DA (hum.) engaged to be
married

ENRODAR vr. to become tangled,
rolled up

ENROLLAR vr. to become tangled

ENSARTAR (vulg.) va. & vr. to insert one's penis into a vagina

ENSEÑAR: ENSEÑAR LA OREJA to show
one's bad side, reveal one's
defects; to reveal one's true
colors; ENSEÑAR UNA PELICULA
(Ang?) to show a movie

ENTABICAR (slang) va. to jail,
lock up in jail

ENTABLAZÓN f. obstruction, severe
constipation

ENTACUACHADO -DA (var. of) entacuchado -da

ENTACUCHADO -DA (slang) well-dressed,
dressed up (coll.)

ENTELIGIR (var. of) inteligir

ENTENDER (see HACER ENTENDER)

ENTERRAR va. to stick with a pointed instrument; vr. to stick a
pointed object into oneself
(usually through accident):
"Me enterré una astilla en el
pie"

ENTONADO -DA: ANDAR ENTONADO -DA
to be drunk

ENTONCE (var. of) entonces

ENTOSEQUIDO -DA (Eng.) intoxicated,
drunk

ENTRACALADO -DA in debt

ENTRACALAR va. to put into debt; vr.
to become indebted, accumulate
debts

ENTRADA inning (in baseball); permission officially given by the
father of a girl to a boy desir-
ous of visiting her at home;
VENIR DE ENTRADA Y SALIDA to
visit or call upon someone briefly

ENTRADERA: ENTRADERA Y SALIDERA (ref.
to person) gadabout

ENTRADITO -TA slightly drunk

ENTRADO -DA slighty drunk

ENTRADOR -DORA mf. dare-devil, taker
of risks

¡ÉNTRALE!   interj. (used to encourage or stimulate) Go at it!,
Do it!: "Entrale, no le tengas miedo!"

ENTRAR va. to tackle, take on (e.g.
a job, a challenge, etc.)

ENTRE: ENTRE MÁS ... MÁS the more
... the more; ENTRE MENOS ...
MENOS the less/fewer ... the
less/fewer

ENTRESACAR va. to thin hair (as
done by barbers to customers
so requesting)

ENTRESEMANA fsg. weekdays

ENTRETENER va. to delay; vr. to be
delayed

ENTRIEGO, ENTRIEGAS, etc. (vars.
of) entrego, entregas, etc.
(pres. ind. of entregar)

ENTRINCAR: ENTRINCAR LOS DIENTES
to clench one's teeth

ENTRO (var. of) adentro adv.

ENTRÓN -TRONA mf. dare-devil,
taker of risks, dreadnought

ENTUMIDO -DA (var. of) entumecido -
da

ENTUMIR vr. to get cold feet (fig.),
shy away from something

ENVITADO -DA (var. of) invitado -da

ENVITAR (var. of) invitar

ENVOLTIJO (var. of) envoltorio
'bundle'

ENVOLVER (Eng.) va. to involve
(someone in something:) "Querían
envolverlo en ese problema"; vr.
to become involved in: "Siempre
se envuelve en mucho mugrero"

ENYERBADO -DA bewitched, hexed

ENYERBAR va. to bewitch, hex

ENVUELTOS mpl. enchiladas

ENZOQUETAR va. to muddy up, splat-
ter with mud; vr. to get
muddied up

¡EPA! or ¡EPALE! interj. Watch
that!, Hey!, Careful!, etc.

EPAZOTE m. wormseed (Chenopodium
embrosioides)(herbal tea used
to treat stomach ache or as
a vermicide)

EPISODIO motion picture presented
in serial form (e.g. in 15
parts, one each week)

ERJOSTES (Eng.)fsg. stewardess,
airline hostess (ant.)

ERO (rus.) (var. of) soy (1st
pers. sg. pres. indic. of ser)

ERUTAR (var. of) eructar

ÉSA ES DE AY or ÉSE ES DE AY (general expression of approval)
(slang) Right on! (slang),
That's right!

¡ÉSA(LE)! or ¡ÉSE(LE)! (slang)(interj. used to call someone's
attention) Hey you!

ESCALERA (hum.) tall person, daddy
long legs (coll.)

ESCAME m. fear, terror

ESCAMOSO -SA fearful, frightened

ESCANDALOSO -SA squeamish

ESCANSAR (var. of) descansar

ESCANTE m. short while, moment:
"Espérame un escante"

ESCARAPELAR va. to chip off; vr.
to get chipped off

ESCARBAR to dig, excavate deeply
(not merely 'to scratch' as
in Std.)

ESCARCHA cold weather, cold season

ESCOBÓN (slang, hum.) m. guitar

ESCOCH (Eng.) m. Scotch whiskey;
ESCOCH TEIP (Eng.) m. scotch
tape

ESCONDIDAS: JUGAR A LAS ESCONDIDAS
to play hide and seek (child's
game)

ESCOR (Eng.) m. score

ESCORCÉS (var. of) escocés

ESCRACHAR (Eng.) va. to scratch
(slang= to cancel, eliminate)

ESCREBIDO -DA (rus.) (var. of)
escrito -ta (ppart. of escribir)

ESCREBIR (var. of) escribir

ESCREPÓN (Eng.) m. shoe with thick
soles (scrape)

ESCRECHAR (Eng.) va. to scratch (cf.
ESCRACHAR)

ESCRIBIDO -DA (rus.) (var. of) escrito -ta (ppart. of escribir)

ESCRÍN or ESCRIN (Eng.) m. ice cream

ESCRÍN (Eng.) m. movie screen

ESCUADRA pistol (usually automatic);
gun (in general); (fig.) square
shooter, honest person; square
deal, honest treatment

ESCUELA (Ang.) classes, school day:
"No hay escuela hoy" (Std. no
hay clases hoy); ESCUELA ALTA
(Ang.) high school

ESCUETO -TA quiet, tranquil

ESCUINCLE mf. child

ESCULCÓN -CONA (pej.) snoop, person
who enjoys searching through
others' possessions without
permission

ESCUPE (slang) m. gun

ESCUPIDA (slang) (fig.) gun blast

ESCUPIDERA (slang) pistol, gun

ESCURA (Eng.) motor scooter;
child's (motorless) scooter

ESCURECER (var. of) o(b)scurecer

ESCÚRER (Eng.) m. scooter, motorcycle; child's (motorless)
scooter

ESCURO -RA adj. (var. of) oscuro-ra

ESGADO -DA sideways, crossways: "El
carro quedó esgado en medio de
la calle" 'The car was left in
a diagonal position in the mid-
dle of the street'

ESLECS (Eng.) mpl. slacks, pants

ESO: EN ESO at that moment, just
then: "En eso llegó María"
'Just then María arrived'

ESPALDA: ESPALDA MOJADA wet-back
(illegal immigrant from Mexico)

ESPALDAR m. headboard; back of a
chair

ESPATEAR or ESPATIAR (Eng.) va. to
spot, recognize

ESPAUDA or ESPAURA (Eng.) (< yeast
powder) baking powder

ESPELEAR or ESPELIAR (Eng.) va. to
spell (words)

ESPELETEAR or ESPELETIAR (Eng.)
(vars. of) espelear, espeliar

ESPERANZA: ¡QUE ESPERANZA(S)! interj. (used to express strong
doubt as to whether something
will take place) That'll be
the day!

ESPICHADITO -TA (Eng?< speech?)
quiet, repressed, not talkative

ESPICHE (Eng.) m. speech, discourse

ESPINECHE (Eng.) m. spinach

ESPINIENTO -TA or ESPINILLENTO -TA
pimpled, beset with facial
pimples

ESPIRINA (var. of) aspirina

ESPÍRITO (var. of) espíritu

ESPORTE (Eng.) m. sport

ESPRÍN (Eng.) m. spring (Std.
resorte); spring (Std. prima-
vera)

ESPUÉS (var. of) después

ESQUECHAR (Eng.) va. to sketch,
draw, design

ESQUECHE (Eng.) m. sketch, design

ESQUINADO -DA or ESQUINIADO -DA adj.
placed at an angle (usually ref.
to a piece of furniture)

ESQUINAR or ESQUINIAR va. to place
at an angle or in a corner of
a room

ESQUINEAR or ESQUINIAR (slang) vn.
to go along with (fig.), assent
to

ESQUIPEAR or ESQUIPIAR (Eng.) va.
to skip (i.e., to miss, e.g. a
class, a lesson, an appointment); va. & vn. to skip, jump,
hop

ESQUITE m. popcorn

ESTACA: POLLITO DE ESTACA person
approaching old age; adult or
person approaching adulthood

ESTACAR (Eng.) va. to stack, pile up

ESTACIÓN: ESTACIÓN DE GASOLINA (Ang?)
f. gas(oline) station

ESTADO: ESTADO DE LA ESTRELLA SOLI-
TARIA Lone Star State (i.e.,
Texas); ESTADO INTERESANTE
(euph.) pregnancy

ESTAFEATE or ESTAFIATE m. medicinal
herb used for stomach disorders

ESTAMPA (Ang.) stamp, postage stamp

ESTAQUITA mumbletypeg (children's
game played with a jack-knife)

ESTAR: ESTAR A MANOS to owe nothing to anyone, be even; to have
avenged oneself; ESTAR A TODA
MADRE (for something to be)
terrific, tremendous; ESTAR A
UNA Y UN PEDAZO to be penniless, stone broke (coll.);
ESTAR BUENO to suffice, be e-
nough:"¡ Ya está bueno!" 'That's
enough!'; ESTAR CALIENTE (Ang.)
to be hot (said of the weather;
Std. hacer calor); ESTAR COMO
LA FREGADA to be as _____ as
can be (e.g., 'to be as ugly as
sin', 'as mean as a junkyard
dog', etc.--ref. usually to any
negative quality known both to
speaker and listener) ESTAR COMO
LA JODIDA to be as _____ as can
be (usual ref. to a negative
characteristic of which both
speaker and listener are cognizant, e.g.:) "Ella está como
la jodida" 'She's as ugly as
sin'; ESTAR CON EL ESPOSO/ESTAR
CON LA ESPOSA (euph.) to be having sexual intercourse; ESTAR
CON FAMILIA to be pregnant;
ESTAR CURADO -DA DE SUSTO fear-
less (ref. to person who does
not frighten easily); ESTAR DE
AQUE(LL)A (slang) to be tremendous, terrific, great, etc.;
ESTAR DE LADO (coll.) to be
in a good mood; ESTAR DE LA
PATADA (slang) to stink, smell
highly; to be incorrigible; to
be very ugly, homely (usually
ref. to women); ESTAR DIOQUIS
(see DE HOQUIS); ESTAR EN CALLE
to be destitute, in extreme
poverty; ESTAR EN LA CHILLA to
be destitute, down and out,
desperate; ESTAR EN LA LÍNEA /
LINIA to be drunk; ESTAR EN
TODO (MENOS EN MISA) to mind
everyone's business but one's
own, attend to everyone's affairs but one's own; ESTAR
FEBRERO / ESTAR MARZO to be
crazy (also: ESTAR FEBRERO LOCO
Y MARZO OTRO POCO, id.) ESTAR
FRÍO (Ang.) to be cold (said
of the weather; Std. hacer frío)
ESTAR HASTA EL COPETE to be

fed up, to have stood as much
as possible; to be extremely
drunk; ESTAR HASTA LAS MANITAS
to be extremely drunk; ESTAR
LA PATRIA MUY POBRE/ESTAR LA
PATRIA MUY FREGADA to be in
a poor financial situation, be
at the end of one's rope (fig.):
"¿Vas a comprar el carro?--No
puedo, está muy fregada la patria"; ESTAR MADRE (slang)
(for something to be) terrific,
tremendous, super, great, etc.;
ESTAR MALO EL CUENTO (for things
to be in a bad state:) "¡Está
malo el cuento!" 'Things have
come to a pretty pass!' (coll.);
ESTAR PADRE (,BATO -TA) (slang)
(iron. expression used to indicate that one's feelings have
been hurt; the implication is
that revenge will be taken or
poetic justice will prevail);
ESTAR PAREJOS to be tied, end
up in a tie; ESTAR PONIÉNDO-
SELA A ALGUIEN to be having
sexual relations with someone;
ESTAR QUE HASTA/ESTAR QUE NOMÁS
to be very tense, fit to be
tied, on pins and needles (fig.),
at one's wits' end (etc.); to
be very ugly/beautiful/drunk
(etc.-- ref. to an extreme
manifestation of an obvious
quality known to both speaker
and listener); ESTAR QUE SE LO
LLEVA EL DIABLO / ESTAR QUE SE
LO LLEVA JUDÁS / ESTAR QUE SE
LO LLEVA EL TREN / ESTAR QUE
SE LO LLEVA LA CHINGADA to be
very tense, fit to be tied, on
pins and needles, at one's wits
end; ESTAR SALADO -DA to be
having a stroke of bad luck;
to be jinxed, unlucky; ESTAR
TAMAÑITO -TA to be edgy, be on
pins and needles (as in anticipation of something to happen
momentarily); ESTAR TIRADO -DA
to be abed, lying in bed (usual
ref. to sick or lazy person);
ESTAR TORCIDOS not to be on
friendly terms (see also TOR-
CERLE LA CARA A ALGUIEN); ESTAR
TRES PIEDRAS to be terrific,
tremendous, very beautiful,
etc.
ESTARA or ESTÁRER (Eng.) m. starter
(on an automobile)
ESTAREAR or ESTARIAR (Eng.) va. to
start (an automobile)
ESTE (used as a stalling device,
i.e., inserted when the speaker cannot think of what to say

next)
ESTECHE HUEGUEN (Eng.) m. station
wagon (type of car)
ESTILACHO (slang) style, fashion
ESTILLA (var. of) astilla
ESTIRADA act or result of growing
taller (usually said with ref.
to teenagers): "No reconocí a
tu hijo; se dio una estirada
tremenda" 'I didn't recognize
your son, he had grown so
much'
ESTIRAR va. ESTIRAR IGUAL to co-
operate, pull together (coll.);
ESTIRAR LA PATA (slang) to die;
ESTIRARLE AL EXCUSADO to flush
the toilet; vr. to grow taller
(usually said with ref. to
teenagers)
ESTIRÓN (slang) m. DARSE UN ESTIRÓN
to grow like a weed (fig.), grow
considerably and suddenly (u-
sually said with ref. to teenagers)
ESTEPLES (slang) (Hispanization of)
Staples, Texas
ESTÉRICO -CA (var. of) histérico -
ca
ESTO (see A TODO ESTO)
ESTÓGAMO: (var. of) estómago; ESTÓ-
MAGO SUCIO indigestion, dys-
pepsia; "infected stomach"
ESTOR (Eng.) m. store, shop
ESTRAIQUE (Eng.) m. strike, work
stoppage; strike (in baseball)
ESTRAIQUEADO or ESTRAIQUIADO (Eng.)
strike-out
ESTRAIQUEAR or ESTRAIQUIAR (Eng.)
va. to strike at and miss a
pitched ball (in baseball); to
strike someone out (baseball);
vn. to strike, go on strike
(Std. estar de huelga, ponerse
de huelga)
ESTRAMBÓLICO -CA (var. of) estram-
bótico -ca 'strange, unusual,
eccentric, queer'
ESTRELLAR vr. to faint, see stars
(coll.); vr. to excel, shine
(in a game, etc.)
ESTROC (Eng.) m. stroke, cerebral
hemorrhage
ESTROPOJO (var. of) estropajo
ESTRUJAR va. to shake violently
ESTRUJÓN m. violent shaking (u-
sually admininstered to a person)
ESTUATA or ESTUATUA (vars. of)
estatua
ESTUFA: ¡ESTUFAS CALIFORNIA! (slang)
Knock it off!, Quiet down!,
Shut up!; ¡YA ESTUFAS! (id.)
ESTUFEAR or ESTUFIAR (slang) va. to
sniff the residue of powdered

narcotic drugs

ESTULE (Eng.) (slang) m. stoolie (slang), stool pigeon (slang), person who betrays one's companions by serving as a police informer

ESTULEAR or ESTULIAR (Eng.) va. to "stool" on someone, serve as a police informer (cf. ESTULE)

ESTUTO -TA (vars. of) astuto -ta

ESTUVO (3rd pers. sg. pret. of estar): ¡YA ESTUVO! That's it!, We've got it made!, The job's done! (etc.)

EXAMINACIÓN f. exam (in a school subject)

EXCLUIGO (var. of) excluyo (1st per. pres. sg. ind. of excluir)

EXCUSADO: EXCUSADO DE AFUERA outhouse, outdoor toilet

EXCUSAR (Ang.) va. to pardon, forgive

ÉXITO (Ang.) exit, way out

EXPERENCIA (var. of) experiencia

EXPLOTAR (Ang.) va. to explode, detonate; vn. (fig.) to explode with anger

EXPRÉS (Ang.) m. express (i.e., express train, express bus); carriage pulled by one or two horses

EXTRA f. spare tire

EXTRAORDENARIO -RIA (var. of) extraordinario -ria

EXTRAVIADO -DA half-crazy, slightly tetched (coll.)

EXTRORDINARIO -RIA (var. of) extraordinario -ria

F

FACHAS fpl. unkempt and messy appearance: "Andaba de unas fachas que daba lástima" 'He looked so messy that one felt sorry for him'

FACHAZO (slang) alcoholic drink; shot of liquor

FACULTOSO -SA usurper of privileges, taker of rights one has not been authorized to enjoy

FAIN (Eng.) adj. fine, okay, all right

FAJA belt used for medicinal or therapeutic purposes; corset

FAJAR va. to spank; to beat (with a belt); to put a collar on someone (fig., i.e. to control)

FAJAZO blow administered with a belt

FAJERO wrapping or swaddling cloth for newborn babies; belt for medicinal or therapeutic purposes (esp. to hold in the navel of the newborn child)

FALDA shirt tail; part of a woman's slip accidentally showing: "Te sale la falda, métetela"

FALDÓN m. fender (automobile)

FALTAR (slang) FALTARLE A ALGUIEN UN TORNILLO to be daffy, have a screw loose (slang), be someone crazy

FALSEAR or FALSIAR: FALSEÁRSELE A ALGUIEN LA RODILLA to sprain one's knee

FALSEO sprain

FALLAR: FALLARLE A ALGUIEN EL COCO to go off one's rocker (slang), become slightly crazy

¡FALLÁU! (Eng.) (interj.) (slang) Far out! (indicating approval of something)

FAMA: DAR FAMA to praise, eulogize

FAMILIA: ESTAR CON FAMILIA to be pregnant

FANEAR or FANIAR (Eng.) va. to fan (baseball slang), strike out; FANEAR EL AIRE to attempt and fail to hit the ball (baseball)

FANTOCHE mf. presumptuous or pretentious

FARMACÉTICO (var. of) farmacéutico

FAROLAZO: ECHARSE UN FAROLAZO (slang) to drink down a shot of hard liquor

FARUCAS (slang) Falfurrias, Texas

FAUBOL or FÁUBOL (Eng.) m. foul ball (in ball sports, e.g., in baseball, said of a ball hit to the left or the right of the field of play)

FAUL (Eng.) m. foul (in sports competitions)

FEDERAL (<feo) (slang) adj. ugly

FEDERICO -CA (slang) ugly (cf. FEDERAL); crazy, insane, lunatic; fsg. federal police, federal troops

FEILAR or FEILEAR or FEILIAR (Eng.) va. to fail, flunk (someone in a school subject); va. & vn. to fail (in a school subject)

FENDA (Eng.) fender (automobile); (slang ant.) hair heavily greased and combed straight back on the sides, "DA" haircut, "fenders" (slang ant.)

FÉNDER (Eng.) f. (var. of) fenda

(Eng.)

FENÓMENO -NA big-headed, large-headed; m. monstrosity

FEO: OLER FEO to stink (said of persons or things); PONERSE FEO to become dangerous, threatening, to turn bad (said of weather): "¿Trajiste tu capa?--¿Por qué preguntas?--Porque se está poniendo feo el cielo"

FEÓN -ONA (var. of) feúcho -cha

FEREAR or FERIAR va. & vn. to barter; make change for: "Por favor, feréame este dólar"

FERIA change, money due from a larger monetary unit; loose change, assortment of coins; TENER FERIA to be flushed, have a great deal of money; to have more money than one customarily has on one's person

FERNI (nickname for) Fernando

FEYO -YA (var. of) feo -a

FIANCE m. (var. of) fianza

FICHA bottle cap; slug; adj. broke, without money; ANDAR FICHA (LISA) to be stone broke, completely without money; CIERTAS FICHAS certain so-and-so's

FICHAR va. to look for money

FICHAZO change, money returned from a larger monetary unit

FICHERA (slang) whore, prostitute

FIEBRE: FIEBRE DEL VALLE f. valley fever, coccidiodomycosis

FIERRITO hat pin

FIERRO (var. of) hierro; FIERROS mpl. tools of a barber's trade; CAMINO DE FIERRO railroad

FIERROCARRIL (var. of) ferrocarril

FIESTERO -RA fond of going to parties

FIFÍ or FIFIRICHE or FIFIRUCHO (slang) effeminate (male), faggot, pansy, swish, Miss Nancy, Miss Molly, nelly (etc.) (slang)

FÍJESE or FÍJESE NOMÁS Fancy that!, Can you imagine that! (expressions of surprise or incredulity)

FIL (Eng.) m. field (ref. to both athletic and agricultural fields); field = specialty (i.-e., academic "field", academic major)

FILA (slang) wife; knife; CARGAR or TRAER FILA to carry a knife, a switchblade, etc.; SACARLE LA FILA A ALGUIEN to pull a knife on someone

FILDEAR or FILDIAR vn. to play the position of fielder (in baseball)

FILDEO act or technique of fielding (in baseball)

FÍLDER (Eng.) m. fielder (in baseball)

FILERA knife

FILEREAR or FILERIAR va. to knife, cut with a knife

FILERO knife

FILETEAR or FILETIAR (slang) va. to knife, cut with a knife

FILORAZO knife wound (usually one inflicted in a knife fight)

FILOREAR or FILORIAR (vars. of) filerear, fileriar

FILOSA (slang) knife

FINA (dim. of) Josefina (see also PEPA)

FINCA building, edifice

FINCAR va. to construct a building

FISGADERA act of snooping or peeping

FISGÓN -GONA mf. peeping tom, person who snoops or peeps on others (observes them surreptitiously)

FITO (nickname for) Adolfo

FLACO -CA thin (usually ref. to animals)

FLACÓN -CONA somewhat thin (usually prefaced by medio: MEDIO FLACÓN / MEDIO FLACONA)

FLANQUEAR or FLANQUIAR (Eng.) (vars. of) flonquear, flonquiar

FLETEAR or FLETIAR (Eng.) va. to flatten (a tire, by letting the air out) (a person, by knocking him/her down with a blow of the fists); vr. to go flat: "La llanta se flatió"

FLET (Eng.) m. flat, flat tire; ANDAR FLET to be flat broke (coll.), completely without money; adj. flat, out of tune (ref. to musical instruments)

FLIPEAR or FLIPIAR (Eng.) va. to flip, flip over; vr. (slang) to go crazy, flip one's lid (slang)

FLIRTIAR (var. of) flirtear

FLOCHAR (Eng.) va. to flush

FLOJÓN -JONA somewhat lazy (often prefaced by medio: MEDIO FLOJÓN/MEDIO FLOJONA)

FLONQUEAR or FLONQUIAR (Eng.) va. to fail, flunk (someone in a school subject); v. & vn. to fail (in a school subject)

FLOR (slang) f. homosexual, pansy (pej.)

FLORE (dim. of) Florinda
FLORIAR (var. of) florear
FLORINDO (slang) homosexual
FLOTAR: FLOTARSE UNA (slang) to drink a beer: "Se flotó una"
FLOUT (Eng.) m. float (Std. carro alegórico)
FLU (Eng.) f. influenza
FLUNQUEAR or FLUNQUIAR (Eng.) (var. of) flonquear, flonquiar
FOCO: FOCOS mpl. eyeglasses
FODONGO (Eng. <Ford) old battered-up car
FÓLDER (Eng.) m. folder (envelope or filing apparatus)
FONAZO (slang) (Eng.) fun, enjoyment
FONCHAR vn. to cheat in a marble game by placing or pushing the marble shooter closer to the target (see also HACER FONCHE)
FONCHE: HACER FONCHE: to cheat in a marble game by placing or pushing the marble shooter closer to the target
FONDONGO (slang) buttocks, ass (vulg.)
FONE (Eng.) adj. mf. funny, amusing
FONES or FONIS (Eng.) mpl. comic strips, funnies (coll.)
FONO (var. of) teléfono
FORCITO (Eng.) old battered-up car (cf. FODONGO)
FOREHUÉS(T) or FOROHUÉS(T) (Hispanization of) Fort Worth, Texas
FOREHUOR (Hispanization of) Fort Worth, Texas
FORIHUÁN or FORITÚ (slang) (Eng.) m. male homosexual (cf. CUARENTAIDÓS/CUARENTAIUNO)
FORJE (slang) m. female figure, woman's body
FORMAL m. (Ang?) formal (dance, gathering, etc.); TRAJE FORMAL m. formal evening wear
FORNITURA (Eng.) (infreq.) furniture
FORTIGO or FORTINGO (Eng.) old battered-up car (cf. FODONGO)
FORRO (slang) good-looking person; mpl. (said of two people who resemble each other): "Son forros" 'They're look-alikes'
FRAGO (slang) cigar
FRAILECILLO or FRAILECÍO blister bug, blister beetle (meloidae)
FRAJEAR or FRAJIAR (slang) va. to smoke
FRAJO (slang) cigarette; FRAJO DE SEDA (slang) marihuana cigarette
FRANQUE (Eng.) (dim. of) Frank or Francisco
FRANQUE (Eng.) adj. frank, honest
FREGADA -DO penniless, down and out, destitute; (almost always adj.)

(said of a woman who looks prematurely old as the result of excessive sexual activity); tricky, roguish, damned (fig.): ESTAR COMO LA FREGADA to be as _____ as can be (e.g., 'to be as ugly as sin', 'as mean as a junkyard dog', etc.--ref. usually to any negative quality known both to speaker and listener); HUERCO FREGADO damned little brat; m. shady dealer, sneaky person; f. hard time, difficult time; IRSE A LA FREGADA (usually a command:) ¡Vete a la fregada!" 'Go to hell!', 'Get the hell out of here!'; LLEVÁRSELO A ALGUIEN A LA FREGADA to die; to fall onto hard times, be ruined (often financially): "Se lo llevó a la fregada porque no hizo lo que debía"; NO IMPORTARLE A ALGUIEN UNA FREGADA not to give a damn (about something): "A mí no me importa una fregada" 'I don't give a damn about it'
FREGADAL m. much, many, large quantity (of something): "Tiene un fregadal de huercos" 'He has a huge bunch of kids' (fig., i.e., a large family)
FREGADAZO blow with the fist or any other object
FREGADERA action of washing dishes; harassment, annoyances; nagging; "thingamagig" (coll., said when one fails to remember the name of a particular object); junk, trash
FREGADITO -TA adj. m. deceitful (usually prefaced by medio: MEDIO FREGADITO); adj., mf. ruthless opportunist
FREGADIZA severe beating; hard time, difficult time
FREGADOR -DORA mf. deceiver, cheater; freeloader; opportunist
FREGAR va. to cheat; to take advantage of; vn. to bear the brunt of, be forced to take the lion's share (of a job), have a real work out with; DE A TIRO LA FRIEGAS (FRIEGA/FRIEGAN etc.) (used to reprimand for abusive behavior) 'You're really something else' 'You're a real lulu' 'You're really just too much' (all used ironically and with critical intent); FREGAR LA BORREGA to bother, pester, annoy;

PARA ACABARLA DE FREGAR to make
matters worse, on top of all that
(fig.); YA NI LA FRIEGAS (FRIEGA,
FRIEGAN, etc.) (set expression
used to censure abusive behavior)
FREGAZO blow with the fist or any
other object
FREGÓN -GONA complainer, chronic
bitcher (slang); bothersome, annoying; fraud, cheat, ruthless
opportunist; (coll.) the boss,
the big cheese
FREGUIZA (see DAR UNA FREGUIZA, LLE-
VAR UNA FREGUIZA)
FREIMIAR (Eng.) va. to frame (coll.)
conspire to have convicted
FREJOLES (var. of) frijoles
FRENTAZO bumping together of two
foreheads
FRENTE: EN FRENTE DE LA GENTE (Eng?)
in public: "Lo regañaron en
frente de la gente"
FRENTUDO -DA big-browed; broad-faced
FRESCO male homosexual
FRIADOR -DORA m.,f. refrigerator
FRIAR (var. of) freír 'to fry' (va.
& vn.) (friar is conjugated like
criar)
FRIFOL (var. of) frijol
FRIFOLERO -RA (var. of) frijolero -ra
FRIJOLERO -RA fond of eating beans
FRÍO: FRÍO -A (slang) dead; FRIO DE
LA MATRIZ "cold womb", fri-
gidity, lack of (feminine) sex-
ual desire; female sterility;
(TIEMPO DE) FRÍO winter, winter
time (the cold season)
FRISA (Eng.) freezer (type of re-
frigerator)
FRISCAR (Eng.) va. to frisk, search
a person for hidden objects
FRISER (Eng.) m. & f. freezer (type
of refrigerator) (cf. FRISA)
FRIYAR (var. of) friar
FRUNCIR: FRUNCIRSELE A ALGUIEN (EL
CULO) (slang, vulg.) to be a-
fraid
FRUTA (slang) m. male homosexual
FUCHE or FUCHEFUCHE or FUCHI or
FUCHIFUCHI interjs. Phew! (used
to express disgust, repulsion,
etc.); TENER FUCHIFUCHI to
be afraid
FUEGO (var. of) juego 'game'
FUEREÑO -ÑA stranger, someone not
from the particular locality,
outsider
FUERTE m. influential person, someone with "pull"; male to whom
all women are attracted; lucky
person, someone who "has it
made"; boss, strong man (fig.);
HACERSE FUERTE to show great
strength (often under emotion-

al strain); to rise to the occasion
FUERTÍSIMO -MA (var. of) fortísimo -
ma
FUERZA: A FUERZA QUE SÍ most likely, in all likelihood, more
likely than not: "¿Tendrán
frío los gatos?--A fuerza que
sí" 'Are the cats cold?--
More likely than not.'; A TODA
FUERZA in full swing: "El baile
esta a a toda fuerza" 'The
dance was in full swing'; HACER
FUERZA to faze, affect: "Se
murío su mamá y ni fuerza le
hace" 'His mother died and it
doesn't affect him in the least'
FULEAR or FULIAR (Eng.) va. to fool,
deceive
FULTAIM (Eng.) adv. full-time
(Std. horario completo, tiempo
completo)
FUMADA act of smoking a cigar or
cigarette
FUNDILLO or FUNDÍO (slang, vulg.)
piece of ass (vulg.): "Tiene
allí su fundillo cuando lo
quiere" 'He's got a piece of
ass ⊏ opportunity for sexual
relations⊐ right there when-
ever he wants it'
FUNDILLON (m.) -LLONA (f.) or FUN-
DILLOTE (m.)-TA (f.) big- bot-
tomed (coll.) (said of person
with a large buttocks)
FUNDILLUDO -DA adj. and mf. (ref.
to person with a sexually-
appetizing rear end)
FUNTA (var. of) junta
FURRIAS mfpl. (pej.) (said of persons) base, mean, despicable;
clumsy; lusterless, dull, un-
interesting; sloppy, careless;
(said of things) shoddily-made
FUTBOLERO (Eng.) football player

G

GABA (abbrev., var. of) gabacho -cha
GABACHERO -RA (pej.) gringoized,
gringo-like; (pej.) gringo-lov-
er, (person) obsequious to grin-
gos
GABACHO -CHA (pej.) Anglo-Saxon,
gringo
GABARDINO -NA (pej.) (var. of) gabacho -cha

GABINETE: GABINETE (DE COCINA)
kitchen cabinet
GABO -BA (pej.) (var. of) gabacho
-cha
GACHO (usually pej.) crude; mean,
base; bad; ugly; ridiculous;
¡QUÉ GACHO! How humiliating!,
How disgusting!, TORCER MUY
GACHO to die a horrible death
GAI (Eng.) (slang) m. guy, fellow
GAITA trick
GALLAZO (slang), shot, puff or "fix"
of a narcotic drug
GALLETA cookie; GALLETA DE SODA
saltine cracker
GALLINA: GALLINA PORPUJADA (type of
child's game)
GALLO (slang) guy, fellow; hero; he-
man, stud (coll.); street sere-
nade; (slang) blood issuing from
a wound received in a fight;
mpl. articles of hand-me-down or
second-hand clothing; DORMÍRSELE
EL GALLO A ALGUIEN to fail in
the sex act, lose one's erection
(said of a man); SACAR GALLO to
show off a new possession (esp.
an article of clothing)
GALLÓN -LLONA brave; terrific, tremendous; m. he-man, stud (coll.)
GAJO cotton
GALGO -GA thin; sickly-looking
GANAR vn. to go toward, head toward:
"Ganó para el río" 'He headed
off toward the river'
GANAS: GANAS TIENES You'd like that,
wouldn't you: "La maistra te va
a flonquiar. --Ganas tienes."
GANCHAR va. to hook onto (an ob-
ject); to force commitment; to
hook, trap (as into marriage);
vr. to become engaged to be
married; to get married
GANCHO (clothes) hanger
GANDAYA uneaten food that is thrown
away after a meal
GANGA (Eng.) gang, group of delin-
quent youths; circle of friends
GANGOSO -SA hair-lipped
GÁNGSTER (Eng.) m. gangster, hoodlum
GARABATOS mpl. poor or unintelligi-
ble handwriting, scribblings
GARACHE (Eng.) m. garage
GARAJE m. filling station, gasoline
station
GARCÍA: ACÁ GARCÍA (hum.) toilet:
"Voy acá García" 'I'm going to
the toilet' (play on words: a
cagar + [Gar] -cía)
GARGANTA: DOÑA GARGANTA agressive,
influential, powerful woman;
shrew
GARITA customs house (on a border

between two countries)
GARNUCHO fillip (flip) with one's
fingers against someone's head
GARRA fsg. old cheap clothes;
ESTIRAR GARRA or SACAR LA GARRA
(slang) to gossip; to run some-
one down (slang), speak ill of
someone; ESTAR MALA DE LA GARRA
/ TENER or TRAER LA GARRA to
be having one's menstrual period
(ref. to women); TIRAR GARRA to
dress up, dress elegantly
GARRANCHAR va. to slash, gash
GAR(R)AR (vars. of) agarrar
GARRASPERA (var. of) carraspera
GARRERO vendor of second-hand clothing; dealer in second-hand
clothing; piles of rags
GARRIENTO -TA ragged
GARROTE (slang) m. large male organ,
big penis; (see also LIMOSNERO
Y CON GARROTE)
GARROTEAR or GARROTIAR va. to rout,
defeat decisively in a sports
match (usually in baseball); to
batter, beat up; to collect
many hits off a pitcher (in
baseball)
GARROTERO batter (baseball); slug-
ger, batter successful in hit-
ting
GARROTIZA severe beating (usually
administered with a club); shel-
lacking, decisive defeat in a
game (usually baseball)
GARRUÑO scratch
GAS: ACABÁRSELE A ALGUIEN EL GAS
(Ang?, fig.?) to run out of
gas, lose one's stamina; (see
also DARLE AL GAS); PEDAL DE
GAS accelerator
GASELÍN m. (var. of) gasolina
GASELINA (var. of) gasolina
GASOFA (slang) gasoline; GASOFA DE
LA BUENA (slang) premium gaso-
line
GASOLÍN (Eng.) m. gasoline
GATA maid, female servant
GATO (slang) fraidy-cat, fearful
person; CORBATA DE GATO (slang)
bow tie
GENTE: HASTA DÓNDE LLEGA LA GENTE
(set expression) My, what some
people are capable of!
GENTECITA rabble, bunch of lower-
class persons
GENTIAZO or GENTILLAZO multitude of
people
GIOMETRÍA (var. of) geometría
GLADIOLA (Eng.) (Std. gladiolo)
GLOBO (slang) (type of barbituate
pill swallowed for narcotic
effect)
GLU or GLUFA (Eng.) f.: HACER(SE)

A LA GLU(FA) to sniff glue (for
the mildly narcotic effect it
produces)
GLUFO -FA high from sniffing glue
(cf. GLU); mf. glue-sniffer
GODORNIZ (var. of) codorniz f.
GOGOTE (var. of) cogote m.
GOLAR (var. of) volar
GOLEAR or GOLIAR (Eng.) vn. to make
a goal (in an athletic contest,
e.g. in soccer)
GOLFO (Eng.) golf (game of golf)
GOLPANAZO severe, heavy blow
GOLPE: DARLE EL GOLPE AL CIGARRO /
DARLE EL GOLPE AL CIGARRILLO
to inhale a cigarette or cigar
GOLPIAR (var. of) golpear
GOLPIZA series of blows; severe
beating
GOMA paste (sticking paste)
GOMITADERA (var. of) vomitadera
GOMITAR (var. of) vomitar
GÓMITO (var. of) vómito
GORDO -DA f. & adj. (coll.) preg-
nant; SALIR GORDA to get preg-
nant; f. thick corn tortilla;
CAER GORDO to be repugnant,
repellent: "Ese tipo me cae
gordo"
GORILA or GORRILA f. (cf. Std. mf.)
GORILÓN -LONA or GORRILÓN -LONA large
and ponderous person
GORUPERO place infested with gorupos
(chicken fleas)
GORUPIENTO -TA infested with gorupos
(chicken fleas)
GORUPO chicken flea
GORRA (slang) heroin capsule
GOTA (slang) gasoline; (see also
SUDAR)
GOTEADOR or GOTIADOR m. eye-dropper,
medicine dropper
GOYO -YA (dims. for, resp.) Gregorio
-ria
GRÁBOL (Eng.) m. gravel
GRACIAS: PARA ESAS GRACIAS if that's
the way it's going to be, if
that's how it is: "Mañana vamos
a tu casa a celebrar la fiesta.
--Muy bien, traigan su guajolote.
--Újule, para esas gracias mejor
nos lo comemos en casa."
GRACIA(S): ¡QUÉ GRACIA(S)! Thanks
a lot! (iron.) Thanks for noth-
ing
GRADACIÓN (var. of) graduación f.
GRADAR (var. of) graduar
GRADO (Ang.) grade, mark in a school
subject; HACER GRADOS to receive
grades, make a certain grade:
(Ang.) "Hice puras 'A's el se-
mestre pasado" 'I made straight
A's last semester'; year or level
in school: "Pedro está en el

segundo grado"
GRAJEA sleet
GRAJEAR vn. to sleet
GRAMO (slang) packet of heroin
GRAMPA (var. of) grapa
GRANDE advanced in years, old; MÁS
GRANDE older (Std. mayor);
(slang) m. a thousand dollars
(Ang? 'one grand'); CASA GRAN-
DE (slang) the big house
(slang), penitentiary
GRANDOTOTE or GRANDOTOTOTE adj. mf.
extremely large, immense, gar-
gantuan
GRANIENTO -TA full of sores
GRANIZAZO major hail storm
GRANJEAR or GRANJIAR to fawn, flat-
ter, do favors so as to ingra-
tiate oneself or receive favors
in return
GRANO sore, open skin lesion; ulcer;
wound
GRASA shoe paste; DAR GRASA to ap-
ply shoe paste (in order to
shine shoes)
GREÑERO -RA disheveled and unkempt
hair: "Trae un greñero de la
mierda" (vulg.) 'He's got a
messy head of hair'
GREVE or GREIVE or GREIVI (Eng.) m.
gravy
GRIFA (slang) marihuana
GRIFO -FA marihuana user; adj. mf.
kinky (ref. to hair)
GRIPA (var. of) gripe
GRITADERA or GRITADERO (vars. of)
gritería
GROCERÍA (Eng.) grocery store
GROCERÍAS (Eng.) fpl. groceries,
food, provisions
GRULLA cold air; police, police
force; adj. ugly: "¡Tu madre!
--¡La tuya, que está más gru-
lla!" (exchange of insults
among children)
GUACHA (Eng.) wrist watch; washer
(used in plumbing)
GUACHAR (Eng.) va. to watch
GUACHATERIA (Eng.) washateria, laun-
dromat
GUACHE (var. of) guacha (Eng.) f.
GUACHIMÁN (Eng.) m. watchman, guard
GUAFLERA (Eng.) waffle maker, ma-
chine for making waffles
GUÁFOL (Eng.) m. waffle
GUAIFA (Eng.) (slang, hum.) wife
GUAIN (Eng.) (slang) m. wine
GUAINERO -RA (Eng., cf. GUAIN) ha-
bitual drinker of wine; heavy
drinker (of any alcoholic bev-
erage)
GUÁIPER (Eng.) m. windshield wiper
GUAJOLOTE mf. (fig.) fool, idiot
GUAMAZO hard blow (with the fist or

other object) (see also GÜEMAZO, HUAMAZO, HUEMAZO)

GUANGO -GA loose-fitting; flabby; VENIRLE A ALGUIEN GUANGO -GA to compare unfavorably (often in the physical sense): "Ese tipo me viene guango" 'That guy is a pushover for me' (i.e., it will be easy for me to defeat him in physical combat)

GUANTADA blow or slap

GUAPO -PA industrious; intelligent; talented

GUAREAR or GUARIAR (slang) va. to say hello to; to plan to meet

GUATO festivity; commotion

GUATOSO -SA noisy

GUAYÍN (Eng.) m. wagon drawn by horses

GÜELAR (var. of) volar

GÜELDEAR or GÜELDIAR (vars. of) hueldear or hueldiar

GÜELITO -TA (var. of) abuelito -ta

GÜELO, GÜELES, etc. (vars. of) huelo, hueles, etc. (pres. ind. conjugation of oler)

GÜELTA (var. of) vuelta

GÜELVA, GÜELVAS, etc. (var. of) huela, huelas, etc. (pres. subj. of oler)

GÜELVO, GÜELVES, etc. (vars. of) vuelvo, vuelves, etc. (pres. ind. of volver)

GÜEMAZO hard blow, slap (cf. GUAMAZO)

GÜENO -NA (var. of) bueno -na

GUENGSTA (Eng.) m. (cf. GÁNGSTER)

GÜERCO -CA (var. of) huerco -ca

GÜERGÜENZA (var. of) vergüenza

GÜERINCHE or GÜERINCHI (pej.) blond, fair-complexioned (cf. GÜERO)

GÜERO -RA blond, fair-complexioned; mf. Anglo-Saxon

GÜERTA (var. of) huerta

GÜERRA (see DAR GÜERRA)

GÜESO (var. of) hueso

GÜETE (var. of) cuete m. 'gun'

GÜETEAR or GÜETIAR va. to shoot

GÜEY (var. of) buey mf.

GUIA steering wheel (automobile)

GÜICHOL (var. of) huichol m.

GÜILA (var. of) huila

GÜILE (Eng.) (dim. of) William

GÜINCHIL (Eng.) m. windshield (automobile)

GUINDO dark red color

GÜINE (Eng.) m. wienie, wiener sausage; COMER GÜINES (slang, tag question equivalent to Eng. "...or something?") "¿Estás loco o comiste güines?" 'Are you crazy or something?'; (vulg.) m. penis, male member (euph.)

GUISAR va. to fry

GÜIZA (var. of) huiza

GUSGO -GA (slang) glutton, chow hound (coll.) (cf. BUSGO -GA)

GUSJEAR or GUSJIAR (slang) va. to eat, "chow down" (slang)

H

HA, HAMOS (vars. resp. of) he, hemos (1st pers. sg. and pl. of pres. ind. haber)

HABER: HAY: "Y ¿qué hay con eso?" 'So?', 'So what?', 'What about it?'

HABLADA f. offensive word; innuendo, insinuation; fpl. ECHAR HABLADAS to make sarcastic remarks; to offend

HABLADERIA (var. of) habladuría

HABLADERO -RA m. chatter, excessive talk; mf., adj. boastful, bragging

HABLADOR -DORA m., f. liar; gossiper

HABLANTINO mf. (var. of) hablantín

HABLAR va. to call, telephone: "Te hablan por teléfono" 'Someone's calling you on the phone'; vn. to gossip; to speak ill of someone; HABLARLE A UNA MUJER to ask a woman to go steady; to tell a woman how one feels about her (romantically); HABLAR NOMÁS POR NO DEJAR to talk just to be talking (for no particular reason); HABLAR PA' TRAS (Ang.) to talk back to, answer in a sassy manner: "No le hables pa' tras a tu papá" 'Don't talk back to your dad'; HABLAR RECIO to speak loudly

HACER va. to figure, imagine, assume: "Yo te hacía en el centro" 'I figured you were downtown'; HACER AGUA (Std. hacer aguas menores) to urinate; HACER A ALGUIEN VER SU FORTUNA to give someone a hard time; HACER A LA LEY to win over (to a particular way of thinking): "Tú no le puedes decir nada. Él ya la hizo a su ley." 'You can't tell her anything. He already won her over.'; HACER A(L) TROCHEMOCHE to do a half-assed job (slang), do poorly, do with a lick and a promise (coll.); HACER APRECIO to pay attention; HACER ATOLE (see ATOLE); HACER BARRANQUE-ÑA to assemble and carry a-long a large quantity of items HACER BOLA to fluster, confuse; HACER BORUCA to fluster, confuse; HACER BUENO (Ang.) to re-place, "make good" (ref. to replacement of belongings lost or destroyed); HACER CARGOS to place charges against; HACER CAQUIS/HACER CAQUIS MAQUIS (euph.) to go potty (euph.), do number two (euph.), defecate (said of infants or small chil-dren); HACER COMO AGUA to do effortlessly; HACER CHICHARRÓN to burn to a crisp; HACER CHILLAR to cause to cry; to anger; HACER ENTENDER to get through after repeated efforts (coll.), succeed in getting (someone) to listen to reason; HACER GARRAS to tear to shreds; HACER JALE (slang) to steal; to cheat; to work; to make ad-vances to a member of the op-posite sex; HACER JALÓN (slang) to make advances to a member of the opposite sex; HACER JAMBER-GA/JAMBORGA/JAMBÓRGUER DE (slang) to make mince-meat of (coll.), beat up soundly (in a fight); HACER LA BARBA to flatter; HACER LA LUCHA to try to convince, try to get some-one to change his/her mind; HACER LA PALA to accompany; HACER LA PARADA to humor, go a-long with, tolerate, put up with; HACER LOS TAMALES DE CHIVO to cheat on one's spouse, commit adultery; HACER MAJE to fool, deceive; HACER OJO to cast a spell upon, cast the evil eye upon; HACER PEDO (slang) to make trouble; to harass; to make advances to a member of the opposite sex; to make a scene, an uproar: "Jorge estaba haciendo pedo en la cantina"; HACER PICADILLO to grind; to squash; HACER PLACER to be courteous and attentive; to humor, go along with: "Mejor es que le hagas placer al jefe para que no te desocupe"; HACER POR (var. of) hacer el esfuer-zo por; HACER TOPILLO (slang) to make a fool of; HACER UNA (MALA) PARADA to do someone a

bad turn, play a dirty trick on; vn. HACER A LA GLU(FA) to sniff glue (for mildly narcotic ef-fect); HACER BIEN (Ang.) to do will, earn money in copious amounts; to be wise, act pru-dently: "Haces bien en no de-círselo"; HACER BORLOTE (slang) to make trouble; to make noise; make a scene (slang), cause an uproar; to make advances to a member of the opposite sex; HACER BUCHES(DE SAL) to fill one's mouth with warm salt wa-ter so as to kill germs and lessen the pain of a toothache; HACER (LA) CACA (vulg.) to de-fecate (Std. cagar); HACER CARR-ITO to harp on the same sub-ject, talk incessantly about the same topic; HACER CHAPUZA A ALGUIEN to cheat someone; HA-CER COMO QUE to pretend, act as if, feign: "Haz como que te pegué muy recio" 'Act as if I struck you real hard'; HACER CORAJE(S) to throw fits of anger, throw a tantrum; HA-CER COSITAS (euph.) to have sexual relations; HACER CUACHA (vulg., slang) to make mince-meat of (fig.), beat up sound-ly (in a fight); HACER DE LAS SUYAS to blunder as usual; to misbehave as always; HACER DE-SATINAR A ALGUIEN to make some-one lose his cool (slang), cause someone to become very angry and quite disoriented; HACER DINERO (Ang.) to make money, get rich; HACER DINERO A MANOS LLENAS to make money hand over fist (fig.), make large quantities of money, get very rich quick; HACER EL CÁLIZ to try, make an effort: "No sabe si puede ganar, pero quiere hacer el cáliz"; HACER EL CUERPO to defecate; HACER FUERZA to faze, affect: "Se murió su mamá y ni fuerza le hace." 'His mother died and it doesn't affect him in the least'; HACER GASTOS to spend money (usually unexpectedly and at times unnecessarily); HACER GENTE A ALGUIEN to treat an undeserving person decently; HACER GRADOS (Ang.) to receive grades, make a certain grade (Std. sacar notas): "Esteban está haciendo muy malos grados"; HACER HAMBRE to work up an ap-

petite; HACER LA CRUZ to make
one's first sale of the day
(ref. to storekeepers); HACER
LA CHI(S) (euph.) to urinate,
make "wee-wee" (euph., also
baby talk); HACER LA PERRA
(slang) to loaf, while away the
time; HACER MAL MODO to slight,
be rude to; HACER PANTOMINAS to
create a scene, make trouble,
make a spectacle of oneself:
"No te contentaste hasta que
hiciste tus pantominas" 'You
just weren't happy until you
could make an idiot of yourself in public'; HACER PAPELES
id. to HACER PANTOMINAS supra;
HACER PEDO (vulg.) to make a
fuss, raise a stink, create
trouble; HACER PENDEJO -JA A
ALGUIEN to cheat on someone,
deceive (e.g., one's spouse,
fiancé(e) etc.); HACER PINI-
NOS (for a baby to make amusing and endearing little ges-
tures); (for a baby to begin
to take his/her first steps);
HACER (LA) PIPI / HACER (LA)
PIPI (slightly euph.) to urinate, "make water" (euph.)
(esp. said of and to children)
HACER POR to try to; HACER
RONCHA to run up one's winnings in a game of chance after
starting out with a very small
amount of money; HACER SUERTES
to do magical tricks; HACER
TIEMPO (Ang.) to do time in jail,
comply with one's jail term;
(Ang.) to "make time" with the
object of one's affections, engage in a display of affection
toward; HACER TRACALADA to make
much noise, raise a ruckus; HA-
CER TRAMPA to resort to crooked tactics (e.g., in a business
deal); HACER TROMPAS to put on
a sad or annoyed facial expression; HACER VACA to run up one's
winnings in a game of chance
after starting out with a very
small amount of money; vr. HA-
CERLA DE to play the role of:
"Luis Aguilar la hace de trampe"
'Luis Aguilar plays the role of
the villain'; HACERLE PEDO A
ALGUIEN (vulg.) to make a play
for someone (with amorous intentions); HACERLE PLÁTICA A AL-
GUIEN to strike up a conversation with someone; HACERSE BO-
CA CERRADA to pretend to be
quiet and reserved; HACERSE BO-
CA CHIQUITA to pretend to be

a small eater; HACERSE CACHETÓN
-TONA to ignore an assignment;
to conveniently forget a debt
or a commitment (see also HA-
CERSE CHATO); HACERSE CIRCO to
make a fool of oneself; HACERSE
CHATO-TA to ignore an assignment; to conveniently forget
a debt or commitment; HACERSE
CHINCHE to act stingy, miserly;
to overstay one's welcome; HA-
CERSE DE: ¿QUÉ SE HIZO DE ___?
(fixed expression) 'Whatever
became of ____?' HACERSE DEL
ROGAR (var. of hacerse de rogar 'to want to be coaxed');
HACERSE FUERTE to arm oneself
with fortitude and patience to
face difficult times, be strong
enough to ward off difficult
situations; HACERSE GACHO to be
unpleasant; HACERSE GRANDE to
act big, act superior, give
oneself airs; HACERSE LA CAS-
QUETA to masturbate; HACERSE
LA GRAN CACA (vulg. and offensive) to act like a big shit
(vulg.), put on airs; HACERSE
LA GRAN COSA to put on airs,
act presumptuously; HACERSE LA
PUÑETA (vulg., slang) to do a
hand job (coll.), masturbate;
HACERSE MOSQUITA MUERTA to give
the (false) impression that
one is reticent, quiet and reserved; HACERSE PATO to retract
(a statement), renege, back
down; HACERSE PA'TRAS (Ang.)
to back out, renege; to take
back, apologize for; HACERSE
PESADO EL BULTO (fig., coll.)
(for one's responsibilities to
become burdensome); HACERSELA
(vulg., slang) to pull on it
(coll.), masturbate; HACÉRSELE
DOLOR A ALGUIEN HACER ALGO for
it to hurt (fig.) someone to do
something (ref. to ungenerous
attitude): "Se te hizo dolor
darme un pedacito de manzana"
'It hurt you to give me a little piece of the apple'; HACÉR-
SELE EL CUERPO CHINITO to get
goosepimples (goosebumps);
misc. (fixed expressions); HA-
CERLA (Ang?) to make it, arrive
(fig.), be successful: "El
bato ese ya la hizo" 'That guy
has got it made'; NO LE HACE
'It doesn't matter'; NO LE HA-
GAS leave well enough alone;
¿QUÉ LE HACE? 'What does it
matter?' 'So what?'; QUE MAN-
DADO HACER (set expression used

to indicate any quality in excess): "Está más loco que mandado hacer" 'He's crazier than
a hoot owl'; ¡QUÉ SUAVE (LE HA-
CES/HACE/ HACEN)! Nice going!
(iron.), That's a fine howdy
do!; TENERLA HECHA (Ang?) to
have it made (to have achieved
a level of accomplishment sufficient to insure future success)
HACHA: ¡HIJO DEL HACHA! interj.
(mildly euph. though considered
lower-class)
HAIGA (var. of) haya (3rd pers.
subj. of haber); ¡BIEN HAIGA!
'Good for you!' (expression of
approbation); YA TE LO HAIGA/
YA SE LO HAIGA/ YA SE LOS
HAIGA (set expression of ad-
monition, warning, etc.):
"¿Estudiaron?--No.-- Ya se
los haiga."
HALLAR: HALLARSE EN LA CALLE to
be broke, penniless; NO HALL-
ARSE to be ill at ease, un-
comfortable, not to feel at
home (fig.): "Estoy impuesto
a la ciudad; no me hallo en los
pueblos chiquitos"
HAMBORGUESA (var. of) hamburguesa
(Eng.)
HAMBRE: MUERTO -TA DE HAMBRE (fig.
and ironic: said with ref. to
a greedy, selfish person)
HAMBRIADO -DA famished, very hungry
HARINA: SER HARINA DEL MISMO COSTAL
to share the same characteristics, be cut from the same
cloth (fig.)
HOMBRE: EL HOMBRE DE LA HORA (Ang.)
the man of the hour (coll.),
the person currently held
in highest regard
HAMBREADO -DA or HAMBRIADO -DA hungry; starving
HAMBRIENTO -TA stingy, mean
HARTADA act and effect of over-eat-
ing: "Se murió de la gran hartada que se dio"
HARTO -TA glutton
HARTÓN -TONA glutton
HASTA: HASTA PA' VENTAR PA' RIBA
(=hasta para aventar para arriba) with much to spare, with
many to spare, in excess;
HASTA QUE NO until (the no is
superfluous): "No nos vamos
a ir hasta que no lo hagas"
'We won't go until you do it';
HASTA QUE SE LE/TE/NOS/LES HIZO
or HASTA QUE SE LE (etc.) CUM-
PLIÓ He/she (etc.) finally got
what he/she had wanted (=fi-

nally realized his/her goals)
HECHO -CHA: HECHO -CHA BOLA very
flustered, very confused; HECHO -
CHA MADRE / HECHO -CHA MÁQUINA
adv. quite rapidly; TENERLA HE-
CHA (Ang.) to have it made
(coll.), be very successful:
"Ya la tienes hecha"
HELADA beer (in cans or bottles)
HELADO popsicle
HERVIENDO (var. of) hirviendo
(ger. of hervir)
HESPITAL m. (var. of) hospital
HESTÉRICO -CA (var. of) histérico -ca
HESTORIA (var. of) historia
HIELERA refrigerator; ice-box (ant.)
HIELERÍA ice plant (place where ice
is made and sold), ice house
(id.)
HIELERO ice man (vendor and deliverer of ice) (ant.)
HIERBA (slang) marihuana; (slang)
mf. & adj. mean, base, low;
HIERBA ANÍS (var. of) anís;
HIERBA COLORADA dock herb (Ru-
mex crispus) (prepared as a solution and gargled to treat
tonsilitis); HIERBA DEL BURRO
burro bush herb (Hymenoclea sp.)
(prepared as a solution and
applied to arthritic areas and
infected cuts); HIERBA DEL INDIO
desert milkweed (Asclepias sp.)
(prepared as a tea and used to
treat kidney ailments); HIERBA
DEL MANZO swamp root (Anemopsis
californica) (prepared as a tea
and used to treat stomach ache);
HIERBA DEL PASMO spasm herb
(Haplopappus larincofolius)
(prepared as a tea and either
drunk or inhaled in the treatment of pasmo); HIERBA MALA
(var. of) mala hierba; Y DEMÁS
HIERBAS (fixed expression) and
so on and so forth (=Std. y así
sucesivamente)
HIERBAJAL or HIERBAJAR or HIERBAZAL
(vars. of) herbazal m.
HIERBERO grassland (=herbazal);
herbalist
HIJO: ¡HIJO! interj. (varies in
meaning according to intensity
and type of articulation: from
mild--Damn!--through strong--
Son of a bitch!--esp. when followed by a prep. phrase e.g.:)
¡HIJO DE CABRÓN!, ¡HIJO DE LA
CHINGADA! (This last is esp.
strong: 'Mother-XXXXXX' bastard!', etc.); HIJO DEL HACHA
(see HACHA); HIJO DE POLICÍA
person to whom no attention has
been paid or who has not re-

ceived any share of something:
"¿Acaso soy hijo de policía?"
(ref. to traditional popular
antipathy towards the police);
HIJO DE LA GUAYABA (see GUAYABA);
¡HÍJOLE! (see also ¡JÍJOLE!)
interjs. (vary in meaning ac-
cording to intensity and situa-
tion, from a mild 'Damn!'
through something much strong-
er)
HINCHAR: HINCHÁRSELE A ALGUIEN
(slang) to do what one damn
well pleases:"¿Cuándo te vas
a ir? -- Cuando se me hinche"
HINDIDURA (var. of) hendedura
HIPROCRESÍA (var. of) hipocresía
HITO -TA (var. of) hijito -ta
HOCICÓN -CONA loud-mouthed; foul-
mouthed
HOGADO -DA (var. of) ahogado -da
HOGAR (var. of) ahogar va.
HOJARASCA type of sweetroll
HOJELATA (var. of) hojalata
HOMBRAZO he-man, stud (slang)
HOMBRE (can also be used as vocative when addressing a woman:)
"No hombre, ni siquiera sabía
que estabas enferma"
HOMBRERA woman strongly attracted
to men
HOMBRO: METER HOMBRO (slang) to
lend a helping hand, put one's
shoulder to the wheel (fig.,
coll.)
HOQUIS (orthog. var. of) oquis
HORA (var. of) ahora
HORA: A LA HORA DE LA HORA / A
L'ORA DE L'ORA at the moment
of truth, at the time of cri-
sis, when all is said and
done (coll.)
HORALE interj. Knock it off!; Move
it!, Hurry up!, (etc.); That's
it! (=You're right!); (with
interrogative intonation:)
How about it?, What do you say
to that?, And ... ?
HORCADO -DA (var. of) ahorcado -da
HORCAR (var. of) ahorcar
HORITA or HORITITA or HORITITITA
(etc.) (vars. of) ahorita (etc.)
HORONGO (vars. of) jorongo
HORQUETA slingshot
HORQUÍA or HORQUILLA clothes pin
HOTEL: HOTEL MUNICIPAL (hum.) coun-
ty or city jail
HOY: HOY EN LA NOCHE tonight
HOYITO: HOYITO DEL CHI urinary
opening (female)
HUACHA (var. of) guacha
HUACHAR (Eng.) va. to watch, ob-
serve, watch out; ¡HUÁCHALO!
(slang) Watch out!, Be careful!

HUACHETERÍA (Eng.) washeteria, self-
service automatic laundry
HUACHIMÁN (var. of) guachimán
HUAFLERA (var. of) guaflera
HUAINO -NA (var. of) guaino -na
HUAMAZO (Eng?) (var. of) guamazo
et al.
HUANGO (var. of) guango
HUARACHAZO (slang) dance
HUARACHE (slang) mf. Mexican
citizen
HUAREAR or HUARIAR (vars. of)
guarear, guariar
HUATO (var. of) guato
HUATOSO -SA (var. of) guatoso -sa
HUAYÍN (Eng.) (var. of) guayín m.
HUAYO (dim. of) Eduardo (see also
Yayo)
HUELDEAR or HUELDIAR (Eng.) va. to
weld, solder
HUELVA, HUELVAS, etc. (vars. of)
güelva, güelvas, etc. (in turn
vars. of) vuelva, vuelvas, etc.
(pres. subj. of volver)
HUEMAZO (var. of) güemazo (see also
GUAMAZO et al.)
HUENO -NA (var. of) bueno -na
HUERCO -CA kid, brat, young child
HUERFANATO or HUERFANATORIO (vars.
of) orfanato orphanage
HUERTE (var. of) fuerte
HUESO: HUESOS mpl. (slang) dice;
HUESO SABROSO funny bone
(coll.) (point near the elbow
where the nerve may be pressed
against the bone to produce a
tingling sensation)
HUEVO: A HUEVO forcibly, by force;
HUEVO HUERO (coll.) rotten egg;
¡HUEVOS! (interj.) Hell no!
(strong negative); HUEVOS RAN-
CHEROS Mexican-style scrambled
eggs with peppers, onions, to-
matoes, etc.; TENER HUEVOS
(vulg.) to have balls (semi-
vulg. & slang), possess considerable strength of charac-
ter, intestinal fortitude
HUEVÓN -VONA (pej.) lazy, no account (coll.), good-for-nothing
HUEVONADA laziness
HUEVONEAR or HUEVONIAR (coll.) vn.
to loaf, be idle
HUEY (var. of) buey m.
HUICHACA billiard pocket
HUICHOL m. wide-brimmed straw hat
HUIFA (Eng.) (slang) wife (see also
GUAIFA)
HÚIGA, HÚIGAS, etc. (vars. of) huya,
huyas, etc. (pres. subj. of
huir)
¡HUIJE! interj. (expression used
to make fun of someone or to

provoke to anger) (see also IJE,
IJI)
HUILA or HUILACHA (slang, pej.)
prostitute, whore; two-dimen-
sional quadrangular kite
HUIMBLE (Hispanization of) Wimberly,
Texas
HUINE (Eng.) (var. of) güine m.
HUIQUÉN (Eng.) m. week-end
HUIRIHUIRI (slang) gossip, idle
talk
HUIRLOCHA (slang) jalopy, old car
HUISCLE m. (var. of) whiski (Eng.)
HUÍVORA (child language var. of)
víbora
HUIZA (slang, pej.) whore, prosti-
tute; (non-pej.) girlfriend;
fiancée
HULE m. inner tube; floor linole-
um; shoe sole; (slang) con-
dom, rubber (slang); (slang)
QUEMAR HULE to burn rubber
(slang), accelerate a car ra-
pidly from a standing position
HUMADERA (var. of) humareda
HUMADO -DA (var. of) ahumado -da
HÚNGARO -RA gypsy
HURGONEAR or HURGONIAR va. to
shake violently
HUYAR (var. of) aullar vn.
HUYIR (var. of) huir vn.

I

ICIR (var. of) decir
IDEAR or IDIAR vn. to idle the
time away by daydreaming about
things beyond one's means to
acquire or achieve
IDEOMA (var. of) idioma m. (f.)
IDEOSO -SA or IDIOSO -SA daydreamer
(cf. IDEAR, IDIAR)
IDIOMA (often f.: LA IDIOMA)
IDIOSO -SA fancier, aficionado (of
something)
IDO -DA or MEDIO -DA nuts (slang),
crazy, cuckoo (slang)
IGLE (PAS) (coll., Hispanization of)
Eagle Pass, Texas
IGNORAR (Ang.) va. to ignore, not
to pay attention to (Std. no
hacer caso)
IGUALADO -DA social-climber (ref.
to person, often overbearing,
who tries to achieve a superior social level)
IGUALAR vr. to social climb (coll.),
try to achieve a superior so-

cial level
ILUMINIO (var. of) aluminio
INACIO -CIA (vars. of) Ignacio -cia
INCONVINIENTE (var. of) inconvenien-
te
INFLUENCIA (var. of) influenza
INFRIAR (var. of) enfriar
INGLESADO -DA (non-pej.) Anglo-ized,
Anglo-like
INSPECTAR (Ang.) to inspect (Std.
inspeccionar)
INSTRUCTAR (Eng.) va. to instruct,
teach
INSTRUCTEAR or INSTRUCTIAR (vars.
of) instructar (Eng.)
IMPERIAL f. type of bleached cot-
ton cloth
IMPIDIR (var. of) impedir
IMPLEMENTO (Ang.) tool, implement
IMPLIADO -DA (var. of) empleado -da
IMPONER va. to accustom, train, get
(someone) used to: "No lo
impusiste a trabajar, por eso
es tan huevón"; vr. to get used
to, accustomed to; to be depen-
dent on (someone)
IMPRUVEAR or IMPRUVIAR (Eng.) va. &
vn. to improve
IMPUESTO -TA accustomed, used to
INCENSO (Eng?) incense (Std. incienso)
INCOMTAX (Eng.) m. income tax
INCONTRAR (var. of) encontrar
INCORDIO (slang) chicken's egg
INDECCIÓN (var. of) inyección f.
INDIADA (pej.) disorderly mob; ill-
bred persons belonging to the
same clan, etc.
INDIGESTO -TA: SENTIRSE INDIGESTO -
TA to feel bloated; to feel one
has a stomach disorder
INDIVIDO -DA (var. of) individuo -
dua
INFANTE mf. (poss. Ang.) infant,
baby
INFECCIÓN: INFECCIÓN DE LA SANGRE
(euph.) syphilis
INFILDA or INFILDER (Eng.) m. in-
fielder (baseball)
INFLENCIA (var. of) influencia
INOCENTE adj. (euph.) (ref. to
various degrees of mental re-
tardation:) "Los niños ino-
centes no pueden asistir a la
escuela con los demás niños"
INORANTE (var. of) ignorante
INORAR (var. of) ignorar
INSULTATIVO -VA (vars. of) insulta-
dor -dora
INSULTO digestive indisposition
(upset stomach, etc.)
INTELIGIR vn. (for someone to be
good at something:) "Le intelige a las matemáticas" 'He's
very good at math'; INTELIGIR-

SE CON to be in charge of:
"¿Quién se intelige con este
negocito?" 'Who's in charge
of this business?'

INTERO -RA (var. of) entero -ra

INTILIGENTE (var. of) inteligente

INTONADO -DA up on (coll.), tuned
in (slang), abreast of the latest news and happenings

INTRODUCIR (Ang.) va. to introduce,
present (two people previously
unacquainted to each other)
(Std. presentar)

IR: IR ACÁ GARCÍA (slang) to go to
the toilet (see discussion s.
GARCÍA); IR A DALLAS (slang)
to have sexual intercourse, come
across (slang), put out (slang)
(play on words: DALLAS = DAR-
LAS 'to give out with one's
sexual favors, come across with';
commentary: the expression is
pr. ir a dal las, the last two
words representing a rough His-
panicization of the name of the
Texas city, Dallas); IR A PA-
TÍN / IR A PATINA (slang) to
go on foot; IR CAYENDO POCO A
POQUITO to come around bit by
bit, yield (cease to resist)
little by little; IR CHISQUEADO -
DA or CHISQUIADO -DA to run at
top speed, go like a bat out of
hell (coll.); IR DE JILO (slang)
to run rapidly, go like a bat
out of hell (coll.); to go directly (without stopping) to
one's destination; IR DE PERLA
to have a good time; to have
good luck: "Le dieron el primer
premio. --¡Caray, le fue de
perla!"; IR DIOQUIS (see DIO-
QUIS, DE HOQUIS); IR HECHO CHILE
(slang) to run rapidly, go like
a bat out of hell (coll.); IR
HECHO MÁQUINA to be going very
rapidly; IRLE A (coll.) to bet
on: "¿Quién va a ganar?--Pues
yo le voy al campeón" ' ...--
Well I bet on the champ'; IR
PA' TRAS (Ang.) to go back,
fail to keep (i.e., one's word,
a promise, etc.); vn. to return:
"Se fue pa' tras pa' México";
IRSE A LAS GREÑAS to go at one
another in a fight which involves
pulling hair (usually said of
two women); ÍRSELE A ALGUIEN EL
SUEÑO to lose one's sleepiness,
get over one's tiredness; ÍRSELE
A ALGUIEN LA MANO to slip up,
lose control; to miscalculate;
ÍRSELE A ALGUIEN LA VOZ to hit
a sour note while singing;

IRSELE LA ONDA A ALGUIEN to go
off on a tangent; ÍRSELE A AL-
GUIEN LAS PATAS (slang) to slip
up, lose control of oneself,
lose one's head; to throw cau-
tion to the wind (often used
in a sexual context, e.g.,
"Mírala, está gorda, se le fue-
ron las patas"); SI A ÉSAS VA-
MOS If that's the case, If
that's how things stack up:
"Si a ésas vamos, yo también
puedo usar dos camisas por día"
VÁMONOS A LA FREGADA Beat it!,
Scram!; ¿VAMOS LLEGANDO ...?
How's about stopping off ...?:
"¿Vamos llegando a ca Pedro?"
'How's about stopping off at
Pedro's house?'; Y VAMOS QUE
even though: "Y no terminó su
tesis el pendejo ese, y vamos
que le dimos dos años" 'And
that S.O.B. didn't finish his
thesis, even though we gave
him two years';

IRRIGAR (Eng.) va. to irrigate

ISTAFIATE (var. of) estafeate, estafiate

IXTLE m. fiber of the century plant
(used to make lariats, etc.)

IZQUIERDISTA mf., adj. left-handed
person (Std. izquierdo -da)

J

JABALÍN m. (ref. to person whose
hair stands straight on end, as
in a crewcut)

JABLA (var. of) jaula

JACALEAR or JACALIAR vn. to habitually go around visiting one
home after another in order to
bear tales and gossip

JACALERA woman who goes from house
to house bearing tales and gossip; busy-body (coll.)

JAIBOL (m.; pl. JAIBOLES) or JAIBOLA
(f.) (Eng.) highball (cocktail)

JAIBOLEADA or JAIBOLIADA (Eng.)
cocktail party

JAIC (Eng.) m. hike, long walk in
the countryside

JAIGUEY or JAIHUEY or JAÍHUEY (Eng.)
m. highway

JAINIAR (slang) vn. to make love,
engage in the sexual act; to

engage in sexual foreplay, make out (slang)

JAINO -NA (slang) m. boy friend; fiancé; f. girl friend; fiancée

JAIPO (Eng.) (slang) needle used to inject narcotic drugs into the veins of the human body; mf. or JAIPO (m.) -PA (f.) person who "mainlines" narcotic drugs into his/her veins

JAITÓN - TONA (Eng.) high-toned (coll.), snobbish; stylish; elegant

JALADO -DA (slang) drunk; f. pull, jerk (cf. JALAR)

JALADOR -DORA hard-working, diligent, industrious

JALAR va. (slang) to steal; vn. (coll.) to work; vr. JALARSELA (vulg., slang) to masturbate: "Lo pescaron jalándosela" 'They caught him pulling away at it!; ¡JÁLALE! interj. (slang) Hurry up!, Move it!

JALE (coll.) m. work, job; HACER JALE; (coll.) to work; (slang) to steal

JALEA (slang) adj. very elegant, dressed to kill (usually with ANDAR: "Anda muy jalea") (poss. Ang?< jelly bean, ant, slant=elegant, well dressed)

JALETINA (var. of) gelatina

JALÓ (Eng.) hello

JALÓN: ANDAR DE JALÓN (slang) to be on the make (slang), be out looking for a date or a sexual partner; DE UN JALÓN once and for all; all at once: "Se tomó todo el vino de un jalón" 'He drank the wine down in a single gulp'; HACER JALONES to flirt, make passes at a member of the opposite sex; HACERLE JALÓN A ALGUIEN to make passes at someone (with amorous intentions)

JALONEAR or JALONIAR va. to jerk; to pull

JALLAR (var. of) hallar

JAMBADO -DA (slang) stolen, ripped off (slang)

JAMBAR (slang) to steal

JAMBERGA (hum., m. & f.) or JAMBORGA (m. & f.) or JAMBÓRGUER (m.) (Eng.) hamburger; HACER JAMBERGA (et al.) DE (slang) to make mince-meat of (someone), beat up soundly (in a fight)

JAMBO -BA (slang) m.,f. thief; adj. thieving

JAMBÓN - BONA (slang) m., f. thief; adj. thieving

JAMÓN m. bacon; (slang) JAMON TORTILLA straight-forward and honest person

JANDO (slang) money

JAQUETA (Eng?, Ang?) jacket, coat

JARDÍN INFANTIL m. kindergarten

JARIA (slang) hunger

JARIPEO (type of rodeo)

JAROCHA or JARUCHA lively and alert (said of women)

JASPE (slang) m. meal (dinner, supper, etc.)

JASPEAR or JASPIAR (slang) va. to eat

JASPIA (slang) hunger

JATANA (slang) guitar

JAULA (slang) jail, cage (coll.)

JAULE (slang) m. burglary

JEDER (var. of) heder

JEDIONDEZ (var. of) hediondez f.

JEDIONDO -DA (var. of) hediondo - da

JEFA (slang) wife; mother

JEFE (slang) m. father

JETEAR or JETIAR vn. to pout

JEY FÍVER (Eng.) m. or f. hay fever

JI interj. (slightly euph.) (< jijo = hijo, q.v.)

JIEDO, JIEDES, JIEDE, JEDEMOS/JIÉDEMOS, JIEDEN (vars. of) hiedo, hiedes, etc. (pres. ind. of heder)

JIJO (var. of) hijo; interjs.: ¡JIJO! (varies in intensity according to degree of emphasis, type of intonation, etc.); ¡JIJO DEL HACHA! or ¡JIJO DE LA MAÑANA! or ¡JIJO DE LA GUAYABA! (all vary in intensity, though all tend to be fairly euphemistic--'Golly Moses!' is an average gloss for most); ¡JIJOLE! interj. (varies in meaning according to intensity and situation, from a mild 'Damn!' through something much stronger)

JILO: ANDAR DE JILO to be in a hurry; IR DE JILO to pass by in a hurry; interj. ¡JILO! (rather euph.) Gosh!, Gee!; ¡JILO DE LA CHINGADA! (not quite as strong as the correspondent ¡Hijo de la chingada!); ¡JILO E LA MAÑANA! (var. of) ¡Jijo de la mañana!

JINCAR (var. of) hincar

JIORGE (var. of) Jorge

JIPO -PA (Eng.) hippopotamus; (n. & adj.) obese; m. "Hippo Size" (soft drink manufactured in San Antonio, Texas)

JIRA (Eng.) m. & f. heater, heating

device

JIRICUA pie baldness, vitiglio

JIRIMIQUEAR or JIRIMIQUIAR vn. to whimper

JIRIOLA: IR(SE) DE JIRIOLA (slang) vn. to cut classes, not to attend school

JIT (Eng.) m. hit, musical success, successful musical composition; base hit (baseball)

JITAZO (Eng.) (slang) tremendous hit, exremely popular musical composition

¡JITO! interj. (euph.) Golly!, Gosh!

JOCOQUE m. curdled milk; yogurt

JODARRIA (slang) harassment

JODEDERA (slang) harassment; nagging

JODER va. to deceive, cheat; to take sexual possession through deception; PARA ACABARLA DE JODER (set expression) To make matters worse, As if that were not enough

JODIDO -DA down and out, desitute; in poor health; (coll.) out of one's gourd (slang), crazy: "Pues ese tipo está jodido si cree que vamos a hacer todo esto en quince minutos"; ESTAR COMO LA JODIDA to be as ____ as can be (usual ref. to a negative characteristic of which both speaker and listener are cognizant, e.g.:) "Ella está como la jodida" 'She's as ugly as sin'

JODÓN -DONA ruthless, opportunistic; deceptive; EL MERO JODON (slang) the big boss, the head honcho (slang)

JOGAR (rus.) (var. of) jugar

JOL (Eng.) m. hall, corridor

JOLA (slang) money

JOLINO -NA short, not tall, not long

JOM (Eng.) m. home base (baseball)

JOMRÓN (Eng.) m. home run (baseball)

JONCHAR (Eng? < to hunch?) va. & vn. to cheat in a game of marbles by moving the marble shooter closer to the target

JONCHE: HACER JONCHE (id. to JONCHAR)

JONDO (local rendition of) Hondo, Texas

JONDO -DA (var. of) hondo -da

JONE or JONI (Eng.) (vocative, term of endearment) honey

JONQUI (Eng.) (pej.) mf. honky, hunky (both pej.), Anglo-Saxon

JONRÓN (Eng.) (var. of) jomrón m.

JOROBAS msg., fsg. (also adj.) (var. of) jorobado -da

JORONCHE (slang) mf. hunch-back

JOSCO -CA (var. of) hosco -ca; m. (fig.) bad boy

JOSLA (Eng? < hustler?) adj. keen; neat, terrific, swell, etc.

JOSLEAR or JOSLIAR (Eng? cf. JOSLA) va. & vr. to steal: "Se joslió dos dulces" 'He stole two bars of candy'

JOTINGO -GA (slang) m. faggot, male homosexual; f. lesbian

JOTITO (slang) young male homosexual

JOTO -TA (slang) m. fag, male homosexual; f., dike, lesbian

JOTQUEY (Eng.) m. hot cake (type of pancake)

JOVENTUD (var. of) juventud f.

JUAN (slang) m. cockroach (see also TALTASCUAN et. al.)

JUANI (dim. of) Juan

JUANITA (slang) marihuana

JUAQUÍN (var. of) Joaquín

JUARILES (also orthog. var. JUARILEZ) (slang) Ciudad Juárez, México

JUDÁS: ESTAR UNO QUE SE LO LLEVA JUDAS to be very angry, very hot under the collar (coll.); ME LLEVA JUDÁS (set expression) Well I'll be, Well I'll be darned

JUEGAR (rus.) (var. of) jugar

JUEGO (var. of) fuego

JUERTE (var. of) fuerte

JUEZ DE PAZ (Ang.) m. justice of the peace

JUGADA (ref. to a woman who has frequently indulged her carnal appetites, who has "played around" a lot

JUGARSE PLANCHA to be slow to react (because of lack of preparation, laziness, etc.)

JUGUETÓN -TONA (hum.) m. adulteror; f. adultress

JUI, JUI(S)TE(S), JUE, JUIMOS, JUERON (vars. of) fui, fuiste, etc. (pret. of ser/ir)

JUILA (Eng? < wheeler?) bicycle

JUISQUE (Eng.) m. whiskey

JUIZA (var. of) huiza

JULIA (slang, underw.) police wagon, paddy wagon (coll.); ambulance

JUM (Eng.) (var. of) jomrón m.

JUMADERA (var. of) humadera, humareda

JUMAR (var. of) fumar

JUMARADA (var. of) humarada

JUMEDAD (var. of) humedad f.

JUMO (var. of) humo

JUMRÓN (Eng.) (var. of) jomrón m.

JÚNIOR (Eng.) m. and adj. junior (see also YÚNIER et al.)

JUNRÓN (Eng.) (var. of) jomrón m.

JUNTAR vr. to become reconciled

(usually ref. to lovers,
husbands and wives, etc., who.
have separated)
JUNTO: ANDAR JUNTOS to go steady
(coll.) (ref. to boy and girl
who date each other exclusively);
JUNTO DE (var. of) junto a:
"Vive junto de su hermano"
JUQUEAR or JUQUIAR (Eng.) vn. to
play hookey, absent oneself
from school (see also JUQUI)
JUQUI (Eng.) m. hookey, unexcused
absence from school; JUGAR JUQUI
to play hookey, absent oneself
from school without permission
JURA (slang) fsg. policeman; fpl.
police force
JURGONEAR or JURGONIAR (vars. of)
hurgonear, hurgoniar
JUSTICIA (slang) fsg. police force
JUT m. (Eng.) hood (aut.)

K

KANSES (Eng., var. of) Kansas
KARMESA (orthog, var. of) carmesa

L

LABERINTO scandal; noise; intrigue
LABERINTOSO -SA squeamish; exagger-
ating; mf. rabble rouser
LABIO: LABIO CUCHO harelip
LABIOSO -SA mf. flatterer; smooth
talker (coll.)
LABOR f. cultivated field; field
used for farming
LA: LA DE MALAS (coll.) bad luck:
"Le tocó la de malas" 'He had
some bad luck'
LADO: BUSCARLE A ALGUIEN POR SU
LADO to approach someone from
his good side (fig.), get some-
one in a good moment; EL MEJOR
LADO (Eng.) someone's best side,
most appealing personality
traits; EL OTRO LADO (coll.)
Mexico; (see also DARLE A AL-
GUIEN POR SU LADO; ESTAR DE
LADO)

LADRERÍA barking of dogs
LAGARTIZO (var. of) lagartijo
LAGARTO -TA alligator
LAIRA (Eng.) f. lighter, cigarette
lighter
LALO -LA (dims. of) Eulalio -lia
LAMBEACHE or LAMBIACHE (vulg.) ass-
kisser (vulg.), flatter, obse-
quious person (mf.)
LAMBECULOS (var. of) lameculos mfsg.
LAMBEHUEVOS (vulg.) mfsg. apple-
polisher, ass-kisser (vulg.)
LAMBER (var. of) lamer
LAMBICHE (var. of) lambeache, lambiache (mf.)
LAMBIDA (var. of) lamida
LAMBIÓN -BIONA mf. flatterer,
apple-polisher, ass-kisser
(vulg.)
LAMBIZQUE mf. (coll.) freeloader,
person who avoids paying
LAMBIZQUIAR (var. of) lambuzquiar
LAMBUZCO -CA hollow leg (coll.),
person perpetually looking for
something to eat; person perpetually eating
LAMBUZQUEAR or LAMBUZQUIAR va. to
nibble at food in between meal-
times; to go around looking
for food to eat in between meal-
times; vn. to be obsequiously
and hypocritically courteous
LAMEACHE or LAMIACHE (vars. of)
lambeache, lambiache (mf.)
LAMECULOS (vulg.) mfsg. flatterer,
apple-polisher, ass-kisser
(vulg.)
LAMER (vulg.) va. to kiss ass
(vulg.), ingratiate oneself
(with someone)
LAMPAREAR or LAMPARIAR (slang) va.
to look at: "Está lampariando
a las batas que pasan"
LAMPREADO -DA or LAMPRIADO -DA
roasted; roasted with a beaten
egg covering
LAMPREAR or LAMPRIAR va. to roast
meat; to cover a roast with
beaten eggs
LANA (slang) money; LANA MORADO:
ANDAR LANA MORADO (slang) to
be in love with (play on words:
lana morado = ena-morado)
LANERO -RA wool worker; person who
gathers the sheep's wool from
the ground and places it on a
platform where it is bundled
LÁNGARA sly, astute, cunning:
"Pedro es una lángara"
LANUDO -DA flushed with money (ref.
to person carrying around an
unaccustomed amount of money
or to a person suddenly much
richer than before)

LAO (var. of) lado

LÁPIZ msg. & mpl. (word wrongly interpreted as already bearing the plural marker, thus") "Traigo un lápiz...no, parece que traigo dos lápiz"

LAQUIAR (Eng.) va. to lock shut

LARGADO -DA estranged, abandoned (by a spouse): "Pobre María está largada iy con tanta familia!"

LARGAR va. to abandon (leave) one's spouse, run away from one's mate: "Juan largó a su esposa"

LÁSTICO (var. of) elástico

LASTIMADA action and effect of injuring or hurting (physically or emotionally)

LASTIMÓN m. (var. of) lastimada

LATA (see DAR LA LATA)

LATIDO stomach spasms or palpitations

LAVADERO act of washing clothes

LAVADO douche

LAZAZO blow with a rope

LAZO clothesline

LEACHO (var. of) liacho

LECIÓN (var. of) lección f.

LECTRICIDAD (var. of) electricidad f.

LECHE f.(vulg.) (male) semen, sperm; LECHE AGRIA sour milk, curdled milk; MOSCA EN LECHE dark-complected person married to (or associating with) a fair-skinned person)

LECHUDO -DA (slang) lucky

LECHUZA bat

LEIDO -DA (var. of) leído -da (ppart. of leer)

LEJECITOS (iron.) adv. quite far away, quite a distance

LENCHO -CHA lame; ANDAR LENCHO to be lame; to be foolish

LENCHO -CHA (dim. of) Lorenzo -za

LENGÓN - GONA (var. of) lenguón -guona

LENGONEAR or LENGONIAR (slang) vn. to gossip; to chat, converse

LENGUA (slang) necktie; BULLIR LA LENGUA to gossip; to talk excessively; ECHAR LENGUA to work excessively; to walk a long distance on a wild goose chase (coll.), walk a long distance in vain; LENGUA DE ZAPATO shoe's tongue (Std. lengüeta de zapato); LENGUA GRANDE big-mouthed (coll.), talkative, garrulous; LENGUA, LENGUA PA' LORENZO (set expression used to poke fun at someone who has walked a long distance on a wild goose chase,

i.e., without accomplishing his objective); TENER LENGUA MOCHA to talk very little; TENER LENGUA SUELTA to talk frequently; to be garrulous; TIRAR LENGUA (slang) to talk too much, be very garrulous

LENGUÓN -GUONA m., f. liar; malicious gossiper; foul-mouthed, filthy-mouthed

LENTODOS (slang) mpl. eyeglasses

LEÑA (slang) marihuana

LEÑITO (slang) marihuana cigarette

LEÓN, LEONA greedy; ambitious; unrelenting in the pursuit of something: "Ella es una leona para las estampillas; nunca deja de pedírnoslas cuando viene de compras"; TIRAR A LEÓN to ignore, not pay attention to

LEPE (coll.) mf. brat, squirt, annoying young child; short-legged, heavy-set person

LER (var. of) leer

LES: JUGAR A LA LES to play tag; TRAER LA LES (also TRAERLA) to be "it" in a game of tag (LES <Eng. last, i.e., 'Last one in is the loser'?, or perhaps <lass 'young girl'?)

LEVANTADA pick-up, woman who allows herself to be solicited for sexual activity: "Tú eres pura levantada" 'You're nothing but a pick-up'

LEVANTAR: LEVANTAR ACEITE (slang) to blow off steam (coll.), get angry; LEVANTAR CHANCLA / LEVANTAR CHANCLE (slang) to move rapidly, really "pick up one's feet" (coll.); LEVANTAR EL ALARME / LEVANTAR LA ALARMA to raise an alarm, give warning; LEVANTAR LA BANDERA (Ang.) to raise the flag (i.e., run the flag up the flag-pole) (Std. izar la bandera); LEVANTARSE CON LAS GALLINAS (Ang?) to get up with the chickens (fig.), arise very early in the morning

LEVANTE (slang) mf. pick-up, person "picked up" (usually in an anonymous fashion) by another for subsequent sexual activity; act of picking up for subsequent sexual activity

LEVANTÓN m. boost in one's morale: "Hay que darle un levantón, está muy triste"

LEY (slang) fsg. police force; METER A LA LEY / METER EN LA LEY to bring suit against (someone)

LEYER (var. of) leer

LIACHO badly-tied bundle (e.g., of clothes)

LIAL (var. of) leal

LICAR (slang) va. to look at, observe: "Está licando la tienda que piensa robar;" to see

LICO (dim. of) Federico

LICOREAR or LICORIAR (slang) va. to look at, observe; to see (cf. LICAR)

LICUADOR m. blender, machine used to blend food

LICHA (dim. of) Alicia

LIEBRE (slang) f. odd job

LIMA (slang) shirt

LIMAR (slang) va. to degrade, humiliate

LIMBURGO (slang) Edinburg, Texas

LIMOSNERO -RA: LIMOSNERO Y CON GARROTE (ref. to person who wants to have his/her cake and eat it too, one who wants a mile when offered an inch, etc.)

LIMPIO -PIA (slang) cleaned-out, stone broke, penniless

LINAR (var. of) alinear

LINDA (slang) vagina; QUITAR LA LINDA to cause to lose one's virginity, to deflower (said of women): "Si no te cuidas te van a quitar la linda"

LÍNEA penny pitching (mild type of gambling game); (Ang.) line, falsehood used to convince: "Le estaba dando una línea" 'He was handing (feeding) her a line'; ANDAR EN LA LÍNEA / ESTAR EN LA LÍNEA (coll.) to be drunk; TIRAR LÍNEA (slang) to flatter, "hand someone a line" (slang)

LINIA (var. of) línea

LINOLIO (var. of) linóleo

LINTERNA small store or business; (slang) eye; (coll.) fire-fly

LÍO (Eng.) Leo (proper name)

LIÓN (var. of) león m.

LIONA (slang) jail

LIPESTIC or LIPESTIQUE or LIPISTIC or LIPISTIQUE (Eng.) m. lipstick

LIQUEAR or LIQUIAR (Eng.) va. to lick; vn. to leak

LIQUELLAR (slang) va. to see; to look

LIRA (slang) guitar

LÍRICO -CA self-taught (ref. to persons who play instruments "by ear" or to persons who recite poems etc. from memory without having learned them from a script); a born ____ (ref. to someone who is said to have inherent talent for something, e. g.:) "un músico lírico" ' a

born musician'

LIS m. (Eng.) lease, rental contract

LISA (slang) shirt

LISTERINA (Eng.) mouth-wash (in general) (loan metonymy Listerine)

LISTONES mpl. children's game played thus: the children divide into two bands; band one decides upon a particular color, which band two then tries to guess by knocking on an imaginary "door" and participating in the following dialogue: "Tantan.--¿Quién es? (response from band two) -- La vieja Inés.-- ¿Qué quería? -- Un listón. -- ¿De qué color?" At this point the second band names a color. If named correctly, band two receives a point; if not then it is the turn of band one to guess the color

LITO -TA (dims. of) Carmen (mf.), Carmelito (m.), Carmelita (f.)

LIVIANO -NA adj. (ref. to persons with a bad reputation); f. woman of ill repute

LOBATISMO (Ang.) cub scouting

LOBI (Eng.) m. lobby, hall, vestibule

LOBICA (slang, Hispanization of) Lubbock, Texas

LOBO (hum. slang, Hispanization of) Lubbock, Texas

LOBO (fig.) astute and clever person

LOCARIO -RIA (slang) crazy

LÓCAT (slang, Hispanization of) Lockhart, Texas

LOCO -CA (slang) drunk; m. (slang) dollar bill; ANDAR LOCO -CA (slang) to be high on narcotic drugs; LOCO DE ATIRO crazy through and through; LOCO -CA ENMAIZADO -DA (coll.) crazy old fool, doddering old idiot; TIRAL AL LOCO (slang) to ignore: "Se enojaron porque los tiraron al loco"; ¡QUÉ LOCO! or ¡QUÉ LOCOTE! (slang) (set expression used to praise an accomplishment:) "Gané el primer premio. --¡Qué loco!"

LOCOTE: ANDAR LOCOTE (slang) to be high on narcotic drugs

LOGO (var. of) luego (adv.)

LONAS fpl. overalls, coveralls (type of men's workclothes)

LONCHAR (Eng.) vn. to eat lunch (see also LONCHEAR, LONCHIAR)

LONCHE (Eng.) m. lunch (light midday meal); sandwich (Std. emparedado): "¿Cuántos lonches quieres hoy?"; ECHARLE A ALGUIEN SU LONCHE (slang) to tell someone off, bawl someone out (slang); "¡Qué bueno que le echó su lonche; lo merecía!"; ECHARSE A ALGUIEN DE LONCHE to defeat someone in a sports competition; to beat someone up in a fight

LONCHEAR or LONCHIAR (Eng.) vn. to eat lunch (see also LONCHAR)

LONCHERA (Eng., cf. LONCHE) lunch pail, lunch bucket (container used to carry one's lunch to work)

LONCHERÍA (Eng., cf. LONCHE) lunch- room; small café

LONDRE or LONDRI (Eng.) m. laundry, place where clothes are cleaned; laundry, dirty clothes to be cleaned

LONJONUDO -DA very fat and flabby

LORE: ¡JI LORE! (Eng. Lordy, dim. of Lord) interj. (euph.) Lordy me! (cf. other interjs. with JIJO)

LOS (slang) Los Angeles, California: "Ese bato es de Los" 'That guy is from Los Angeles'

LOS (var. of) nos (1st pers. pl. object pron.): "Él siempre que los ve los pide que véngamos a casa" 'Every time he sees us he asks us to come over to his house'

LOSOTROS -TRAS (var. of) nosotros - tras

LUCARIO -RIA (var. of) locario -ria

LUCAS (slang) adj. mfsg. crazy, foolish; TIRAR A LUCAS (slang) to ignore

LUCE or LUCI (dim. of) Lucía

LUCIR vr. to show off, act ostenta- tiously

LUCHA (dim. of) Lucía, Luz

LUCHA: HACERLE LA LUCHA A ALGUIEN to try to convince someone (usually against his/her will), try to get someone to change his/her mind

LUCHISTA mf. go-getter (coll.), a- gressive person

LUCHÓN -CHONA (id. to LUCHISTA supra)

LUEGO: LUEGO LUEGO or LUEGO LUEGUITO adv. right away, immediately

LUENGA (var. of) lengua

LULI (Hispanization of) Luling, Texas

LUIS MORALES (hum.) m. man with low moral standards (bilingual play on words: loose morals)

LUISA MORALES (hum.) f. woman with low moral standards (bilingual wordplay, cf. LUIS MORALES supra)

LUMBRE: SER MUY LUMBRE (said of a person who wears things out,

i.e., clothes, or who puts them in a state of disrepair in a short time); SACAR LUMBRE to harp on the same subject, talk incessantly about the same to- pic

LUMBRE f. light, match (for light- ing cigarettes, etc.): "Dame lumbre" 'Give me a light'

LUMBRERO -RA firefighter, fireman

LUMBRIZ (fig.) mf. thin (person) (var. of lombriz, a form which is seldom heard in Texas)

LUNA menstruation period; ESTAR MALA DE LA LUNA to be having one's (menstruation) period

LUNADA moonlight party

LUP (Eng.) m. loop

LUPE (dim. of) Guadalupe (m., f.)

LUQUIS (slang) mf. crazy person

LURIO -RIA or LURIAS (mfsg.) (slang) crazy: "Ese bato está lurias" 'That guy is crazy'

LUTO: TRAER LUTO (fig.) to have dirty fingernails

LL

LLAMAR vr. to go back on one's word, retract a promise: "Car- los se llamó, por eso estoy enojado"

LLAMÓN -MONA person who goes back on his/her word, fails to car- ry out a promise

LLANTA (fig., hum.) doughnut; (fig., slang) "spare tire" (slang), role of fat around a person's waist; fpl. gifts given at a wedding

LLANTÓN -TONA (slang, pej.) U.S. black person

LLEGAR: LLEGARLE A ALGUIEN to get to someone, get the best of someone; ¿VAMOS LLEGANDO ... ? How's about stopping off ...?: "¿Vamos llegando a ca Pedro?" 'How's about stopping off at Pedro's house?'

LLENAR va. & vr. to soil, dirty, stain (esp. clothes): "Le llenaste la camisa de jugo" 'You stained his shirt with juice'; vn. LLENAR DE _____ to have enough _____,e.g., LLENAR DE SUEÑO to have enough sleep

LLEVAR va. LLEVAR PA' TRAS (Ang.)

to return, take back; to retract
(e.g., a promise), go back on
(one's word); vn. LLEVAR UNA
FREGUIZA to have a hard time of
(something); vr. to kid around
(slang), direct humor towards
(someone) with apparent offensive intent though never with
genuine malice; LLEVARLA to
pay for, be given the responsibility for, have to shoulder the
blame for: "Cuando el hogar se
desbarata la mujer es la que
la lleva" 'When a home breaks
up it's the woman who pays for
it'; to take out on: "Todo el
día el profesor mira a las mu-
chachas bonitas y después cuando llega a casa es la mujer la
que la lleva" 'All day the pro-
fessor is looking at pretty
girls and then when he gets
home he takes it out on his
wife'; LLEVARSE A ALGUIEN EL
TREN / LLEVARSE A ALGUIEN LA
CHINGADA / LLEVARSE A ALGUIEN
LA JODIDA (vulg.) (fixed expressions): "¡Me lleva la
chingada!" 'Well I'll be doubled
damned!'; (also used in the
sense of 'to find oneself in
a tight spot': "¡Ya me llevaba
el tren!" 'I was really in
trouble then!'); LLEVARSE A
ALGUIEN to get the best of
one in a business deal, "take"
someone (slang): "Ese chico sí
que te llevó" 'That boy really
got the best of you'; (slang)
to knife (someone); LLEVARSE
DE ENCUENTRO to run over (someone)
LLORADA act of crying: "Tuvo su
buena llorada" 'He had a real
good cry'
LLORAR: YA NI LLORAR ES BUENO No use
crying over spilled milk
LLORETAS mfsg. crybaby, whimperer
LLORIDO cries, act of crying: "Nos
despertaron sus lloridos" 'His
crying woke us up'
LLORONA (slang) patrol car (police);
fire engine; siren (of a fire
engine or a police car); LA
LLORONA: ghost-woman who,
according to folk legend, killed
her baby and afterwards threw
it into the water; when she died
she was forced to atone for her
crime by wandering along the
banks of the river, mourning
the child; many towns and vil-
lages are said to have their
own "local Lloronas" who haunt

the banks of the local stream
LLOVEDERO -RA mf. heavy rainfall,
cloudburst; continuous rainfall

M

MACALEN (Hispanization of) McAllen,
Texas
MACALILILILIÁ children's game in
which the participants form two
human chains facing each other;
a type of sung dialogue trans-
pires, during which one child
and then another asks something
of a child from the other group
MACANAZO blow with a blackjack
MACANEAR or MACANIAR va. to strike
over the head with a blackjack
or other heavy instrument
MACÁNICO -CA (var. of) mecánico -ca
MACANO -CA adj. cheap, common,
ordinary; f. cheapskate, parsimonious person; blackjack
(weapon)
MACETA (slang) head; (slang) hand;
slow poke, person who acts or
learns slowly
MACITA beautiful and desirable woman; (slang, often vocative)
sweet mamma
MACIZAR va. to secure something for
oneself, appropriate
MACIZO (slang) boy friend; gang
leader; favorite son (ref. to
local or regional politicians
who enjoy considerable popular-
ity)
MACUACHE mf. useless person
MACUCO -CA old
MACUECO -CA left-handed
MACHACAR: MACHACAR LA MUELA (slang)
to eat
MACHETE adj. (var. of) machetón -
tona; m. (slang) tomboy; mfpl.
KID MACHETES (Eng. 'kid' +
machetes) (ref. to person who
does everything wrong)
MACHETEAR or MACHETIAR va. to do a
job clumsily, leave a job half
done
MACHETÓN -TONA lazy; clumsy, awkward
MACHÍN -CHINA strong; outstanding,
excellent
MACHITO type of Mexican food prepared in the same way as the
chittling and consisting of the
same ingredients (pig entrails)

MACHO adj. very masculine, studly (slang); m. type of roast dish of liver, sweetbreads and other meat; adv. A LO MACHO in a manly manner: "Pórtate a lo macho" 'Act like a man' ; NO APEARSE DE SU MACHO / NO BAJARSE DE SU MAHCO to be unyielding, stubborn (in an opinion or on a stand one has taken)

MACHÓN -CHONA adj. (var. of amachón -chona 'stubborn'); f. woman who acts mannishly; tomboy

MADAMA (Eng.) madame (title of address which maids give to the women they work for)

MADERA flattery; MADERA GACHA flattery, adulation; falsehood, lie; interj. ¡MADERA (GACHA)! Hog wash!, Bull roar!; (see also DAR MADERA)

MADEREAR or MADERIAR va. to flatter; to lie, deceive; vr. to pass the time; to boast, brag

MADRERA or MADERÍA lumber yard

MADERISTA mf. braggart; liar; flatterer

MADRE f. (slang) shapely and sexy woman; ACÁ LA MADRE DE LOS BURROS / ACÁ LA MADRE DE LOS CABALLOS adv. very far away; DAR EN LA MERA MADRE / DAR EN TODA LA MADRE (slang) to beat up severely (usually in a fist fight); ECHARLE A ALGUIEN LA MADRE / MENTARLE A ALGUIEN DE LA MADRE to insult someone by referring to his/her mother (in however veiled or cryptic a fashion); ECHAR MADRES to curse, speak obscenities; EN LA MADRE where it hurts (coll.), in a vulnerable spot (physical or emotional): "Le van a dar en la madre"; ¡MADRE SANTA! interj. (fairly euph.) Good Lord! Heavens!; NO IMPORTARLE A ALGUIEN MADRE not to give a damn about anything; NO TENER MADRE (expression used as mild or hum. criticism of someone's boldness or bad behavior); NO VALER MADRE not to be worth a damn; ¡PURA MADRE! interj. Hell no!, The hell (you say)!; ¡QUÉ PADRE MADRE! (slang) What a gorgeous hunk of woman!; (see also: A TODA MADRE s. TODO, DAR EN LA MADRE, DE A MADRE)

MADRECITA (slang) beautiful and sexy woman

MADRUGUERO -RA early riser

MAGACÍN or (orthog. var.) MAGAZÍN (Eng.) magazine, periodical

MAGUE (dim. of) Margarita (Eng. Maggie?)

MAIESTRO -TRA or MAISTRO -RA (var. of) maestro -tra

MAIQUE (Eng.) (dim.) Mike (< Michael)

MAIQUE pron. I; me; mine (probable hum. substitution of MAIQUE Mike, Eng., + my/mine)

MAIZ (var. of) maíz m.

MAJE adj. (slang) dumb, ignorant; HACERLE MAJE A ALGUIEN to make a fool of someone

MAJADERO -RA loud mouth (coll.) (ref. to boisterous and aggressive talker)

MAL adv./adj. MAL AVERIGUADO -DA hot-tempered, easily provoked; MAL DADO -DA damaging (ref. to a hard blow to the body's more vulnerable parts); MAL DE HIEL gall bladder disease; MAL DE LA SANGRE (euph.) syphilis

MALAJOS interj. (used to express impatience) Dammit to hell!; ¡MALAJOS SEAS! Damn you!

MALAMÉ m. corn, maize; chicken feed

MALANCO -CA somewhat rotten (fruit); sick; slightly under the weather (coll., ref. to persons who are mildly sick); mean, base, vile; SALIR MALANCO -CA to turn out to be bad (ref. to persons, e.g., a bad spouse, a bad son, etc.)

MALANCON -CONA sick, ill; disreputable (ref. to persons); SALIR MALANCÓN -CONA (id. to SALIR MALANCO -CA)

MALAVERIGUADO -DA pugnacious, quarrelsome

MALCREADAR or MALCRIADAR to talk back to, be insolent with: "No le malcriadees a tus mayores" 'Don't talk back to your elders'

MALCRIADO -DA sassy, impudent

MALDICIENTO -TA (var. of) maldiciente

MALDITO -TA superior: "Ella se cree muy maldita" 'She thinks she's really some big deal' (coll.)

MALE (Eng.) Molly (personal name)

MALECITO slight but bothersome cold in the head; cold on the verge of becoming flu

MALES (mpl.) (var. of) malas 'enfermedades'; ¿CÓMO SIGUE DE MALES? (set expression) How are things with you?; PARA COLMO DE MIS MALES (set expression) To make things worse, As if that weren't enough

MALETA baby's excrement found on a diaper

MALETUDO -DA baggy (ref. to person wearing baggy pants)

MALHAYA or MALHAYA SEA interjs. Cursed be ... ! "¡Malhaya sea el día en que naciste!"

MALI (Eng.) (var. of) Male 'Molly'

MALIA or MALILLA m. male actor who plays the "heavy" (villain) in movies; adj. cruel

MALICIÓN (rus.) (var. of) maldición f.

MALINCHE mf. & adj. bad, evil; turncoat, betrayer

MALO -LA adj. MALA DIGESTIÓN (pleonasm for) indigestion; MAL GENIO bad tempered; MAL HABLADO -DA foul-mouthed, given to insults; MALA REATA / MALA RIATA m. tough guy (coll.), mean bastard: "No hay que negarlo, es mala riata"; MALA YERBA (fig.) bad seed, person marked for tragedy or bad deeds from birth onward; untrustworthy person; DE MALAS at least: "De malas no perdí todo el dinero"; LA DE MALAS bad luck: "Le tocó la de malas" 'He had some bad luck'

MALORA mf. & adj. perverse, malevolent: "Pedro es un malora"; f. evil deed

MALPASADO -DA ill-nourished; irregularly fed

MALPASAR vr. not to eat regularly

MALTRATADO -DA beat, beaten down (ref. to someone who shows all the signs of having lived a hard life); f. reprimand, scolding

MALVA adj. astute, clever

MALLATE (orthog. var. of) mayate

MALLUGADO -DA (var. of) magullado-da

MALLUGAR (var. of) magullar

MALLUGÓN m. (var. of) magullón / magulladura / magullamiento

MAMA (Eng.) mamma (Std. mamá)

MAMACITA (slang) pretty girl

MAMADA act of sponging off of someone (coll.), living at someone else's expense

MAMADERA sinecure

MAMADOR -DORA sponger (coll.), parasite, person who lives off a sinecure

MAMÁ GRANDE grandmother (Std. abuela)

MAMALECHE f. hopscotch (children's game) (see also BEBELECHE)

MAMALÓN -LONA (slang) m. male homosexual; f. lesbian

MAMAR va. & vn. to sponge (coll.), live off of someone else's work or income; MAMAR CHICHE to be fed from the breast (said of babies): "El bebé mama chiche, no necesita botella"; to sponge (coll.) (id. to MAMAR); MAMAR Y DAR TOPE to have one's cake and eat it too (coll., ref. to the desire to receive the maximum possible)

MAMASES (var. of) mamás (pl. of mamá) fpl.

MAMASOTA (slang) beautiful woman

MAMI (Eng.) f. mommy, mamma

MAMIS fsg. (var. of) mami

MAMÓN m. baby's pacifier

MANA (var. of) hermana; (often used in the vocative and then not necessarily to one's own sister): "Oye, mana" 'Listen woman'

MANCILLA (var. of) manecilla

MANCORNÍA / MANCORNILLA or MANCUERNÍA (usually fpl.) cufflinks

MANCHA NEGRA black sheep (fig.), member of a family who brings disgrace upon the rest

MANDA religious vow; PAGAR UNA MANDA to fulfill a religious vow

MANDADERO -RA errand boy/girl; messenger

MANDADO errand; order (i.e., of groceries, at or from a store); groceries, foodstuffs

MANDAR: MANDAR A LA CHINGADA / MANDAR AL DIABLO / MANDAR A LA FREGADA / MANDAR A LA PORRA to tell (someone) to go to hell (coll.), dismiss someone in extreme anger; MANDAR A LA CHINITA POR TU AMOR (euph. var. of MANDAR A LA CHINGADA et al.) to tell someone to go to "heck"; MANDAR MUY LEJOS to tell someone to go fly a kite (fig.), tell someone off, get angry at someone; ¿QUIÉN TE MANDA? (¿QUIÉN ME MANDA? etc.) Who told you to get involved in this business?

MANEA brake (on a vehicle); ECHAR LA(S) MANEA(S) to apply the brakes, put the brakes on (lit. and fig.; fig.= to restrain)

MANEADO -DA or MANIADO -DA limited in talent, with limited competency

MANEAR or MANIAR va. to brake

MANEJADOR -DORA m., f. (Ang.) manager; MANEJADOR -DORA DE LA CIUDAD (Ang.) city manager

MANEJERA handlebars (on a bicycle); steering wheel (on a car); any

type of handle; ÍRSELE A ALGUIEN
LA MANEJERA to lose control of
the steering wheel

MANFLOR -FLORA m. male homosexual;
f. lesbian

MANGA (slang) attractive (adj. ref.
to persons); sharp dresser
(coll.), person who dresses sty-
lishly; fpl. ARISCAR MANGAS to
roll up one's sleeves (for any
reason, but esp. in preparation
for a fist fight)

MANGAZA (slang) girl with an attractive figure

MANGO -GA mf. handle (of a kitchen
utensil; of any apparatus); m.
(slang) penis; PAJUELEARLE EL
MANGO A ALGUIEN to be good at
something, excel: "A Godofredo
le pajuela el mango pa' jugar
beisbol"

MANIJAR (var. of) manejar

MANIJERA (var. of) manejera

MANIL (slang) m. money

MANITA: DAR (UNA) MANITA to lend a
helping hand; ANDAR HASTA LAS
MANITAS to be very drunk

MANITO (var. of) hermanito; ANDAR
MANITOS to be real buddy-buddy
(slang), be on very friendly
terms

MANO (var. of) hermano; (coll.)
friend, buddy, pal; (also used
as a verbal stalling device, i.
e., inserted when the speaker
cannot think of what to say
next); fpl. CHOCAR (LAS) MANOS
to shake hands; ESTAR A MANOS /
PONERSE A MANOS / QUEDARSE A
MANOS to owe nothing to anyone, be even (coll.); to have
avenged oneself; IRLE A ALGUIEN
A LA MANO to discipline a child
by spanking him/her; ÍRSELE A
ALGUIEN LA MANO to slip up,
lose control; to miscalculate;
MANO A MANO on equal terms,
even, tied; METER MANO (vulg.)
to engage in manual coitus,
insert one's finger into a
vagina to simulate copulation;
to engage in enthusiastic and
vigorous sexual foreplay; PA-
SÁRSELE A ALGUIEN LA MANO
(var. of ÍRSELE A ALGUIEN LA
MANO, supra); SALIR A MANOS to
break even in a game of chance

MANOPLA (slang) hand

MANOSEADA or MANOSIADA (ref. to a
woman who has indulged her carnal appetites frequently, a
a woman who has been "handled"
frequently

MANOSEADERA or MANOSIADERA act of

"handling" a woman; sexual foreplay

MANOSEADOR or MANOSIADOR m. (ref.
to man who "handles" or engages
in sexual foreplay with a woman)

MANOSEAR or MANOSIAR va. to handle,
pet, paw (etc., i.e., engage in
vigorous sexual foreplay)

MANOSEO (id. to MANOSEADERA, supra)

MANQUE conj. (var. of) aunque

MANTELITO table napkin

MANTENIDO -DA m. gigolo; f. kept
woman, mistress

MANTEQUÍA (var. of) mantequilla

MANTIA (var. of) mantilla

MANZANEAR or MANZANIAR va. to seek
to gain favor through gifts

MAÑANEAR or MAÑANIAR (slang) va. to
steal

MAÑANITAS fpl. early morning serenade on the occasion of someone's birthday, typically sung
outside the house of the cele-
brant

MAPA or (more frequently) MAPE (both
m.) (Eng.) mop (cf. MOPE et al.)

MAPEADA or MAPIADA action and effect
of mopping (Eng., cf. MAPA,
MAPE et al.)

MAPEADOR or MAPIADOR (Eng.) m. mop;
person who mops floors, mopper
(see also MAPERO -RA)

MAPEAR or MAPIAR (Eng.) va. to mop
(see also MOPEAR et al.)

MAPERO -RA (Eng.) person who mops
floors, mopper (see also MAPEA-
DOR et al.)

MÁQUINA car, automobile; (coll.)
fire engine; locomotive; HECHO -
CHA MÁQUINA (coll.) adv. very
rapidly (see also A TODA MÁQUI-
NA); MÁQUINA DE (CORTAR) ZACATE
lawn mower

MAQUIS or MAQUISHUEL (slang, Hispanization of) Maxwell, Texas

MARACA (slang) dollar, dollar bill

MARAVIOSO -SA (var. of) maravilloso
-sa

MARCA person ostracized by his/her
own peers or compatriots

MARCADO (var. of) mercado

MARCADO -DA scar-faced

MARCAR va. to brand, scar

MARCHANTA woman customer

MARCHO (slang) convict, prisoner

MARGAYATES mpl. confusion, disorder

MARÍA JUANITA (slang) marihuana

MARICOCAIMORFI (slang) mf. person
who habitually uses marihuana,
cocain and morphine

MARIGUANA (var. of) marihuana

MARIGUANO -NA or MARIHUANO -NA habitual marihuana user

MARIJUANA (var. of) marihuana

MARIOLA (slang) marihuana
MARIPOSA (slang) prostitute
MARITATA mf. street vendor, peddler
MARMAJA (slang) money
MAROMA sommersault (see also MARO-
  META)
MAROMEAR or MAROMIAR va. to set a
  trap for, seek to entrap; vn.
  to turn sommersaults; (fig.) to
  betray
MAROMEO act of betrayal
MAROMETA sommersault (see also MA-
  ROMA)
MAROTA tomboy, slightly masculine
  girl
MARQUETA (Eng.) market; meat market
MARQUETERO -RA (Eng., cf. MARQUETA)
  clerk in a store or market;
  butcher
MARTIAR or MARTILLAR (slang) to eat
MARTILLO or MARTÍO (slang) food
MARZO (slang) daffy, screwy, slight-
  ly crazy; FEBRERO LOCO Y MARZO
  OTRO POCO a little bit crazier with each passing day
MARRANA (pej.) bitch (term of insult); MARRANA CUINA (pej.) fat
  and ugly old bitch (insult di-
  rected at a woman)
MARRAR (var. of) amarrar
MARROQUIANO -NA (var. of) parroquiano
  -na
MARRULLERO -RA lazy, sluggish
MÁS: MÁS AL RATO (pleonasm) (var.
  of) al rato; MÁS ANTES (pleonastic var. of) antes 'before,
  beforehand'; MÁS DESPUÉS (pleonasm) (var. of) después; MÁS
  MEJOR (pleonastic var. of) mejor
  'better'; MÁS QUE QUIÉN SABE QUÉ
  a lot, a great amount: "Ahora
  la ama más que quién sabe qué";
  MÁS NADA (var. of) nada más:
  "No tengo más nada acá conmigo"
  'I don't have anything else with
  me here'; MÁS _____QUE QUIÉN
  SABE QUÉ (coll.) more _____
  than you could possibly imagine;
  ENTRE MÁS ____ MÁS the more
  ____ the more
MASA (slang) mf. slowpoke, lethar-
  gic person; flabby, blubber-
  bellied (coll.)
MASACOTA or MASACOTE f. disorganized
  mixture, jumble of various items
MASCADA scarf
MÁSCARA (coll.) woman with an ugly
  face
MASERO -RA vendor of ready-made
  dough for tortillas
MASES (Hispanization of) Mathis,
  Texas
MASOTA beautiful and sexy woman,

red hot mamma (slang)
MASUDO -DA doughy, not well-baked
  (ref. to pastry or other dough
  product)
MATA: plant (any plant in general);
  LA MERA MATA the real McCoy
  (coll.), the genuine article
MATABURROS msg. (coll.) dictionary,
  lexicon; cheap grade of whiskey
MATAGUSANOS msg. worm-killer, medicine used for purposes of de-
  worming people or animals; any
  de-worming agent
MATALOTE m. type of spine-backed
  fish
MATAMOSCA m. (var. of) matamoscas
  'flyswatter'
MATANZA slaughter-house
MATATENA children's game in which
  stones are thrown in the air
MATE: DARLE A ALGUIEN EN EL MERO
  MATE to hit someone right where
  it hurts
MATÓN -TONA m. (slang) gangster;
  self-styled lady killer, Don
  Juan type; f. wicked and evil
  woman; m., f. killer, assassin,
  murderer
MATRACA mf. chatterbox (coll.),
  person who talks incessantly
MATRALLADORA (var. of) amatralladora
  (in turn var. of) ametralladora
MATRIMONIAR vr. to get married
MATRIZ (slang) f. prostitute
MATUTENA (var. of) matatena
MAULA adj. clever, astute; TRAER
  MAULA (coll.) to be up to some-
  thing, have something up one's
  sleeve (coll.)
MAYATE (pej.) mf. U.S. black person
MAYESTRO -TRA (var. of) maestro -tra
MAYOR (Ang.) m. mayor (of a city)
  (Std. alcalde)
MAYOTE m. nag, old horse
MAYUGAR (var. of) magullar
MAZORCA (slang) fsg. teeth, set of
  teeth
MAZUMA (slang) money (<mazuma, ant.
  English <Yiddish, slang of the
  1930's)
MEADERA frequent urinating
MEADERO (var. of) meadera
MECANEAR or MECANIAR vn. to do
  mechanical work, work as a
  mechanic
MECATAZO whiplash, lash of a whip
MECATE: ANDAR COMO BURRO SIN MECATE
  to run wild and free, do as one
  pleases; CADA CHANGO A SU MECATE
  Y A DARSE VUELO (lit. 'each
  monkey to his rope and start
  swinging') every man for himself, let each person do his
  own thing (slang)

MECETA (var. of) maceta
MECO -CA lower-class person; person
　　in a bad mood; MECOS mpl.
　　(vulg.) semen, seminal fluid
MECHA (Ang.) match (for lighting
　　fire) (Std. cerilla, fósforo)
MECHACHITO -TA (vars. of) muchachito
　　-ta
MECHAR (Eng.) va. to match, compare
　　(one thing with another); to
　　match, harmonize (attempt to
　　make two items harmonize with
　　each other)
MECHAS fpl. disheveled hair, "mop"
　　of hair (coll.); AGARRARSE A LAS
　　MECHAS / AGARRARSE DE LAS MECHAS
　　to pull one another's hair in a
　　fight; IRSE A LAS MECHAS / IRSE
　　DE LAS MECHAS to pass from a
　　verbal to a physical battle
　　(esp. one in which hair is pull-
　　ed)
MECHUDO -DA person with long and
　　unkempt hair; hippie
MEDECINA (var. of) medicina
MEDIAGUA: ESTAR MEDIAGUA to be
　　drunk
MEDICINA: MEDICINA DE LA BOTICA/
　　MEDICINA DE LA FARMACIA patent
　　medicine
MEDIERO -RA sharecropper (unequal
　　"partner" on a ranch or farm")
MEDIO nickel, five-cent piece
MEJICLE (slang) Mexico
MEJOR: A LA MEJOR (Std. a lo mejor);
　　MÁS MEJOR (pleonasm) better
　　(Std. mejor); MEJOR MITAD (Ang.)
　　f. wife
MELA (nickname for) Carmela
MELA (slang) human head
MELE (nickname for) Guillermo
MELENA (slang) head (body: neck
　　upward)
MELITAR (var. of) militar m. 'sol-
　　dier'
MELÓN m. hornless or dehorned bull;
　　or MELONA f. (slang) human head
MEMBRECIA membership
MEME (Eng.) Mamie (woman's name)
MEMO (nickname for) Guillermo
MENARDE or MENARVE (Hispanization
　　of) Menard, Texas
MÉNDIGO (var. of) mendigo. (latter
　　is infrequently used in Texas);
　　m. rogue, trickster; adj. mf.
　　MÉNDIGO -GA cheap, stingy;
　　mean, base, wicked
MENEADA or MENIADA or MENEADERO -RA
　　or MENIADERO -RA mf. the act
　　of stirring (esp. a liquid in
　　a container): "Dale una meniada
　　al caldo" 'Stir up the soup'
MENEAR: MENEARLAS or MENEAR LAS
　　NALGAS to wiggle one's hind

quarters
MENIJAR (var. of) manejar
MENIU (Eng.) m. menu
MENJURGE (var. of) mejunge m.'dis-
　　orderly pile of objects jumbled
　　together'
MENORAR (var. of) minorar
MENOS: DE MENOS at least (Std. a
　　lo menos, por lo menos); ENTRE
　　MENOS BURROS, MÁS OLOTES /
　　MIENTRAS MENOS BURROS, MÁS OLO-
　　TES the fewer people, the more
　　there is to go around (often
　　said with ref. to food); ESTAR
　　EN TODO MENOS EN MISA be mind-
　　ing everybody's business except
　　one's own; ENTRE MENOS _____,
　　MENOS _____ the fewer _____,
　　the fewer _____
MENSO -SA ignorant; foolish
MENSUAL (slang) (hum. var. of menso
　　-sa)
MENTIDERA (coll.) several lies at
　　once, string of lies
MENTIR vn. to be wrong, be in
　　error: "Pues, vino a las ocho...
　　No, miento, vino a las ocho y
　　media"
MENTIRITAS: DE MENTIRITAS in make-
　　believe fashion
MENTOLATO (Eng?) mentholatum
MENUDO soup or stew made with var-
　　ious types of tripe and well
　　seasoned, esp. with salt; menu-
　　do is popularly known as an
　　efficacious hangover cure
MEÓN, MEONA m., f. person who uri-
　　nates frequently, weak-bladdered
　　(coll.)
MERO: EL MERO BEBÉ the one and only
　　(coll.); EL MERO MERO / EL MERO
　　PETATERO (slang) the big boss,
　　the big cheese, the head honcho
　　(slang); the real McCoy, the
　　genuine article (slang); EL
　　MERO JODÓN (slang) the big boss,
　　the head honcho (slang); YA
　　MERO / YA MERITO almost, nearly
MES m. menstrual period; TENER EL
　　MES to have one's (menstrual)
　　period
MESA: SALIR POR DEBAJO DE LA MESA
　　to always come out on the short
　　end of the stick (fig.), always
　　fail in whatever one attempts
MESMO (var. of) mismo
MESTRO -TRA (var. of) maestro -tra
¡MÉTELE! interj. Hit 'em!; Hurry
　　up!; Get to work! (etc.)
METER va. to stick, sting (slang),
　　charge excessively for: "Le
　　metieron quinientos dólares por
　　esa carrucha" 'They stung him
　　$500 for that old heap'; A LA

QUE ME METÍ A fine mess I got
myself into; A TODO METER full
speed ahead, very rapidly; (adj.)
stupendous, exceptional, marvel-
ous (etc.); METER A ALGUIEN
EN BOLA to get someone into
trouble, involve someone in a
conflict; METER A ALGUIEN EN LA
LEY to bring a lawsuit against
someone; METER A ALGUIEN EN
UN TRABAJO to use one's influence to obtain a job for someone;
METERLE A ALGUIEN UNA PALIZA /
REATIZA / PORRIZA (etc.) to
give someone a severe beating;
vn. METER CABALLO (slang) to
put in a bad word (about someone), speak ill of; METER EL
CODO (slang) to put in a good
word for someone, speak well of;
METER HOMBRO to help out, lend
a helping hand; to put in a good
word for someone, speak well of;
METER MANO (vulg.) to engage
in manual coitus, insert one's
finger into a vagina to simulate
copulation; to engage in enthusiastic and vigorous sexual
foreplay; METERLE DURO / METERLE
MUCHO to do something to excess
(esp. the drinking of alcohol):
"Le mete duro a la tomada" 'He
really drinks heavily'; vr. to
consume, eat up: "Me metí dos
platos de frijoles"; to cover
territory, travel: "Me metí 20
millas en una hora"; METERSE EN
EL EJÉRCITO/CUERPO AÉREO/MARINA
(etc.) to enlist in the army
(etc.); METÉRSELA DOBLADA A AL-
GUIEN to get the best of someone in a business deal, a sports
competition, etc.: "A Pedro se
la metieron doblada en es juego";
METÉRSELE A ALGUIEN EN LA CABEZA
(coll.) to get (something) into
one's head, for an idea to occur
to someone; to be bullheaded
about something
METICHE or METICHI mf. busybody,
meddler
METIDO -DA: ESTAR MUY METIDO -DA
CON ALGUIEN to be very involved with someone (esp. in a love
affair); ESTAR MUY METIDO -DA
EN ALGO to be very absorbed in
something; f. (vulg.) act of
fornication (see also DAR UNA
METIDA)
METRALLADORA (var. of) ametralladora
MEXICANO-AMERICANO (Ang.) Mexican-
American (Std. mexicoamericano)
MÉXICO: MÉXICO VEN POR TU GENTE
(expression of disapproval

directed at Mexican-Americans
who are making a spectacle of
themselves); MÉXICO VIEJO (Old)
Mexico (as distinct from New
Mexico, U.S. state)
MEZQUINO wart
MEZQUITE (slang) m. month
MÍ (pers. pron.): A MÍ ¿QUÉ?/¿A MÍ
QUÉ ME DA? What's that to me?,
What concern's that of mine?
(expresses indifference)
MIADERA (var. of) meadera
MIAR (var. of) mear
MICAILA (var. of) Micaela (woman's
name)
MIEMBRECÍA (var. of) membrecía
MIENTRAS: MIENTRAS MENOS at the
very least (Std. cuanto menos);
POR MIENTRAS for the time
being, meanwhile
MIÉRCOLES (euph.) msg. feces, "num-
ber two" (euph.--the word that
miércoles avoids is mierda);
¡MIÉRCOLES! interj. (mildly
euph.) Damn!, Hell!
MIERDA (vulg.) excrement, feces
(also with ref. to persons:)
(vulg.) Son-of-a-bitch, No-good
bastard (etc.)
MIGRA (slang) immigration service
(U.S.); U.S. border patrol
MIGUEL (slang) (pers. pron.) I; me
(hum. identification between mí
and Miguel)
MILAGRO: ¡QUÉ MILAGRO! 'What a
pleasant surprise!'
MILITARIO (var. of) militar (n. &
adj.)
MILO -LA (dims. of) Emilio -lia
MILQUE (Eng.) f. milk
MIMELA (slang) (pers. pron.) I (Std.
yo) (cf. MIGUEL, supra)
MINE (dim. of) Minerva, Herminia
MINGO (dim. of) Domingo
MIÓN, MIONA (var. of) meón, meona
MIRA (Eng.) f. meter (e.g., parking
meter)
MIRAMONTE (slang) (3rd pers. sg.
pres. ind. of mirar)
MIRAR: MIRAR ADELANTE PARA (Ang.)
to look forward to, anticipate;
ESTAR DE MÍRAME Y DÉJAME (pej.,
said with ref. to a homely woman): "Esa mujer está de mírame
y déjame"; ¡MIRA NOMÁS! (interj.
of surprise:) Well I'll be damned!, Will you look at that!
MIRELES (slang) (pers. pron.) I
(Std. yo) (1st pers. sg. subject
pron.) (cf. MIGUEL, MIMELA et
al.)
MIROJEAR or MIROJIAR va. to peep,
sneak a look at, glance at
covertly and often with lust

aforethought

MISA: LA MISA (hum. or else mock Eng. for) La Mesa, Texas

MISA: MISA DE GALLO (var. of) misa del gallo; ESTAR EN TODO MENOS EN MISA to mind everyone else's business but one's own

MISIÓN (re-Hispanization of) Mission, Texas

MISIRICORDIA (var. of) misericordia

MÍSPERO (var. of) níspero (Japanese plum tree)

MISTEAR or MISTIAR (Eng.) va. to miss; to fail to attend (e.g. a class); to feel the absence of: "Te misteo mucho, vuelve pronto"; to fail to hit (e.g. a target): "Le mistié al pajarito con mi rifle"

MÍSTER (Eng.) m. mister, Mr.

MITA Y MITA (var. of) mitá y mitá (mitad y mitad) half and half (as when one person shares something with another)

MITO: CORTAR EL MITO (slang) to silence, shut up: "Le cortaron el mito" 'They shut him up'

MITOTE m. uproar, din; disturbance; trouble; noisy party, loud festivity

MITOTEAR or MITOTIAR va. to stir up, incite; vn. to make trouble, raise hell (coll.), to go on a wild spree

MITOTERO -RA adj. rowdy, noisy; troublesome, hard to handle; mf. instigator, rabble rouser, troublemaker

MIXEAR or MIXIAR (Eng.) va. to mix (see also MIXTEAR et. al.) (note: of the four variants, mixiar is the most prevalent)

MIXTEAR or MIXTIAR (Eng.) va. to mix

MOCA (Eng?) mug (e.g. for drinking coffee)

MOCO: TIRAR MOCO (slang) to cry; (see also DAR EN EL MOCO)

MOCHA switch-engine (locomotive used to shuffle cars in a trainyard)

MOCHACHO -CHA (var. of) muchacho -cha

MOCHAR (Eng?) va. & vn. to mooch off of (slang), sponge (coll.), live off the earnings of others; ¡MÓCHATE! (slang) Bug off!, Get out of here!, Cut out! (slang)

MOCHERA camp-follower (woman who resides near a military base so as to be proximate to the amorous attentions of military personnel, who often pay her for services rendered)

MOCHO -CHA (said of someone missing an extremity, i.e., one-handed, one-armed, one-legged); m. soldier (usually of low rank); adj. impudent, sassy

MOFLA or MOFLE (Eng.) m. muffler (aut.) (Std. silenciador m.)

MOGOTE m. brush land, brush country

MOJADO -DA illegal immigrant to the U.S. from Mexico, wetback (pej.)

MOJARRA mf. illegal immigrant to the U.S. from Mexico, wetback (pej.)

MOJO (var. of) moho 'rust'

MOJÓN m. solid drenching, thorough soaking

MOJOSO -SA (var. of) mohoso -sa 'rusty'

MOLCAJETE: CARA DE MOLCAJETE (slang) (pej.) (insult used to indicate a very ugly face)

MOLCAS (var. of) molcajete; CIERTAS MOLCAS (used to ref. to person whose name one wishes to avoid mentioning; cf. CIERTOS ELOTES)

MOLER: MOLER GENTE to bother (someone), make a nuisance of oneself: "¡Cómo te gusta moler gente!"

MOLÓN -LONA m., f. pest, bothersome person; complainer

MOLOTE m. bun of hair, topknot

MOLLEJA pocket watch

MOLLERA: MOLLERA CAÍDA fallen fontanelle (the soft part of a baby's skull which sometimes "falls" or retracts before becoming fully hardened); MOLLERA CERRADA (fig.) (ref. to person who is slow to learn)

MOLLETE m. cake baked in the shape of a loaf

MOMIO -MIA dunderhead, blockhead, dolt

MOMIO (var. of) momia

MOMPES (Eng.) mpl. mumps

MONA (dim. of) Ramona

MONARCO movie theater, cinema (<?, perhaps mono, q.v., or, through metonymy Monarco, name of a particular theater)

MONEADA or MONEADERA or MONIADA or MONIADERA act of being or attempting to be cute or amusing

MONESTERIO (var. of) monasterio

MONI (msg.) or MONIS (mpl.) (Eng.) money

MONITO -TA (rus.) (var. of) bonito -ta

MONITA paper doll, cartoon cut-out doll

MONO (slang) movie theater, cinema; movie, film; APRETARLE A ALGUIEN EL MONO to bewitch someone;

MONO DE AGUA　fireplug; SER
　　MUY MONO -NA to dress very
　　elegantly
MONONTEROS　(var. of) montoneros mpl.
　　'gang of attackers'
MONQUIAR (Eng.) (slang) vn. to
　　monkey around with, engage in
　　often meaningless activities
　　for the sake of killing time
MONSTRO -TRA　(vars. of) monstruo -
　　trua
MOPE　(Eng.) m. (infrequently used
　　var. of mape)
MOPEADA or MOPIADA　(vars. of) ma-
　　peada, mapiada (Eng.)
MOPEADOR -DORA or MOPIADOR -DORA
　　(vars. of) mapeador -dora,
　　mapiador -dora (Eng.)
MOPEAR or MOPIAR　(vars. of) mapear,
　　mapiar (Eng.)
MOQUEADERA or MOQUIADERA　act of
　　crying; nasal drip
MOQUEAR or MOQUIAR (slang) vn. to
　　cry; to drip (said of noses)
MOQUERA or MOQUERIA　act of crying;
　　nasal drip
MOQUETAZO　punch in the nose
MOQUIENTO -TA (var. of) mocoso -sa
MORA　(slang) juvenile detention
　　home, house of correction for
　　boys or girls; fpl. PESCAR EN
　　LAS MORAS　to catch (someone)
　　red-handed, catch in the act
MORAS:　LAS MORAS (Spanish name for)
　　Brackettville, Texas
MORDELÓN -LONA (pej.) policeman (m.),
　　policewoman (f.) (usually ref.
　　to corrupt policemen, i.e.,
　　those who accept mordidas)
MORDIDA　bribe; pay-off, kick-back
MORE　(Hispanization of) Moran, Texas
MORETEADO -DA or MORETIADO -DA
　　bruised, covered with bruises
MORETEAR or MORETIAR　va. to bruise;
　　vr. to bruise oneself
MORFINIENTO -TA　user of narcotic
　　drugs (esp. morphine)
MORIDO -DA　(var. of) muerto -ta
　　(ppart. of morir)
MORIENDO　(var. of) muriendo (ger.
　　of morir)
MORIERA, MORIERAS, etc. (vars. of)
　　muriera, murieras, etc. (past
　　subj. conjugation of morir)
MORIERON　(var. of) murieron (3rd
　　pers. pl. pret. of morir)
MORIÓ　(var. of) murió (3rd pers. sg.
　　pret. of morir)
MORMACIÓN　f. nasal obstruction
MORMADO -DA　nasal (ref. to sound
　　of the voice of a person with
　　a temporary articulatory de-
　　fect resulting from a stopped-
　　up nose, a throat inflamation,

etc.)
MORMAR　vr. to contact an inflama-
　　tion of the nasal passages,
　　the throat, etc. (and which
　　serves to nasalize or other-
　　wise distort the vocal quality)
MORMULLO　(var. of) murmullo
MORMURAR　(var. of) murmurar
MORO or MORONDEL　(slang, Hispaniza-
　　tion of) Martindale, Texas
MOROSAICO　(Eng.) motorcycle
MORRAGIA　(var. of) hemorragia
MORRALUDO　(ref. to man wearing bag-
　　gy pants)
MORRO -RRA　short and chubby
MORROCOYO　(slang) any type of in-
　　sect
MORTIFICACIÓN　f. worry, preoccupa-
　　tion
MORTIFICAR　va. & vr. to worry
MOSCA　(fig.) pest, bothersome per-
　　son; MOSCA EN LECHE dark-com-
　　plected person married to (or
　　associating with) a fair-skin-
　　ned person; POR SI LAS MOSCAS
　　just in case
MOSQUERÍO　swarm of flies
MOSQUIENTO -TA　fly-ridden, abound-
　　ing in flies
MOSQUITA MUERTA　person who pretends
　　to be timid and reserved but is
　　not; wolf in sheep's clothing
　　(fig.), person pretending to
　　be harmless
MOTA　f. moss balls on trees (type
　　of tree fungus); LA MOTA
　　(slang) (Spanish name for)
　　Hunter, Texas
MOTA　(slang) marihuana
MOTEA or MOTELLA　(rus.) (var. of)
　　botella
MOTEADO -DA or MOTIADO -DA (var. of)
　　goteado -da or gotiado -da;
　　(slang) ANDAR MOTIADO -DA to
　　be high from using marihuana
MOTEAR or MOTIAR　(slang) vn. to
　　smoke pot (slang), smoke mari-
　　huana
MOTEL　(Eng.) m. motel
MOTO　(slang) mf. marihuana freak,
　　habitual user of marihuana
MOTORCICLETA　(var. of) motocicleta
MOTOSAICA　m. (Eng.) motorcycle
MOVER:　MOVER LA JICOTERA to stir
　　things up, get things moving
　　(coll.); vr. MOVERSE DE CASA
　　(Ang.) to move, change resi-
　　dences　(Std. mudarse de casa);
　　NO LE MUEVAS Leave well enough
　　alone
MOVIDA:　MOVIDA CHUECA (slang)
　　crooked move, unsavory deal;
　　illicit love affair; TENER MO-
　　VIDA (slang) to have plans for

a sexual assignation

MOYOTE m. mosquito

MU (var. of) muy

MUCHACHON -CHONA m. boyish; f. girl-
ish: "Se ve muy muchachón"
'He looks very boyish'

MUCHAR (var. of) mochar 'to cut
(off)'

MUCHAR (var. of) mochar

MUCHITO -TA (var. of) muchachito -
ta

MUEBLE (rus.) m. automobile, car

MUELA fpl. CONTAR LAS MUELAS to
pull the wool over one's eyes
(fig.), deceive: "A mí no me
cuentes las muelas; tú me
robaste ese dinero"

MUELÓN -LONA m., f. bothersome person, pest

MUERTO -TA: m. adj. CAER(SE) MUERTO
to drop dead; (slang) to pay
up, pay, cough up (slang);
ESTAR MUERTO -TA to be unaware
of a fraud or a deception; to
be adamant, stubborn, hard to
convince; MUERTO -TA DE HAMBRE
(fig.) (said of a greedy and
selfish person); NO TENER EN
QUÉ CAERSE MUERTO to be totally broke, penniless

MUGRAR (rus.) va. to dirty, make
dirty; vr. to get dirty, dirty
oneself

MUGRE f. (word used to name something whose name the speaker
has forgotten, 'whatchamacallit',
'thingamagig','gizmo', etc.);
prostitute

MUGRERO junkyard (fig.), place filled up with useless and dirty
objects; botch-job, work badly
done

MUJER: MUJER DE LA CALLE (pej.)
street-walker, prostitute;
MUJER JUGADA / MUJER PASEADA or
PASIADA / MUJER PATEADA or
PATIADA woman with a lot of
mileage on her (coll.), woman
with considerable sexual experience

MUJERERO (var. of) mujeriego

MUJERINGO (pej.) effeminate, sissy,
fruity (slang)

MULO -LA: SER MULO -LA (fig.) to
be stubborn; f. (Eng.) (ant.
slang) money

MULETA: AGUANTAR MULETA (v.s.
AGUANTAR)

MUNCHO -CHA (var. of) mucho -cha

MUNINCIPAL (var. of) municipal

MURIR (var. of) morir

MÚSICA: TENER or LLEVAR LA MÚSICA
POR DENTRO (said of an intro-
verted person) to have one's

real self hidden; MÚSICA DE
BOCA harmonica, mouth organ

MUSIQUERO -RA musician

MUSTIO -TIA ill-humored; dull,
lusterless

N

NA (var. of) nada 'nothing'

NACIONAL mf. Mexican, Mexican national, someone from Mexico;
mpl. (coll.) beans, frijoles

NACHO -CHA (dim. of) Anastasio -sia

NACHO (Eng., <natch, naturally)
(slang) naturally, sure thing
(coll.), you bet (coll.)

NADA: NADA VALE There's nothing to,
The ____ is insignificant ....
(expression used to indicate
that one thing is of little
importance compared to something else, which is worse:)
"Nada vale la borrachera, lo
peor es la cruda" "Being drunk
is nothing, the worst part is
the hangover'

NADIEN (var. of) nadie (pron.)

NAGUA or NAHUA fsg. (vars. of)
naguas fpl. 'petticoat';
'skirt'

NAGUAS fpl. (var. of) enaguas fpl.

NAIDE(N) (vars. of) nadie (pron.)

NAIFA (Eng.) knife

NAILÓN (Eng.) m. nylon

NALGAS: NALGAS PELONAS (vulg.)
(hum.) bare-assed: "Él anda
con las nalgas pelonas" 'He's
going around bare-assed'; (see
DAR LAS NALGAS)

NALGATORIO (hum.) big buttocks

NALGÓN -GONA (var. of) nalgudo -da

NALGUEADA or NALQUIADA spanking

NALGUEAR or NALGUIAR va. to spank;
to pat someone on the buttocks

NANA baby-sitter

NANDO -DA (dims. of) Fernando -da

NAPQUETÍN (Eng.) m. napkin (Std.
servilleta)

NAQUEADO -DA or NAQUIADO -DA (Eng.)
knocked out, unconscious (see
also NOQUEADO et al.)

NAQUEAR or NAQUIAR (Eng.) va. to
knock out, render unconscious;
vn. to knock on a door

NAQUIN (Eng.) m. napkin

NARANJADO -DA (var. of) anaranjado -

-da

NARANJAS (slang) adv. no (negative
    response to a question):
    "¿Vienes conmigo? ---¡Naranjas!"
NARANJILES (slang) adv. no (negative
    response to a question) (cf.
    NARANJAS)
NARANJO (Hispanization of) Orange
    Grove, Texas
NARCO (slang) member of the narcotics
    squad of the police force; de-
    tective (in general) (Eng?,
    nark)
NARIZ f. SER NARIZ to be a busy-
    body (coll.), be overly inter-
    ested in the affairs of others
    (see also NARIZÓN -ZONA); fpl.
    NARICES DE TÍSICO good sense of
    smell: "Tienes unas narices de
    tísico" (often said in exaspera-
    tion, as by a mother to a child
    who has succeeded in smelling
    out a cake that was to be kept
    whole until dinner time)
NARANJA DULCE f. children's game in
    which the following verse is
    sung by a moving circle of par-
    ticipants: "Naranja dulce, li-
    món partido / Dame un abrazo
    que yo te pido"; one child is
    stationed inside the circle,
    and when he/she succeeds in em-
    bracing one of those forming
    part of the circle, that child
    enters the center and is re-
    placed by its former occupant
NATO (dim. of) Natividad or Natalio -
    lia
NATURAL m. "regular" haircut, how-
    ever defined (traditionally a
    cut in which the hair does not
    cover the ears or descend be-
    low the collar line)
NAYOTAS (slang) fpl. nose
NAVAJEAR or NAVAJIAR va. to cut
    with a knife
NAVAJERO -RA flatterer; knife
    wielder (person whose favorite
    weapon is a knife)
NECEDERA (var. of) necedad 'foolish-
    ness'
NECESIDAD fpl. HACER LAS NECESI-
    DADES (euph.) to go to the
    bathroom (for purposes of fecal
    or urinary evacuation)
NECIO -CIA annoying, bothersome;
    fussy, fidgety, irritable: "Yo
    creo que el niño tiene calen-
    tura porque está muy necio"
    'I think the child has a tempera-
    ture because he's very fussy'
NECITAR (var. of) necesitar
NEGRADA large group of U.S. black
    persons

NEGRITA elderberry (Sambucus mexi-
    cana) (prepared as a tea and
    used to treat colic)
NEGRO (pej.) mpl. CENA DE NEGROS
    any disorderly gathering
NEI mf. Inez
NEJO -JA dirty; yellowed (ref. to
    old tortillas)
NEL or NELA or NELA CANELA (slang)
    no (negative response to a
    question)
NELO -LA (dim. of) Manuel -la
NEQUIN (Eng.) f. napkin
NETA (Eng.) net (tennis or volley-
    ball net)
NETO (dim. of) Ernesto
NI: NI MADRE (coll.) not a thing,
    not a single mother-lovin'
    thing (slang): "¿Qué hay en
    la hielera? -- Ni madre"; NI
    PELIGRO not a chance, fat
    chance (slang); NI POR AHI TE
    PUDRES (said to a friend or
    close relative who has not vi-
    sited you in a while) 'What's
    become of you?'; NI SOCA not
    a bit, not at all
NICLE (Ang.) m. five-cent piece
NIERVO (var. of) nervio
NIEVE f. ice-cream (Std. helado);
    NIEVE DE PALITO eskimo pie,
    ice-cream on a stick; f. co-
    caine
NIEVERIA (var. of) nevería
NIEVERO (var. of) nevero 'ice-cream
    vendor'
NIGACHURA or NIGASURA or NIGUESURA
    (Eng.) sling shot, nigger's
    shooter (ant. slang)
NIGUAS (slang) no (negative response
    to a question)
NINGUNEAR or NINGUNIAR (slang) va.
    to kill, wipe out (slang), off
    (slang)
NINO -NA (dims. of) Bernardino -
    dina
NIÑO: EL NIÑO MÁS (ref. to person
    whose name one wishes to avoid
    mentioning; cf. CIERTOS ELOTES
    (VERDES), MOLCAS); NIÑO DEL
    OJO pupil (of eye)
NIUNCA (var. of) nunca
NIUQUIS (slang) New Braunfels, Tex-
    as (see also NUIQUIS)
NO: ¡NO DIGO! interj. I told you
    so!, Didn't I tell you?!; How
    about that? (indicates admira-
    tion for a thing, a feat, etc.);
    ¿NO QUE NO? Didn't you say
    that ...?: "¿No que no te ca-
    sabas?" 'I thought you said
    you were never going to get
    married!; ¿NO QUE NO, CHIQUITO
    -TA? I thought you told me

you weren't (going to do what-
ever you said you weren't)
NOBLADO -DA (var. of) nublado -da
NOCAUT (Eng.) m. knockout (in box-
ing) (see also NACAUT)
NOCHE late at night, late hours of
the night: "Vino muy noche"
'He came very late last night'
NOCHEBUENA Poinsetta plant (Euphor-
bia pulcherrima)
NOCHECITA adv. fairly late at
night
NODRIZA nurse (in general) (Std.
enfermera)
NOJADO -DA (rus.) (var. of) enojado
-da
NOJAR (var. of) enojar
NOJOTROS -TRAS (rus.) (var. of)
nosotros -tras
NOMÁS adv. just; only; no sooner;
AQUÍ NOMÁS / AY NOMÁS just so-
so: "¿Cómo le va?-- Ay nomás";
How about that?, What do you
think of that (often a slightly self-congratulatory response
to a compliment); NO NOMÁS not
just; not only; NOMÁS EN CUAN-
TO (var. of) en cuanto 'as
soon as'; NOMÁS NO (resolute
negative reply to a request or
a suggestion): "¿Nos puedes
hacer ese favor? -- ¡Nomás no!";
(iron.) Yes indeed, Yes sirree:
"¿Se lo llevaron a la cárcel?--
Nomás no"
NOPALERO -RA person employed to cut
nopales or to clear land covered with nopales
NOQUEAR or NOQUIAR (Eng.) va. to
knock out (in boxing); vn.
to knock on a door (see also
NAQUEAR et al.)
NORIA well (in general, e.g., NORIA
DE AGUA 'water well', NORIA
DE ACEITE 'oil well'); drain
NORTEADO -DA or NORTIADO -DA crazy,
nutty, cracked (coll.)
NORTEAR or NORTIAR va. to drive
crazy; vr. to go crazy
NORTECITO cold front accompanied
by strong winds from the north
NOVIERO -RA easily enamored, quick
to fall in love (ref. to person who flits from novio -via
to novio -via)
NUBLAZÓN f. (var. of) nublado
'storm cloud'; cloudiness
NUBLINA (var. of) neblina
NUECERA person (invariably a woman)
who works in a pecan factory
as a processor, packager, etc.
NUECERÍA pecan factory, pecan processing plant
NUEVAS fpl. news (i.e., informa-

tion forming part of a newspaper account or media broadcast)
NUEVECÍSIMO -MA very new, brand
new
NUEVECITO -TA very new, brand new
NUIQUIS (slang) New Braunfels, Texas (see also NIUQUIS)

Ñ

ÑANGO -GA thin, scrawny
ÑUDO (var. of) nudo

O

OBEDENCIA (var. of) obediencia
OCEANO or OCIANO (vars. of) océano
ODIOSO -SA incorrigible; overbearing
OFECINA (var. of) oficina
OFENDOR -DORA m.,f. (Eng.) offender;
juvenile delinquent
OFICINA (Ang.) political office,
elective office (e.g., mayor,
congressman, etc.): "¿Pa'
qué oficina estás corriendo?"
'What office are you running
for?'
OFRECIDO -DA apple-polisher, flatterer; f. woman who is prone
to throwing herself at a man's
feet, putting herself thereby
at his mercy
OIDO -DA (var. of) oído -da
ÓJALA, (var. of) ojalá
OJALÁ Y (var. of) ojalá (que):
"Ojalá y vengas pronto" 'I
hope you come soon'
OJETE (vulg.) anus; adj. stingy,
cheap, parsimonious
OJO: OJOS CAPOTUDOS bulging eyes,
pop eyes (slang); drooping eye-
lids; OJO DE BOTÓN buttonhole;
OJO DE CHÍCHARO (slang) alert,
sharp; OJO DE VENADO deer's
eye (Muzuna sloani) (used as
an amulet for protection a-
gainst El Ojo--the Evil Eye)

HACER OJO to cast a spell on someone, give someone the mal de ojo; QUEDARLE A ALGUIEN EL OJO: "¿Cómo le quedó el ojo?" 'How does that grab you?' (slang), 'How do you like that as a result?'; TRAER A AL-GUIEN ENTRE OJOS to have one's eye on someone, be watching someone for any little slip (misbehavior)

OLO, OLES, OLE, etc. (vars. chiefly rus.,of) huelo, hueles, huele, etc. (pres. indic. conj.of oler)

OLOTE m. corn-cob (ear of corn with husk and grains removed); ENTRE MENOS BURROS MÁS OLOTES the less you eat the more there'll be for someone else (often said as a reprimand to a child who refuses to eat)

OLLA (slang) buttocks,ass; PATA-LEARLE or PATALIARLE A ALGUIEN LA OLLA to kick someone in the ass; to beat someone up in a fight

OMBLIGÓN -GONA ponderous, heavy-set (ref. to persons); (said of a person with a large navel)

ONDA trend of the moment (in style, thought, speech, etc.), latest fad; ESTAR EN LA ONDA to be up-to-date, "with it" (slang); EN ONDA turned on, "with it", up-to-date

ONDE (var. of) donde

ONQUE (rus.) (var. of) aunque

¿ONTÁ? (rus.) (var. of) ¿Dónde está?

¡OPA! or ¡ÓPALE! Hey!, Hey you! Watch out!; uff! (grunt issued when lifting a heavy object)

OQUIS (var. of) de oquis, dioquis (advs.) (see also ANDAR DIOQUIS, ESTAR DIOQUIS)

ORA (var. of) ahora

¡ÓRALE! interj. Hurry up!; That's it, That's right!; fine by me, okay, sure; Throw it!, Let's have it!, Over here!; Stop it!, Knock it off! (coll.); ORALE ÓRALE Do it right now!

ORALIA (slang) (var. of) órale

ORDEN m. (Ang.) any request for merchandise (Std. pedido)

ORDENAR (Ang.) va. to order, re-quest merchandise (Std. pedir)

OREJA handle (on a pitcher, a mug, etc.); telephone receiver and mouthpiece; hearing aid; fpl. (slang) yes (affirmative response to a question); APA-CHURRAR OREJA / PLANCHAR OREJA / TRAMPAR OREJA (slang) to sleep; PARAR (LA[S]) OREJA(S) to

perk up one's ear(s), listen attentively (usually so as to hear what one should not); TIRAR OREJA (slang) to listen

ORGULLECER (var. of) enorgullecer

ORILLA: ESTAR DE ORILLA to be in a good mood; SER DE ORILLA to be temperamental, mercurial

ORILLAR vr. to pull over to the curb of the street (when driv-ing a car)

ORINADA act of urinating

ORITA (var. of) ahorita 'right now'

ORMI (Eng.) m. army

ORQUESTRA (var. of) orquesta

ORUTAR (var. of) eru(c)tar

ORUTO (var. of) eru(c)to

OTATE m. bamboo pole or stick (Bambu arundinacea)

OTRO: EL OTRO CACHETE (DE LA CARA) or EL OTRO LADO (DEL CHARCO) Mexico; mpl. SER DE LOS OTROS (slang) to be a (male) homo-sexual; fpl. SER DE LAS OTRAS to be a lesbian

OVAROLES (Eng.) mpl. overalls (type of work pants) (see also OVEROLES)

OVEN (Eng.) m. oven (Std. horno)

OVEROLES (Eng.) mpl. overalls (type of work pants)

ÓVULOS mpl. vaginal suppositories (which may be used as contra-ceptives)

OYÍ, OYISTE, OYIMOS (vars. of) oí, oíste, oímos (1st pers. sg., 2nd pers. sg. and 1st pers. pl. pret. forms of oír)

OYIDO -DA (var. of) oído -da

P

PA' (var. of) para (prep.)

PACA bale; pack

PACA (var. of) para acá: "Ven pacá" 'Come here'

PACENCIA (var. of) paciencia

PACIENTA (var. of) paciente f.: "El paciente y la pacienta tenían mucha pacencia"

PACITO (dim. of) papacito 'daddy' (term of endearment in child language)

PACO -CA (dim. of) Francisco -ca

PACOIMA (slang) square (slang), person not up-to-date, not "with" whichever current trends

PACÓN (Eng.) m. popcorn
PACHANGA (coll.) party, festivity
PACHOCHA (slang) money
PACHORRAS mf. slowpoke
PACHORRUDO -DA slowpoke
PACHUCO -CA Chicano "zoot-suiter"
　　of the 1940's; m. boy or f.
　　girl from El Paso, Texas; EL
　　PACHUCO (slang) El Paso, Texas.
　　(There are several possible ex-
　　planations of the word's origin:
　　that it is a deliberate defor-
　　mation of Paso with probable
　　support from the Mexican city
　　of Pachuca, or that the deforma-
　　tion of Paso may form part of the
　　well-known process whereby nick-
　　names beginning with c derive
　　from syllables whose initial
　　consonant is s, thus: Chente
　　<Vicente.)
PACHUQUISMO linguistic oddity said
　　to be typical of pachucos
PADED f. (child language var. of)
　　pared
PADER (var. of) pared f.
PADRASTO (var. of) padrastro
PADRE (slang) adj. keen, terrific,
　　neat, etc.: ESTÁ PADRE (,BATO
　　-TA) (slang) (iron. expression
　　used to indicate that one's
　　feelings have been hurt; the
　　implication is that revenge
　　will be taken or poetic justice
　　will prevail); ¡QUÉ PADRE MADRE!
　　(slang) What a broad!, What a
　　doll! (ref. to a very attractive
　　woman); PADRE DE MÁS DE CUATRO
　　(slang) he-man, stud, macho
PADROTE (slang) m. pimp; gigolo
PAENTRO or PA'ENTRO (vars. of) para
　　adentro
PAFUELA (var. of) pajuela
PAFUELAZO (var. of) pajuelazo
PAFUELEADA or PAFUELIADA (vars. of)
　　pajueleada or pajueliada
PAFUELEAR or PAFUELIAR (vars. of)
　　pajuelear or pajueliar
PA' FUERA (see DAR PA' FUERA)
PAGADOR -DORA m., f. person who
　　settles debts promptly
PAGO pay, wages
PAGRE (rus.) (var. of) padre
PAGRECITO (rus.) (var. of) padrecito
PAGULEAR or PAGULIAR (slang) to
　　pay (see also paulear or pau-
　　liar)
PAI (Eng.) m. pie
PAINE (rus.) (var. of) peine m.
PAIPA (Eng.) pipe, smoking pipe;
　　waterpipe
PAIS (var. of) país m.
PAISA mf. (var. of) paisano -
　　na

PAJAREAR or PAJARIAR (slang) va.
　　to look; to see; to watch,
　　keep an eye on (coll.)
PÁJARO (slang) jail bird, prison
　　inmate; PÁJARO -RA NALGON -
　　GONA (slang) person with a
　　large posterior, fat ass (vulg.)
PAJUELA woman of easy virtue, whore
PAJUELAZO whipping, (physical)
　　blow; shot or gulp of liquor
PAJUELEADA or PAJUELIADA whipping
PAJUELEAR or PAJUELIAR va. to whip;
　　PAJUELEARLE A ALGUIEN (EL MANGO)
　　PARA HACER ALGO: to excel at
　　doing something: "A Roberto
　　le pajuelea el mango pa enseñar
　　idiomas"; PAJUELEARLE EL CALLO
　　A ALGUIEN (said of feet which
　　smell badly): "A Primitivo le
　　pajuelea el callo"
PAL (var., i.e., contraction, of)
　　para el: "¡Vámonos pal centro!"
PALABRA: PALABRA MALA swearword,
　　dirty word
PALABROTA very erudite and learned
　　word
PALE (Eng.) m. pal, friend
PALEDAR (var. of) paladar m.
PALERO -RA (coll.) cover, cover-up
　　agent, person who covers up
　　the unintentional or deliberate
　　mistakes of others
PALETA popsicle; ice-cream on a
　　stick
PALÍO (var. of) palillo 'toothpick'
PALITO game resembling cricket;
　　(euph.) penis; ECHAR UN PALITO
　　to have sexual intercourse;
　　DULCE DE PALITO lollipop; mpl.
　　(usually pl.) clothes pins
PALIZA (see DAR UNA PALIZA)
PALO tree; (slang) penis; interj.
　　Wham!, Crash!; PALO BLANCO
　　aspen tree; SER DE PALO to be
　　insensitive, hard as a rock
　　(coll.)
PALOMA butterfly
PALOMÍA (var. of) palomilla
PALOMILLA gang, street corner gang;
　　circle of friends
PALOMITA moth
PALOTAZO blow with a rolling pin
PALOTE m. rolling pin; (vulg.)
　　large penis
PALLÁ or PA' ALLÁ (vars. of) para
　　allá: "¿Onta Jorge?-- Se jue
　　pallá" 'Where's Jorge?-- He
　　went over there'
PALLAMAS (orthog. var. of) payama(s)
　　(see also pijama)
PAMITA tansy mustard herb (Descu-
　　rainia pinnata) (prepared as a
　　tea for the treatment of em-
　　pacho)

PAN (vulg., slang) vagina (see also PANOCHA, PANOCHO; PAN (DE) DULCE sweetbread; PAN DE HUEVO type of sweetbread in semispherical form; PAN DE MAIZ or PAN DE MAIZ cornbread; type of old-fashioned dance

PANA lint, fluff

PANASCO -CA fat

PANCA (var. of) para la casa de: "¿Onta Chente? --Se jue pancá su buelita"

PANCHO -CHA (dims. of) Francisco -ca

PANCHO -CHA: PANCHO RIATA tough guy, mean bastard: "Ése es un pancho riata de verdad"; SER MUY PANCHO -CHA to be lacking in good taste, esp. with ref. to clothes: "Ése es muy pancho pa vestirse" 'That guy's got lousy taste in clothing'; (in general) to be lusterless, plain, dull, colorless; to be unsophisticated

PANDEADO -DA or PANDIADO -DA (vars. of) pando -da

PANDEAR or PANDIAR vr. to retract, take back: "Cuando se lo reclamaron, se pandió" 'When they confronted him with what he had said, he took it back'

PANDO -DA tilted, lopsided; (slang) drunk, looped

PANECIO (var. of) panecillo

PANEL (Eng.) m. panel van (type of small truck similar to a delivery van)

PANITA lint, fluff

PANOCHA or PANOCHO (slang) vulva

PANOCHUDA (vulg.) adj. ref. to woman with a large vagina

PANQUEQUE (Eng.) m. pancake

PANTALETAS fpl. woman's panties

PANTALÓN m. (usually mpl.) PANTALONES CORTOS shorts, short pants; PANTALONES DE CUCHILLA bell-bottom(ed) trousers; PANTALONES DE PECHERA bib overalls; PANTALONES DE PLITS (Eng.) pleated trousers (Std. pantalones de pliegue); PANTALONES PEGADOS overalls (work trousers)

PANTALONUDO -DA (ref. to person with baggy pants)

PANTAS (Eng.) fpl. pants, trousers

PANTASMA (var. of) fantasma

PANTERA adj. elegant, groovy, (slang) (said. esp. of attractive and noticeable woman): "¡Qué pantera!"

PANTIÓN (var. of) panteón 'cemetery'

PANTOMINA (var. of) pantomima

PANTOMINA: HACER PANTOMINAS to make a scene (coll.), make a public spectacle of oneself, make a fool of oneself: "No te asilenciaste hasta que hiciste tus pantominas" 'You didn't shut up until you could make a scene in public'

PANZAZO (var. of) panzada 'push or shove with one's belly'

PANZONA (vulg.) knocked up (vulg.), pregnant

PANZONCITA (hum.) (ref. to a chubby woman who is pregnant)

PANZONZOTA (ref. to woman who is enormously pregnant)

PAÑO handkerchief

PAPA: ¡LA PAPA! interj. Great!, Terrific!, Swell!; PAPA MACEADA or PAPA MACIADA or PAPA MOLIDA mashed potatoes; fpl. ECHAR PAPAS to lie, tell lies

PAPACHADO -DA (var. of) apapachado -da

PAPACHADOR -DORA (var. of) apapachador -dora

PAPACHAR (var. of) apapachar

PAPACHOS m. (usually pl.) fondling, pampering, indulging; HACER PAPACHOS to pamper, fondle, spoil (said of children), indulge

PAPA GRANDE or PAPÁ GRANDE m. grandfather

PAPALOTE m. paper kite; windmill; propeller

PAPALOTEAR/PAPALOTIARLE A ALGUIEN PARA HACER ALGO to excel at doing something: "A Nino le papalotea pa pichar"

PAPASES (var. of Std. pl.) papás mpl.

PAPASOTE (slang) m. handsome man; sexy male; sugar daddy; daddy-o (slang)

PAPEL (Ang.) m. newspaper; PAPEL DE CHINA tissue paper (used for packing gifts); mpl. HACER PAPELES to make a spectacle of oneself or play the fool in public, create a scene in public; PAPEL PICADO confetti

PAPELERIA establishment that buys used papers and magazines for recycling

PAPELERO -RA m. newsboy, newspaper seller; adj. mf. showoff; braggart; fraud; person prone to making scenes in public or to making a fool of him/herself; exhibitionist; mess of papers, scattered papers

PAPERO -RA liar; pretender

PAPI (Eng.) m. pappy, daddy

PAPIRO paper (in general); newspaper, periodical; PAPIRO DE CÍTICEN (Ang.) citizenship paper, document attesting to citizenship

PAPIS (Eng.) msg. (var. of) papi

PAPITA little white lie, falsehood of generally minor proportions

PAPULAR (Eng.) (var. of) popular adj.

PAQUETE m. the best part of anything; first prize; mf. opportunist

PAQUETUDO -DA (slang) excellent, topnotch

PARA: PARA ACABARLA DE FREGAR to make matters worse, on top of all that (fig.); PA(RA) ESAS GRACIAS in that case: "Vete por el perro. -- ¿Dónde está y qué hago con él cuando lo encuentre? --Bueno, pa' esas gracias yo voy mejor"

PARADA dirty deal, unfair bargain; HACERLE A ALGUIEN UNA (MALA) PARADA to play a dirty trick on someone; give someone a dirty deal; HACERLE LA PARADA A ALGUIEN to go along with someone's stand (position on an issue) or joke

PARADO -DA adj. m. on foot; standing; adj. mf. DEJAR A ALGUIEN PARADO -DA (in baseball) to strike someone out without a chance (i.e., with pitches so aimed that the batter has no chance to even swing at the ball); to stand someone up, fail to keep an appointment or show up for a date; f. TRAERLA PARADA to have a hardon (slang, vulg.), have an erection

PARALIS (var. of) parálisis msg.

PARAR: ¡PÁRE(N)LE AHÍ! interj., coll.: Knock it off!, That's enough of that!; va. to stand something up perpendicularly; PARARLE EL ALTO A ALGUIEN / PARARLE LOS PEDOS A ALGUIEN to put a stop to someone's abusive behavior, put someone down (slang); PARARSE EN UNA BODA to stand up for (the bride/the groom) at a wedding, participate as one of the nuptual couple's sponsors; vr. to leave a sick bed upon getting well; NO PARARLE LA COLA A ALGUIEN: "Llámale por teléfono a ver si está en casa, porque a ése nunca le para la cola"

'Call him up to see if he's at home, because he's constantly on the go'

PARCHE mf. disagreeable person; leech, sponge, person who lives off of others

PARDE (rus.) (var. of) padre m.

PARDI (Eng.) m. (var. of pare/pore) party

PARE m. (Eng., var. of pore) party

PARED: PARED VERDE (slang) f. Walgreen's drug store (national chain of stores)

PAREJO -JA: ESTAR or QUEDAR PAREJO -JA CON ALGUIEN to be even with someone, owe nothing to someone: "Aquí está lo último que te debo; quedamos parejos ahora"; to be tied, end up in a tie (with someone); SER PAREJO -JA to be honest, honorable

PARENTRO (var. of) para adentro 'inside'

PARIÁN m. large market; marketplace

PARIENTE (Ang.) m. (usually mpl.) parent(s)

PARNA (Eng.) m. partner (usually term of non-pej. address towards a U.S. black person)

PARPAREAR or PARPARIAR (vars. of) parpadear

PÁRPARO (var. of) párpado

PARQUE m. role of tape used as "ammunition" for cap guns; PARQUE DE ANIMALES zoo; PARQUE DE PELOTA (Ang.) baseball stadium, baseball park

PARQUEADERO or PARQUIADERO (Eng.) parking place; parking lot; act of parking a car

PARQUEADO -DA or PARQUIADO -DA (Eng.) parked (ref. to cars, or, hum. to persons, e.g., "parked" or seemingly immobile in a chair)

PARQUEAR or PARQUIAR (Eng.) va. to park; vr. (slang) to sit down, "park oneself in a chair; to remain seated at great length, thus overstaying one's welcome

PARQUETE (var. of) paquete m.

PARTE: PARTES (fpl.) DE CARRO auto parts

PARTIDO -DA m. SER BUEN PARTIDO to be a good partner (esp. in a sports competition); f. part (in one's hair); (vulg.) vagina

PARTO: SEGUNDO PARTO afterbirth (placenta and membranes)

PARRANDA group of drunken revelers

PARRANDEAR or PARRANDIAR vn. to go on a drunk, go on a drinking

spree
PARRIBA or PA' ARRIBA (vars. of)
para arriba
PASADA: DE PASADA in passing:
"Dale el libro de pasada" 'Give
him the book as you go by'
PASADERO -RA or PASADOR -DORA adj.
m., f. passable (ref. to a job
accomplished, commitments ful-
filled, the physical attributes
of persons, etc.)
PASAR va. PASAR BRACA (Ang?) to
give someone a break (opportunity); PASAR ALGO to be able
to eat food without vomiting
after an attack of stomach disorder: "El enfermo ya está
pasando la comida"; vn. PASAR-
LA to be getting along in a
so-so fashion, just getting by:
"¿Cómo le va? --Pasándola";
PASARLA BIEN to be doing well;
PASARLA MAL to be doing poorly:
PASAR UN BUEN TIEMPO (Ang.)
to have a good time (Std. diver-
tirse); PASÁRSELE A ALGUIEN LA
MANO (var. of írsele a alguien
la mano)
PASEADO -DA or PASIADO -DA f. ESTAR
MUY PASEADA/PASIADA (ref. to
women) to have a lot of mileage,
to have indulged oneself freely
in sexual relationships: "Esa
mujer está muy pasiada"
PASEADOR -DORA or PASIADOR -DORA
m., f. (said of someone fond
of "doing the town," going out
on a spree)
PASEANDO or PASIANDO (see s. ANDAR:
ÁNDATE PASIANDO)
PASEÑO -ÑA person from El Paso, Tex-
as
PASEO parade, procession
PASGUATO -TA idiot, numbskull
PASIAR (var. of) pasear
PASIÓN fpl. (slang) "¿QUÉ PASIONES?"
'What happened?' (deformation
of ¿Qué pasó?)
PASITO adv. (said of rivers suf-
ficiently empty of water to
allow crossing without having
to take one's clothes off)
PASO: EL PASO DEL ÁGUILA (Hispani-
zation of) Eagle Pass, Texas
PASOTE (slang) m. handsome man,
sexy male; sugar daddy; daddy-o;
¿QUÉ PASOTES (CON LOS ZAPATO-
TES)? (slang) What's wrong?,
What happened? (deformation of
¿Qué pasó?, cf. PASIÓN)
PASTA hay, feed for livestock
PASTERO cowboy who rides the bounda-
ries of a ranch to check whether
everything is running smoothly

PASTILLA or PASTÍA (slang) money;
money traditionally thrown to
children by godparents at a
baptism
PASTOR -TORA m., f. stupid; discourteous; countrified, hickish,
farm-fresh (coll.)
PASTORELA traditional theatrical
representation of the birth of
Christ performed around Christmas time
PASTORES: LOS PASTORES traditional
Christmas pastoral play which
depicts the visit of the shep-
hards to the stable at Beth-
leham
PASTURA (slang) tobacco
PATA: fpl. DE PATAS: ECHARLE A
ALGUIEN DE PATAS to throw
someone out feet first
PATADA (Ang.) kick (of a firearm),
recoil; kick (obtained from alcohol or drugs), thrill; (see
also AGARRAR PATADA, DAR LA
PATADA, DAR PATADAS DE AHOGADO,
ESTAR DE LA PATADA)
PATALEAR or PATALIAR: PATALEARLE
LA OLLA A ALGUIEN (slang) to
kick someone in the ass
PATERO -RA smuggler (esp. one using
small rafts--patos--to smuggle
goods across the Río Grande)
PATI (dim. of) Patricia
PATÍN m. wooden scooter used by
children (see also A PATÍN)
PATITAS (see DE PATITAS)
PATO bedpan; small raft with canvas
sails used in fording rivers
(esp. the Río Grande/Río Bravo,
by illegal immigrants from
Mexico to the U.S.); (slang,
vulg.) homosexual, faggot
(slang); weakling, effeminate
male
PATÓN (slang) m. policeman, "flat-
foot" (slang)
PA' TRAS (var. of) para atrás
'again' (adv.): "¡Entra pa'
tras!" 'Come on back in again!'
(see also: DAR PATRÁS, HACERSE
PATRÁS, IR PATRÁS, LLEVAR PA-
TRÁS, PASAR PATRÁS, VENIR PA-
TRÁS)
PAULEAR or PAULIAR (slang) va. to
pay
PAVICO diaper
PAYAMA(S) (Eng.) m(pl.) pajamas
PEDAL: PEDAL DE GAS accelerator
PEDICHE or PEDICHI adj., mf. per-
sistent, demanding, bothersome
PEDIDERA repeated asking, tiresome-
ly constant requests for some-
thing
PEDIÓRICO (var. of) periódico

PEDIR: PEDIR EMPRESTADO -DA (var. of)
pedir prestado -da; PEDIR LA
ENTRADA (see ENTRADA); PEDIR UN
OJO Y LA MITAD DEL OTRO to ask
for an excessive amount of something

PEDO fight; uproar; drunkenness, in-
ebriation; PEDO -DA adj. drunk;
ECHARLE UN PEDO A ALGUIEN to
scold, warn: "Le echó un pedo
porque llegó tarde"; PARARLE A
ALGUIEN LOS PEDOS to put a stop
to someone's abusive behavior;
to put someone in his/her place;
¡PURO PEDO! (slang, vulg.)
Bull roar! (vulg.), The hell
you say!; ¿QUÉ PEDO TE CARGAS?
(slang) What are you trying to
prove?, What are you up to?;
TRAERLE A ALGUIEN AL PURO PEDO
to harass someone; (see also
ANDAR PEDO, HACER PEDO)

PEDORRA: CHINCHE PEDORRA stinkbug
(any insect of the Pentato-
midae family)

PEDORREAR or PEDORRIAR (slang) va.
to scold, give a warning to;
vr. (vulg.) to fart continuous-
ly

PEDORRERA (vulg.) continuous breaking of wind: "Le agarró una
pedorrera de la fregada" 'He
really farted up a storm'
(slang)

PEDRADA innuendo, insinuation:
"Esa pedrada no curvió" (lit.)
'That (intended) curve ball
didn't curve' = 'Your attempted
insinuation was actually a direct accusation'

PEGAR: ANDAR PEGANDO to get along
well together (ref. to persons);
PEGARLE (DE MÁS) (AL CUENTO /
AL RELATO) to add something
(usually a mendacious element)
to a story or a narration; PE-
GARLE EL SUEÑO to get sleepy:
"Al niño le pegó el sueño como
a las doce"

PEGOISTIA or PEGOITES mf. pest (ref.
to person who imposes his/her
presence upon others against
their wishes) (see also PEGOSTE)

PEGOSTE mf. pest (id. to PEGOISTIA)

PEGOSTEAR or PEGOSTIAR va. & vr. to
smear with a sticky substance

PEINADOR m. vanity table (low table with a mirror, piece of
bedroom or bathroom furniture
also serving as a dressing table

PELADAJE m. crowd of pelados,
group of lower-class people
(who are usually acting in an

"ill-bred" fashion)

PELADO -DA lower-class person; ruf-
fian, bully

PELADORA gold digger (fig.), woman
in search of a wealthy husband
or boy friend

PELAR va. to give a haircut to; vr.
to get a haircut; vr. to flee,
leave in a great hurry; to peel
off, flake; PELÁRSELA to pull
back the foreskin of one's penis; PELAR GALLO (slang) to die;
PELAR (EL) OJO to open one's
eyes wide so as to stare fixed-
ly at something; PELAR EL DIEN-
TE / PELAR (LOS) DIENTES to
smile mockingly; to bare one's
teeth (as in anger)

PELEA boxing; boxing match

PELEONERO -RA or PELIONERO -RA pugnacious

PELERÍO pile of hair, great abundance of hair: "Barre ese
pelerío que dejaste en el piso"

PELIAR (var. of) pelear

PELÍCOLA (var. of) película

PELITOS mpl. hair of the genital
zone; soft hair on the human
body

PELIZCADA (var. of) pellizcada

PELIZCAR (var. of) pellizcar

PELIZCO (var. of) pellizco

PELIZCÓN (var. of) pellizcón

PELMAS mfsg. slowpoke

PELO: stature, height (of person):
"Juan y Jorge son del mismo
pelo"; ALZÁRSELE A ALGUIEN EL
PELO / ALZÁRSELE A ALGUIEN LOS
PELOS to stand on end (said
of one's hair): "Se le alza-
ron los pelos"; PELO CHINO
curly hair; PELO DERECHO (Ang.)
or PELO LISO straight hair
(as opposed to kinky or curly
hair); PELO PARADO hair
standing on end, standing
straight up (as in a crew-cut);
PELO QUEBRADO naturally curly
or wavy hair

PELÓN PELÓN PELACAS / PELÓN PELACAS,
CUIDA LAS VACAS/ PELÓN PELACAS,
CUIDA LAS VACAS, YO LAS ENGORDO
Y TÚ LAS ENFLACAS (expressed
used to poke fun at persons--
usually boys--who wear crew
cuts)

PELÓN -LONA skinhead, person with
hair cut close to the scalp
(as in a crewcut); difficult,
hard to resolve; PELÓN -LONAS:
NALGAS PELONAS (vulg.) (hum.)
bare-assed: "Él anda con las
nalgas pelonas" 'He's going a-
round bare-assed'

PELOTA: CARGAR PELOTA POR / TRAER
PELOTA POR (slang) to really
have the hots for, be passionately in love with: "Se ve
que ese bato carga pelota por
su chava" 'You can see that that
guy really has the hots for his
chick'; EN PELOTAS (vulg.)
naked

PELOTAZO m. (ref. to both men and
women as adj.) astute, sly,
sharp

PELUCA (hum.) hair; ANDAR or ESTAR
PELUCAS (slang) to be cleaned
out, broke (usually as a result
of having lost one's money in a
game of chance)

PELUCAR (slang) va. to clean someone out in a game of chance

PELUDO -DA physically mature; large
in size

PELUQUERO -RA habitual winner in a
game of chance

PELUSA riff-raff, ill-behaved lower-class types

PELLÍN m. buttocks

PENAR: ANDAR PENANDO (said of a
soul clothed as a ghost which
roams the earth, fulfilling an
unfinished commitment or right-
ing a wrong which circumstances
did not permit it to right during its lifetime)

PENCO -CA child born out of wedlock

PENDEJADA foolish or stupid act

PENDEJIAR (var. of) pendejear

PENDEJO -JA: HACERSE (EL/LA) PEN-
DEJO -JA to play dumb, pretend not to know or understand;
HACER PENDEJO -JA A ALGUIEN to
fool someone; to cheat, defraud

PENDEJÓN -JONA (pej.) stupid idiot,
ignoramus

PENDIENTE: ESTAR CON EL PENDIENTE
DE ALGUIEN to be worried about
someone: "Estoy con el pendiente de María porque todavía no
ha llegado"; TENERLE A ALGUIEN
CON EL PENDIENTE to have someone worried (about someone):
"¿Ya llegó María?--No, aún me
tiene con el pendiente" 'Did
María arrive? -- No, I'm worried about her'; TENER PEN-
DIENTE DE ALGUIEN to be worried about someone: "Tengo
pendiente de Jorge, porque
llora tanto"

PENE or PENI (Eng.) m. penny, one-
cent piece; f. (slang) penitentiary (reduction of penitenciaría)

PENITENCIA (var. of) penitenciaría

PENQUEQUE (Eng.) m. pancake (see
also PANQUÉ et al.)

PEPA (slang) clitoris: "La pepa es
donde la mujer siente más sen-
sación sexual"

PEPE -PA m. (dim. of) José, f.
(dim. of) Josefa and Josefina
(see also Fina); ¡AY TÚ PEPE!
(etc.--see AY)

PEPENAR: PEPENARLE A ALGUIEN UNOS.
GOLPES to hit someone

PEPETORIA or PEPITORIA (vars. of)
pipitoria

PEPEYENDO breaking wind (ger.)
(the ger. is the only form used
of the consequently hypotheti-
cal verb pepeyer)

PERCURAR (var. of) procurar

PERDER: PERDER LA CAMISA (Ang.) to
lose one's shirt (coll.), lose
a considerable amount of money

PERFILADO unravelled sewing

PERICO -CA mf. talkative person,
chatterbox (coll.), gossip;
f. (slang) radio

PERIÓRICO (var. of) periódico

PERIQUEAR or PERIQUIAR (slang) vn.
to talk incessantly, chatter

PERIQUERA (slang) upper gallery of a
movie theater

PERLA (see IR DE PERLA)

PERSINAR (var. of) persignar

PERSONAL m. poll tax

PERRA (see HACER LA PERRA)

PERRILLA sty, inflamation on the
eyelid

PERRO -RRA f.: LA PERRA DE CUATRO
LLANTAS (hum.) greyhound bus;
PERRO CALIENTE (Ang.) hot dog
(type of sausage); PERRO CHATO
bulldog; SER COMO EL PERRO /
LA PERRA QUE NO TIENE NI DEJA
TENER to have a dog-in-the-
mangerish attitude (ref. to a
selfish person); f. SUERTE
PERRA very bad luck; TRABAJAR
COMO PERRO to work quite hard

PERRODA (var. of) pedorra (also
chinche pedorra)

PERRÓN -RRONA m., f. bully; malicious person

PERRUSQUILLO -LLA or PERRUSQUÍO -
QUÍA drunk; lower-class person

PESADO -DA (Ang.) (slang) adj. (ref.
to the very latest in extra-
vagant and "far-out" popular
music= Eng. slang expression
heavy music); PONERSE PESADO -
DA to get nasty (coll.), act
in an unpleasant manner

PESAR: PESARLE A ALGUIEN LAS BOLAS
/ EL BUCHE/LAS PELOTAS (vulg.)
to be (very) lazy

PESCADO fish in general (cf. Std. pez 'live, uncaught fish')

PESCAR: PESCAR A ALGUIEN EN LA MENTIRA / PESCAR A ALGUIEN EN LAS MORAS to catch red-handed (coll.), discover someone's involvement in a criminal act, in a falsehood, etc.; PESCARLE A ALGUIEN LA NOCHE to be overtaken by night fall

PESCUEZO: TENER EL PESCUEZO TORCIDO to have a crick in one's neck

PESCUEZÓN - ZONA or PESCUEZUDO -DA (vars. of) pescozudo -da

PESETA twenty-five cent piece; repugnant and repellent person (see also CAER PESETA)

PESETUDO -DA repugnant, repellent

PESTE: ECHAR PESTES to raise a stink (fig.), make trouble

PESUÑA: GRAN PESUÑA (slang) foot; toe-nail

PESO dollar (U.S. currency)

PESPUNTE (see A PESPUNTE)

PESTAÑA: TIRAR PESTAÑA (slang) to sleep

PESUDO -DA rich, well-to-do

PETACA automobile trunk

PETACONA large and shapely woman

PETATE m. small rug, mat

PETATEAR or PETATIAR (slang) vr. to die, kick the bucket (slang)

PETATERO -RA: EL MERO PETATERO/LA MERA PETATERA the boss, the big cheese (coll.)

PETATÓN -TONA EL MERO PETATÓN/ LA MERA PETATONA the boss, the big cheese

PETICOUT (Eng.) m. petticoat

PETRA (dim. of) Petrona

PEYER (var. of) peer vn.

PEZÓN: PEZÓN ENLECHADO engorged nipple, caked breast

PIATÓN -TONA (var. of) peatón -tona

PICADILLO confetti (see also HACER PICADILLO)

PICADO -DA adj. ready for more, stimulated, excited (ref. to person whose appetite has been whetted by something); DIENTE PICADO tooth with a cavity; ¡QUÉ PICADO! (fixed expression) You'd like that, wouldn't you? (used iron.)

PÍCAP (Eng.) m. (var. of) pícop

PICAR va. to provoke, incite, needle (fig.); to bug (slang), annoy, bother: "¿Qué te pica?" 'What's bugging you?'; PA' QUE SE PIQUE(N) / PA' QUE TE PIQUES (slang) Eat your heart out! (slang), Put that in your pipe and smoke it (slang); PICARLE A ALGUIEN LOS OJOS to make a fool out of someone; vr. to become excited by something and to want more of it, get a taste of something and go to extremes to satisfy the appetite (cf. PICADO); to get angry; to inject oneself with drugs; to hurry, move quickly; ¡PÍCALE! Move it! Hurry up!;¡PÍCATE! interj. (an incitement to envy, approx.) Put that in your pipe and smoke it!

PICLE (Eng.) m. pickle

PICO: CERRAR EL PICO to keep silent; to become silent, shut up (coll.)

PICÓN -CONA m. act of provoking someone to anger; mpl. DAR PICONES to tease, make jealous needle (coll.); adj. mf. (ref. to instigator, i.e., person who enjoys needling or inciting to anger; ref. to person easily aroused to anger or otherwise incited)

PÍCOP (Eng.) m. pick-up truck (see also PÍCAP)

PICORETA child's toy metal trumpet

PICOSO -SA adj. spicy (ref. to food which "burns" the inside of the mouth)

PICOTE mf. chatterbox (coll.), excessive talker

PICUDO -DA card sharp (person expert and somewhat unscrupulous at playing cards)

PICHA (vulg.) penis; (Eng.) m. pitcher (baseball) (see also PÍCHAR); PICHA-QUECHA-NACA (composite ref. to game of baseball) (Eng.) (cf. QUECHA)

PICHADA (Eng.) pitch (in baseball)

PICHAR (Eng.) va. & vn. to pitch (baseball)

PICHEO (Eng.) act of pitching (baseball)

PÍCHER (Eng.) m. pitcher (baseball)

PICHICATO -TA stingy, miserly

PICHICUATE m. water snake (genus Natrix)

PICHÓN -CHONA m., f. born loser (coll.), person who always loses or comes out last; easy to defeat; easy to deceive; m. (vulg.) penis

PICHONEAR or PICHONIAR va. to effortlessly defeat a novice in a sports competition; vn. to engage in active sexual foreplay

PICHUDO (slang) cocksman (vulg., hum.) (ref. to man with a large penis)

PIDEMOS (var. of) pedimos (1st pers. pl. pres. indic. of pedir)

PIDICHE or PIDICHI (vars. of) pediche, pedichi

PIDIR (var. of) pedir

PILDORIENTO -TA (slang) user of narcotic pills

PIEDRA: fpl. gallstones; PIEDRAS EN
LA VEJIGA gallstones; ESA PIEDRA
NO CURVEÓ (id. to ESA PEDRADA
NO CURVEÓ, q.v. supra); ESTAR
TRES PIEDRAS (slang) to be tre-
mendous, terrific, very nice
(ref. to persons and things)

PIEDRADA (var. of) pedrada

PIEDRERÍA (var. of) pedrería

PIEDRIZA stoning, act of throwing
stones

PIERDA (var. of) piedra f.

PIERDADA (var. of) pedrada

PIERNA: MÁS PUEDEN LAS PIERNAS
QUE LOS BRAZOS (v.s. BRAZO)

PIERNUDO -DA large-legged; f. woman
with attractive legs

PIESES mpl. (var. of) pies (mpl.
of pie 'foot')

PIEZA: AGARRAR ALGO DE UNA PIEZA
(v.s. AGARRAR); CAMBIAR LA
PIEZA to stop harping on the
same topic, cease to talk about
the same thing: "Por fin cam-
bió la pieza y comenzó a hablar
de algo diferente"

PILDOREAR or PILDORIAR vr. to in-
gest narcotic pills: "Ese bato
se pildorea" 'That guy is a
pillpopper'

PÍLDORO -RA (slang) (person) high
on narcotic pills

PILIAR (var. of) pelear

PILÍCULA (var. of) película

PILINGO -GA small child; child small
for his/her age, pee-wee (slang)
(see also PILINGUACHE et al.,
PIRRONGO -GA); f. (vulg.) penis

PILINGUACHE or PILINGUACHI or PILIN-
GÜE mf. (vars. of) pilingo -ga

PILMAMA baby sitter

PILÓN m. additional amount, premium (a "little extra" given to
someone who has made a purchase);
DE PILÓN free, gratis

PILONGA (slang, vulg.) male sex organ, penis (cf. PILINGA)

PILOTEAR or PILOTIAR va. & vn. to
drive a car

PILLIDO sharp cry

PIMIENTITO -TA (hum.) half-pint
(coll.), person of very short
stature

PIMPO (Eng.) pimp, whoremaster

PIMPÓN (Eng.) m. ping-pong, table
tennis

PINCEL (see A PINCEL)

PINCHE adj. mean, base, despicable;
m. punk, hoodlum; mpl. clothes

pins

PINCHURRIENTO -TA weak-willed,
easily swayed

PINGA (vulg.) penis (cf. PRINGA);
mf. tricky person

PINGO mischievous person, little
devil (coll.)

PINGUAS fpl. (usually pl.) narcotic
pills; LLEVAR PINGUAS (slang)
to behave mischievously

PINGUITO -TA malicious; mischievous

PININOS (usually mpl.) baby's first
steps (when just learning to
walk)

PINTA (slang) jail, penitentiary

PINTAR va. to dye one's hair; vr.
escape, run off, leave rapidly

PINTERO -RA painter (Std. pintor m.)

PINTO -TA very dark-skinned though
without negroid facial features;
PINTO -TA VIEJO -JA jailbird
(coll.), person often jailed;
PONER PINTO A ALGUIEN to
heap with insults, tear to
pieces (fig.), tell someone
off in no uncertain terms

PINTORREGEAR or PINTORREGIAR vr. to
use cosmetics to excess

PINTOTE m. type of yellow catfish

PINTURA: PINTURA PA' LAS UÑAS nail
polish; NO PODER VER A AL-
GUIEN NI EN PINTURA not to be
able to stand the sight of someone, hate someone intensely

PIOCHA pointed beard; (slang) nice-
looking, attractive; swell,
great, keen, excellent (etc.)

PIOJERO or PIOJERA swarm of lice

PIÓN, PIONA (var. of) peón, peona
m.,f.

PIONILLO croton (Croton coresianus)
(herb prepared as a tea and
used in treating colic)

PIOR (var. of) peor

PIOSOL (Hispanization of) Pearsall,
Texas

PIPA (Ang.) pipe for conducting
gases or fluids (Std. tubo)
(cf. PAIPA)

PIPI or PIPÍ (euph.) f. penis; HA-
CER (LA) PIPI/PIPÍ (mildly
euph.) to urinate, "go pee-pee"
(euph., said esp. of and to
children)

PIPIÁN (slang) m. food (in general)

PIPILÍN (var. of) pipirín m.

PIPILISCO -CA near-sighted

PÍPILO (slang) gigolo; effeminate
man; male homosexual

PIPIRÍN (slang) m. food (in general) (cf. PIPILÍN)

PIPITORIA adj. (used only in the
following fixed expression:)
RAZA PIPITORIA (pej.) (ref. to

Mexicans or Mexican-Americans);
f. type of candy made with
brown sugar and pumpkin seeds
PIQUENIQUE (Eng.) m. picnic
PIQUETAZO (var. of) picotazo
PIQUETE provocation, insult; DARSE
UN PIQUETE (slang) vr. to inject narcotic drugs; ECHAR PI-
QUETES to insult; ESTAR DE
PIQUETE to be on unfriendly
terms; PIQUETE DE AGUJA (hum.)
fornication; SER DE PIQUETE to
have a hot temper; to enjoy inciting others to anger; to be
easily offended, quick to take
offense; (slang) to be a drug
addict
PIQUETEAR or PIQUETIAR (Eng.) va. to
picket (as a factory, by workers
on strike); to boycott
PIQUINIQUE (var. of) piquenique m.
PIQUITO kiss; small mouth
PIRATA (slang) drunk, soused; mf.
thief
PIRATÓN -TONA (slang) very drunk,
smashed (slang)
PIRFANTEAR or PIRFANTIAR va. & vr.
to dress up, dress elegantly
PIRINOLA top (child's toy); penis
PIRUJO -JA sly, astute, clever
PIRULERO -RA vendor of pirulí
(type of caramel candy); JUAN
PIRULERO (type of children's
game)
PIRRINGO -GA small child (see PILON-
GO et al.)
PISAR (slang) va. to fromp (slang),
fornicate (with); (Ang?) to step
on the gas (coll.), accelerate
a car
PISÓN m. (var. of pisotón?=) step,
heavy tread, heavy footstep
PISOTEADA or PISOTIADA trampling
PISPIS: TENER PISPIS to be afraid
PISPORRA or PISPORRIA bump on the
head
PISTE m. alcohol
PISTEADERA or PISTIADERA act of
drinking alcohol
PISTEAR or PISTIAR va. & vn. to
drink alcohol
PISTO -TA drunk, inebriated; m.
alcohol; ECHARSE UN PISTO to
take a drink of alcohol; m.
money; small quantity of anything
PISTÓN -TONA very drunk, ploughed
(slang)
PISTUDO -DA wealthy
PITA dagger
PITAR va. & vn. to honk (the horn
of a car); to blow on a whistle,
blow on any wind instrument
PITAZO -ZA clever, shrewd; wise,

intelligent
PITO -TA (id. to PITAZO -ZA)
PIZARRO asbestos siding (used in
the construction of buildings)
PIZCA harvest (usually ref. to cotton crop harvest)
PIZCADOR -DORA m., f. cotton picker
PIZCAR va. to pick cotton; to pick
up, collect, glean
PLANCHA JUGARSE PLANCHA to be slow
to react (because of lack of
preparation, laziness, etc.)
PLATA (see A PLATA LIMPIA)
PELOTAZO astute, clever, alert:
"Juanita es un pelotazo; cuidado con ella"
PLACA false teeth, dental plate;
plaque (clay-like substance
that accumulates between teeth);
(slang) police force, cops,
"the badge"
PLACER: HACERLE PLACER A ALGUIEN
to treat someone well, be very
courteous toward someone; to
humor someone
PLANCHA wallflower (fig.), shy and
retiring person; person who
fails to take advantage of op-
portunities; HACERSE PLANCHA
to overstay one's welcome; TI-
RAR PLANCHA to be left holding
the bag (fig.), be abandoned
(as by one's boy- or girlfriend)
PLANCHADA fsg. (var. of) planchado
msg. 'clothes to be ironed'
PLANCHAR: PLANCHAR OREJA (slang)
to sleep
PLANIAR (var. of) planear
PLANTA: PLANTA DE HUEVOS (Ang.)
eggplant
PLANTADO -DA stood up, jilted;
dressed elegantly; f. hard slap
on the face
PLÁNTANO (var. of) plátano
PLANTAR vr. to dress elegantly; to
overstay one's welcome, visit
for longer than one should;
PLANTÁRSELA A ALGUIEN to hit
someone with one's fist or with
the palm of one's hand
PLANTÍA or PLANTILLA first base-
man's glove (baseball)
PLASTA lazy person; slow-moving
person; hair oil; adj. greasy
PLATICADA chat, conversation
PLATICADERA lively conversation
PLATICADOR -DORA chatterbox, ex-
cessive talker
PLATICAR va. to tell a story
PLATICÓN -CONA fond of talking
PLATO phonograph record; base (in
baseball); COLMARLE A ALGUIEN
EL PLATO to exhaust someone's

patience; ECHARSE AL PLATO to take advantage of someone; to seduce sexually; to kill

PLEBE f. mob of lower-class people; lower-class people in general; gang of children; children in general

PLEGÓN: ECHARLE A ALGUIEN UN PLEGÓN to tell someone off

PLEIT (Eng.) m. home plate (baseball)

PLEITO boxing; boxing match

PLIT (Eng.) m. (usually mpl. PLITS) pleat

PLOCHA (var. of) piocha

PLOGA f. or PLOGUE m. (Eng.) plug (e.g., electric plug); (vulg.) mistress, kept woman

PLOGUE f. (Eng.) (vulg.) mistress, kept woman, bed-mate

PLOGUEAR or PLOGUIAR (Eng.) va. to plug, plug in (Std. enchufar); (Eng.) (vulg.) va. to fornicate

PLOMAZO pistol shot

PLOMEAR or PLOMIAR (slang) va. & vn. to shoot with a pistol

PLOMO -MA gray (color); m.,f. slow-moving person who dislikes work; SER (MUY) PLOMO -MA to be (very) slow to react to a given situation

PLUJEAR or PLUJIAR (Eng.) va. & vn. to plunge

PLUMA prostitute; woman of easy virtue, run-around (coll.)

POBRAR (var. of) probar va.

POCA or PÓCAR (Eng.) m. poker (card game) (see also PÓQUER)

POCITO (hum.) vagina

POCO: ¡A POCO! (fixed expression of surprise: You don't say!, Really?!; (expression of doubt): "¡A poco crees que me vas a engañar!" 'So you think you're going to cheat me!'; POCO A POQUITO (var. of) poco a poco

POCHISMO Spanish word or construction reflecting English influence (cf. POCHO -CHA)

POCHO -CHA (pej.) "gringoized" Mexican; (pej.) Mexican-American, Chicano

PODER: PODERLAS to be influential; to be a favorite (e.g., in political circles, among members of the opposite sex, etc.): "Él es de los que las puede"; PODERLE A ALGUIEN to wound, hurt; to displease, annoy: "Le pudo lo que le dije" 'What I said hurt him'; PUEDE QUE perhaps, maybe

PODO (slang) marihuana

POETA (slang, ant.) jitterbug

(person who enjoys dancing the jitterbug, a popular dance of the 1940's)

POLECÍA (var. of) policía

POLI f. police

POLICÍA: HIJO DE POLICÍA (v.s. HIJO)

POLIS f. insurance policy

POLIS (Eng.) m. policeman; f. police force

POLITIQUIAR (var. of) politiquear

PÓLIZA (Ang.) policy, course of action

POLO -LA (dims of) Hipolito, Apolonio, Leopoldo -da

POLQUEAR or POLQUIAR (var. of) polcar

POLQUERO -RA person who enjoys polkas

POLVADERA (var. of) polvareda 'dust cloud'

POLVEADO -DA or POLVIADO -DA all powdered up, covered with powder

POLVEAR or POLVIAR vr. to powder oneself, cover oneself with powder (e.g., to powder one's nose)

POLVERO -RA (vars. of) polvareda; f. powder puff

POLVITO: ECHAR POLVITOS to hex, bewitch (see also POLVO)

POLVO: ECHAR POLVOS to hex, bewitch

POLVOSO -SA (var. of) polvoroso -sa

POLLITO: POLLITO DE ESTACA (=pollo -lla q.v. infra)

POLLO spit, phlegm

POLLO -LLA or POLLÓN -LLONA person entering a subsequent stage in his/her life, e.g., an adolescent about to become an adult; can also ref. to someone whose physique is advanced for his/her chronological age, e. g., an adolescent with a body that is already adult

POMPA (Eng.) faucet; pump (Std. bomba)

POMPAÑERO -RA (rus.) (var. of) compañero -ra

POMPE or POMPI (dims. of) Pomposa

POMPEADOR -DORA or POMPIADOR -DORA (slang) swinger (person who enjoys a very active and adventuresome sex life) (cf. POMPEAR)

POMPEAR or POMPIAR (Eng.) va. to pump; (vulg.) to fornicate

POMPIADO -DA (slang) tired, exhausted

PONCHAR (Eng.) va. to puncture; to punch; vr. to go flat (said of an aut. tire)

PONCHE: ESTAR PONCHE (slang, Eng.) to be punchy, punch-drunk (analogy with behavior of a groggy boxer); (slang) to be crazy

PONCHE or PONCHI (Eng.) m. punch, blow with the fist

PONCHI (var. of) ponche adj.

PONE (Eng.) m. pony (see also PONI)

PONER vr. (var. of) oponerse

PONER: va. to supply, provide, furnish: "El padrino va a poner el salón" 'The best man is going to furnish the dance hall' ESTAR PONIÉNDOSELA A ALGUIEN (see ESTAR); PON (var. of) supon (< suponer); PONER DE PATITAS EN LA CALLE to fire, dismiss (from a job) in short order; to run off, tell to leave (usually ref. to the manner in which one common law partner tells the other to depart); PONER EL CARRO EN REVERSA to shift into reverse gear; PONER CUIDADO to pay attention; PONER A ALGUIEN AL ALBA (slang) to alert someone, put someone on guard; PONER A ALGUIEN DEL ASCO to heap insults upon someone: "Pobrecito, lo pusieron del asco"; PONER A ALGUIEN EN MAL to speak ill of someone, discredit, run down (fig.); PONER A ALGUIEN PINTO to heap insults on someone; PONER COLA (slang) to "tail" someone (coll.), have someone followed; PONER DE LA BASURA to heap with insults, shout insults at: "Se metió a la casa porque la estaban poniendo de la basura"; PONER (EL) DEDO to accuse, point the finger at; PONER GORRO to harass; PONERLE EL OJO MORADO A ALGUIEN to give someone a black eye; PONER NOMBRE to name, give a name to: "¿Cómo le pusieron?" 'What name did they give him?'; PONER PA' TRAS (Ang.) to put back, fail to promote (as a child in school); to put back, return to a place (as a glass to a cupboard); PONER UN HASTA AQUI to draw the line (fig.), indicate the limits beyond which a particular form of behavior is unacceptable; vr. PONERSE ÁGUILA (slang) to become alert, be on the alert; PONERSE CABALLÓN -LLONA (slang) to get high on alcohol or narcotic drugs; PONERSE (CON) to challenge, mess

around with: "No te pongas con él" 'Don't mess around with him'; PONERSE CON UNO DEL TAMAÑO DE UNO to pick on someone one's own size; PONERSE CUETE to get drunk; PONERSE CHANGO to become alert; PONERSE DEL ASCO to get extremely dirty; PONERSE EL AIRE PESADO for a situation to become tense; PONERSE EN EL AVISPERO to become alert; PONERSE EN LA LÍNEA/LINIA to get drunk; PONÉRSELA A ALGUIEN to hit someone (fig.), succeed in obtaining money through pressure or artful persuasion: "Si no te cuidas, te la van a poner"; PONÉRSELAS to get drunk: "Anoche se las puso, por eso todavía no se levanta"; PONERSE LAS BOTAS to have a ball (fig.), have a good time; PONERSE PESADO -DA to get tough with, act insultingly towards: "Hórale, no te pongas tan pesado" 'Don't get so tough'; PONERSE TRUCHA / PONERSE TRUCHE (slang) to become alert, get wise (slang)

PONI (Eng.) m. pony

PONÍ, PONISTE(S), PONIÓ, PONIMOS, PONIERON (vars. of) puse, pusiste, etc. (pret. conj. of poner)

¡PÓNELE!, ¡PÓNGA(N)LE! interj. Get to work!, Get busy!, Get with it!, Hurry up! (etc.); ¡PÓNELE JORGE AL NIÑO! interj. Get to work, Get busy! (etc.)

POPE (Eng.) m. puppy, infant dog

POPULACIÓN (Ang.) f. population, number of inhabitants within a given area

POQUEAR or POQUIAR (Eng.) vn. to play poker

PÓQUER (Eng.) m. poker (card game) (see also POCA et al.)

POR: DE POR SÍ It's bad enough as it is (without your making it worse): "De por sí que hace frío y tú dejas la puerta abierta" 'It's cold enough as it is, and you have to go and leave the door open'; POR LA BUENA willingly; POR LA MALA by force; POR MIENTRAS meanwhile; POR SÍ LAS MOSCAS just in case; POR SÍ O POR NO just in case: "Vamos a cerrar la puerta por sí o por no" 'We're going to shut the door, just in case'

PORA m. man encharged with maintaining sheep-shearing equipment

PORAZO (Eng., cf. PORE) blow-out

(slang), large noisy party

PORE (Eng.) m. party

PORO (var. of) pero conj.

PORTABLE (Eng.) adj. portable (Std. portátil)

PORTAMONEDA fsg. (var. of) porta-monedas fpl.

POS (var. of) pues conj.

POSTA ball bearing; pellet; rail-road tie

POSTE tall; skinny; (vulg.) m. rod (slang,vulg.), large penis

POSTEMILLA abscess in the mouth

POSTERO -RA (pej.) cedar chopper (lower- or working-class cen-tral Texas Anglo-Saxon); poor white (in general)

POSTOTES (Eng.) mpl. Post Toasties (brand name of type of break-fast cereal); dry breakfast cereal (in general)

POZO (slang) solitary confinement cell in a jail

POZOL(E) m. drink made from corn and sugar

PRAI: LA PRAI (Hispanization of) La Pryor, Texas

PRACTICIAR (Eng?) (var. of?) prac-ticar 'to practice'

PRÁTICA (var. of) práctica

PREBA (var. of) prueba

PREBAR (var. of) probar

PRECINCTO or PRECINTO (Eng.) pre-cinct (electoral)

PRECULA (Eng.) pre-cooling system in vegetable cannery, used to keep vegetables fresh and un-spoiled

PRECUPAR (var. of) preocupar

PRECURAR (var. of) procurar

PREGUNTAR: PREGUNTAR UNA PREGUNTA or PREGUNTAR UNA CUESTIÓN (Ang.) to ask a question (Std. hacer una pregunta)

PRENCEPAL (var. of) principal

PRENCIPIO (var. of) principio

PRENDER va. to hook on (=cause to be addicted to) narcotic drugs

PRENDIDO -DA hooked on (addicted to) narcotic drugs

PREVILEGIO (var. of) privilegio

PRICULA (Eng.) (var. of) precula

PRICULERO -RA (Eng.--see PRECULA/PRICULA) worker in the pre-cooling section of a vegetable processing plant

PRIETO -TA (term of endearment)

PRIMERO: DE PRIMERO at the begin-ning

PRINCIPAL (Ang.) m. principal of a school (Std. director de escue-la)

PROBE or PROBRE (var. of) pobre 'poor'

PROCURAR va. to look after, watch over: "Juan la procura mucho a su hermanita"; to make a play for, seek to gain the affections of: "Jorge anda procurando a esa chavala"; to seek out the company of, go look for

PRODUCÍ, PRODUCISTE, etc. (vars. of) produje, produjiste, etc. (pret. forms of producir)

PROFESIONISTA (var. of) profesional

PRONTA adj. f. (sole ref. to women) (said of a very young adoles-cent girl who begins to "run around with" men)

PRONTO: AHORA PRONTO recently

PRONUNCIAR (Ang.) va. to declare that something is so (Std. declarar): "Yo los pronuncio casados" 'I now pronounce you man and wife'

PROPETARIO -RIA (var. of) propie-tario -ria

PROTESTANTE -TA m., f. Protestant (Std. protestante mf.)

PROVISIÓN fsg. groceries

PUCHA: ¡LA PUCHA! interj. Oh yeah?! (simultaneous indica-tion of doubt and defiance)

PUCHAR (Eng.) va. to push, shove

PUCHE (Eng.) m. push, shove

PUCHI interj. Whew! (expresses distaste towards an awful smell)

PUEBLO downtown, business section of a city

PUELA frying pan

PUERTA (interj., vulg.) (used to indicate that a woman is re-vealing, whether intentionally or not, those parts of her body which, should not be shown, esp. the vaginal region); DAR PUERTA to show off something new; (said of women) to show (uncover) the vaginal region, whether intentionally or not; DE PUERTA nice, good, super (expression of approval)

PUERTAZO (var. of) portazo

PUERTERO -RA (var. of) portero -ra

PUERTÓN (var. of) portón m.

PUJAR vn. to grunt

PUJIDO grunt

PUL (Eng.) m. pool, billiards; (Eng.) pull, influence (usually political)

PULGA fpl.: ¡ÚJULE, PA' MIS PUL-GAS! (fixed expression of annoyance:) 'That's the last thing I needed!'

PULGIENTO -TA flea-ridden, lousy (in the literal sense)

PULIAR (Eng.) va. to pull

PULMAN (Eng.) m. pullman

PUNTADA   very appropriate joke or story; fpl. ¡QUÉ PUNTADAS! What crazy ideas!

PUNTÍA (var. of) puntilla

PUNTO -TA: SER PUNTO -TA to be cooperative, accommodating; to to be game, willing to try something; mpl. ANDAR DE PUNTOS (v.s. ANDAR)

PUÑETA: HACERSE LA PUÑETA (vulg.) to masturbate; f. masturbation

PUÑETEADA or PUÑETIADA (vulg.) masturbation

PUÑETEAR or PUÑETIAR (vulg.) va. to masturbate

PUÑETERO -RA (vulg.) fond of masturbation

PURGACIÓN f. gonorrhea, clap (slang)

PURO -RA utter, absolutely; only, nothing but (e.g.,: "Pura perica!" 'Nothing but talk!')

PUTEAR or PUTIAR vn. to solicit customers (said of prostitutes)

PUTO (slang) male homosexual, fag (slang)

Q

QUÉ: ¡QUÉ ESPERANZA(S)! interj. (used to express strong doubt as to whether something will take place:) That'll be the day!; ¡QUÉ BONITO!, ¿NO? (iron.) That's a fine howdy do!; ¡QUÉ GRACIA! (iron.) Why, that's nothing!; ¿QUÉ HÚBOLE? or ¿QUIÚBOLE? (slang) What's up?, What's happening? (phrases often used in greeting); ¿QUÉ LE HACE? What's the difference? What does it matter? So what? (fixed expressions); QUE NI QUÉ for sure, certainly, without doubt: "Ese niño se va a enfermar, que ni qué"; ¿QUE QUÉ? Huh? Whatcha say? (discourteous); ¡QUÉ SI! (stress on qué) I should say so!, Absolutely!: "¿La besó el novio? --¡Qué si!"; ¿QUÉ TAL? (indication of pleasant surprise upon hearing good news) How about that?, Imagine that!; ¿QUÉ TANTO? How much? (Std. ¿Cuanto?); SER QUÉ DE: ¿QUÉ

ES UD. DE MARÍA? How are you related to María?; YO QUE TÚ (YO QUE ÉL, etc.) If I were you (If I were him, etc.)

QUEBRADO -DA (Ang.) broke, penniless; (Ang.) f. break, opportunity; first shot in a game of pool; DAR QUEBRADA to give someone an opportunity: "¡Dame una quebrada nomás!" 'Just give me a break!'

QUEBRANZAS fpl. (hum.) taxes

QUEBRAR: SER DE ESOS QUE NO QUIEBRAN NI UNA TAZA/NI UN PLATO not to be able to hurt a fly (coll.), be extremely gentle

QUECHA (Eng.) m. catcher (baseball) (see also QUECHE et al.)

QUECHAR (Eng.) va. to catch (a ball, in baseball); vn. to play the position of catcher (in baseball)

QUECHE or QUECHER (Eng.) m. catcher (in baseball) (see also QUECHA)

QUEDAR va. to fit, match, harmonize with, go well with: "Este traje le queda bien" 'This suit fits him well'; vn. to match, harmonize: "¿Le queda ese pantalón a ese saco?" 'Do those pants match that coat?'; to matter, concern, involve: "¿A mí qué me queda de eso?" 'What's that to me?/ How does that involve me?'; vn. to die: "Allá quedó" 'He died then and there' 'That was the end of him'; vr. to end, terminate: "La vista se quedó donde se besaron" 'The movie ended where they kissed each other'; AY QUE QUEDE let it rest, let it be (etc.): QUEDAR A LA MEDIDA (for clothes) to fit to a T: "El sombrero le quedó a la medida" 'The hat fit him to a T'; QUEDAR AL PELO to fit to a T: "La chaqueta le quedó al pelo" 'The coat fit him to a T'; QUEDAR EN DONDE MISMO to make no progress, make little headway; to not better oneself, not improve; QUEDAR EN NADA to amount to nothing, turn out to be a failure; to fail to reach an agreement or solution; to be abandoned: "¡Qué pasó con el programa? --Quedó en nada"; QUEDAR HECHO PEDAZOS / QUEDAR COMO TRAPO MOJADO to be dead tired, end up dead tired (as after vigorous activity); QUEDAR PAREJOS to be tied, end up in a tie; QUEDAR-LE A ALGUIEN vn. to be some-one's business, be of interest to someone: "¿A ti qué te queda eso?" 'What business is that of yours?'; vr. QUEDARSE SÚPITO -TA to fall fast asleep as soon as one lies down; vr. QUEDAR(SE) TIESO -SA to die; vr. QUEDARSE LIMPIO -PIA to become broke (penniless), get cleaned out (slang); QUEDARSE TAMAÑITO -TA to be left on pins and needles, become nervous in anticipation of; QUEDÁRSELE to retain (a thought): "Eso no se me queda a mí, por más que lo estudie" 'I can never remember that, no matter how much I study it'; SIN QUE ME QUEDE NADA (SIN QUE TE etc. QUEDE NADA) all modesty aside, if I say so myself: "¡Qué bien escribí esta carta!, sin que me quede nada"; vr. TÚ ¿DÓNDE TE QUEDAS? You're no better, You're just as bad

QUEDRÉ, QUEDRÁS, etc. (vars. of) querré, querrás, etc. (future conj. of querer)

QUEDRÍA, QUEDRÍAS, etc. (vars. of) querría etc. (cond. conjugation of querer)

QUEHACEROSA or QUIHACEROSA adj. & f. woman who enjoys doing housework

QUEJÓN -JONA plaintive, complaining; querulous

QUELA (dim. of) Ángela or Micaela

QUEMADO -DA suntanned; f. burn, scald

QUEMADORA incinerator

QUEMAR vr. to be close to the solu-tion of, be near to a hidden ob-ject one is seeking (usually in a game); to get a sun tan; TRAER QUE QUEMAR (slang) to have cigarettes in one's possession

QUEMAZÓN m. fire (Std. incendio); an object that has been burned; VENTA DE QUEMAZÓN fire sale (sale of merchandise minimally damaged by a fire in the store)

QUEMÓN m. burn; (fig.) burn, insult; DAR QUEMONES (slang) to attempt to anger, to taunt, to needle (coll.)

QUÉMPAR or QUÉMPER (Eng.) m. camper (recreational vehicle)

QUEN (rus.) (var. of) quien

QUENEDE (Hispanization of) Kenedy, Texas

QUENO -NA (dims. resp. of) Eugenio, Eugenia

QUENQUE adv. piggyback; m, piggy-back ride; SUBIR AL QUENQUE to climb on (someone's back) for a piggyback ride

QUEQUE or QUEIQUE (Eng.) m. cake; ¡AIRE AL QUEQUE! interj. Beat it!, Scram!, Get out of here!

QUEQUITO (Eng.) cupcake

QUERENDÓN -DONA loving, affection-ate; (ref. to person who forms close attachments easily)

QUERMES (var. of) quermés or quer-mese m. 'church bazaar'

QUERO, QUERES, etc. (vars. of) quiero, quieres, etc. (pres. indic. conj. of querer)

QUESO (slang) smegma that collects around the lower part of the head of an uncircumcised child's penis

QUETA (dim. of) Enriqueta

QUIEN: ¿A QUIÉN Y A CUÁNTOS? What concern is that of anyone's?; ¿QUIÉN TE LO MANDA? I told you so!

QUIHACER (var. of) quehacer m.

QUIMONA (var. of) quimono

QUINCEAÑERA or QUINCIAÑERA girl who is just turning fifteen and in whose honor a "coming-out" party is traditionally given

QUINDA or QUINDER (Eng. < German) m. kindergarten

QUINESVIL (Hispanization of) Kings-ville, Texas

QUINIPA (Hispanization of) Knippa, Texas

QUINO (dim. of) Joaquín

QUINTA small park-like area contain-ing a gazebo, a band platform, etc., in the center, which is used for meetings or recreation-al purposes

QUIQUE (dim. of) Enrique

QUIRE (Eng.) mf. kitty, kitten

QUIRO -RA (Eng.) kiddo, bud, bub (slang) (terms of endearment, also vocatives)

QUIT (Eng.) Kid (used, at times maliciously, as a prefix to a series of sobriquets denoting physical attributes, e.g., QUIT JOROBAS ⌊said to a hunch-back⌋

QUITAR va. QUITAR LA LINDA (slang) to deflower (euph.), cause to lose one's virginity (said of women): "Si no te cuidas te van a quitar la linda"; vr. to stop, cease, subside (esp. with ref. to weather phenomena): "Ya se quitó l'agua" 'It's stopped raining now'; QUIEN QUITE Y perhaps: "Quien quite y vengan temprano" 'Perhaps they'll come early'; NO SE LE QUITA You can't take that away from him (fig.), You've got to give him his due: "No se le quita, de veras sabe sus cosas" 'You've got to hand it to him, he really knows his stuff'

R

RABO: VIEJO RABO VERDE (see VERDE)
RABÓN -BONA (hum.) short-statured; overly short (ref. to articles of clothing shorter than is appropriate): "Ese vestido le queda muy rabón" 'That dress is too short for you'; PANTALONES RABONES highwater pants (hum.) pants not reaching the ankle
RACHAR (Eng.) va. to rush, crowd up upon (esp. in sports)
RADIODERÍA (var. of) radiador (aut.)
RAFA or RAFE or RAFEL (dims. of) Rafael
RAID (Eng.) m. ride (in a car)
RAIHUOT (Hispanization of) Redwood, Texas
RAITAR or RAITEAR or RAITIAR (Eng.) vn. to ride (in a car), go for a ride, go riding
RAITÓN (Eng.) m. ride (in a car)
RAIZ (var. of) raíz f.
RAJADA (vulg.) vulva
RAJADA (var. of) rajadura
RAJAR vr. RAJARSE CON to denounce, squeal (slang), betray to: "Ya no tengo nada que ver con él porque se rajó con la policía" 'I don't have anything to do with him anymore because he squealed to the cops'
RAJETA(S) mfsg. (mfpl.) (most often used as an adjective) tattle-tale, betrayer, denouncer, squealer (slang); breaker of promises: "Todo el mundo sabe que ella es muy rajetas"
RAJOLEAR or RAJOLIAR vr. to back down, take back (a promise)
RAJÓN -JONA coward; tattle-tale, betrayer, stool pigeon (slang); breaker of promises
RALEA bunch of disorderly and ill-bred persons
RALO -LA weak, flavorless (commonly ref. to coffee or other beverage)
RAMAS fpl. bushes

RAMFLA (slang) jalopy, old battered-up car
RANCHERO -RA adj. shy, bashful, "countrified"; country; regional: MÚSICA RANCHERA country music (the Mexican and Chicano equivalent of the Anglo-American "country and western" music)
RANCHO small rural farming community; (Eng.) ranch (Std. hacienda); HACER RANCHO to overstay one's welcome, continue to visit for too long; adj. DE RANCHO countrified, cornfed (coll.), farm-fresh, hickish, from the sticks: "Tu primo es muy de rancho" 'Your cousin is quite farm-fresh'; SER PURO RANCHO to be very countrified, straight from the farm (fig.), a hick from the sticks (coll.)
RANFLA (orthog. var. of) ramfla
RANQUEAR or RANQUIAR (Eng.) va. to rank, arrange, classify
RAPTAR (Ang.) va. to rape (Std. violar)
RAPTO (Ang.) rape
RAQUETA (Eng?) racket, illegal business operation
RASCADA or RASCADERA act or effect of scratching
RASCARRABIAS mfsg. irritable and easily annoyed person
RASCÓN m. (id. to RASCADA supra)
RASCUACHE mf. punk, worthless person
RASGUÑADA (id. to RASCADA supra)
RASGUÑÓN m. scratch
RASPA adj. & f. riff-raff, ill-bred person: "Había mucha gente raspa ahí"; stingy, parsimonious; f. snow cone (shaved ice, to which is added a sweet fruit flavoring)
RASPADA act and effect of scraping
RASPADORA apparatus used to make scraped ice (esp. for snow cones --see RASPA)
RASPOSO -SA scratchy, uneven (ref. to surfaces), bumpy
RASQUERA itching sensation
RASTRILLAZO blow delivered with a rake
RASTRILLO (slang) comb
RASURADA act or effect of shaving
RATO: A POCO RATO shortly, soon thereafter; MÁS AL RATO (pleonasm) (var. of) al rato
RATÓN: SER RATÓN DE UN AGUJERO to be a one-woman man or a one-man woman (i.e., to be completely uninterested in any member of the opposite sex except one's spouse)
RATONERA (fig.) old and decrepit

house, squalid or depressing
dwelling; swarm of mice or rats;
den of thieves, hang-out for criminal or other low-life elements
RATONERO (var. of) ratonera 'mouse
hole', rat hole' (also fig. 'old
house')
RAUN(D) (Eng.) m. round (period of
time into which a boxing match
is divided); DAR UN RAUND to
go for a whole round, be able
to last for a whole round (boxing)
RAYA pay, wages, paycheck; penny-
pitching (game won by person who
pitches a penny closest to a
designated line)
RAYADO -DA (said of person carrying
large sums of money or various
other valuable possessions);
scratched: "Ese disco está rayado" 'That record is scratched'
RAYAR (rus.) va. to write; to pay
wages; vr. to come into money
or property; to hit a streak of
good luck; RAYARSE EL DISCO to
sound like a broken record (said
of any conversation in which the
speaker wears out the listeners
by harping on the same subject):
"¡Cállate, ese disco ya se rayó!"
RAZA (collective ref. to persons of
Hispanic background in general;
also ref. esp. to Mexican-Americans; note: the word may have
negative or pej. connotations to
older Mexican-Americans): "En
esa escuela había pura raza"
'There were nothing but Mexican-
Americans in that school'
REAJUSTE m. period of adjustment
REAL m. unit of currency equal to
twelve and a half cents, hence
only used in multiples of two
or more, with ref. to U.S. currency; thus DOS REALES= $.25,
CUATRO REALES= $.50, OCHO REALES=
$1.00
REALIZAR (Ang.) va. to realize, become aware of (Std. darse cuenta
de)
REATA or RIATA (vulg.) penis; interj.
Pow! (accompanies the administra-
tion or simulation of a blow,
usually with the fist); SER
BUENA REATA/RIATA (coll.) to be
a good Joe (coll.), be considered a good fellow by others; (see
also PANCHO RIATA)
REATAL or RIATAL m. large quantity
of something
REATAZO or RIATAZO blow with the
fist; mpl. severe beating,
whipping, thrashing (see also

DAR REATAZOS)
REATIZA or RIATIZA severe beating
(see also DARSE UNA REATIZA)
REBAJAR va. to belittle, disparage;
humiliate; to reduce in price;
(also REBAJAR DE PESO) to lose
weight, reduce
REBAJE or REBAJO reduction of price,
discount
REBALOSO -SA· (rus.) (var. of) res-
baloso -sa
REBATAR (var. of) arrebatar
REBORUJO noise; confusion, commotion,
melee
REBOTAZO big bounce
REBUSTO -TA (vars. of) robusto -ta
RECA (Eng.) wrecker (Std. camión
grúa)
RECAR (Eng.) va. to wreck (usually
a car); vr. to have a wreck
RECARGADO -DA arrogant, presumptious

RECARGAR vr. to brag, boast; RE-
CARGÁRSELAS to brag, boast
RECARGUISTA mf. braggart
RECAR (Eng.) va. to wreck
RECEBIR (var. of) recibir
RECLAMAR va. to confront (i.e.,
to confront someone with the
truth): "Voy a reclamarle la
verdad"; "No dijo nada cuando se
lo reclamé"
RECLE: AL RECLE (slang) in a while
RECOGIDO -DA adopted child; foster
child
RECONOCIENCIA recognition; acknowl-
edgment; gratitude, apprecia-
tion
RECORTADO -DA low on funds (see also
ANDAR RECORTADO -DA DE DINERO)
RECORTAR va. to denigrate, put
down (a person), speak ill of;
to trim a small amount (of hair);
to lay off, disemploy
RECORTE m. newspaper clipping;
slight hair trim
RECRECIÓN (var. of) recreación f.
RECULÓN m. sudden jerk made by a
car when the accelerator is de-
pressed rapidly
RECHANCHO -CHA selfish, egocentric
RECHINAR vr. RECHINÁRSELE A ALGUIEN
EL CUERPO to get goose pimples
(goose bumps)
RECHINCHE stingy, parsimonious (cf.
CHINCHE)
REDEPENTE (var. of) de repente
REDETIR or REDITIR (var. of) derr-
etir
REDICULEZA or RIDICULEZA (vars. of)
ridiculez f.
REDÍCULO (var. of) ridículo
RÉFERI (Eng.) m. referee
REFERIR va. to recall a favor one

has done (for someone): "A mí
no me gusta que refieran nada"
'I don't like for people to recall the favors they've done
me'

REFÍN (slang) m. food

REFINAR (slang) va. to eat

REFUEGA wild and volatile woman

REGADERA shower-bath; (ref. to any
messy room full of misplaced
objects)

REGANCHAR (var. of) reenganchar va.
to contract for work (often
for agricultural work, field
work, etc.)

REGANCHE (var. of) reenganche m.
(used with the following variant
meanings:) bonus given to a
(farm) worker in advance of the
start of the job

REGANCHISTA mf. payer of the reganche (q.v.) bonus

REGAÑADA bawling out, scolding

REGAR: REGARLA to make a mess of
things, foul things up, do a
poor job; to create problems; to
be foolish; REGÁRSELA to make
trouble

REGRESAR va. to return an object
to its owner

REGÜELTO -TA (var. of) revuelto -ta

REIMUNDO (var. of) Raimundo

REIR (var. of) reír

REJA (slang) jail

RELACIÓN f. buried treasure

RELAJAR va. to ridicule, make a
fool of; vr. to ridicule oneself

RELAJE m. trick, joke; cruel teasing, humiliation

RELATIVO -VA (Ang.) relative (person one is related to by blood
or other kinship ties)

RELÍS m. sharp cliff, precipice;
(Eng.) m. release (from a job,
from prison, from responsibility,
etc.)

RELÓ (var. of) reloj m.

RELOJ DE ALARMA (Ang.) m. alarm clock

REMODELACIÓN f. remodeling (of a
house or other edifice)

REMOVER(SE)LE A ALGUIEN LA CONSCIEN-
CIA to be bothered by one's
conscience: "Se le removió la
consciencia"

REMPLE (slang) m. car, automobile

REMUDA herd of horses

REMUDERA lead horse, horse which
wears a bell in a herd of
horses

REMUDERO cowboy in charge of watching the horses at night

REMUEQUES mpl. excessive and taste-
less adornments

RENDIR vn. to suffice, be enough
(usually used in the negative):
"Veinte tortillas no rinden a-
quí; debes hacer más"

RENEGAR vn. to protest, complain,
grumble

RENEGÓN -GONA m., f. constant complainer

RENTAR (Ang?) va. to lease, rent,
offer for rent: "Voy a rentar
esta casa el mes que viene porque me hace falta el dinero"

RENTERO -RA (Ang?) renter, person
who pays money for the privi-
lege of using or occupying)

REPELAR vn. to complain, grumble

REPELIDO act of complaining, grumbl-
ing

REPELÓN -LONA complainer, grumbler

REPETIR vn. to belch, burp (esp.
said of babies)

REPIOCHA adj. mf. extremely beautiful; terrific, swell (coll.)

REPITIR (var. of) repetir

REPUÑOSO -SA selfish

REQUE (Eng.) m. wreck (of an automobile)

REQUEAR or REQUIAR (Eng.) va. to
wreck (a car); vr. to have a
wreck (see also RECAR)

RÉQUER (Eng.) m. wrecker (Std. camión grúa)

REQUINTADO -DA (var. of) arrequintado -da

RES f. numbskull; CAER LA RES (ref.
to someone who has been fooled,
taken in, deceived): "¿Sabes
que Samuel se casó con ésa de
quien te hablé antes? -- ¡Uh,
pues cayó la res!"

RESACA artificial lake or reservoir

RESBALÓN m. affair (amorous); AN-
DAR EN EL RESBALÓN to be having an affair; RESBALÓN -LONA
shrewd, clever, slippery (fig.);
teasing

RESEDÁ (var. of) reseda

RESEQUEDAC f. dryness

RESONGAR to talk back rudely (esp.
to one's elders)

RESORTES mpl. suspenders (for trousers)

RESPINGAR vn. to complain; to kick
(as a burro); to blow one's top
(slang), get angry

RESPINGÓN -GONA m., f. habitual
complainer

RESPONSABLIDAD f. (var. of) responsa-
bilidad

RESPONSALIDAD f. (var. of) responsa-
bilidad

RESTA (slang) restaurant

RESURADA (var. of) rasurada (cf.
resurar)

RESURAR (Eng?, combination of 'razor'
with Std. rasurar?) va. to shave;
vr. to shave oneself

RESVIL (Hispanization of) Reedville,
Texas

RETACAR va. to fill a container
tightly up to the very top; vr.
to stuff oneself (said of someone who overeats)

RETEJILADO -DA very rapid: "La chota
lo paró porque iba retejilado";
in quick succession: "Perdieron
cinco juegos retejilados" 'They
lost five games in quick succession'

RETESUAVE (slang) adj. mf. great,
super, keen, tremendous

RETINTO -TA very dark-skinned (though
without other specifically Negroid features)

RETOBAR or RETOBEAR or RETOBIAR vn.
to talk back impudently (esp.
to older persons, to one's parents, etc.)

RETOBÓN -BONA m., f. sassy back-talk-
er (ref., esp., to young person
who consistently talks back to
older people)

RETRA (slang) m. (var. of) retrato

REVERSA (Ang.) reverse gear (vehicle);
DARLE DE REVERSA (A UN VEHÍCULO)
to back up (reverse) (a vehicle);
(fig.) to back up (backtrack)
when one has made a mistake

REVOLVER va. to confuse, muddle; vr.
to become confused, muddled:
"No digas nada ahorita; me voy
a revolver si no te callas";
REVOLVÉRSELE A ALGUIEN EL ES-
TÓMAGO to get an upset stomach

REVUELTO -TA upset (said of stomach)

REZUMBAR: REZUMBARLE A ALGUIEN (EL
APARATO / EL MANGO) PARA HACER
ALGO to excel at doing something: "A Chente le rezumba
(el mango) para jugar al pimpón"

RIACLO (slang) AL RIACLO in a while

RIAL (var. of) real

RIATA (var. of) reata

RIATAZO (var. of) reatazo

RIATIZA (see REATIZA, DAR UNA REATI-
ZA)

RICÉS (Eng.) m. recess (play period
during the school day)

RICHE (Eng.) (dim. of) Richard

RIDETIR or RIDITIR (vars. of) derretir (see also DIRRETIR, REDE-
TIR et al.)

RIDÍCOLO -LA (var. of) ridículo -la

RIELES (slang) mpl. woman's legs
(hum.)

RIELOTES (slang, hum.) mpl. woman's
legs

RIFA card reading (form of fortune

telling); ECHAR RIFAS to read
the cards

RIFAR vr. to excel at something

RIFLE m. ESTAR COMO RIFLE to be
in superb physical condition
for any undertaking (esp. for
the sex act)

RILEY or RÍLEY (Eng.) m. relay
(race)

RILLO (var. of) río 'river'

RIN (Eng.) m. ring; rim

RINCONAR (var. of) arrinconar

RINCONERA quack midwife

RINCHE (Eng.) m. Texas Ranger (pa-
ramilitary state police corps
member)

RING (Eng.) m. ring (boxing, Std.
cuadrilático)

RINGUEAR or RINGUIAR (Eng.) va. to
ring (a bell)

RIR (var. of) reír (see also REIR)

RISIÓN -SIONA m., f. ridiculous;
brunt of jokes

RISIONADA anything that provokes
laughter

RITMO rhythm method (of birth control)

RIUMA (var. of) reúma

RIUMÁTICO (var. of) reumático

RIUMATISMO (var. of) reumatismo

RIYO ,RIYES, RIYE, RIYEMOS/REYIMOS,
RIYEN (vars. of) río, ríes,
etc. (pres. ind. of reír)

ROBÓN -BONA m., f. thief; adj.
thieving, larcenous

ROCHE or ROCHO m. (Eng. < roach <
Sp. cucaracha) roach, cockroach
(see also RUCHO)

RODIADO -DA (var. of) rodeado -da

RODIAR (var. of) rodear

ROGÓN -GONA m., f. person who constantly begs for favors; person
who enjoys being coaxed to do
things; f. brazen hussy (coll.),
woman who does not hesitate to
make advances at men

ROGAR: HACERSE DEL ROGAR (var. of)
hacerse de rogar 'to want to be
coaxed'

ROL (Eng.) m. bread roll; hair roll,
hair roller

ROL m or ROLA f. (slang) automobile

ROLA (slang) phonograph record;
song

ROLADO -DA (slang) asleep; lying
down

ROLANTE (slang) m. automobile

ROLAR (slang) vn. to sleep; vr. to
go to bed, go to sleep

ROLE (slang) (Eng?) m. hair roller;
automobile (see also ROL, ROLA);
sleep (state or act of sleeping)

ROLETA (var. of) ruleta

ROLIAR (slang) (Eng.) va. to roll

someone (slang), steal from someone while he/she is asleep or
drunk

ROMANCE (Eng.) m. romance, love

ROMO -MA short-statured

ROMPER va. to tear (Note: verb
does not mean 'to break' as in
Std.; for the "Texas" equivalent
of 'to break' see QUEBRAR); vr.
ROMPERSE LA CABEZA to hurt oneself in the head

ROMPIDO -DA (var. of) roto -ta (ppart.
of romper)

RONCADERA loud snoring; combined
snoring of many persons

RONCÓN -CONA person who snores frequently

RONCHA: HACER RONCHA to run up one's
winnings in a game of chance
after starting out with very
little money

ROPA: ROPA DE ABAJO underwear, un-
derclothes; ROPA DE SALIR dress
clothes, "Sunday best" (coll.)

ROQUIROL (Eng.) m. Rock 'n' Roll
(the music; the dancing appropriate thereunto)

ROSA: ROSA DE CASTILLA herb rose
(Rosa sp.) (its petals are prepared as a tea and taken as a
mild purge)

ROSADO -DA irritated (skin); chapped
(lips): "Traigo la piel rosada
aquí en el pescuezo"; ANDAR RO-
SADO -DA to have a skin irritation in a "certain place" (euph.
--when the irritated part of the
body in not mentioned it is
assumed to be the anal region)

ROSAR (var. of) dorsal m.

ROSAS (var. of rosetas?) fpl. popcorn

ROSQUITA (var. of rosquilla?) ring-
shaped pastry

ROST (Eng.) m. roast (roasted meat);
roasting pan

ROSTICERÍA (Eng., roast) place
where roast meat is sold; restaurant which specializes in
roast meat

ROTADO -DA (ppart. of rotar, q.v.
infra) ruptured (with a hernia)

ROTADURA rupture (with a hernia)
(see also ROTURA)

ROTAR va. & vr. ("var." of romper,
apparently a back formation from
the Std. ppart. of romper, i.e.,
roto) (Note: rotar is used in
all the expected tenses and
modes and is fully regular in
its conjugation: Uds. rotan,
rotaron, rotaban, rotarán,
rotarían, que roten, que
rotaran, etc.)

ROTURA rupture (with a hernia)

ROYER (var. of) roer va.

ROZAR vr. to chap one's skin (esp.
the lips)

ROZÓN m. slight scratch, break, or
irritation of the skin; flaying
of the skin

RUBE (dim. of) Rubén

RUCAIBA (slang) mother, ole lady
(slang)

RUCAILO -LA old person

RUCO -CA (slang) m. old man; husband;
boy friend; boy (in general);
f. old woman; wife; girl friend;
girl

RUCHO (Eng. <roach,< Sp. cucaracha)
roach, cockroach (see also
ROCHE, ROCHO)

RUFIANO -NA overly-familiar, overbearing

RUEDA: RUEDA DE LA FORTUNA Ferris
wheel; RUEDA DE SAN MIGUEL
type of children's game

RUIDO: BUSCARLE RUIDO AL CHICHARRÓN
(see CHICHARRÓN)

RULA (Eng.) ruler (measuring instrument)

RUMALDO (var. of) Romualdo

RUMBADO -DA strewn, scattered (often with ref. to possessions
such as toys, clothes, etc.,
left every whichwhere in a
room)

RUMBAR va. to carelessly strew or
scatter things about

RUNRÚN m. gossip

RUÑIR va. to gnaw; to eat away at

RURE or RURI (Eng.) Rudy (dim. of
Rudolph)

RUSCO -CA stingy, parsimonious

RÚSTICO -CA lusterless, dull, un-
interesting (ref. to persons)

RUTERO -RA newspaper deliverer, m.
paperboy

S

SABER: NO SABER DAR SANTO Y SEÑA
DE ALGUIEN to be unable to
tell where someone is; NO SABER
EN DONDE ESTÁ UNO not to know
whether one is coming or going
(fig.), to be highly confused;
PARA QUE SEPAS (SEPAN, etc.)
(set expression of defiance).
So there!; QUE QUIÉN SABE QUÉ

very, extremely, _____-er than
a _____ (used in comparative expressions:) "Está más loco que
quién sabe qué" 'He's crazier
than a loon'; SABER A QUE ATE-
NERSE to know the score (slang),
know in advance what the situation is; SABER LO QUE ES AMAR A
DIOS EN TIERRA AJENA to know
firsthand what trouble really
is; SABER LOS SECRETOS DE AL-
GUIEN (said, hum., when drinking from someone else's glass);
SEPA DIOS or SEPA EL BURRO DE
LOS MECATES (expressions indicating incredulity) God
only knows!, Who can say?!
SABO (rus.) (var. of) sé (1st pers.
indic. of saber)
SABROSO -SA superior to others,
hot stuff (slang): "Él se cree
muy sabroso" 'He thinks he's
really something'
SACAR va. to throw in someone's
face (fig.) the favors one has
done for that person: "Vete,
a mí no me gusta que me saquen
los favores que me hacen"; to
inherit (as physical or personal
traits): "María sacó la nariz de
su mamá" 'María inherited her
mother's nose; to make (money),
earn: "Con esta chamba no vamos
a sacar ni para pagar por los
frijoles" 'With this job we're
not even going to make enough
to pay for the beans'; vr. to
get (what one deserves): "Eso
es lo que se sacan por andar
molestando gente" 'That's what
they get for going around bothering people'; vr. to weasel out
(slang), cleverly find a way
out of a responsibility or commitment; to move quickly aside
to avoid a blow; DE AHI NO TE
SACAN (DE AHÍ NO LO etc. SACAN)
(set expression) No one can make
you yield on that point (ref.
to stubborn person unwilling to
be convinced); SACAR AIRE to
burp (a baby); SACAR DAGA CON
to show off something new (esp.
an article of clothing); SACAR
LA GARRA to gossip; SACAR
LUMBRE to harp on the same
subject, talk incessantly about
the same topic; SACARLE A ALGUIEN
LA COLORADA to give someone a
bloody nose (see also COLORADA);
SACARLE (LA VUELTA) A ALGO/AL-
GUIEN to dodge, avoid something/
someone: "El jefe siempre nos
da mucho trabajo y por eso le

sacamos (la vuelta) cuando lo
vemos venir"; SACARLE A ALGUIEN
LOS TRAPOS/TRAPITOS AL SOL /
SACARLE A ALGUIEN LOS TRAPOS/
TRAPITOS A REMOJAR to hang out
someone's dirty linen (fig.),
bring the skeleton(s) out of
someone's closet (fig.); SACAR-
LE CANAS A ALGUIEN to give
someone gray hairs; SACAR PA-
TADA (Ang.) (slang) to get a
kick out of (something): "Él
es de los que sacan su patada
de las drogas" 'He get his
kicks from drugs'; ¡SÁCATE!
interj. Pow!; ¡SÁCATE LA DAGA!
Get to work!; Get with it!;
Your turn to pay!
SACATE (orthog. var. of) zacate m.
SACATEADA or SACATIADA evasive act,
avoidance
SACATEAR or SACATIAR va. to avoid,
evade, side-step, duck, dodge
SACATÓN -TONA (coll.) m.,f. free-
loader
SACÓN -CONA m.,f. shirker, avoider
of responsibilities
¡SÁCOTE! (var. of) ¡SÓCATE! (q.v.)
SACUDIR vr. to try to shake off
the blame from oneself, attempt
to exculpate oneself
SAFADO -DA (orthog. var. of) zafado
-da
SAFAR (orthog. var. of) zafar
SAFO(S) (orthog. var. of) zafo(s)
SAIN (Eng.) m. sign, placard, post-
er
SAINAR or SAINEAR or SAINIAR (Eng.)
va. to sign (Std. firmar)
SAL: ECHARLE A ALGUIEN LA SAL to
jinx, bring bad luck to
SALADO -DA jinxed, cursed with bad
luck
SALAMANQUEZCO salamander
SALAMÓNICOS (slang) San Marcos,
Texas
SALARETE m. bicarbonate of soda;
baking powder
SALIDA: SALIDA DE LOS DIENTES
teething; VENIR DE ENTRADA Y
SALIDA to call on someone
briefly, stop by for a brief
visit
SALIDERA Y ENTRADERA constant leav-
ing and entering, coming and
going
SALIDERO -RA gad-about, person who
is always "out on the town"
SALIDOR -DORA m., f. person who enjoys going out on the town
(coll.), frequent seeker of
night-life entertainment
SALIR: SALIR A LUZ (Ang?) to come
to light, become apparent;

SALIR A MANOS to break even in
a game of chance; SALIR CANUTO
to attempt to defer payment on
merchandise or services after
these have been delivered or
performed: "Le corté el sacate
y me salió canuto" 'I cut his
grass and then he promised to
pay me some other day'; SALIR
DE SU CUIDADO to give birth:
"Tu tía ya salió de su cuidado";
SALIR DIOQUIS (see DE HOQUIS,
DIOQUIS); SALIR GORDA to get
pregnant; SALIR PA' FUERA (euph.)
to go to the bathroom (euph.=
to urinate or defecate) (see
also IR PA' FUERA); SALIR POR
DEBAJO DE LA MESA to always
come out on the short end of
the stick, always fail in whatever one attempts; SALIR SO-
BRANDO to be superflous, re-
dundant; to be academic; to be
useless or of little or no importance (often said with ref.
to help offered after a problem
has been solved); SALIRSE to
spill one's seed (coll.), for
the man to withdraw the penis
before ejaculation so as to avoid
pregnancy
SALUBIDAD f. (var. of) salubridad
SALVAR (Ang.) va. to save (money)
SANABABICHE or SANABABICHI (Eng.)
(vulg.) m. son-of-a-bitch
SAN ANTON (slang) San Antonio, Texas
SAN ANTOÑO (var. of) San Antonio,
Texas
SAN CUILMAS (hum.) San Antonio,
Texas; (hum.) (any town one
wishes to burlesque)
SANAR (euph.) vn. to give birth,
deliver
SANCHAR va. to cheat on one's
spouse, commit adultery
SÁNCHEZ m. the "third person" in
an amorous triangle (ref. to
the male lover of the other
man's wife)
SANCHO -CHA adj. adulterous; m.
adulteror; f. adultress; mf.
animal raised as bottle-fed
(in the absence of or rejection
by the animal's mother)
SAN FELIPE DEL RÍO (original Spanish name of) Del Rio, Texas
SANGRE (slang) adv. no (negative
response); SANGRE DÉBIL anemia
(coll.) SANGRE DE CHANGO mer-
curochrome; SANGRE DE CHINCHE
unpleasant, repulsive (ref.
to persons); SANGRE POBRE
anemia; TENER LA SANGRE LIVIANA
to be pleasant, agreeable, well-

liked
SANGRIAR (var. of) sangrar
SANGRÓN -GRONA disagreeable, re-
pugnant (ref. to persons);
conceited
SÁNGÜICH(E) or SÁNGÜICHI or SÁNHUICH
(E) (Eng.) m. sandwich
SANTA CLOS (Eng.) m. Santa Claus
(Std. Padre Noel)
SANTO mpl. DARSE UNO DE SANTOS to
be grateful, to thank one's
lucky stars; NO SABER DAR SANTO
Y SEÑA DE ALGUIEN to be unable
to say what became of someone
who is unaccountably absent)
SAPO frog; (orthog. var. of) zapo
SAPOLTURA (var. of) sepultura
SARAMPIÓN: SARAMPIÓN DE TRES DÍAS
German measles, rubella
SARDERA camp-follower (prostitute
who establishes herself near a
military base); woman very fond
of soldiers
SARDINA (fig.) low man on the totem
pole, person whose job is of
minimal importance
SARDO (slang) soldier; sergeant
SARSA (var. of) salsa
SARTÉN m. (var. in gender of sartén
f.)
SARRUCHAR (var. of) serruchar
SARRUCHE m. (var. of) serrucho
SARRUCHO (var. of) serrucho
SASTRERÍA dry-cleaners (Std. tinto-
rería)
SASTRERO -RA tailor (Std. sastre)
SATÍN m. (var. of) satén 'satin'
SÁTIRO -RA senile old person
SAURINO -NA (var. of) zahorí 'for-
tune teller, soothsayer'
SAXOFÓN (var. of) saxófono m.
SECADOR m. napkin
SECIÓN (var. of) sección f.
SECO: VENIRSE EN SECO to engage in
coitus interruptus, have an
ejaculation elsewhere than in-
side the woman's vagina
SECONDARIA (var. of) secundaria
(most typically escuela secon-
daria)
SECTIEMBRE (var. of) septiembre
SEDAL m. type of strong string
(used in fishing line, for
flying kites, etc.)
SEDAZO screen door; window screen
SEGUIDA: EN SEGUIDA (DE) along-
side, next door (to): "Vive
en la casa de en seguida" 'He
lives in the house next door'
SEGUIDO adv. frequently, often
SEGUNDO (see DE SEGUNDO 'second
hand')
SEGURANZA insurance
SEGURO safety pin (Std. imperdible):

SEGURO QUE SÍ of course, naturally (see also DE SEGURO 'for
sure'); SEGURO QUE NO of course
not, by no means
SEGUROLA interj. (slang) Yessir,
Yes indeed
SEMÁFARO (var. of) semáforo
SEMÁSFORO (var. of) semáforo
SEMBRAR (slang) va. to bury a corpse
SEMÍA (var. of) semilla
SEMOS (var. of) somos (1st pers.
pl. pres. ind. of ser)
SENCÍO -CÍA (var. of) sencillo -
cilla
SENSE or SENSÉN m. game of marbles;
the ring in that game (played
in essentially the same fashion
as the game of "marbles," i.e.,
the object is to knock out
marbles from the center of the
ring)
SENTADERAS (var. of) asentaderas
fpl.
SENTADOR -DORA (Ang.) baby sitter
SENTENCIA (Ang.) sentence, combination of words constituting a
complete utterance (Std. oración,
frase)
SENTENCIADA: TENÉRSELA SENTENCIADA
A ALGUIEN to place someone under warning, indicating that
revenge will be carried out at
some future time: "Mira, Concha,
cuídate que ya te la tengo sentenciada" 'Watch out, Concha.
The day you're least expecting
it I'm going to get my revenge
on you'
SENTENCIAR: SENTENCIÁRSELA A ALGUIEN
(id. to tenérsela sentenciada,
see s. SENTENCIADA)
SENTIDO outer ear (Std. oreja)
SENTIR: SENTIR BASCAS to gag, feel
nauseated
SENTÓN m. hard flop experienced
when one sits down abruptly
SEÑORITA virgin: "Ella todavía es
señorita, gracias a Dios"
SEPO (var. of) sé (1st pers. sg.
pres. ind. of saber) (see also
SABO)
SEPULGRO (var. of) sepulcro
SER: ¡NO VAYA A SER (TAN DE REPENTE)!
That'll be the day! (general ex-
pression of incredultiy); SER
ALGO DE ALGUIEN to be related
to someone: "¿Qué es Carlos de
Jorge?" 'How is Carlos related
to Jorge?'; SER DE AGUA (v.s.
AGUA); SER DE DULCE (v.s. DULCE);
SER DE LOS OTROS (v.s. OTRO);
SER DE ORILLA (v.s. ORILLA);
SER DE PALO (v.s. PALO); SER
LUMBRE (v.s. LUMBRE); SER POR

DE MÁS to be useless, be in
vain: "Es por de más tratar de
darle consejos" 'It's useless
to try to give him advice';
SEA POR DIOS so be it (fixed
expression indicating resigna-
tion); SI ES DE QUE if: "Ire-
mos si es de que viene temprano"
'We'll go if he comes early';
TÚ LO SERÁS (UD. LO SERÁ, etc.)
The same to you! (expression
used to return an insult)
SERENATEAR or SERENATIAR va. to
serenade
SERENATERO -RA serenador, person
who serenades
SERVICIO (euph.) chamber-pot
SERVIENTE m. -TA f. (var. of) sir-
vienta
SÉSGALE (interj.) Stop that!; Cut
it out!, Stop bothering me!
SESO mpl. TENER (BUENOS) SESOS to
be intelligent
SESONAR (slang) to sniff glue (for
a mildly narcotic effect)
SETEAR or SETIAR (Eng.) va. to set
(esp. with ref. to hair)
SEYA, SEYAS, etc. (vars. of) sea,
seas, etc. (pres. subj. of ser)
SHAINEAR or SHAINIAR (Eng.) (var.
of) chainear or chainiar (Note:
digraph "sh" pronounced as pa-
latal sibilant [š])
SHO (Eng.) (var. of) cho (Eng.)
SÍ: (NO) DAR DE SÍ (used more in the
negative) (not) to be reasonable, yield, be compromising,
easy to convince; DE POR SÍ QUE
as it is, as things (now) stand:
"No hables de él; de por sí que
no quiere venir a la fiesta"
'Don't talk about him; as things
now stand he surely won't want
to come to the party'; TRAER DE
POR SÍ to be born with: "Ese
talento lo trae de por sí" 'He
was born with that talent'; Y
TÚ SI (Y ELLA etc. SI) (iron.)
Yeah, I'll bet, That'll be the
day: "Me voy a casar mañana.--
Y tú sí"
SÍA (var. of) silla
SIEMPRE after all, anyway, still:
"¿Siempre te vas?" 'Are you
still going to go?'/'Are you
going, after all?'
SIETECUEROS msg. watery blister on
the sole of the foot (caused,
according to popular tradition,
by stepping barefoot in horse
urine)
SIGUIR (var. of) seguir
SILABARIO (slang) (expansion-disguise of sí) adv. yes

(affirmative response)

SILENCITO -TA quiet; taciturn

SILINDRO (slang) (expansion-disguise of sí) adv. yes (affirmative response)

SÍMBULO (var. of) símbolo

SIMÓN or SIMÓN, LEÓN or SIMONACHO (all slang) (expansion-disguises of sí) adv. yes (affirmative response)

SIMPLE adj. (euph.) mentally retarded (cf. INOCENTE)

SIMPLETÓN -TONA (Eng?) m., f. simpleton, idiot, fool

SINC (Eng.) m. sink, washbasin (see also sinque)

SINGLISTA mf. player of a singles match in tennis

SINÓ (var. of) sino 'but, but rather'

SIÑOR -ÑORA (rus.) (var. of) señor, señora

SINQUE (Eng.) m. sink, washbasin (see also SINC)

SINSONCLE or SINSONTLE or SINSONTE m. mockingbird (see also CENZONCLE et al.)

SINTAR (var. of) sentar

SINTARAZOS (slang) (expansion-disguise of sí) adv. yes (affirmative response)

SINTEMOS (var. of) sentimos (1st pers. pl. pres. ind. of sentir)

SINTIR (var. of) sentir

SINVERGÜENZO (var. of) sinvergüenza

SÍQUELE (Eng.) (interj.) Sic 'em! (expression of encouragement said to dogs)

SIRANDA "spanking" (neologism used as a pseudo-noun solely within a specific context: "Bueno, si quiere siranda" 'Well, if you want a spanking...') (derived from the phrase "Bueno, si quieres ir, anda," said to a child who asks permission to go somewhere knowing in advance that his/her parents have already denied that permission; in a sense siranda is a form of disguised speech to prevent the child from losing face in front of a playmate)

SIROL or SIROL SIROLACHO (slang) (expansion-disguise of sí) adv. yes (affirmative response)

SIRVIR (var. of) servir

SIRRE m. (var. of) sirle or sirria 'dung, manure' (esp. of cows, sheep, goats)

SISOTE m. boil (skin inflamation); sore; ringworm

SISTA (Eng.) sister (female sibling); Sister (nun)

SO (rus.) (var. of) soy (1st pers.

sg. pres. ind. of ser)

SO (Eng.) conj. so 'therefore' (Std. así que)

SOBADOR -DORA m. masseur; f. masseuse

SOBAJAR va. to humiliate, shame

SOBITA mf. son-of-a-bitch (Eng. < S.O.B. plus -ita)

SOBRANDO (see SALIR SOBRANDO)

SOBRES (usually mpl.) overshoes; (slang) adv. yes (affirmative response)

SOCA: NI SOCA (slang) not a bit, not at all; (Eng.) f. sucker, all-day sucker (type of hard candy mounted on a stick and ingested through sucking)

SOCADO -DA (Eng.) soaked, cleaned out (in a game of chance) (cf. SOCAR); (see also ANDAR SOCADO -DA)

SOCAR (Eng.) va. to soak (slang), clean out (slang), win all of someone's money in a game of chance

SOCAS (see ANDAR SOCAS)

¡SÓCATE! (interj.) Wham!, Pow!

SOCROSO -SA dirty, filthy

SODERÍA soft-drink bottling plant

SODERO -RA person who bottles soda (soft drinks) in a bottling plant; person who sells or delivers soft drinks; person fond of consuming soft drinks

SODONGA (slang) soda water, soft drink

SOFACEAR or SOFACIAR vn. to lie on a sofa

SOFBOL or SÓFBOL (Eng.) m. softball (baseball played with a larger, softer ball); f. softball (the ball itself)

SOFLAMERO -RA finicky; oversensitive, touchy

SOFOQUE mf. heckler

SOLANO -NA (slang) alone, unaccompanied

SOLAR m. patio; yard (either front or back yard or else both considered as a single space)

SOLDADERA camp-follower

SOLECITAR (var. of) solicitar

SOLECITO intense heat

SOLIMAS (slang) (expansion-disguise of sólo or a solas) alone

SOLOLOY m. (var. of) celuloide

SOLTAR va. to let out, expand (the size of clothes); vn. to fade (clothes), come off (color on utensils)

SOLTURA diarrhea, loose bowels

SOMBREAR or SOMBRIAR vr. to move into or stay in the shade

SOMBRERÓN -RONA or SOMBRERUDO -DA

person (usually male) who habitually wears a large hat
SOMBRÍA (var. of) sombrilla
SONADO -DA (slang) turned on (slang),
under the influence of narcotic
drugs
SONAJEAR or SONAJIAR va. to spank
or whip a child
SONAR va. to spank: "Le sonaron
fuerte" 'They gave him a sound
spanking'; to pay; vr. to beat
up; to spank: "Al niño se lo
sonaron"
SONCEAR or SONCIAR (orthog. vars.
of zoncear or zonciar
SONCERA (orthog. var. of) zoncera
SONGA (Eng.) (slang) song
SONSERA (orthog. var. of) zoncera
SONSEAR or SONSIAR (orthog. vars.
of) zoncear or zonciar
SONSO -SA (orthog. var. of) zonzo
-za
SOÑALIENTO -TA (var. of) soñoliento
-ta
SOÑAR (slang) vr. to put oneself
under the influence of marihuana
SOPA mf. convict, jailbird (coll.);
¡SOPA! interj. Pow!, Wham!;
SOPAS adv. yes (affirmative
response) (slang)
SOPEAR or SOPIAR vn. to use tor-
tillas or pieces of bread (rather
than forks and spoons) as eat-
ing utensils
SOPERA soup bowl; bowl for any pur-
pose
SOPETÓN (see DE UN SOPETÓN 'in one
gulp')
SOPITAS fpl. pieces of cornmeal
tortillas mixed with scrambled
eggs and bits of onion
SOPLADO -DA bloated; heavy, fat
SOPLAR va. to punish with a whip-
ping or with blows
SOPLETE m. harsh scolding
SOPLETÓN or SOPLÓN m. punishment
through a severe beating or
whipping
SOPLO heart murmur
SOPONCIO uneasiness; despair
SOPORA (Eng.) mf. supporter (Std.
partidario -ria)
SOPORTAR (Ang.) to support, back up,
be a partisan of (Std. apoyar);
to sustain, maintain; to finance
SOPORTE (Ang.) m. support, backing,
partisanship (Std. apoyo)
SOPRESA (var. of) sorpresa
SOQUEADO -DA or SOQUIADO -DA (Eng.)
(vars. of) socado -da; (see also
ANDAR SOQUEADO -DA et al.)
SOQUEAR or SOQUIAR (Eng.) (vars. of)
socar (Eng.)
SOQUETE (orthog. var. of) zoquete m.

SORDEQUE m., SORDECA f. (slang)
(disguise of sordo) deaf person
SORPRENDIENTE (var. of) sorprendente
SORRASTRO -TRA dissipated; degener-
ate
SOSPIRAR (var. of) suspirar
SOSPRESA (var. of) sorpresa
SPICH (Eng.) m. speech, discourse,
oration (see also ESPICHE)
STAR (var. of) estar 'to be' (re-
sultant conjugation:) stoy,
stas, sta, etc. (pres. ind.)
and ste, stes, ste, etc. (pres.
subj.) (see also TAR)
STEPIAR (Eng.) vn. to step (Std.
plantar el pie)
STIMROLA (Eng.) steamroller
STORIA (rus.)(var. of) historia
STRAIQUE (Eng.) m. (var. of) estrai-
que (Eng.)
STRAIQUIAR (Eng.) (var. of) estraiquear, estraiquiar
SUADERO (var. of) sudadero
SUATO -TA foolish, stupid
SUAVE (slang) easy, unconcernedly
(see AGARRARLA SUAVE); (slang)
nice, cool (slang), okay:
"(Es) tá suave, bato" 'Cool,
man'; DARLE A ALGUIEN LA SUAVE
to humor someone; to flatter
someone; ¡QUE SUAVE (LE HACES/
HACE/HACEN)! Nice going!
(iron.), That's a fine howdy do!
SUAVIZAR vr. to regain one's composure, to "cool it" (slang)
SUBAJAR va. to discredit, run someone down (coll.)
SUBE Y BAJA or SUBEIBAJA m. teeter-
totter
SUBIR: SUBIR PA(RA) ARRIBA (pleonasm) to go up, ascend; SUBÍR-
SELE A ALGUIEN EL/LO INDIO to
lose one's temper; to get very
angry; SUBÍRSELE LA TOMADA A
ALGUIEN to get tipsy, high on
alcohol
SUDADA act and effect of sweating
SUDAR: SUDAR LA GOTA GRUESA (var.
of) sudar la gota gorda to
sweat blood, overtax oneself
SUDÓN -DONA m., f. person who sweats
easily, profusely, and often;
m. act and effect of sweating
SUEÑO: LLENAR DE SUEÑO to have
enough sleep
SUEÑAL m. considerable tiredness
or sleepiness
SUERA (Eng.) sweater (see also
SUÉTER)
SUERTE fpl. magic tricks; HACER
SUERTES to do magic tricks;
SUERTE CHAPARRA / SUERTE PERRA
very bad luck; SUERTE LOCA
good luck

SUERTERO -RA lucky, fortunate
SUERTUDO -DA lucky, fortunate
SUICH or SUICHE (Eng.) (elec.)
    switch
SUICHE or SUICHI (Eng.) m. switch
    (electric) (Std. interruptor m.)
SUIDADANIA (var. of) ciudadanía
SUIDADANO -NA (var. of) ciudadano -na
SUIMEAR or SUIMIAR (Eng.) vn. to
    swim
SUIMIMPUL (Eng.) m. swimming pool
SUMBAR (orthog. var. of) zumbar
SUMIR vr. to get into debt
SUPCIO -CIA (var. of) sucio -cia
SUPRENTENDENTE or SUPRINTENDENTE mf.
    (vars. of) superintendente mf.
SURA   quarter, twenty-five cent piece;
    CAERLE SURA A ALGUIEN not to be
    liked by, be disagreeable or
    distasteful to (said of persons):
    "Ese tipo me cae sura" 'I can't
    stand that guy'
SURE (Eng.) m. sewer
SUROTO -TA (slang) unpleasant, annoy-
    ing; f. petty thief
SUR(R)UMATO -TA (orthog. vars. of)
    zurumbato -ta (see also ZURUM-
    BATICO -CA)
SUSIRIO (var. of) susidio
SUSTITUIGO (var. of) sustituyo (1st
    pers. sg. pres. ind. of sustitu-
    ir)
SUSTITUYIR (var. of) sustituir
SUSTO (an illness which, according
    to popular belief, is caused by
    a traumatic experience, result-
    ing in symptoms of nervous ten-
    sion, loss of appetite, etc.);
    CURAR DE SUSTO to cure (by
    sorcery) the after-effects of
    susto or any frightening expe-
    rience; ESTAR CURADO -DA DE
    SUSTO (said of a person who
    doesn't scare easily)
SUT (Eng.) m. suit (Std. traje)
SWINGUEAR or SWINGUIAR (Eng.) to
    swing (slang), enjoy oneself as
    the jet set does (frequent con-
    notation: to participate ac-
    tively in sex of an often exotic
    variety)
SUIDAD f. (var. of) ciudad
SUPITO -TA fast-asleep

T

TA, TAMOS, TAN (see s. TOY)
TABACEADO -DA or TABACIADO -DA weak;
    tired, played-out (see also
    TABAQUIADO -DA)
TABAQUIADO -DA (slang) weak etc. (id.
    to TABACEADO -DA)
TABIQUE (slang) m. jail
TABIRO (slang) jail
TABLA: TABLA MARINA surfboard;
    ESTAR / QUEDAR / SALIR TABLAS
    to be tied (e.g. in a sports
    competition); to be even, break
    even
TABLITA shoe with a pointed toe
TACOTILLO tumor; boil (skin irrita-
    tion)
TACUACHE m.(var. of) tlacuache;
    adj. mf. drunk, inebriated
TACAUCHITA or TACUACHITO (type of
    polka)
TACUCHE m. suit of clothes; clothes
    (in general), wardrobe; (slang)
    worthless bum, good-for-nothing
    person
TACUCHO (var. of) tacuche 'suit of
    clothes'
TACHO -CHA (dim. of) Anastasio -sia
TADRE (var. of) tarde (adv. and f.)
TAFETAN m. adhesive tape
TAIPEAR or TAIPIAR (Eng.) to type,
    typewrite va.
TAIPIADOR -DORA (Eng., cf. TAIPEAR)
    m., f. typist; f. typewriter
TAIPISTA (Eng.) mf. typist
TALACHE m. (var. of) talacho 'pick-
    axe'
TAL: TAL POR CUAL mf. so-and-so
    (oblique ref. to person one
    does not wish to name): "Nunca
    me ha gustado ese tal por cual"
TALARAÑA (var. of) telaraña
TALON -LONA m. f. (slang) thief,
    hustler (coll.); m. fifty-cent
    piece, half-dollar
TALONEAR or TALONIAR (slang) va.
    to steal; to hustle (slang)
TALTASCUAN m. cockroach (see also
    JUAN, TAPAJUAN, TAPASCUAN,
    TASCALCUAN et al.)
TALLADOR m. washboard
TALLA joke, witty anecdote; (Eng.)
    tire (aut.); (Eng.) tie, neck-
    tie; (Eng.) railroad tie
TALLAR va. to scrub, wash (e.g.

clothes); TALLARSE LOS OJOS to
rub one's eyes
TALLARÍN -RINA (Eng.?<tired?) tired
TALLE (slang) m. work; job
TALLUDO -DA stubborn; tough, resist-
ant; old, aged; flexible as re-
gards the truth, moderately
mendacious
TAMALADA tamale bake (social event
at which tamales are the main
dish)
TAMALES mpl.: HACERLE A ALGUIEN
LOS TAMALES DE CHIVO to deceive
one's spouse in an adulterous
affair
TAMAÑITO -TA (see ESTAR TAMAÑITO -
TA, QUEDARSE TAMAÑITO -TA)
TAMBO (slang) jail
TAMBORERO -RA (var. of) tamborilero -
ra   drummer
TAMBORETEADO -DA or TAMBORETIADO -
DA tired, worn-out; beaten up
(in a fight)
TAMBORETEAR or TAMBORETIAR va. to
beat up (in a fight)
TAMBORIZA: DARLE A ALGUIEN UNA
TAMBORIZA to beat someone to
a pulp in a fight
TAMIÉN (var. of) también
TANATES mfsg. strong-willed person
TANDO (slang) hat
TANQUE mf. (fig.) fat person; m.
(slang) jail
TAN-TAN (onomatopoeic) knock-knock
(sound made when knocking at a
door)
TANTEADA or TANTIADA estimate, cal-
culation
TANTITO -TA (dim. of) tanto -ta:
"Échale tantita sal" 'Just
throw in a little bit of salt';
a moment, a second: "Espérate
tantito" 'Wait a second'
TANTO -TA: EN TANTO QUE NADA in the
twinkling of an eye: "Lo hizo
en tanto que nada"; ¿QUÉ TANTO?
How much? (Std. ¿cuánto?); UN
TANTO a little bit, a fixed
amount: "Le podemos dar un
tanto ahora y mañana lo demás"
TAPA (slang) hat; (see also VOLAR-
SE LA TAPA)
TAPADO -DA constipated; narrow-
minded; unyielding, uncompro-
mising; naive
TAPAJUÁN m. cockroach (see TALTA-
SCUÁN et al.)
TAPAR va. to constipate: "El pan
me tapó" 'The bread constipated
me'; vr. to become constipated
TAPASCUÁN m. cockroach (see TALTA-
SCUÁN et al.)
TAPÓN -PONA m., f. short, stocky
person; m. ECHARLE A ALGUIEN UN

TAPON to tell someone off
TAQUERO -RA person who prepares and
sells tacos
TAR (var. of) estar (see also STAR)
TARÁNTULA (fig.) mf. hairy person
TARDEADA or TARDIADA late afternoon
party (usually held out-of-doors)
TARDECITO -TA adv. a little bit
late; very late (iron.)
TARECUA (slang) shoe
TARIS (slang) m. jail
TARLANGO (slang) hat
TARTANA old car, jalopy
TARUGADA foolish action
TARUGO -GA fool, idiot
¡TAS! or ¡TAS TAS! interj. Pow!,
Wham!, Bang! (imitation of
sound of bullets)
TASAJEAR or TASAJIAR va. to slice
(esp. meat)
TASAJILLO or TASAJÍO type of cactus
plant with very prickly leaves
TASCALCUÁN m. cockroach (see TAL-
TASCUÁN et al.)
TASINQUE m. sheep-shearer (person
who shears sheep for a living)
TATAJUÁN m. cockroach (see TALTAS-
CUÁN et al.)
TATEMA meat roasted in the hot em-
bers of a fire (esp. ref. to
heads of animals cooked in this
fashion)
TAUN (Eng.) m. town; downtown, city
center
TAUR m. (var. of) ataúd
TAURERÍA funeral home
TAVÍA (var. of) todavía
TAXA (Eng.) tax (esp. income tax)
TAXACIÓN (Eng.) f. taxation
TAYA (orthog. var. of) talla (Eng.)
TÉ (slang) m. marihuana
TECATO -TA (slang) junkie, heroin
user
TECLA (slang) cigarette butt
TECOL (slang) (abbrev. of) tecolote
m.
TECOLOTA (slang) cigarette butt
TECOLOTE (slang) m. policeman; owl;
night watchman
TECORUCHO old tumble-down-house
TECURUCHO (var. of) tecorucho
TEIP (Eng.) m. tape
TEIPIAR (Eng.) va. to tape
TEJABÁN m.or TEJABANA small old
house, often in disrepair,
covered with a tile roof
TEJÓN -JONA m., f. (hum.) short-
statured; (euph.) TEJONES SI
NO HAY LIEBRES (untranslatable
--tejones is euph. for "Te
jodes ...", thus the last four
words constitute nonsense
syllables; the literal transla-
tion is 'Badgers if there are

no hares')

TELA (dim. of) Estela

TELE (abbrev.) f. television; woman's breast; baby bottle, nursing bottle

TELEFÓN (Eng.) m. telephone (Std. teléfono)

TELEFONAZO: ECHAR UN TELEFONAZO to make a telephone call, to phone someone

TELEFONEADA or TELEFONIADA telephone call

TELEFONIAR (var. of) telefonear

TELEVÍ f. (abbrev. of) televisión

TELEVIGENTE m. (var. of) televidente

TEMBELEQUE (var. of) tembleque mf. adj.

TEMOLOTE m. (var. of) tejolote 'stone pestle'

TEMPLETE m. badly-built construction armature (scaffolding)

TEMPONEAR or TEMPONIAR va. to be accustomed to

TENCHA (dim. of) Hortensia, Cresencia

TENDAJERO -RA storekeeper (esp. ref. to owner of a grocery store)

TENDAJO small store (esp. small grocery store)

TENDEDERO or TENDERADA act of hanging out clothes to dry on a clothesline

TENDIDO -DA: ESTAR TENDIDO -DA to be lying in state (said of a dead person in a funeral parlor)

TENDIDA act of hanging out clothes to dry on a clothesline (cf. TENDEDERO ET AL.); clothes hung out to dry

TENDER: TENDER LA CAMA (Std. hacer la cama)

TENER: NO TENER EN QUÉ CAERSE MUERTO -TA to be destitute, dirt-poor; TENER BOCA CHICA to be taciturn, speak infrequently; TENER (UN) BUEN TIEMPO (Ang.) to have a good time, enjoy oneself; TENER CARRITO to harp on the same subject, talk constantly about the same thing; TENER CUERPO DE TENTACIÓN Y CARA DE ARREPENTIMIENTO to have a beautiful body and a homely face (ref. to women); TENER EL ALMA EN EL CUERPO to wear one's heart on one's sleeve (fig.), allow one's emotional state to be very noticeable; TENER FON / TENER UN FONAZO (Eng.) to have fun, have a good time; TENER HUEVOS (vulg.) to have a lot of guts (coll.),

have sufficient bravery for; TENER LA CARA DE HACER ALGO to have (sufficient) audacity to do something; TENER LA SANGRE DE CHINCHE to be repugnant to, be repellent to; TENER MALA LA TOMADA: "Tiene mala la tomada" 'When he drinks he really gets his Irish up' (ref. to person-- Irish or not--who habitually becomes belligerent or pugnacious after having had a few alcoholic drinks); TENERLA HECHA (Ang?) to have it made (to have achieved a level of accomplishment sufficient to insure future success); TENER A ALGUIEN DE SU CUENTA to have someone on a string (fig.), have someone in a position of dependency: "Ya déjalo, ya lo tuviste bastante de tu cuenta"; TENER LENGUA SUELTA to be garrolous, speak frequently; TENER (UN) MAL TIEMPO (Ang.) to have a bad time, not to enjoy oneself; TENER MUCHA LENGUA to be very talkative; TENER QUE DARLE A ALGUIEN EN EL CODO to have to make someone pay for something (ref. to difficulties in getting a stingy person to pay; cf. CODO); TENER UN TORNILLO SUELTO (Ang?) to have a screw loose, to be slightly crazy

TENIS mpl. (Eng?<tennies--slang for tennis shoes?) tennis shoes; COLGAR LOS TENIS (slang) to die

TENTADERA repeated act of touching, feeling, pawing (excessive handling by one person of another)

TENTÓN -TONA m., f. person given to excessive and repeated touching, feeling, fondling, etc. (cf. TENTADERA)

TEÓRICA (slang) talk, chatter

TEORICAR (slang) va. & vn. to talk, chatter, jabber

TEPALCATES mpl. odds and ends of little value

TEPASCUÁN m. cockroach (see TALTASCUÁN et al.)

TEPOCATE m. (coll.) kid, runt (small child of unprepossessing appearance)

TEQUILERO -RA seller of tequila

TERALAÑA (var. of) telaraña

TERE (dim. of) Teresa

TERREGAL m. dust cloud

TERRERO dust cloud

TERROSO -SA dusty

TESÓN: AGARRAR TESÓN CON   to harp on (a subject); to use or wear (repeatedly): "Agarró tesón con la corbata nueva" 'He kept on wearing the new tie'

TESTAL m. round ball of dough constituting the proper amount of masa (q.v.) needed to make a single tortilla

TESTEAR or TESTIAR (Eng.) va. to test, examine

TESTO -TA full, stuffed

TETERA (var. of) tetero 'baby bottle'; sinecure; act of drinking alcohol; AGARRAR LA TETERA to talk to the bottle (coll.), become an alcoholic

TIATRO (var. of) teatro

TIBÓN m. (Eng.) T-bone steak

TICHA (var. of) ticher (Eng.) mf.

TICHAR (Eng.) va. & vn. to teach

TICHER (Eng.) mf. teacher

TIEMPAL m. long period of time, coon's age (slang): "Hace un tiempal que no lo veo" 'I haven't seen you in a coon's age'

TIEMPECITO bad weather; plenty of time, time to spare

TIEMPO (Ang.) time, clock time (Std. hora): "Ya es tiempo de ir" 'Ya es la hora de ir'; (see also BUEN TIEMPO, MAL TIEMPO)

TICURUCHO (var. of) tecorucho

TIENDA fly (of trousers); TRAER LA TIENDA ABIERTA to have one's fly open

TIENDERO -RA (var. of) tendero -ra

TIERNÍSIMO -MA (var. of) ternísimo -ma

TIERRA: CAERLE TIERRA A ALGUIEN to be taken by surprise: "Estaban jugando a los dados cuando les cayó tierra. Fue la policía" 'They were playing dice when they were taken by surprise. It was the cops'; SABER LO QUE ES AMAR A DIOS EN TIERRA AJENA (see s. SABER)

TIERRAL m. large cloud of dust; large amount of dust

TIERROSO -SA (var. of) terroso -sa

TIESO -SA: (fig.) QUEDAR(SE) TIESO -SA to die

TÍGUERE -RA m., f. (var. of) tigre mf.

TIJERA: SER CORTADAS POR LA MISMA TIJERA (said of persons having the same characteristics) to be cut from the same cloth (fig.)

TILA (dim. of) Otilia

TILICHES mpl. stuff, junk, old bits of odds and ends

TIMBA (slang) capsule of heroin

TINA pail (usually one of galvanized iron)

TINACO large elevated tank for the storage of drinking water (often the water supply for an entire municipality)

TINIADO -DA (Eng.) (slang) high from sniffing paint thinner (which produces a slightly narcotic effect)

TINTO -TA (slang) U.S. black person

TÍO: TÍO SAMUEL (Eng.) Uncle Sam (symbolic representation of the United States); TÍO TACO (pej.) Mexican-American who has "sold out" (slang) to Anglo society, accepts its values, and generally opposes militant Chicano politics

TIPAZO Adonis, extremely handsome man

TIPO -PA adj. elegantly dressed; ANDAR (MUY) TIPO -PA to be elegantly dressed

TÍQUETE (Eng.) m. ticket (entrance pass), receipt, etc.; ticket (list of political candidates); traffic ticket

TIQUETERÍA (Eng., cf. TÍQUETE) large number of tickets (defs. 1 & 3)

TIQUETERO -RA ticket-seller

TIRACHO -CHA (slang) U.S. black person

TIRADERO disorderly collection of items left scattered about a room

TIRADO -DA disorderly, helter-skelter, unkempt; f. hunting (with a firearm); (vulg.) fornication, sexual intercourse; DAR UNA TIRADA (vulg.) to fornicate; ESTAR TIRADO -DA to be abed, lying in bed (usual ref. to sick or lazy person)

TIRANTE adj. mf. stiff (slang), dead

TIRANTITAS fpl: LLEVÁRSELAS TIRANTITAS to keep a tight rein on someone: "A sus hijos se las lleva tirantitas"

TIRAR: va. (slang) to use, come out with (coll.): "Está tirando mucho totacho" 'He's using a lot of English'; TIRAR A LEÓN / LIÓN to pay no attention to, ignore; TIRAR AL LOCO (slang) to ignore; TIRAR A LUCAS (slang) to ignore; to ditch (slang), leave unaccompanied; TIRAR ALTO to aspire to a lucrative or prestigious position or career, to shoot for the stars (fig.);

TIRAR BESOS to throw kisses (usually at an audience or at children, as along a parade route); TIRAR FLORES to compliment; TIRAR LÍNEA (Ang?) to feed someone a line, tell someone an embellished version of the truth; vn. TIRAR (LA) BASURA (mildly euph., slang) to defecate; TIRAR BONQUE (slang) to sleep; TIRAR CHANCLA/TIRAR CHANCLE (slang) to dance; TIRAR (EL) AGUA (slang) to urinate; TIRAR GARRA (slang) to dress well; TIRAR GRITOS to shout, yell; TIRAR PESTAÑA (slang) to sleep; TIRAR PLANCHA (slang) to be left holding the bag (slang), be abandoned (e.g., a woman waiting in vain for her fiancé at the church on their putative wedding day); TIRAR ZOQUETE (mildly euph., slang) to defecate; TIRARLA PA' (slang) to head for, go toward a destination: "Ése, ¿pa' onde la tira?" 'Hey you, where ya goin'?"; TIRARLE A TODO to try one's hand at everything; TIRARLE A TODO Y NO DARLE A NADA to be Jack of all trades and master of none (coll.), be able to do many things but none well; TIRAR MOCO (slang) to cry; TIRAR NAILON (slang) to dance; TIRAR PLAYA (slang) to take a bath; to take a showerbath; TIRAR SALIVA (hum.) to talk; vr. TIRARSE A LA CALLE / TIRARSE A LA PERDICIÓN to go wrong, take the road to perdition; to become a prostitute; TIRARSE LA MANTECA (slang) to let the cat out of the bag (coll.), tell a secret; TIRARSE UN PEDO (vulg.) to expel anal gas

TIRICIA sadness

TIRILÍ (slang) juvenile delinquent (see also TIRILÓN, TIRILONGO)

TIRILÓN -LONA (slang) juvenile delinquent

TIRILONGO -GA (slang) (id. to TIRILÍ, TIRILÓN -LONA)

TIRO shooting marble used in the game of marbles; cue ball (in pool or billiards); (see also A TIRO DE QUE, A TODOS TIROS, DE A TIRO/DEL TIRO)

TIRÓN: VIVIR A(L) TIRÓN to have a hard time making ends meet, barely eke out a living

TIRONEAR or TIRONIAR (slang) to make love; to pull at each

other's limbs and clothes in a fight or in fun

TIS f. (var. of) tisis (q.v.)

TÍSICO: NARICES DE TÍSICO extra-keen sense of smell

TISIS adj. (var. of) tísico -ca 'tubercular'

TITIRITEAR or TITIRITIAR (vars. of) tiritar

TIVÍ (Eng.) m. television. T.V. (abbrev.)

TIZÓN -ZONA dark-complexioned person

TLACHICHINOLE m. type of herb (Kohleria deppeana) prepared in solution and used as a vaginal douche

TO or TOO (vars. of) todo 'all'

TOALLA napkin, table napkin

TOALLITA protective cover for furniture surfaces (tables, chests of drawers, etc.)

TOAVÍA (var. of) todavía

TOCADOR m. large cloth draped over chest of drawer for decorative effect

TOCAR: YA LE TOCABA His number was up, He was destined to die

TOCINO ham

TOCHAR (Eng.) va. to touch

TOCHDAUN or TOUCHDÁUN (Eng.) m. touchdown (in football)

TODO (see TIRARLE A TODO Y NO DARLE A NADA); (see also ESTAR EN TODO)

TOFUDO -DA (Eng.) (slang) tough, rough, (ref. to aggressive persons)

TOÍTO -TA (var. of) todito -ta

TOLACO or TOLECO (slang) fifty-cent piece, half-dollar

TOLIDO or TOLIRO (slang) toilet

TOLOLOCHE m. string bass, bass viol (Std. contrabajo)

TOLÓN (slang) m. fifty-cent piece, half-dollar

TOMADA or TOMADERA act of drinking alcohol; TENER MALA LA TOMADA: "Tiene mala la tomada" 'When he drinks he really gets his Irish up' (ref. to person--Irish or not--who habitually becomes belligerent or pugnacious after having had a few alcoholic drinks)

TOMADOR -DORA m., f. habitual drinker; alcoholic

TOMAR va. & vn. to drink alcoholic beverages; TOMAR AL CABO to carry out, execute (Std. llevar a cabo); TOMARLE SABOR A ALGO to enjoy something

TOMATE (slang) m. eye, eyeball; TOMATE DE FRESADILLA small-

sized tomato which remains green
  when ripe
TOMATEAR or TOMATIAR (slang) va. &
  vn. to see; to look
TOMATERA tomato-packing factory
TONADITA singsong intonation
TONCES (var. of) entonces
TONE (Eng.<Tony?) (dim. of) Antonio
  -nia
TONTARREAJE or TONTARRAIJE m. bunch
  of idiots, aggrupation of fool-
  ish persons
TONTIAR (var. of) tontear 'to talk
  nonsense, act foolishly'
TONINO -NA heavy-set person
TOÑO -ÑA (dims. of) Antonio -nia
TOPE mpl. DARSE TOPES to bump
  heads; to try to outdo each
  other (said of two persons)
TOPILLO or TOPIO: HACER TOPILLO
  (slang) to make a fool of
  someone
TOQUE (slang) m. puff on a cigarette (esp. on a marihuana
  cigarette)
TORCADISCOS (var. of) tocadiscos
TORCER va. (slang) to draft into
  the army; (slang) to jail,
  put in jail; TORCERLE LA CARA
  A ALGUIEN to snub someone;
  vn. (slang) to die; TORCER MUY
  FEO or TORCER MUY GACHO to die
  a horrible death; vr. to
  have a falling out with someone: "Jorge y Julio se tor-
  cieron, pero ya se conformaron";
  TORCERSE EL PESCUEZO vr. to
  twist one's neck; to sprain
  one's neck
TORCIDO -DA angry; (slang) jailed
TORCHA (var. of antorcha?) (slang)
  match (for lighting fire to
  an object)
TOREAR or TORIAR: TOREARLA (slang)
  to defy the law; (slang) to do
  the town, go out on a spree;
  vr. to make the attempt
TÓRICA (var. of) teórica
TORITO: TORITO DE LA VIRGEN horned
  toad
TORNILLO or TORNIO: ANDAR DE TOR-
  NILLO to be in a bad mood;
  TENER UN TORNILLO SUELTO (Ang?)
  to have a screw loose (slang),
  be slightly crazy
TORQUE or TORQUI (Eng.) m. turkey
TORTA: TORTA DE PAN loaf of bread
TORTEAR or TORTIAR va. to applaud;
  vn. to slap one's hands back
  and forth while making tortillas
TORTILLA: TORTILLA DE AZÚCAR flour
  tortilla prepared with sugar
  and cinnamon; TORTILLA DE HA-

RINA flour tortilla; TORTILLA
  DE MAÍZ/MAIZ corn-meal tortilla; TORTILLA DE MASA corn-
  meal tortilla; (see also HACER
  TORTILLA)
TORTILLERÍA place where tortillas
  are made and sold
TORÓN -RONA m., f. adj. strong
  and heavy-set, bull-like
  (usually applied to male persons)
TORZÓN m. sharp internal pains
  (in person's intestine, etc.)
TORRE: DARLE A ALGUIEN EN LA TORRE
  (slang) to hit someone where
  it hurts (coll.); to beat someone up in a fight
TOSTA (slang) fifty-cent piece,
  half-dollar
TOSTÓN (slang) fifty-cent piece,
  half-dollar; CAERLE TOSTÓN
  A ALGUIEN not to be liked by,
  to be repugnant to: "Ese bato
  me cae tostón" 'I don't like
  that guy'
TOTACHA (slang) the English language; Pachuco speech style
  (the Spanish typically spoken
  by Pachucos); Chicano slang
  (in general)
TOTACHAR (slang) vn. to speak
  using Chicano slang (cf. TO-
  TACHA); to switch codes, speak
  in a "mixture" of Spanish and
  English, alternate between
  Spanish and English
TOTACHO (var. of) totacha
TOTORUSCO -CA awkward, graceless;
  coarse-featured
TOVIERON (var. of) tuvieron
  (3rd pers. pl. pret. of tener)
TOXIDO (Eng.) tuxedo
TOY, TAS, TA, TAMOS, TAN (vars. of)
  estoy, estás, está, etc. (pres.
  indic. forms of estar)
TOY (var. of) todo y '____ and all':
  "Se lo comió con toy todo"
  'He ate it, ____ and all'
  (____=whichever item of food)
TRABAJANTA babysitter
TRABAJAR va. to bewitch, hex:
  "Parece que te están trabajan-
  do desde que volviste del
  viaje, pues te estás portando
  muy mal"
TRABAJO: TRABAJO COCHINO (Ang?)
  (slang) dirty work (slang),
  criminal undertaking
TRÁCALA debt
TRACALADA uproar, din
TRACALERO -RA person frequently in
  debt
TRACO shoe
TRADUCÍ, TRADUCISTE, etc. (vars. of)

traduje, tradujiste, etc. (pret. conjugation of traducir)

TRAER va. to have (ref. to physical condition or part of the body): "Traes los ojos chinitos" 'You have sleepy eyes'; TRAER CARGA (slang) to be carrying narcotic drugs; TRAER (MUCHO) EMPALME to be (heavily) bundled up, be wearing (a considerable amount of) heavy clothing; TRAER DE POR SÍ to be born with: "Ese talento lo trae de por sí" 'He was born with that talent'; "Es malo de por sí" 'He was born bad'; TRAER ENTRE OJOS to have one's eye on someone (fig.) keep a watch out for someone, observe someone with interest; TRAER LA EDUCACIÓN EN LAS PATAS / TRAER LA EDUCACIÓN EN LOS PIES not to behave like an educated person (said of any ill-mannered recipient of a higher academic degree); TRAER A ALGUIEN AL PURO PEDO (slang) to harass, annoy someone; TRAER PELOTA (vulg.) to be passionately in love with someone, have the "hots" for someone; to be carrying the torch for someone; TRAER PURO CLAVO (slang) to be loaded with money, be in the money; TRAER QUE QUEMAR (slang) to have cigarettes in one's possession; TRAER TIEMPO (see s. TIEMPO); TRAER TRAGO to have a few drinks under one's belt (slang), to have been drinking alcohol for quite a while: "Ese ya trae trago" 'He's already had a few'; TRAER TROTE (coll.) to have something up one's sleeve, be up to something: "¿Qué trote traes?" 'What are you up to?'; TRAERLA to be "it" in the game of tag; vr. ¿QUÉ TRAES? (fixed expression) What's with you?, What are you up to ? (coll.); TRAÉRSELA A ALGUIEN MUY CERQUITA to keep a tight rein on someone, keep someone on a short leash (fig.)

TRAGADERO -RA act of eating heavily

TRAGANTE m. esophagus

TRAGAR: TRAGARSE LOS AÑOS to look younger than one's years

TRAGO alcohol in general

TRAIBA, TRAIBAS, etc. (vars. of) traía, traías, etc. (imperfect conjugation of traer)

TRAIDO -DA (var. of) traído -da

(ppart. of traer)

TRAIDRÉ, TRAIDRÁS, etc. (vars. of) traeré, traerás, etc. (future conjugation of traer)

TRAIDRÍA, TRAIDRÍAS, etc. (vars. of) traería, traerías, etc. (conditional conjugation of traer)

TRAILA (Eng.) trailer (Std. remolque)

TRAIR (var. of) traer

TRAJEADO -DA or TRAJIADO -DA elegantly dressed

TRAJIAR (var. of) trajear

TRAJIERA, TRAJIERAS, etc. (vars. of) trajera, trajeras, etc. (past subj. conjugation of traer)

TRAMA wheat flour bread

TRAMADOS mpl. (slang) pants, trousers

TRAMOS: mpl. (slang) pants; TRAMO FREGÓN (slang) zoot suit (type of clothing affected by hoodlum elements in the 1930's and 1940's)

TRAMPA or TRAMPE (Eng.) m. tramp, bum; villain in a movie

TRAMPAR OREJA (slang) to sleep

TRAMPEAR or TRAMPIAR va. to hunt animals; to trap animals; vn. to enter without paying (as into a movie theater)

TRANCA: ECHAR LA TRANCA (see s. ECHAR)

TRANCALERO -RA (var. of) tracalero -ra

TRANVÍ m. (var. of) tranvía

TRAPEADA or TRAPIADA sponge bath

TRAPEAR or TRAPIAR (Eng.) va. to trap (see also TREPEAR); va. to give a spong bath; vr. to take a sponge bath

TRAQUE (Eng.) m. railroad track

TRAS interj. Bang!, Crash!

TRAS(H)AMBRIDO -DA undernourished

TRASCULCAR (var. of) esculcar to search (a person), search through (boxes, etc.)

TRASTEAR or TRASTIAR va. to wash dishes, "do" the dishes

TRASTERÍO pile of dirty dishes (waiting to be washed)

TRASTERO closet; storage room; attic

TRAVESÍA shortcut; ECHAR/HACER/ TOMAR UNA TRAVESÍA to take a shortcut

TRAYER (var. of) traer

TREATO (var. of) teatro

TREILA f. or TREILER m. (Eng.) trailer (Std. remolque)

TREILÓN (Eng.) m. large tractor trailer attached to a truck

TREILONA (Eng.) truck

TREINTATREINTA m. thirty-thirty

(type of firearm)
TREMPRANO (rus.) (var. of) tempra-
no
TREN (see A TODO TREN)
TRER (var. of) traer
TRES: LAS TRES three puffs (on a
cigarette); ¡DAME LAS TRES!
'Let me have a puff!'; TRES
PIEDRAS (slang) keen, excel-
lent, great, super (etc.); "El
cho estuvo tres piedras" 'The
show was terrific'
TRES RÍOS (Hispanization of) Three
Rivers, Texas
TREÚNFO (var. of) triunfo
TRIATO or TRIATRO (var. of) teatro
TRIBO m. (var. of) tribu f.
TRILAZO (Eng.) thrill
TRIMIADA (Eng.) trimming (of hair)
TRIMIAR (Eng.) va. to trim (hair)
TRINE or TRINI (dims. of) Trinidad
mf.
TRIPA water hose; (hum.) thin person; AMARRARSE LA TRIPA to
tighten one's belt (fig.),
economize; to endure hunger;
TRIPA IDA blocked intestine;
(folk medicine) belief that
fear can serve to lock or block
intestines
TRIPÓN -PONA small child under the
age of ten
TRIQUI-TRIQUI interj. (Eng.) m.
trick-or-treat! (said by chil-
dren on Halloween as they go
from house to house begging
for candy or other treats)
TRISTE fpl. LAS TRISTES (slang)
three puffs on a cigarette
(cf. TRES)
TRITIAR (Eng.) va. to treat, en-
tertain at one's own expense
TROCA (Eng.) truck (see also TROQUE);
TROCA DE DOMPE dump truck
TROCÓN (Eng.) m. large truck
TROCONA (Eng.) large truck
TROCHEMOCHE: HACER ALGO A(L) TROCHE-
MOCHE to do a half-assed job
(coll.), do something poorly
TROLA (slang) match (for igniting);
cigarette
TROLE (slang) mf. crazy; drunk
TROMPA (slang) mouth; fpl. thick-
lipped person; mfpl. sour
puss (coll.), person having
a grouchy disposition often
accompanied by an unhappy
facial expression; HACER TROM-
PAS / PONER TROMPAS to put
on a sad facial expression; to
be grouchy; (see also DARSE
TROMPA)
TROMPADAS fpl. fist fight
TROMPAZOS (see DARSE TROMPAZOS)

TROMPEZAR (var. of) tropezar
TROMPEZÓN (var. of) tropezón m.
trip, stumble
TROMPÓN -PONA thick-lipped
TRONADERA thunderstorm; repeated
cracks of thunder; volley of
shots from a firearm; volley of
bangs from firecrackers
TRONADO -DA drunk
TRONADOR m. (vulg.) male fond of
engaging with frequency in
amorous activities
TRONAR va. to smoke (esp. marihuana); vn. TRONAR LOS HUESOS
to crack (ref. to bones): "Al
sentarse le truenan los huesos"
'When he sits down his bones
crack'; vr. to kill: "Se
tronaron a González" 'They killed González'; (vulg.) to copulate; to spank; to beat up (in
a fight); to shoot
TRONCO (fig. & vulg.) male sexual
organ (esp. one of larger than
average dimensions); (fig.)
short and chubby person; CAER
COMO UN TRONCO to drop off to
sleep, fall asleep rapidly;
DORMIR COMO UN TRONCO (Ang?)
to sleep like a log
TROQUE (Eng.) m. truck
TROQUERO -RA truck driver
TROSTEAR or TROSTIAR (Eng.) va. to
trust
TROTE: AGARRAR TROTE CON to keep
harping on (a theme); to wear
or do (something) unceasingly
(i.e., to fail to change one's
clothes): "Ya agarraste trote
con esa camisa"; ANDAR AL TROTE
CON to be all wrapped up in
(fig.), completely involved
with: "El niño anda al trote
con el juguete que le compramos"; HACERLE TROTE A ALGUIEN
to make advances at someone;
TRAER TROTE (coll.) to have
something up one's sleeve, be
up to something: "¿Qué trote
traes?" 'What are you up to?'
TRUENAR (var. of) tronar
TRUJE, TRUJISTE, TRUJO, TRUJIMOS,
TRUJ(I)ERON (vars. of) traje,
trajiste, etc. (pret. conjugation of traer)
TRUNCO -CA (Eng.) drunk
TRUNQUIS (Eng.) adj. mf. drunk
TUALLA (var. of) toalla
TUBO (slang) sock, stocking; inner
tube; TUBO DE PLÁSTICO inter-
uterine device, coil, loop
(contraceptive device)
TUERCA: (LLAVE DE) TUERCA monkey
wrench

TUÉTARO (var. of) tuétano
TUNA (Eng.) tunafish (Std. atún m.)
TUPIDO -DA abundant; dense; filled
  to the brim DE BARBA TUPIDA
  heavy-bearded
TURRON m. block, bar: "Cómprame
  un turrón de magnesia" 'Buy me
  a bar of magnesia'

U

UJU or ÚJULE (expression of disap-
  pointment, varying in intensity
  according to intonation, empha-
  sis, etc.)
UGENIO -NIA (var. of) Eugenio -nia
ULALIO -LIA (var. of) Eulalio -lia
ULTIMADAMENTE (var. of) últimamente
ÚLTIMO: AL ÚLTIMO finally, at last
  (Std. por fin, al fin)
UMBLIGO (var. of) ombligo
UNDE (var. of) donde
UNIÓN (Ang.) f. (labor) union;
  fpl. long underwear (Eng? cf.
  union suit)
UNO: UNO TRAS OTRO (slang) (euph.)
  sausage: "Le dieron uno tras
  otro pal refín" 'They gave him
  sausages for dinner'
UNQUE (var. of) aunque
UNTADA (var. of) untadura
UÑA: UÑA DE GATO type of prickly
  shrub
UÑERA (var. of) uñero 'ingrown toe-
  nail' (also 'hangnail')
¡ÚPALE! (interj. used when lifting
  up a child) Up you go!
UROPA (var. of) Europa
URUTAR (var. of) eructar
URZUELA split hair (tip of hair
  which has split in two)
ÚRZULA (var. of) úlcera
URRACA (fig.) (pej.) non-negroid
  person with a very dark com-
  plexion
USEBIO -BIA (var. of) Eusebio -bia

V

VACA (fig.) adj. stupid, unintelli-
  gent (said of persons); HACER
  VACA to run up one's winnings
  in a game of chance after starting with a very small amount of
  money
VACILADA (slang) kidding, joking;
  fooling around, having a good
  time; VACILARSE A ALGUIEN
  to make a fool of someone; to
  play a joke on someone; to kid
  or tease someone; ANDAR EN LA
  VACILADA to have a good time,
  fool around; to flirt; A VACI-
  LAR A CA CHAPA (< a vacilar
  en acas de Chapa): "Vete a
  vacilar a ca Chapa" 'Go tell
  it to the marines' (=Std. a
  otro perro con ese hueso)
  (Note: this saying may be pe-
  culiar to San Antonio, Texas,
  as it involves a local ref. to
  a well-known drugstore on the
  west side of that city; the
  store was torn down in the
  1960's)
VACIAR vr. to bleed to death
VACIL m. fun, amusement (cf. VACI-
  LADA); act of flirting
VACILADOR -DORA m., f. joker, kid-
  der; flirt
VACILÓN -LONA m., f. flirt, person
  who flirts; person who serves
  as comic relief, joker; movie
  cartoon
VACOTA (fig.) clumsy, awkward
VAGONERO man who loads railroad
  cars
VAISA (orthog. var. of) baisa
VALA, VALAS, etc. (vars. of) valga,
  valgas, etc. (pres. subj. of
  valer)
VALER: NO VALER CACA (vulg.) not
  to be worth XXXX, be very
  worthless; VALER MADRE to be
  worthless
VALSEAR or VALSIAR (vars. of)
  valsar
VAMPIRO -RA bloodthirsty person
  (fig.), mercenary
VANELA (var. of) vainilla
VARAÑA (orthog. var. of) baraña
VARO dollar (U.S. currency); peso
  (Mexican currency et alibi)

VÁRVULA (var. of) válvula
VASIJA set of dishes
VEDERA (var. of) vereda
VEGETABLE (Eng.) m. vegetable (Std. verdura
VEJARANO -NA or VEJERANO -NA (blend of viejo and veterano?) (pej.) old person
VEJIGA balloon
VELADORA large votive light
VELIZ (orthog. var. of) velís m.
VENADO -DA square, person not atuned to the latest fads. slang, etc.
VENDIDO -DA (pej.) Uncle Tom, race traitor (very pej. ref. to Mexican-American who has "sold out" to Anglo interests or who always sides with Anglos in ethnic conflicts)
VENIR va. VENIRLE A ALGUIEN MUY AGUADO to be no match for someone: "Ese tipo me viene muy aguado" 'That guy is no match for me'; VENIR A LA MEDIDA to fit to a T: "El sombrero le vino a la medida" 'The hat fit him to a T; VENIR AL PELO (for clothes) to fit to a T: "La chaqueta le quedó al pelo" 'The coat fit him to a T'; VENIR DE ENTRADA Y SALIDA to visit or call upon someone briefly; vn. VENIR PA' TRAS (Ang.) to return, come back (Std. volver); vr. (vulg.) to have an orgasm; VENIRSE EN SECO (vulg.) to have an orgasm outside the woman's vagina; ¿A QUÉ VIENE (TODO) ESO? What are you implying?, Why are you bringing that matter up?; VIENE SALIENDO LA MISMA GATA It's all the same in the end, It comes to the same thing, Same difference; YA VENGO I'll be back soon, I'll see you shortly
VENTA: VENTA DE GARAJE (Ang.) garage sale, sale of miscellaneous objects; VENTA DE QUEMAZON fire sale, sale of merchandise minimumly damaged by a fire in the store
VENTAJOSO -SA opportunistic
VENTO (dim. of) Ventura
VENTOSA (folk medicine) cure for pains in the side of the abdomen supposedly caused by contack with cold air; the cure consists in placing the mouth of a glass over the affected region; the cold air is then supposed to be sucked out by the glass and the patient is cured

VER va. to opine, think about: "¿Cómo la ve?" 'What do you think (about it)?'; AHORA VERÁS (AHORA VERÁN etc.) Now you're in for it, Now you're going to get it (phrases of warning); ESTAR DE VERSE to be acceptable; NO PODER VER A ALGUIEN NI EN PINTURA not to be able to stand the sight of someone, hate someone with extreme intensity; VERLE LA CARA A ALGUIEN to seek out humbly, to ask for forgiveness or reconciliation, to eat crow (fig.); to face someone reluctantly to ask for a favor (expression most often used in the negative); VERLE LA CARA DE PENDEJO A ALGUIEN (slang) to see someone approaching; YA LO VERÁS (YA LO VERÁ etc.) Now you're in for it, Now you're going to get it (phrases of warning): "Te dije que limpiaras el carro y no lo hiciste. Ya lo verás" 'I told you to clean the car and you didn't do it. Now you're in for it'
VERDAD: ¿PA(RA) QUÉ MÁS QUE LA VERDAD? Let's tell it like it is, Why tell anything but the truth?
VERDE mf. greenhorn, inexperienced person
VERDELAGAS(S) or VERDOLAGA (slang) mf. greenhorn, inexperienced person
VERGÜENZOSO -SA (var. of) vergonzoso -sa
VERIGUATA (var. of) averigua ta 'dispute, argument, din, noise'
VERIJÓN -JONA m., f. wide-hipped; clumsy; f. adverse to doing housework
VERNE (Hispanization of) Vernon, Texas
VESITAR (var. of) visitar
VEVA (dim. of) Genoveva
VEVIR (var. of) vivir
VEYA, VEYAS, etc. (vars. of) vea, veas, etc. (pres. subj. conjugation of ver)
VEYO (var. of) veo (1st pers. sg. pres. ind. of ver)
VIA, VIAS, etc. (vars. of) veía, veías, etc. (imperfect conjugation of ver)
VIAJEAR or VIAJIAR (vars. of) viajar
VIANCICO (var. of) villancico
VÍBORA (slang) penis; PICAR LA VÍBORA (slang): "Cuídate, no te vaya a picar la víbora" 'Watch out, don't let them get into your pants' (euph.) (said to a girl about to go out on a date,

warning her not to let the male
persuade her to become engaged
in copulative activities)

VICA (orthog. var. of) bica

VICEPRINCIPAL (Eng.) m. vice principal, assistant director of a
school

VÍCERAS (slang) fpl. sunglasses

VICI- (var. of) vice- (prefix indicating subordinate position,
e.g., vici-presidente = vice-
presidente

VICOCA (orthog. var. of) bicoca

VICTROLA (Eng.) (var. of) vitrola
(Eng.)

VIDE (var. of) vi (1st pers. sg.
pret. of ver)

VIDO (var. of) vio (3rd pers. pret.
of ver)

VIDRIERA (DE CARRO) windshield (of
a car)

VIDRIOS mpl. (slang) eyeglasses;
AY NOS VIDRIOS (slang) Catch
ya later (slang), See you later;
¡POR VIDRIOS! interj. (euph.)
(var. of) ¡Por vida de Dios!

VIEJERO -RA m. woman who chases
around after men; f. man who
chases around after women

VIEJEZ (var. of) vejez f.

VIEJITA (slang) cigarette butt

VIEJO -JA (slang) m. husband; father; f. wife; mother; whore;
attractive woman (in general);
cigarette butt (see also VIEJI-
TA); VIEJO -JA RABO VERDE (var.
of viejo -ja verde)

VIEN (orthog. var. of) bien

VIERNES: CUCHARA DE VIERNES meddler, meddlesome person

VÍGORA or VÍGURA (var. of) víbora

VINAGRÓN m. scorpion (Scorpionida)

VINIR (var. of) venir

VIRDIO (var. of) vidrio

VIRGÜELA (var. of) viruela

VIROL (slang) m. bean (usually
mpl.)

VIRONGUEAR or VIRONGUIAR (orthog.
vars. of) bironguear, bironguiar

VIRONGUERO -RA (orthog. var. of)
bironguero -ra

VIRUELA: VIRUELA LOCA chicken pox

VIRUL mf. or VIRULO -LA one-eyed

VIRULA bicycle

VIS- (var. of) vice- (id. to VICI-,
q.v.)

VISITA: EN VISITAS on a visit,
visiting (Std. de visita);
VISITA DE DOCTOR (var. of visita
de médico 'very brief visit')

VISTA (slang) film, movie; fpl.
(more frequent than fsg.)
motion-picture show, movies:
"Anoche fuimos a las vistas"

'Last night we went to the
movies'

VISTERO -RA movie fan, avid movie-
goer, cinéaste

VISTIR (var. of) vestir

VÍTOR (var. of) Víctor

VITORIA (var. of) Victoria

VITORIANO (var. of) Victoriano

VITROLA (Eng.) victrola, phonograph,
record-player

VIVIDOR -DORA m., f. opportunist

VIVIR: VIVIR A(L) TIRÓN to have a
hard time making ends meet,
barely eke out a living

VODEVILES (Eng.) mpl. vaudeville

VOLADO -DA (said of a person who
reacts quickly and positively
to advances or flattery); very
much in love; ANDAR VOLADO -DA
CON ALGUIEN to be very much
in love with someone

VOLADA: DE A VOLADA or DIAVOLADA
fast, rapidly, quickly

VOLANDO right away, right this
minute: "Traime el papel volando"

VOLANTÍN m. merry-go-round

VOLAR va. (slang) to steal; vr. to
fall in love; to blow one's
brains out, shoot oneself in the
head; vr. to become giddy; to
become infatuated; VOLARLE A
ALGUIEN LA CABEZA to give someone a swell head (fig.), an
exaggerated sense of importance;
to make someone feel dizzy,
light-headed, giddy; VOLÁRSELA
or VOLARSE LA TAPADA DE LOS
SESOS to blow one's brains out,
shoot oneself in the head (see
also LEVANTARSE or SALTARSE LA
TAPA DE LOS SESOS); VOLÁRSELE
A ALGUIEN LA CABEZA to become
dizzy, giddy, light-headed; to
get dizzy spells; to become
confused; VOLÁRSELE A ALGUIEN
LA TAPA to blow one's top,
get angry: "A Rubén se le voló
la tapa de deveras" 'Rubén
really blew his top'; (see also
A VOLAR)

VOLCÁNICO -CA vulcanized; m. patent
medicine, in liquid form, applied to sore muscles

VOLCANIZAR va. to vulcanize

VOLCANO (Ang.) volcano (Std. volcán)

VOLER (var. of) oler

VOLTEADO -DA or VOLTIADO -DA m., f.
homosexual

VOLTEAR or VOLTIAR: VOLTEAR EL ES-
TÓMAGO A ALGUIEN to turn one's
stomach (fig.), be repugnant to;
VOLTEARLE A ALGUIEN LA CABEZA
to give someone a swell head

(fig.), cause someone to assume an exaggerated sense of importance

VOLVER: vn. VOLVER PA' TRAS (Ang.) to return, go back (Std. volver); va. VOLVERLE A ALGUIEN EL ALMA AL CUERPO to regain one's composure after being scared; YA VUELVO I'll be right back, I'll see you shortly

VOLVIDO -DA (var. of) vuelto -ta (ppart. of volver)

VOMITADERA vomiting spell, serial regurgitation

VORRADO (orthog. var. of) borrado

VOZ f. (Ang.) voice (lessons): "Estoy estudiando voz" 'I'm taking voice lessons'

VRIGEN (var. of) virgen f.

VUELO: AGARRAR VUELO to get a running start; (see DE TODO VUELO)

VUELTA: DAR LA VUELTA to drop by (a place), drop over (for a visit): "Mañana no dejes de dar la vuelta" 'Don't forget to come by tomorrow for a visit'; DE VUELTA again; after returning

VUEVO (var. of) huevo

W

WAXEAR or WAXIAR (Eng.) va. to wax (a floor)

Y

Y: ¿Y DIAY (QUÉ)? or ¿Y DE AHÍ (QUÉ)? So? So what?; Y ¿QUÉ HAY CON ESO? So what about it? (coll.)

YA: YA ESTA or YA ESTUVO That's it!, Consider it done (consider the job finished); YA ESTUVO I've got it made, There's no way I can fail; YA LO HUBO or YA LUVO (id. to YA ESTÁ); YA NI YO (YA NI ELLA, etc.) (expression used to shame someone into doing something that another person of lesser ability can do): "¿No puedes hacer esto? ¡Qué vergüenza! Ya ni Linda que es tan joven" 'Can't you do this? That's absurd! Linda can do it and she's much younger than you'; ¿YA SI NO? Well after all, what did you expect (would happen)?; YA TE LO HAIGA or YA TE LO HAYA You will be sorry!; YA, YA (expression of sympathy usually directed at children) There, there, that's all right

YANITORIA (Eng.) janitorial service

YAQUE (Eng.) m. jack (aut.) (Std. gato)

YARDA (Ang.) yard, lawn, plot of grass in front of or behind a house; YARDA DE MADERA (Eng.) lumberyard

YAYO (dim. of) Eduardo (see also HUAYO)

YEC (Eng.) m. jack (Std. gato) (see also YAQUE)

YEDO (slang) marihuana

YEQUEAR or YEQUIAR (Eng.) va. to jack up (a car, a structure, etc.)

YERSE (Eng.) m. jersey, sweater

YES (Eng.) m. jazz

YESCO -CA (slang) marihuana smoker; drug addict; f. marihuana

YET (Eng.) m. jet, jet airplane

YIDO (var. of) ido (ppart. of ir)

YIN (Eng.) m. gin (alcohol); YIN DE ALGODÓN cotton gin

YIP(E) (Eng.) m. jeep

YIR (var. of) ir 'to go'

YIRA or YIRI (Eng.) mf. jitterbug (dance); jitterbugger (person fond of dancing the jitterbug)

YOCHE (Eng., dim. of) George; (Hispanization of) George West (city in south Texas)

YOGA f. or YOGUE m. (Eng.) jug (see also YOQUE)

YOGAS or YOGAS EL CANTINERO (slang) I (1st pers. sg. pron.) (disguise-expansion of Std. yo)

YOLE (dim. of) Yolanda

YOLI (dim. of) Yolanda

YOMPA (Eng?) jumper (type of hunting jacket worn by men)

YÓMPER (Eng?) m. jumper (type of single-piece combination blouse and skirt worn by women)

YONCA (Eng., < junker?) bicycle

YONQUE (Eng.) m. junk; junkyard

YONQUEAR or YONQUIAR (Eng.) va. to junk

YOQUE (Eng.) m. jug (see also YOGA et al.)

YOYO (Eng.) yoyo, type of toy top

which is raised or lowered by
being spun from a string
YUDAR (rus.) (var. of) ayudar
YULA (Hispanization of) Beulah,
Texas
YÚNIER or YÚNIOR (Eng.) m. younger;
youngest of several; Junior
(e.g., "Éste es Juan yúnier"
'This is Juan Jr.', said by a
father in ref. to his identical-
ly-named son)
YUTA (Hispanization of) Utah (U.S.
state)
YUYO (dim. of) Jesús (see also
CHUY)

Z

ZACATAL m. tall dense grass in
great abundance
ZACATE (slang) m. low-grade marihuana
ZACATEADA or ZACATIADA (orthog. vars.
of) sacateada or sacatiada
ZACATEAR or ZACATIAR (orthog. vars.
of) sacatear or sacatiar
ZAFAR: ZAFARSE UN HUESO to dislo-
cate a bone from the socket or
the joint
ZAFO: CON ZAFOS (slang) The same
to you!, Take your words and
eat them (fig., said to take re-
venge for any derogatory remarks
initially directed toward you
by someone else)
ZAMBO -BA bow-legged
ZAMBUTIR (var. of) zambullir
ZANCUDERÍO or ZANCUDERÍA or ZANCUDERO
swarm of mosquitos
ZANORIA (var. of) zanahoria
ZAPETA diaper
ZAPO (slang) shoe (disguise or var.
of zapato)
ZARABANDA spanking
ZARAPE (orthog. var. of) sarape m.
ZIGZAQUEAR or ZIGZAQUIAR (vars. of)
zigzaguear or zigzaguiar
ZÍPER (Eng.) m. zipper
ZONCEAR or ZONCIAR vn. to fool a-
round; to joke
ZONCERA foolishness
ZOPILOTE (slang, pej.) m. policeman
ZOQUETAL m. mudhole
ZOQUETE m. mud; (fig.) good-for-
nothing, worthless person
ZOQUETERA mud-guard (aut.); mudhole

ZOQUETOSO -SA muddy
ZUCA (rus.) (var. of) azúcar
ZUCADERO -RA (vars. of) azucarero
-ra
ZUCARERO -RA (vars. of) azucarero
-ra
ZUMBAR va. to win; to conquer;
(slang) to eat up; ZUMBARLE A
ALGUIEN EL APARATO/EL MANGO
to excel in something (esp. in
sports); ZUMBARLE A ALGUIEN EL
COCO to be daffy, screwy,
slightly crazy
ZUMBIDO gossip, wagging of tongues;
running around (usually in
search of sexual adventures)
ZURUMBÁTICO -CA daffy, screwy,
slightly crazy; dumb, stupid,
ignorant
ZURUMBÁS adj. (var. of) zurumbático
-ca
ZURUM(B)ATO -TA (var. of) zurumbático -ca
ZURRAR vr. to get angry, become
infuriated

Apéndice A: Proverbios y refranes
Appendix A: Proverbs and Sayings

Proverbios y refranes/Proverbs and Sayings

A

¡A BUENA HORA! (iron.) High time!:
"¡A buenahora vas llegando!"
'A fine time to be arriving!'

A BUEN ENTENDEDOR, POCAS PALABRAS
A word to the wise is sufficient

A BUEN HAMBRE NO HAY MAL PAN
Hunger is the best sauce

A BUEN SANTO TE ENCOMIENDAS The
blind are leading the blind (A
fine choice of a guide you've
made)

A CABALLO DADO NO HAY QUE MIRARLE
EL COLMILLO / LOS DIENTES
One should never look a gift
horse in the mouth (also: A
CABALLO REGALADO NO HAY QUE
MIRARLE EL DIENTE id.)

A CADA SANTO SE LE LLEGA SU DÍA
Every dog has his day (Everyone
gets his reward sooner or later)

A GUSTOS SE ROMPEN PANZAS Every
man to his own taste (Arguments
on likes and dislikes often
provoke fights)

A HUEVO NI LOS ZAPATOS ENTRAN You
can lead a horse to water but
you cannot make him drink

A LO DADO NO SE LE BUSCA LADO Don't
look a gift horse in the mouth

A MAL TIEMPO BUENA CARA Keep a
stiff upper lip

A OTRO PERRO CON ESE HUESO Go tell
it to the marines

A QUIEN LE VENGA EL GUANTE, QUE SE
LO PLANTE If the shoe fits,
wear it

A QUIEN MADRUGA, DIOS LE AYUDA The
early bird gets the worm / God
helps him who helps himself

A TODO LE TIRA, Y A NADA LE DA
Jack of all trades, master of
none

A VER SI COMO RONCAN DUERMEN Talk
is cheap / Let's see if they can
deliver the goods

AL FLOJO LO AYUDA DIOS/AL FLOJO DIOS
LO AYUDA/AL PEREZOSO LO AYUDA
DIOS/AL PEREZOSO DIOS LO AYUDA
Some people have all the luck
(comment directed to a lazy
person who has had a much easier
time with a chore than was expected)

AL OJO DEL AMO ENGORDA EL MACHO
A watched pot does boil / If
you want it done right, do it
yourself

AL QUE LE APRIETA EL ZAPATO QUE SE
LO AFLOJE/AL QUE LE APRIETE EL
ZAPATO QUE SE LO AFLOJE God
helps those who help themselves

AL QUE LE DÉ COMEZÓN QUE SE RASQUE
God helps those who help themselves

AL QUE LE DUELA LA MUELA QUE SE LA
SAQUE/AL QUE LE DUELE LA MUELA
QUE SE LA SAQUE God helps
those who help themselves

AL QUE LE QUEDE EL ZAPATO, QUE SE
LO PONGA If the shoe fits,
wear it

AL QUE MADRUGA, DIOS LE AYUDA The
early bird gets the worm / God
helps him who helps himself

AL QUE NO HABLA, DIOS NO LO OYE
Faint heart never won fair lady

ABEJA: s. ESTAR COMO . . .

ABRAZAN: s. DE FAVOR TE . . .

ABRIR EL CORAZÓN To bare one's
heart

ABUELA: s. CUÉNTASELO A TU . . .

ACÁ LA MADRE DE LOS BORREGOS Far,
far away / Way down yonder /
East of the twelfth of never

ACABA: s. LA MUERTE LO ACABA TODO

ACABA: s. QUIEN MAL ANDA, MAL . . .

ACOSTARSE CON LAS GALLINAS (Y LEVAN-
TARSE CON LOS GALLOS) Early
to bed and early to rise / To
go to bed with the chickens and
wake up with the roosters

ACUERDO: s. NO LLORO, PERO ME . . .

AGUANTE: s. NO HAY MAL QUE DURE
CIEN AÑOS . . .

AHORA ES CUANDO, YERBABUENA, LE
HAS DE DAR SABOR AL CALDO
Strike while the iron is hot /
Now is the time to make one's
move

AHORA QUE ENTIERRAN DIOQUIS Get it
whjle the getting's good

AHORA SI BAILA MI HIJA CON EL DOCTOR
/CON EL SEÑOR Now you're talking! (indicates complete accord
between speaker and listener)

AHORA SÍ CHISPAS, QUÉMENME Strike
while the iron is hot / Now
is the tjme to make the move

AHORA VA LA MÍA / LA TUYA / LA
SUYA (etc.) Now it's my turn /
your turn (etc.)

AJENA: s. CUIDA TU VIDA Y DEJA . . .

AMIGO: s. EL QUE PRESTA A UN
AMIGO . . .

AMOLAR: s. PARA ACABARLA DE . . .

AMOR CON AMOR SE PAGA By love is
love repaid / As you sow, so
shall you reap

AMOR DE LEJOS, AMOR DE PENDEJOS
Out of sight, out of mind

AMORES: s. NI BESOS NI APACHURRO-
NES. . .
AMOS: s. ES POR DEMÁS, NADIE PUEDE
SERVIR A DOS . . .
ANDA: s. QUIEN MAL ANDA . . .
ANDAR VUELTA Y VUELTA to pace the
floor
ANDAS: s. DIME CON QUIEN . . .
ANTES DE HABLAR ES BUENO PENSAR
Think before you act / Look
before you leap
ANTES QUE TE CASES, MIRA LO QUE HACES
Look twice before you leap
APAREZCA: s. DE LO PERDIDO . . .
APRIETA: s. EL QUE MUCHO . . . /
QUIEN MUCHO ABARCA . . .
ÁRBOL: s. EL ÁRBOL SE CONOCE POR
SU FRUTA
ARRIBA: s. BUSCAR ALGO DE . . .
ARRIEROS SOMOS Y EN EL CAMINO ANDAMOS
We are all the children of God
(expression used to admonish
someone who is criticizing de-
ficiencies he himself will in-
evitably come to possess)
ARRIESGA: s. EL QUE NO
ASTILLA: s. DE TAL PALO TAL . . .
ATIENDA/ATIENDE: s. QUIEN TIENE
TIENDA . . .
ATOLE: s. CORRERLE A ALGUIEN . . .
AUNQUE LA MONA SE VISTA DE SEDA,
MONA SE QUEDA You can't make
a silk purse from a sow's ear /
Clothes do not make the man
AVENTAR: s. HAY HASTA PARA . . .
AYUDA: s. AL FLOJO LO AYUDA DIOS
AYÚDATE, QUE DIOS TE AYUDARÁ God
helps those who help themselves
AZUL: s. EL QUE QUIERE . . .

B

BAILA: s. POR DINERO BAILA EL
PERRO . . .
BAJÁRSELE A ALGUIEN LA SANGRE A LOS
PIES To be scared stiff
BARRIO AJENO: s. ESTAR COMO PERRO
EN . . .
BIEN: s. EL QUE MAL HAGA, . . .
BITOQUE: s. LA JERINGA . . .
BOCA: s. EL QUE TIENE . . .
BORREGOS: s. ACÁ LA MADRE DE LOS...
BOTICA: s. HAY DE TODO COMO EN . . .
BRINCOS: s. ¿PARA QUE DAR TANTOS
. . . ?
BROCHE: s. CERRAR CON . . .
BUEN: s. A BUEN ENTENDEDOR . . .

BUENA: s. A MAL TIEMPO BUENA CARA
BUENOS: s. CUMPLIR COMO LOS ME-
ROS . . .
BURRA: s. CUANDO DIGO QUE . . .
BURRADA: s. HACER UNA . . .
BUSCAR ALGO DE ARRIBA A ABAJO To
look high and low for something
BUSCARLE TRES PATAS AL GATO To com-
plicate matters

C

CABEZA: s. ECHARLE A ALGUIEN
POR . . .
CADA CHANGO A SU MECATE Y A DARSE
VUELO Let each one mind his
own business and get on with
it / Keep your nose to yourself
CADA OVEJA CON SU PAREJA Birds of a
feather flock together
CADA POBRETE LO QUE TIENE METE
(general meaning: The poor
must use all the resources at
their disposal)
CADA UNO ES COMO DIOS LO HIZO We are
all as God made us
CAE MÁS PRONTO UN HABLADOR QUE UN
COJO A liar is more likely to
slip up than a lame person
CALZÓN: s. PON, PON, PON UN NICLE
PA' JABÓN
CAMARÓN QUE SE DUERME SE LO LLEVA LA
CORRIENTE Opportunity only
knocks once
CAMINO: s. ARRIEROS SOMOS Y EN
EL . . .
CAMPOSANTO: s. VALE MÁS SUCIO EN
CASA . . .
CANASTA: s. QUITARLE A ALGUIEN
LA . . .
CANDIL DE LA CALLE, OSCURIDAD DE LA
CASA A saint abroad and a
devil at home
CANTA Y CANTA Y NADA DE ÓPERA Much
ado about nothing
CÁNTARO: s. TANTO VA EL . . .
CAPITÁN: s. DONDE MANDA . . .
CARA: s. A MAL TIEMPO BUENA CARA
CARO: s. LO BARATO ES . . .
CASA: s. VALE MÁS SUCIO EN CASA ...
CASCARÓN: s. NO SALIR DEL . . .
CASES: s. EL MARTES NI TE . . .
CERRAR CON BROCHE DE ORO To end a
program or event with a bang /
with a grand finale
CIEGO: s. EL AMOR ES . . .
CIEN: s. MÁS VALE UNA TOMA . . .

CIENCIA: s. LA EXPERIENCIA ES LA MADRE DE . . .

COCHINOS: s. EL QUE NO QUIERA RUIDOS . . .

COLA DE RANA: s. SANA, SANA, . . .

COLMARLE A ALGUIEN LA PACIENCIA To cause someone to run out of patience

COLMILLO: s. A CABALLO DADO NO HAY QUE MIRARLE . . .

COMER FRIJOLES Y REPETIR POLLO Weak to perform though mighty to pretend (ref. to person who tries to give the impression that he is better off than he really is)

COMER: s. NO HAY QUE MORDER LA MANO . . .

COMER: s. NO MUERDAS LA MANO . . .

COMEZÓN: s. AL QUE LE DÉ COMEZÓN...

COMO: s. CADA UNO ES COMO DIOS LO HIZO

CON EL TIEMPO Y UN GANCHITO HASTA LAS VERDES SE ALCANZAN All things come to him who waits

CON LA VARA QUE MIDAS SERÁS MEDIDO As you sow, so shall you reap

CONOCE: s. EL ÁRBOL SE CONOCE POR SU FRUTA

CONOCER: s. MÁS VALE LO MALO CONO- CIDO QUE LO BUENO POR . . .

CONSEJO: s. DAR EL . . .

CONSUELO: s. MAL DE MUCHOS, . . .

CORAZÓN: s. ABRIR EL . . .

CORAZÓN: s. OJOS QUE NO VEN, . . .

CORAZÓN: s. PANZA LLENA, . . .

CORAZONES: s. POR LAS ACCIONES SE JUZGAN LOS . . .

CORRERLE A ALGUIEN ATOLE POR LAS VENAS To be extremely patient / To be slow as molasses

CORRIENTE: s. CAMARÓN QUE SE DUERME

CORTITO -TA: s. TRAERLE A ALGUIEN MUY . . .

COSA MALA NUNCA MUERE A bad penny always turns up

COSA: s. DECIR UNA . . .

COSTA: s. HAY MOROS EN . . .

CREER: s. VER ES . . .

CRIE: s. EL QUE NO QUIERA RUIDOS...

CUAL MÁS CUAL MENOS Six of one, half dozen of the other

CUANDO DIGO QUE LA BURRA ES PARDA, ES PORQUE TRAIGO LOS PELOS EN LA MANO When I say it's so, it's because I have the proof right here in my hand

CUANDO MÁS SE TIENE, MÁS SE QUIERE The more one has, the more one wants

CUANDO UNA PUERTA SE CIERRA, OTRA SE ABRE There are other fish in the sea

CUANDO UNO ANDA DE MALAS HASTA LOS PERROS LO MEAN When it rains, it pours

CUANDO YO TENÍA DINERO ME LLAMABAN DON TOMÁS, Y AHORA QUE NO TENGO ME LLAMAN TOMÁS NOMÁS Wealth makes worship / A rich man has many friends

CUENTAS: s. EN RESUMIDAS . . .

CUÉNTASELO A TU ABUELA Tell it to the marines

CUENTO CHINO tall tale, fish story

CUIDA TU VIDA Y DEJA LA AJENA / LA DEL PRÓJIMO / LA DEL VECINO Go mind your own business

CUIDADO: s. SI QUIERES VIVIR SIN . . .

CULECAS: s. SON MÁS LAS . . .

CUMPLIR COMO LOS MERO BUENOS To live up to one's word / To fulfill one's commitments to the letter

CURA: s. LA CURA ES PEOR . . .

CH

CHÁVEZ: s. TÚ SABES QUIEN TRAE LAS LLAVES, . . .

CHINGUES: s. NO ME CHINGUES ...

CHINO: s. CUENTO ...

CHISPAS: s. AHORA SÍ ...

D

DAN: s. POR DINERO BAILA EL PERRO ...

DAÑO: s. HASTA LO QUE NO COMES TE HACE ...

DAR EL CONSEJO Y QUEDARSE SIN ÉL Not to practice what one preaches

DAR GATO POR LIEBRE to deceive some- one, to give someone a song and a dance

DARE: s. MÁS VALE UN TOMA ...

DÉ: s. AL QUE LE DÉ COMEZÓN...

DE FAVOR TE ABRAZAN, Y QUIERES QUE TE APRIETEN They give you an inch and you want a mile

¡DE LA QUE ME ESCAPÉ! That was a close shave / close call!

DE LO PERDIDO A LO QUE APAREZCA Something is better than nothing (lit. 'From having lost it to whatever may appear')

DE MÚSICO, POETA Y LOCO, TODOS TE-
    NEMOS UN POCO Everyone is a
    little bit crazy
DE TAL PALO TAL ASTILLA Like fa-
    ther like son
DE UNA MENTIRA NACEN MUCHAS One
    lie leads to a thousand
DE UN DIA PARA OTRO any day now,
    any time soon
DE UN MOMENTO PARA OTRO any min-
    ute now, any time soon
DEBE: s. EL QUE NADA ...
DEJES: s. NO DEJES PARA MAÑANA ...
DEL ÁRBOL CAÍDO TODOS HACEN LEÑA
    Everyone kicks a man when he's
    down
DEL DICHO AL HECHO HAY MUCHO TRECHO
    Sooner said than done
DECIR POR DERECHO To call a spade
    a spade / To tell it like it
    is
DECIR UNA COSA Y HACER OTRA To say
    one thing and do another
DEJARSE TRATAR CON LA PUNTA DEL PIE
    to let someone walk all over
    you
DERECHITO: s. SANGRE DE PERRITO ...
DERECHO: s. DECIR POR ...
DESEA: s. LA SUERTE DE LA FEA ...
DESHONRA: s. EL SER POBRE NO ES ...
DÍA: s. A CADA SANTO SE LE LLEGA
      ...
DÍA: s. DE UN ...
DIENTE: s. A CABALLO DADO NO HAY
    QUE MIRARLE ...
DIFERENTE: s. LA JERINGA ...
DIGO: s. HAZ LO QUE YO DIGO ...
DIME CON QUIEN ANDAS Y TE DIRÉ QUIEN
    ERES A man is known by the com-
    pany he keeps
DINERO: s. EL QUE PRESTA A UN AMIGO
    ...
DINERO: s. POR DINERO BAILA EL
    PERRO ...
DINERO LLAMA DINERO Money begets
    money / The rich get rich
    (and the poor get poorer)
DINERO TRAE DINERO (id. to DINERO
    LLAMA DINERO)
DIOS: s. A QUIEN MADRUGA, ...
DIOS: s. AL FLOJO LO AYUDA DIOS
DIOS: s. AL QUE MADRUGA, ...
DIOS: s. AL QUE NO HABLA, ...
DIOS: s. AYÚDATE , QUE ...
DIOS: s. CADA UNO ES COMO DIOS LO
    HIZO
DIOS: s. DONDE ...
DIOS: s. EL HOMBRE PROPONE Y ...
DIOS: s. EL QUE NO HABLA ...
DIRE: s. DIME CON QUIEN ANDAS ...
DONDE COMEN DOS , COMEN TRES There's
    always room for one more / Two
    can live as cheaply as one

DONDE DIOS ES SERVIDO On the other
    side of nowhere / Beyond the
    twelfth of never
DONDE MANDA CAPITÁN , NO MANDA MARI-
    NERO Too many cooks spoil the
    broth (There can be only one
    boss)
DOS: s. MÁS VALE QUE HAIGA ...
DUELA/DUELE: s. AL QUE LE DUELA LA
    MUELA ...

E

ECHAR EL GATO A RETOZAR to steal
ECHAR LA CASA POR LA VENTANA to go
    for broke, to shoot the works
ECHARLE A ALGUIEN POR LA CABEZA To
    let the cat out of the bag
    (give someone away, betray some-
    one)
ECHAR MENTIRAS PARA SACAR VERDADES
    To tell a lie and learn the
    truth
EL AMOR ES CIEGO Love is blind
EL ÁRBOL SE CONOCE POR SU FRUTA By
    their fruits ye shall know them
EL BURRO POR DELANTE PARA QUE NO SE
    ESPANTE "Me first" (said to
    a person who always mentions
    his/her name before the names
    of others, e.g., 'Yo y mis a-
    migos lo hicimos')
EL COMAL LE DIJO A LA OLLA: QUÉ
    COLA TAN PRIETA TIENES The pot
    is calling the kettle black
EL HÁBITO (NO) HACE AL MONJE Clothes
    (don't) make the man
EL HOMBRE PROPONE Y DIOS DISPONE
    Man proposes, (but) God dis-
    poses
EL MARTES NI TE CASES NI TE EM-
    BARQUES (folk wisdom:) Don't
    marry or set sail on Tuesdays
EL MUERTO AL POZO Y EL VIVO AL NE-
    GOCIO Let the dead bury the
    dead / Life must go on
EL SER POBRE NO ES DESHONRA Poverty
    is no sin
EL TIEMPO ES ORO Time is money
EL QUE CANTA, SUS MALES ESPANTA He
    who sings chases away his blues
EL QUE LA HACE LA PAGA As you sow
    so shall you reap
EL QUE MAL HAGA, BIEN ESPERE As you
    sow so shall you reap
EL QUE MUCHO APRIETA, POCO ABARCA
    Don't bite off more than you
    can chew

EL QUE NADA DEBE NADA TEME If your
hands are clean you have nothing to fear

EL QUE NO ARRIESGA, NO GANA Nothing ventured, nothing gained

EL QUE NO HABLA DIOS NO LO OYE God
helps those who help themselves

EL QUE NO LLORA NO MAMA One must
speak up to be heard, God helps
those who help themselves

EL QUE NO QUIERA RUIDOS QUE NO CRÍE
COCHINOS/EL QUE NO QUIERE
RUIDOS QUE NO CRÍE COCHINOS
If you can't stand the heat,
stay out of the kitchen (lit.
'He who wants no noise should
not raise hogs')

EL QUE PRESTA A UN AMIGO, PIERDE EL
DINERO Y PIERDE EL AMIGO Neither
a borrower nor a lender be
(lit. 'He who lends money to a
friend loses both money and
friend')

EL QUE QUIERA AZUL QUE LE CUESTE
One must pay for what one wants
(='Take what you want and pay
for it, says God'--Spanish
proverb)

EL QUE RÍE ÚLTIMO, RÍE MEJOR He who
laughs last, laughs best

EL QUE TIENE BOCA A ROMA VA Speak
up loud and you'll draw a
crowd (he who speaks up is
heard / is listened to)

EN BOCA CERRADA NO ENTRAN MOSCAS
Silence is golden

EN LA UNIÓN HAY FUERZA In unity
there is strength, United we
stand, divided we fall

EN RESUMIDAS CUENTAS when all is
said and done

EN TIERRA DE CIEGOS EL TUERTO ES
REY In the land of the blind
the one-eyed is king

ENCUERAS: s. ¿QUÉ ESPERAS QUE NO...

ENFERMEDAD: s. LA CURA ES PEOR ...

ENGAÑAN: s. LAS APARIENCIAS ...

ENSEÑAR LA OREJA to show one's
ignorance

ENTENDEDOR: s. A BUEN ENTENDEDOR ...

ENTIENDES: s. ¿ME ENTIENDES, ...

ENTIERRAN: s. AHORA QUE ...

ENTRARLE PAREJO To go for broke (to
go all out for something)

ERES: s. DIME CON QUIEN ANDAS ...

ES MEJOR ANDAR SOLO QUE MAL ACOMPA-
ÑADO better to travel alone
than to keep bad company

ES MEJOR QUE HAYA UN TONTO Y NO DOS
You've made enough of a fool
of yourself already (and you'll
make more of one of yourself
if you keep doing what you are
doing)

ES POR DEMÁS, NADIE PUEDE SERVIR A
DOS AMOS No one can serve two
masters

ESCAPE: s. ¡DE LA QUE ME ... !

ESPANTA: s. EL QUE CANTA, SUS MALES
...

ESPANTE: s. EL BURRO POR DELANTE ...

ESPERAS: s. ¿QUÉ ESPERAS QUE NO ...

ESTAR COMO LA ABEJA, QUE VOLANDO
PICA (ref. to the person who
enjoys malicious insinuation)

ESTAR COMO PERRO EN BARRIO AJENO To
be like a fish out of the water

ESTAR TAMAÑITO to have one's heart
in one's mouth, to feel "just
so big"

EXPERIENCIA: s. LA EXPERIENCIA ES
MADRE ...

EXPLICO: s. ¿ME ENTIENDES, ...

F

FALTA: s. NUNCA FALTA ...

FAROL DE LA CALLE, OSCURIDAD DE LA
CASA A saint abroad and a sin-
ner at home

FEA: s. LA SUERTE DE LA FEA ...

FEDERICO: s. ¿ME ENTIENDES, ...

FLOJO: s. AL FLOJO LO AYUDA DIOS ...

FREGASTE: s. TE CASASTE, TE ...

FUERZA: s. EN LA UNIÓN HAY FUERZA

FUERZA: s. MÁS VALE MAÑA QUE ...

G

GALVÁN: s. NO LO ENTENDERÁ ...

GALLINAS: s. ACOSTARSE CON LAS ...

GALLO: s. MÁS CLARO NO CANTA ...

GANCHITO: s. CON EL TIEMPO Y ...

GANSO: s. ME CANSO DIJO UN ...

GARROTE: s. LIMOSNERO ...

GATO: s. BUSCARLE TRES PATAS ...

GATO: s. HAY ...

GUANTE: s. A QUIEN LE VENGA ...

GUATEMALA: IR DE GUATEMALA A GUATE-
PEOR/SALIR DE GUATEMALA PARA
IR A GUATEPEOR to go from bad
to worse

GUSTOS: s. A GUSTOS SE ROMPEN PAN-
ZAS

H

HABLA: s. EL QUE NO HABLA ...
HABLADOR: s. CAE MÁS PRONTO UN ...
HABLAR: s. ANTES DE ...
HACER ALGO A COMO DÉ LUGAR to do
    something by hook or by crook
HACER DE LAS SUYAS to be up to one's
    tricks
HACER UNA BURRADA to pull a real
    boner
HACER: s. NO ES LO MISMO DECIR
    QUE ...
HAGO: s. HAZ LO QUE YO DIGO ...
HAIGA: s. MÁS VALE QUE HAIGA ...
HAMBRE: s. A BUEN HAMBRE ...
¡HASTA LO QUE NO COMES TE HACE DAÑO!
    Busybodies never lack a bad day/
    If you look for trouble you
    will find it
HAY DE TODO COMO EN BOTICA (Here)
    there's a little bit of every-
    thing
HAY GATO ENCERRADO There's something
    rotten in Denmark / There's
    something fishy going on
HAY HASTA PARA AVENTAR PA' ARRIBA
    There is enough (here) to take
    care of an army
HAY MOROS EN LA COSTA The walls
    have ears
HAY MUERTOS QUE NO HACEN RUIDOS Y SON
    MAYORES SUS PENAS Silent rivers
    run deep
HAY: s. NO HAY MAL QUE ...
HAZ BIEN Y NO MIRES A QUIEN Charity
    is its own reward
HAZ LO QUE YO DIGO, Y NO LO QUE YO
    HAGO Do as I say, not as I do
HERMOSA: s. LA SUERTE DE LA FEA ...
HERMOSO: s. QUIEN A FEO AMA, ...
HIJA: s. AHORA SÍ BAILA MI ...
HINCAN: s. VEN LA TEMPESTAD Y NO
    SE ...
HIZO: s. CADA UNO ES COMO DIOS LO
    HIZO
HOCICO: s. PERRERO HUEVERO AUNQUE
    LE QUEMEN ...;
HOMBRE: s. NO SÓLO DE PAN VIVE ...
HORA: s. A BUENA HORA ...
HOY: s. NO DEJES PARA MAÑANA LO
    QUE PUEDES HACER...
HUESO: s. A OTRO PERRO CON ESE ...

I

IMPORTA: s. NO IMPORTA QUE NAZCAN
    CHATOS ...
INCOMODA: s. LA VERDAD NO MATA, PERO
    ...
IR POR LANA Y SALIR TRASQUILADO (lit.
    'To go to buy wool and to come
    back sheared'; the sense is that
    one has gone with the intent of
    winning but returns a complete
    loser)

J

JICOTERA: s. MOVER LA ...
JUAN DOMÍNGUEZ: s. NO ME CHINGUES
    ...
JUSTOS PAGAN POR PECADORES The just
    pay for the sins of the guilty

L

LA CURA ES PEOR QUE LA ENFERMEDAD
    The cure is worse than the dis-
    ease
LA ENEMA: s. LA JERINGA ...
LA EXPERIENCIA ES LA MADRE DE LA
    CIENCIA Experience is the mo-
    ther of wisdom
LA GRACIA ES ANDAR ENTRE LAS LLAMAS
    Y NO QUEMARSE The real trick
    is to emerge unscathed from
    flame and fire
LA JERINGA/LA LAVATIVA/LA ENEMA ES LA
    MISMA, SÓLO EL BITOQUE ES DI-
    FERENTE (mildly vulg.) Plus
    ça change, plus c'est la même
    chose
LA MALA YERBA NUNCA MUERE The bad
    penny keeps coming back
LA MENTIRA DURA HASTA QUE LA VERDAD
    LLEGA The truth will always
    come out in the end

LA MUERTE A NADIE PERDONA Death
    pardons no man
LA MUERTE LO ACABA TODO Death puts
    an end to everything
LA SUERTE DE LA FEA LA HERMOSA LA
    DESEA The grass is always
    greener on the other side (lit.
    'The beautiful woman envies the
    good fortune of the ugly one')
LA VERDAD NO MATA, PERO INCOMODA
    The truth sometimes hurts
LAS APARIENCIAS ENGAÑAN You can't
    judge a book by its cover
LADO: s. A LO DADO NO SE LE BUSCA
    ...
LADO: s. SANGRE DE VENADO ...
LADRE: s. NO TENER NI PADRE ...
LADRÓN: s. MÁS PECA LA VÍCTIMA ...
LANA: s. IR POR LANA Y SALIR
    TRASQUILADO
LAVATIVA: s. LA JERINGA ...
LEJOS: s. POCO A POCO SE VA ...
LEÑA: s. DEL ÁRBOL CAÍDO TODOS
    HACEN ...
LIEBRE: s. DAR GATO POR ...
LIMOSNERO Y CON GARROTE Beggars
    can't be choosers
LIMPIO: s. VALE MÁS SUCIO EN CASA
    ...
LO BARATO CUESTA CARO / LO BARATO
    ES CARO Cheap goods cost dear
    in the long run
LO CORTÉS NO QUITA LO VALIENTE Ci-
    vility never detracted from
    valor
LO QUE PASÓ VOLÓ Let bygones be by-
    gones, No use crying over spill-
    ed milk
LOCO: s. DE MÚSICO, POETA Y ...
LOCOS: s. LOS NIÑOS Y LOS ...
LOS NIÑOS Y LOS LOCOS DICEN LA VER-
    DAD Children and crazy people
    always tell the truth / Words
    from the mouth of babes
LUGAR: s. HACER (ALGO) A COMO DÉ
    ...

LL

LLAMAS: s. LA GRACIA ES ANDAR
    ENTRE ...
LLORA: s. EL QUE NO LLORA ...

M

MACHO: s. AL OJO DEL AMO ENGORDA ...
MACHO: s. TAPARLE EL OJO AL ...
MADRE: s. LA EXPERIENCIA ES MADRE
    ...
MADRE: s. NO TENER NI PADRE ...
MAL: s. A MAL TIEMPO BUENA CARA
MAL: s. NO HAY MAL QUE ...
MAL: s. QUIEN MAL ANDA ...
MAL ACOMPAÑADO: s. ES MEJOR ANDAR
    SOLO QUE .../ MÁS VALE ANDAR
    SOLO QUE ...
MAL DE MUCHOS, CONSUELO DE TONTOS
    Misery loves company / Fools
    are comforted by the misfortunes
    of others
MALES: s. PARA ALIVIO DE MIS ...
MAMA: s. EL QUE NO LLORA ...
MAÑANA: s. NO DEJES PARA MAÑANA ...
MANDADOS: s. UNOS NACIERON PARA
    MANDAR ...
MANDAR: s. UNOS NACIERON PARA MAN-
    DAR ...
MANO: s. NO HAY QUE MORDER LA ...
MANO: s. NO MUERDAS LA ...
MÁS CLARO NO CANTA UN GALLO As clear
    as the nose on your face
MÁS PECA LA VÍCTIMA QUE EL LADRÓN
    (roughly equivalent to 'The
    coward dies a thousand deaths,
    the valiant only one', though
    the literal meaning shows a
    variation on that theme: 'The
    victim sins more than the thief--
    because the victim suspects and
    blames everyone whereas the
    thief only sinned during the
    single act of thievery')
MÁS VALE ALGO QUE NADA Every little
    bit helps
MÁS VALE ANDAR SOLO QUE MAL ACOM-
    PAÑADO It is better to be
    alone than in bad company
MÁS VALE LO MALO CONOCIDO QUE LO
    BUENO POR CONOCER Better safe
    than sorry / Better a lean agree-
    ment than a fat sentence
MÁS VALE MAÑA QUE FUERZA The pen is
    mightier than the sword
MÁS VALE PÁJARO EN MANO QUE CIEN
    VOLANDO A bird in the hand is
    worth two in the bush
MÁS VALE QUE HAIGA UN TONTO Y NO DOS
    (roughly equivalent to:) Two
    wrongs do not make a right

(though lit. 'Better for there
to be just one fool than two')
MÁS VALE TARDE QUE NUNCA Better late
than never
MÁS VALE UN TOMA QUE CIEN TE DARÉ A
bird in hand is worth two in the
bush
MATANCEROS: s. NADIE QUIERE SER
CHIVO; TODOS QUIEREN SER ...
ME CANSO / ME CANSO, DIJO UN GANSO /
ME CANSO, DIJO UN GANSO, CUANDO
VOLAR NO PUDO (ritualistic response given--usually by a
child--to someone ordering him/
her to cease any particularly
taxing form of behavior; the
sense of the refrain is "I'll
do what I'm doing as long as I
feel like doing it")
¿ME ENTIENDES, MÉNDEZ, O TE EXPLICO,
FEDERICO? (expression used to
emphasize the speaker's de-
sire to be understood; rough
Eng. equivalent would be 'Ya
see what I mean, Gene, or must
I tell it all, Paul?')
MECATE: s. CADA CHANGO A SU ...
MÉNDEZ: s. ¿ME ENTIENDES, ...
MENOS: s. CUAL MÁS CUAL ...
MENTIRA: s. DE UNA ...
METE: s. CADA POBRETE LO QUE TIENE
METE
MIRA: s. ANTES QUE TE CASES, ...
MIRES: s. HAZ BIEN Y NO ...
MISMA: s. LA JERINGA ...
MISMA: s. SER PÁJAROS DE LA MISMA
PLUMA
MOMENTO: s. DE UN ...
MONA: s. AUNQUE LA ...
MONJE: s. EL HÁBITO (NO) HACE ...
MOSCAS: s. EN BOCA CERRADA NO
ENTRAN ...
MOSCO: s. YA TE CONOZCO ...
MOVER LA JICOTERA to stir things
up, to start a commotion
MUELA: s. AL QUE LE DUELA LA MUELA
...
MUERDE: s. PERRO QUE LADRA NO ...
MUERE: s. COSA MALA NUNCA ...
MUERE: s. YERBA MALA NUNCA ...

N

NACIERON: s. UNOS NACIERON PARA
MANDAR ...
NADA: s. MÁS VALE ALGO QUE ...
NADIE QUIERE SER CHIVO; TODOS QUIEREN
SER MATANCEROS Everyone wants
to be a chief and no one an
Indian
NAZCAN: s. NO IMPORTA QUE NAZCAN
CHATOS ...
NI BESOS NI APACHURRONES SON AMORES
Actions speak louder than words
NO DEJES PARA MAÑANA LO QUE PUEDES
HACER HOY Don't leave for to-
morrow what you can do today
NO ES EL LEÓN COMO LO PINTAN / NO
ES LA LEONA COMO LA PINTAN
Things are seldom what they
seem
NO ES LO MISMO DECIR QUE HACER Actions
speak louder than words
NO ES ORO TODO LO QUE RELUCE All
that glitters is not gold
NO HAY COSA / NO HAY PERSONA TAN MALA
QUE PARA ALGO NO SIRVA There's
a little bit of gold in every
mine / There's some good in
everyone
NO HAY MAL QUE DURE CIEN AÑOS NI
ENFERMO QUE LOS AGUANTE Nothing
can last forever / Everything
must have an end
NO HAY MAL QUE POR BIEN NO VENGA
Every cloud has a silver lining/
It's a blessing in disguise
NO HAY QUE MORDER LA MANO QUE NOS DA
DE COMER Don't bite the hand
that feeds you
NO IMPORTA QUE NAZCAN CHATOS CON TAL
QUE TENGAN RESUELLO Handsome
is as handsome does, You can't
judge a book by its cover (lit.
'It doesn't matter if they're
born flat-nosed just as long as
they can breathe through it')
NO LE ENTENDERÁ GALVÁN If he doesn't
know, nobody will
NO LLORO, PERO ME ACUERDO I may not
be crying, but I can remember
the pain
NO ME CHINGUES, JUAN DOMÍNGUEZ (rough
Eng. equivalent:) Don't try to
cheat, Pete (=Don't try to get
the better of me)

NO MUERDAS LA MANO QUE TE DA DE CO-
MER Don't bite the hand that
feeds you
NO SALIR DEL CASCARÓN (TODAVÍA) To
be (still) wet behind the ears
NO SÓLO DE PAN VIVE EL HOMBRE Man
does not live by bread alone
NO TENER NI PADRE NI MADRE NI PERR-
ITO QUE LE LADRE to be all
alone in this world
NO VENGO A VER SI PUEDO SINO PORQUE
PUEDO VENGO (literally: I
haven't come to see if I am
able but because I know I'm
able, I'm here)
NUNCA: NUNCA FALTA UN YOLOVÍ
There's always going to be
someone watching, There will
always be a witness
NUNCA: s. MÁS VALE TARDE QUE ...

O

OJOS QUE NO VEN, CORAZÓN QUE NO
SIENTE Out of sight, out of
mind
OJOS: s. PELAR TAMAÑOS ...
OLLA: s. EL COMAL LE DIJO A ...
ÓPERA: s. CANTA Y CANTA Y NADA DE
...
OREJA: s. ENSEÑAR ...
ORO: s. EL TIEMPO ES ...
OSCURIDAD: s. CANDIL DE LA CALLE
.../FAROL DE LA CALLE...
OTROS: s. UNOS NACIERON PARA MAN-
DAR ...
OYE: s. EL QUE NO HABLA ...

P

PACIENCIA: s. COLMARLE A ALGUIEN
...
PAGA: s. AMOR CON AMOR SE ...
PAGA: s. EL QUE LA HACE ...
PÁJAROS: s. SER PÁJAROS DE LA MIS-
MA PLUMA
PALABRAS: s. A BUEN ENTENDEDOR...
PAN: s. POR DINERO BAILA EL PERRO
...

PANZA LLENA, CORAZÓN CONTENTO A
full stomach makes a happy
heart / Man ist was man isst
(German proverb)
PANZAS: s. A GUSTOS SE ROMPEN ...
PARA ACABARLA DE AMOLAR On top of
everything else / To top it
all off
PARA ALIVIO DE MIS MALES To make
matters worse / On top of every-
thing else
¡¿PARA QUÉ DAR TANTOS BRINCOS ESTAN-
DO EL SUELO TAN PAREJO?! (ref.
to the folly of excessive pride,
egotism, etc.)
PAREJA: s. CADA OVEJA CON SU ...
PAREJO: s. ENTRARLE ...
PAREJO: s. ¡¿PARA QUÉ DAR TANTOS
BRINCOS ...?!
PASÓ: s. LO QUE PASÓ VOLÓ
PECA: s. MÁS PECA LA VÍCTIMA ...
PECADORES: s. JUSTOS PAGAN POR ...
PEDITO: s. SANA, SANA, COLA DE
RANA ...
PELAR TAMAÑOS OJOS to open one's
eyes very wide (as in astonish-
ment)
PENAS: s. HAY MUERTOS QUE NO HACEN
RUIDOS ...
PENDEJOS: s. AMOR DE LEJOS ...
PEOR: s. LA CURA ES PEOR ...
PERDIDO: s. DE LO PERDIDO ...
PERDONA: s. LA MUERTE A NADIE ...
PERRERO HUEVERO AUNQUE LE QUEMEN EL
HOCICO Once a _____ always a
_____
PERRITO: s. NO TENER NI PADRE ...
PERRITO: s. SANGRE DE PERRITO ...
PERRO: s. POR DINERO BAILA EL
PERRO ...
PERRO: PERRO QUE LADRA NO MUERDE
A barking dog never bites
PERROS: s. CUANDO UNO ANDA DE
MALAS ...
PIE: s. DEJARSE TRATAR CON LA PUN-
TA ...
PIE: s. TE DAN LA MANO Y QUIERES
...
PIERDE: s. EL QUE PRESTA A UN
AMIGO ...
PINTAN: s. NO ES EL LEÓN ...
PLUMA: s. SER PÁJAROS DE LA MISMA
PLUMA
POBRETE: s. CADA POBRETE LO QUE
TIENE METE
POCAS: s. A BUEN ENTENDEDOR ...
POCO A POCO SE VA LEJOS Rome wasn't
built in a day / Little by
little one goes a long way
PODER: s. QUERER ES ...
POLLO: s. COMER FRIJOLES Y REPETIR
...
PON, PON, PON UN NICLE PA' JABÓN,
PA' LAVAR TU CALZÓN Every

little bit helps (expression
hopefully encouraging contribu-
tions into a general fund, as
at a church bazaar, etc.)
POR DINERO BAILA EL PERRO/POR DINERO
BAILA EL PERRO Y POR PAN SÍ SE
LO DAN Money talks
POR LAS ACCIONES SE JUZGAN LOS CO-
RAZONES Actions speak louder
than words
POR UN OÍDO LE ENTRA Y POR OTRO LE
SALE In one ear, out the other
POZO: s. EL MUERTO AL ...
PRESTA: s. EL QUE PRESTA A UN A-
MIGO ...
PRESTADO: s. SI QUIERES VIVIR SIN
CUIDADO, NO PIDAS NUNCA ...
PUERTA: s. CUANDO UNA ...

Q

¿QUÉ ESPERAS QUE NO TE ENCUERAS?
(vulg.) What are you waiting
for, doomsday?
QUERER ES PODER Where there's a
will there's a way
QUIEBRA: s. TANTO VA EL CÁNTARO AL
AGUA HASTA ...
QUIEN: s. DIME CON QUIEN ANDAS ...
QUIEN A FEO AMA, HERMOSO LE PARECE
Love makes even the ugly look
beautiful
QUIEN BIEN SIEMBRA, BIEN RECOGE As
you sow, so shall you reap
QUIEN MAL ANDA, MAL ACABA He who
lives by the sword shall die by
the sword; As you sow so shall
you reap
QUIEN MÁS TIENE, MÁS QUIERE The
more you have the more you want
QUIEN MUCHO ABARCA, POCO APRIETA
Your eyes are bigger than your
stomach
QUIEN NO OYE CONSEJOS NO LLEGA A
VIEJO Heed my advice or pay
the price
QUIEN TIENE TIENDA Y NO LA ATIENDA,
QUE LA VENDA/QUIEN TIENE TIENDA
Y NO LA ATIENDE, QUE LA VENDA
(lit. 'He who has a store and
doesn't attend to business
should sell the store')
QUIERE: s. QUIEN MÁS TIENE,...
QUITARLE A ALGUIEN LA CANASTA To
cut the umbilical cord (=to
withdraw financial or other
type of support)

QUITARSE ALGUIEN LA VENDA DE LOS
OJOS To see things the way
they really are

R

RASQUE: s. AL QUE LE DÉ COMEZÓN ...
RECOGE: s. QUIEN BIEN SIEMBRA ...
RELUCE: s. NO ES ORO TODO LO QUE
...
RESUELLO: s. NO IMPORTA QUE NAZCAN
CHATOS ...
RETOZAR: s. ECHAR EL GATO ...
RÍE: s. EL QUE ...
ROMPEN: s. A GUSTOS SE ROMPEN PAN-
ZAS
RONCAN: s. A VER SI COMO ...
RUIDOS: s. EL QUE NO QUIERA RUIDOS
...
RUIDOS: s. HAY MUERTOS QUE NO HACEN
...

S

SALE: s. POR UN OÍDO LE ENTRA Y
POR OTRO LE ...
SALIR: s. IR POR LANA Y SALIR
TRASQUILADO
SALIR DE GUATEMALA PARA IR A GUATE-
PEOR To go from bad to worse
SANA, SANA, COLA DE RANA, TIRA UN
PEDITO PARA AHORA Y MAÑANA
(expression said to children
when one applies medicine to
their cuts and bruises or when
one simply kisses the wound to
"make it better")
SANGRE: s. BAJÁRSELE A ALGUIEN ...
SANGRE DE PERRITO QUE SE VAYA DE-
RECHITO (said to or by a per-
son trying to hit the target
he is shooting at)
SANGRE DE VENADO QUE SE VAYA POR UN
LADO (said to someone to cause
him to miss a target he is
shooting at)
SANTO: s. A BUEN SANTO ...
SAQUE: s. AL QUE LE DUELA LA MUELA
...
SER PÁJAROS DE LA MISMA PLUMA To be
birds of a feather

¡SI FUERA VÍBORA TE MORDIERA! It's
staring at you right in the
face! (said of a sought object)
SI QUIERES VIVIR SIN CUIDADO, NO
PIDAS NUNCA PRESTADO Neither a
borrower nor a lender be
SIRVA: s. NO HAY COSA TAN MALA QUE
PARA ALGO NO ...
SÓLO: s. LA JERINGA ...
SÓLO EL TIEMPO DIRÁ Only time will
tell
SON MÁS LAS CULECAS QUE LAS QUE ESTÁN
PONIENDO There are more birds
in the barn than eggs in the
nest (expression used to criti-
cize pretense, exaggerated
claims, etc.)
SUCIO: s. VALE MÁS SUCIO EN CASA
...

T

TANTO VA EL CÁNTARO AL AGUA HASTA
QUE SE QUIEBRA The pitcher
went to the well once too often/
You'll get yours (=your just
deserts) sooner or later
TAPARLE EL OJO AL MACHO to keep up
appearances
TARDE: s. MÁS VALE TARDE QUE NUNCA
TE CASASTE, TE FREGASTE A man's
troubles begin when he gets
married
TE DAN LA MANO Y QUIERES EL PIE
They give you an inch and you
want a mile
TEMPESTAD: s. VEN LA TEMPESTAD ...
TENER: s. NO TENER NI PADRE ...
TIEMPO: s. A MAL TIEMPO BUENA CARA
TIEMPO: s. SÓLO EL ...
TIENDA: s. QUIEN TIENE TIENDA ...
TIENE: s. CUANDO MÁS SE ...
TIRA: s. A TODO LE ...
TODO: s. LA MUERTE LO ACABA TODO
TOMA: s. MÁS VALE UN TOMA ...
TOMÁS: s. CUANDO YO TENÍA DINERO
ME LLAMABAN ...
TONTO: s. ES MEJOR QUE HAYA ...
TONTO: s. MÁS VALE QUE HAIGA ...
TRABAJA: s. UNO NUNCA SABE POR
QUIEN ...
TRAERLE A ALGUIEN MUY CORTITO -TA
to keep a tight rein on someone/
to keep someone on a short leash
TRASQUILADO: s. IR POR LANA Y SALIR
TRASQUILADO
TRECHO: s. DEL DICHO AL HECHO ...

TRES: s. DONDE COMEN DOS ...
TÚ SABES QUIEN TRAE LAS LLAVES,
CHÁVEZ You know who runs the
show around here / You know
who's boss, Hoss
TUERTO: s. EN TIERRA DE CIEGOS, ...

U

UNIÓN: s. EN LA UNIÓN HAY FUERZA
UNO NUNCA SABE POR QUIEN TRABAJA
One never knows who will reap
the rewards of one's labor
UNOS NACIERON PARA MANDAR Y OTROS
PARA SER MANDADOS Some were
born to command, others to be
commanded, Some were born to
be chiefs and other Indians

V

VALE: s. MÁS VALE QUE HAIGA ...
VALE: s. MÁS VALE TARDE QUE NUNCA
VALE: s. MÁS VALE UN TOMA ...
VALE MÁS SUCIO EN CASA Y NO LIMPIO
EN EL CAMPOSANTO (approx.
equivalent:) Better a messy
house than an early death (lit.
'It's better to be dirty at
home than clean in the ceme-
tery')
VALIENTE: s. LO CORTÉS NO QUITA
LO ...
VARA: s. CON LA ...
VAYA: s. SANGRE DE PERRITO ...
VAYA: s. SANGRE DE VENADO ...
VEN LA TEMPESTAD Y NO SE HINCAN
They don't know enough to come
in out of the rain
VENADO: s. SANGRE DE VENADO ...
VENDA: s. QUIEN TIENE TIENDA ...
VENDA: QUITARSE UNO LA ...
VENGA: s. NO HAY MAL QUE POR
BIEN ...
VENTANA: s. ECHAR LA CASA POR ...
VER ES CREER Seeing is believing
VERDAD: s. LA MENTIRA DURA HASTA
QUE ...
VERDADES: s. ECHAR MENTIRAS PARA
...
VÍBORA: s. ¡SI FUERA ... !

VÍCTIMA: s. MÁS PECA LA VÍCTIMA ...
VIEJO: s. QUIEN NO OYE CONSEJOS ...
VOLANDO: s. MÁS VALE PÁJARO EN
        MANO ...
VOLÓ: s. LO QUE PASÓ VOLÓ
VUELTA: s. ANDAR ...

Y

YA TE CONOZCO MOSCO I've seen
        through you
YERBA MALA NUNCA MUERE A bad penny
        always shows up
YERBA: s. LA MALA ...
YERBABUENA: s. AHORA ES CUANDO, ...
YOLOVÍ: s. NUNCA FALTA ...

Z

ZAPATO: s. AL QUE LE QUEDE ...
ZAPATOS: s. A HUEVO NI ...

Apéndice B: Verbos en -EAR/-IAR
Appendix B: Verbs in -EAR/-IAR

Verbos en *-ear/-iar*

Uno de los cambios fonéticos de mayor difusión social que se halla en el español de Tejas se relaciona con la terminación verbal -ear. Las dos vocales "fuertes" (bajas) se diptongan por un proceso de simplificación que convierte la e en i. Dicha transformación se realiza en el infinitivo y en los participios pasivos y presentes, así como en muchas formas de los tiempos sencillos. Conjugamos a continuación el verbo desear como ejemplo:

Verbs in *-ear/-iar*

One of the most widespread phonetic variations observable in Texas Spanish (and one which affects the speech of all social levels) concerns verbs whose infinitives end in -ear and -iar in "standard" Spanish. The two "strong" (low) vowels are diphthongized and thereby simplified in a process which converts e into i. This trajectory is observed in the infinitive and in the past and present participles as well as in most forms of the simple tenses. There follows the partial conjugation of the verb desear as an example:

INFINITIVO/INFINITIVE: desiar

PARTICIPIO PASIVO/PAST PARTICIPLE: desiado

GERUNDIO (PARTICIPIO PRESENTE)/PRESENT PARTICIPLE: desiando

PRESENTE DE INDICATIVO/PRESENT INDICATIVE:
    deseo
    deseas
    desea
    desiamos
    desean

PRESENTE DE SUBJUNTIVO/PRESENT SUBJUNCTIVE:

    desee
    desees
    desee
    desiemos / desiamos (la segunda forma se usa más, a pesar
        de no marcarse morfológicamente como subjuntivo /
        the second form is used more, even though it is mor-
        phologically unmarked as a subjunctive)
    deseen

FUTURO DE INDICATIVO/FUTURE INDICATIVE:

    desiaré, desiarás, etc.

POTENCIAL/CONDITIONAL:

    desiaría, desiarías, etc.

PRETÉRITO/PRETERITE:

    desié, desiaste, desió, desiamos, desiaron

IMPERFECTO DE SUBJUNTIVO/PAST SUBJUNCTIVE:

    desiara, desiaras, etc.

IMPERFECTO/IMPERFECT: desiaba, desiabas, etc.

En el polo opuesto encontramos la "descomposición" del diptongo de i mas a, e u o que se halla en los verbos que terminan en -iar en el español "estándar," v. gr. copiar. La ultracorrección convierte la i a e en los tiempos sencillos:

On the other hand we observe the "decomposition" of diphthongs occuring in verbs whose infinitives end in -iar in "standard" Spanish, e.g., copiar. Ultra-correction variously converts i to e in simple tenses:

PRESENTE DE INDICATIVO/PRESENT INDICATIVE:

    copeo, copeas, copea, copiamos, copean

PRESENTE DE SUBJUNTIVO/PRESENT SUBJUNCTIVE:

    copee, copees, copee, copiemos/copiamos, copeen

Parece, por lo tanto, reflejarse en la casilla a la izquierda de la designación de número y persona, una resistencia de parte de ambas conjugaciones variantes hacia toda vocal que no sea la alta i, a menos que se coloque el énfasis en la casilla a la izquierda; en este caso tiene que aparecer la vocal no alta. Así que la distinción entre los verbos -ear e -iar parece haberse eliminado.

In effect, both variant conjugations appear to reflect a resistance in the slot immediately to the left of the designation of number and person towards all but high vowel i unless stress falls on the leftward slot, in which case a non-high vowel must occur. The distinction, then, between -ear and -iar verbs appears to have been eliminated.

Apéndice C: Bibliografía
Appendix C: Bibliography

Bibliografía

Cada una de las siguientes obras de consulta se encuentra anotada (la mayor parte de manera crítica) en: Richard V. Teschner, Garland D. Bills and Jerry R. Craddock, Spanish and English of United States Hispanos: A Critical, Annotated, Linguistic Bibliography, Arlington, Va.: Center for Applied Linguistics, 1975, xxii, 352 pp. Al lector se le recomienda encarecidamente la consulta de esa fuente bibliográfica para más informes tocante las obras aquí citadas tanto como más de 600 libros, artículos, monografías, tesinas, etc. adicionales que versan sobre el español de Tejas, el Sudoeste estadounidense y demás regiones de los Estados Unidos también.

Bibliography

Each of the following secondary sources is annotated (for the most part critically) in: Richard V. Teschner, Garland D. Bills and Jerry R. Craddock, Spanish and English of United States Hispanos: A Critical, Annotated, Linguistic Bibliography, Arlington, Va.: Center for Applied Linguistics, 1975, xxii, 352 pp. The user is urged to consult that source for information on these and more than 600 other books, articles, monographs, dissertations, theses, etc., pertinent to the Spanish of Texas, the Southwest and other regions of the United States as well.

Atwood, E. Bagby. The Regional Vocabulary of Texas. Austin: Univ. of Texas Press, 1962. 273 pp.

Baugh, Lila. "A Study of Pre-School Vocabulary of Spanish-Speaking Children." MA Thesis, Univ. of Texas, Austin, 1933. 129 pp.

Braddy, Haldeen. "Narcotic Argot Along the Mexican Border." American Speech 30.84-90 (1955).

_____. "Smugglers' Argot in the Southwest." American Speech 31.96-101 (1956).

_____. "The Pachucos and Their Argot." Southern Folklore Quarterly 24.255-271 (1960).

Carrow(-Woolfolk), Elizabeth (Sister Mary Arthur). "Comprehension of English and Spanish by Preschool Mexican-American Children." Modern Language Journal 55.299-306 (1971).

_____. "Auditory Comprehension of English by Monolingual and Bilingual Preschool Children." Journal of Speech and Hearing Research 15.407-412 (1972).

Castillo Nájera, Francisco. "Breves consideraciones sobre el español que se habla en Méjico." Revista Hispánica Moderna 2.157-169 (1936).

Cerda, Gilberto, Berta Cabaza and Julia Farias. Vocabulario español de Texas. Univ. of Texas Hispanic Studies, Vol. 5 (Austin: Univ. of Texas Press, 1953). 347 pp. (Reprinted unrevised, Austin: Univ. of Texas Press, 1970.)

Cervantes, Alfonso. "A Selected Vocabulary of Anglicisms Used by First Grade Students of Elementary Schools of Del Rio, Texas." MA Thesis, Southwest Texas State Univ., San Marcos, 1973. vi, 68 pp.

Coltharp, Lurline. "The Influence of English on the 'Language' of the Tirilones." PhD Diss., Univ. of Texas, Austin, 1964. (Subsequently published with occasional revisions as: The Tongue of the Tirilones. University, Alabama: Univ. of Alabama Press, 1965. 186 pp.)

_____. "Some Additions: Lexicon of 'Tongue of the Tirilones.'" In Ralph W. Ewton, Jr. and Jacob Ornstein, eds., Studies in Language and Linguistics 1969-70, El Paso: Texas Western Press, 1970, pp. 69-78.

_____. "'Invitation to the Dance': Spanish in the El Paso Underworld." In Glenn G. Gilbert, ed., Texas Studies in Bilingualism, Berlin: Walter de Gruyter Co., 1969, pp. 18-41.

Cornejo, Ricardo Jesús. "Bilingualism: Study of the Lexicon of the Five-Year-Old Spanish-Speaking Children of Texas." PhD Diss., Univ. of Texas, Austin, 1969. 228 pp.

Elías Olivares, Lucía E. "Study of the Oral Vocabulary of Ten High-School Mexican-American Students in Austin, Texas." MA Thesis, Univ. of Texas, Austin, 1970. 100 pp.

Fody, Michael III. "A Glossary of Non-Standard Spanish Words and Idioms Found in Selected Newspapers of South Texas During 1968." MA Thesis, Southern Illinois Univ., Carbondale, 1969. 154 pp.

Frausto, Manuel. "Vocabulario español de San Marcos, Texas." MA Thesis, Southwest Texas State Univ., San Marcos, 1969. 55 pp.

Galván, Roberto A. "Un estudio geográfico de algunos vocablos usados por los habitantes de habla española de San Antonio, Texas." MA Thesis, Univ. of Texas, Austin, 1949. 142 pp.

_____. "El dialecto español de San Antonio, Texas." PhD Diss., Tulane Univ., New Orleans, 1955. 315 pp.

_____. "Más observaciones sobre el argot de Baranquilla." Hispania 49.483-485 (1966).

_____. "'Chichecano', neologismo jergal." Hispania 53.86-88 (1970).

_____. "More on 'Frito' as an English Loan-Word in Mexican Spanish." Hispania 54.511-514 (1971).

García, Anita H. "Identification and Classification of Types of Common Deviations from

Standard Spanish Made by Representative Native Speakers in South Texas." MA Thesis, Texas A & I Univ., Kingsville, 1969. 110 pp.

García, Lucy. "Vocabulario selecto del español de Brownsville, Texas." MA Thesis, Southwest Texas State Univ., San Marcos, 1972. 64 pp.

González, Gustavo. "A Linguistic Profile of the Spanish-Speaking First-Grader in Corpus Christi, Texas." MA Thesis, Univ. of Texas, Austin, 1968. 83 pp.

_____. "The Acquisition of Spanish Grammar by Native Spanish Speakers." PhD Diss., Univ. of Texas, Austin, 1970. 178 pp.

Harrison, Helene. "A Methodological Study in Eliciting Linguistic Data from Mexican-American Bilinguals." PhD Diss., Univ. of Texas, Austin, 1967. 119 pp.

Ivey, Alfred Joe. "A Study of the Vocabulary of Newspapers Printed in the Spanish Language in Texas." MA Thesis, Univ. of Texas, Austin, 1927. iii, 137 pp.

January, William Spence, Jr. "The Chicano Dialect of the Mexican-American Communities of Dallas and Fort Worth." MA Thesis, Texas Christian Univ., 1971. 242 pp.

Keever, Mary, Alfredo Vásquez and Anna Padilla. Glossary of Words and Expressions, Irregular in Form or Meaning, Encountered in the Examination of Spanish Mail on the Mexican Border. El Paso, Texas: El Paso Office of the United States Office of Censorship, 1945. vii, 46 pp. mimeographed. (Location: Library of Congress, PC 4832 .U5.)

Kelly, Rex Robert. "Vocabulary as Used on the Mexican Border." MA Thesis, Baylor Univ., Waco, Texas, 1938. 39 pp.

_____ and George W. Kelly. Farm and Ranch Spanish. N. place: Authors, 1961. xv, 241 pp.

Kercheville, Francis M. "A Preliminary Glossary of Southwestern and Rio Grande Spanish Including Semantic and Philological Peculiarities." Unpublished ms., Kingsville: Texas A & I Univ., 1967. 71 pp.

Lance, Donald M., ed. and chief contributor. A Brief Study of Spanish-English Bilingualism. Bethesda, Maryland: U.S. Dept. of Health, Education and Welfare, 1969. 104 pp. (ERIC System No. ED 032 529.)

León, Aurelio de. Barbarismos comunes en México. 2 vols. México D.F.: Imprenta Mundial, (1: 1936, 2: 1937). 80 +/92 pp.

Luna, Juanita J. "A Selected Vocabulary of the Spanish Spoken in Sabinal, Texas." MA Thesis, Southwest Texas State Univ., San Marcos, 1970. 101 pp.

Marambio, Juan. "Vocabulario español de Temple, Texas." MA Thesis, Southwest Texas State Univ., San Marcos, 1970. 110 pp.

Marrocco, Mary Anne W. "The Spanish of Corpus Christi, Texas." PhD Diss., Univ. of Illinois, Champaign-Urbana, 1972. 502 pp.

McKee, Okla Markham. "Five-Hundred Non-Dictionary Words Found in the El Paso-Juárez Press." MA Thesis, Univ. of Texas-El Paso, 1955. 75 pp.

Montemayor, Elsa Diana. "A Study of the Spanish Spoken by Certain Bilingual Students of Laredo, Texas." MA Thesis, Texas Women's Univ., Denton, 1966. 106 pp.

Ornstein, Jacob S. "Sociolinguistics and New Perspectives in the Study of Southwest Spanish." In Ralph W. Ewton, Jr. and Jacob Ornstein, eds., Studies in Language and Linguistics 1969-70, El Paso: Texas Western Press, 1970, pp. 127-184.

_____. "Language Varieties Along the U.S.-Mexican Border." In Applications of Linguistics: Selected Papers of the Second International Congress of Applied Linguistics, edited by G.E. Perren and J.L.M. Trim, New York et alibi: Cambridge Univ. Press, 1971, pp. 349-362.

Patterson, Maurine. "Some Dialectal Tendencies in Popular Spanish in San Antonio." MA Thesis, Texas Women's Univ., Denton, 1946. 120 pp.

Ramírez, Carina (Karen). "Lexical Usage of and Attitude Toward Southwest Spanish in the Ysleta, Texas, Area." Graduate Paper, Univ. of Texas-El Paso, 1971. 84 pp. (Circulates through Library, Univ. of Texas-El Paso.)

_____. "Lexical Usage of and Attitude Toward Southwest Spanish in the Ysleta, Texas, Area." Hispania 56.308-315 (1973).

Ramón, René Simón. "Vocabulario selecto del español regional de Del Río, Texas." MA Thesis, Southwest Texas State Univ., San Marcos, 1974. vii, 70 pp.

Reséndez, Víctor. "Vocabulario español de Seguín, Texas." MA Thesis, Southwest Texas State Univ., San Marcos, 1970. 81 pp.

Reynolds, Selma Fay. "Some Aspects of Spanish as Spoken and Written by Spanish-Speaking Students of a Junior High School in (Corpus Christi,) Texas." MA Thesis, Texas Women's Univ., Denton, 1945. 105 pp.

Romano-V., Octavio I. "Donship in a Mexican-American Community in Texas." American Anthropologist 62.966-976 (1960).

Rubel, Arthur J. Across the Tracks: Mexican-Americans in a Texas City. Austin: Univ. of Texas Press, 1966. xxvii, 266 pp.

Said, Sally Eugenia Sneed. "A Descriptive Model of Austin Spanish Syntax." MA Thesis, Univ. of Texas, Austin 1970. 62 pp.

Sawyer, Janet Beck. "A Dialect Study of San Antonio, Texas: A Bilingual Community." PhD Diss., Univ. of Texas, Austin, 1957. 325 pp.

Sharp, John M. "Some El Paso Spanish Etymologies." In Ralph W. Ewton, Jr. and Jacob Ornstein, eds. Studies in Language and Linguistics 1969-70, El Paso: Texas Western

Press, 1970, pp. 207-232.
Simón, Alphonse, O.M.I. Pastoral Spanish. San Antonio: Standard Printing Co., 1945.
xxii, 511 pp.
Vásquez, Librado Keno and María Enriqueta Vásquez. Regional Dictionary of Chicano Slang.
Austin, Texas: Jenkins Publishing Co./The Pemberton Press, 1975. 111 pp.
Wagner, Max Leopold. "Ein mexikanisch-amerikanischer Argot: Das Pachuco." Romanistisches Jahrbuch 6.237-266 (1953-54).
Ward, Hortense Warner. "Ear Marks." Texas Folklore Society. Publications 19.106-116
(1944).
Wesley, Howard D. "Ranchero Sayings of the Border." Texas Folklore Society. Publications 12.211-220 (1935).

Otras fuentes útiles/Other Useful Sources

Aranda, Charles, comp. Dichos: Proverbs and Sayings from the Spanish. Santa Fe, NM:
Sunstone Press, 1975.
Beltramo, Anthony Fred. "Lexical and Morphological Aspects of Linguistic Acculturation
by Mexican Americans in San José, California." Ph.D. diss., Stanford University,
1972.
Blanco, S., Antonio. La lengua española en la historia de California. Madrid: Ediciones
Cultura Hispánica, 1971.
Corominas, J. Diccionario etimológico del español, 4 vols., Madrid: Gredos, 1954.
Domínguez, Domingo. "A Theoretical Model for Classifying Dialectal Variations of Oral
New Mexican Spanish." Ph.D. diss., University of New Mexico, 1975.
Fuentes, Dagoberto, and José A. López. Barrio Language Dictionary: First Dictionary
of Caló. Los Angeles/La Puente, CA: Southland Press/El Barrio Publications; Lubbock, TX: Trucha Publications, 1974.
Gross, Stuart Murray. "A Vocabulary of New Mexican Spanish." M.A. thesis, Stanford
University, 1935.
Kay, Margarita Artschwager; John D. Meredith; Wendy Redlinger; and Alicia Quiroz Raymond.
Southwestern Medical Dictionary: Spanish-English/English-Spanish. Tucson, AZ:
University of Arizona Press, 1977.
Riegelhaupt-Barkin, Florence. "The Influence of English on the Spanish of Bilingual
Mexican American Migrants in Florida." Ph.D. diss., SUNY-Buffalo, 1976.
Ross, Lyle Ronald. "La lengua castellana en San Luis, Colorado." Ph.D. diss., University of Colorado, 1975.
Santamaría, Francisco J., Diccionario de mejicanismos, 1959.
Serrano, Rodolfo G. Dictionary of Pachuco Terms. Bakersfield, CA: Sierra Printers, 1976.
Teschner, Richard V.; Garland D. Bills; and Jerry R. Craddock, eds. Spanish and English
of United States Hispanos: A Critical, Annotated, Linguistic Bibliography. Arlington, VA: Center for Applied Linguistics, 1975.
_____. "Current Research on the Language(s) of U.S. Hispanos." Hispania, 60
(1977):347-58.
Webb, John Terrance. "A Lexical Study of Caló and Non-Standard Spanish in the Southwest." Ph.D. diss., University of California, Berkeley, (Dec.) 1975.